Improving Your Child's Schoolwork

Improving

Your Child's

Schoolwork

1,001 Ideas Arranged from A to Z

Lawrence J. Greene

PRIMA PUBLISHING

PRIMA PUBLISHING·and colophon are trademarks of Prima Communications, Inc.

Library of Congress Cataloging-in-Publication Data

Greene, Lawrence J.
    Improving your child's schoolwork : an A–Z reference guide / Lawrence J. Greene.
        p.   cm.
    Updated ed. of: 1001 ways to improve your child's schoolwork.
    Includes bibliographical references
    ISBN 0-7615-0163-0
    1. Education—Parent participation—United States—Handbooks, manuals, etc.
2. Home and school—United States—Handbooks, manuals, etc.   3. Study skills—
Handbooks, manuals, etc.   I. Greene, Lawrence J.   1001 ways to improve your child's
schoolwork.   II. Title.
LB1048.5.G746   1995
649'.68—dc20   95-24333
                                                                                 CIP

95 96 97 98 99 RRD 10 9 8 7 6 5 4 3 2 1
Printed in the United States of America

How to Order:
Single copies may be ordered from Prima Publishing, P.O. Box 1260 BK, Rocklin, CA 95677; telephone (916) 632-4400. Quantity discounts are also available. On your letterhead, include information concerning the intended use of the books and the number of books you wish to purchase.

This book is for Adelaide and Harold.
You were always there.
This book is also for the newest addition to
our family, Joshua Ryan Greene.
Your mother and I will always be there for you.

Contents

Acknowledgments

THERE ARE MANY WONDERFUL PEOPLE I WANT TO THANK FOR THEIR assistance and support. These include Pamela Wilding, Alison Lucas, Mark Steinberg, Ph.D., Estella Lacey, M.F.C.C., Anne Henshall, Dan Greene, and Evelyn Greene. I am especially indebted to my wife, Dr. Alison Freeman-Greene for her encouragement, incisive suggestions, and love. And then, of course, there are my four exceptional collegues: Robbie Dunton, Elizabeth Gustafson, Joan Cayton-Vidal, and Helen Waugh. You are the consumately talented educational therapists who demonstrate every day how to help children achieve their full potential.

Introduction

What should you do when your child does not complete his homework or neglects to write down his assignments? Should you realistically be expected to help him with a reading, spelling, or math problem? How should you react when your daughter leaves her book reports to the last minute and invariably runs out of time? What should you do if she seems perfectly content to hand in sloppy, illegible assignments or reports with sentence fragments and run-on sentences? How should you respond when she studies diligently, appears to know the material, and then does poorly on the test? Should you commiserate with her, admonish her, or roll up your sleeves and become her tutor?

If you have wrestled with any of these issues, you know the frustration of wanting to help and not knowing how to help. Perhaps, in exasperation, you've felt like screaming: "I'm not a teacher! I haven't been trained to deal with these problems." And perhaps, in desperation, you resorted to the classic weapons that parents use to "motivate" their children: nagging, threats, punishment, and denial of privileges.

Improving Your Child's Schoolwork has been written as a parent resource. The book is predicated on several key assumptions:

- You place great value on your child acquiring a first-rate education.
- You recognize the importance of good academic skills and a good academic track record in a complex, highly competitive, and technologically advanced society.

- You want your child to acquire the tools and resources he needs to achieve and be successful.
- You want your child to establish personal performance goals and performance standards.
- You want your child to be motivated and conscientious.
- You want your child to acquire self-confidence.
- You want your child to be proud of her talents and accomplishments.
- You want your child to develop the intellectual, emotional, and academic resources requisite to prevailing over challenges in school and in life.
- You want your child to be able to analyze problems, evaluate opportunities, learn from mistakes, and bounce back from setbacks.

This preceding list encapsulates the legitimate desires of every concerned and responsible parent. Unfortunately, each year millions of potentially capable students fail to acquire the skills they need to win in a very competitive and demanding world. Some are inadequately educated. Some struggle because of learning problems. Others have acquired a pattern of self-defeating habits. They procrastinate, hand in sloppy work, and do not pay attention to important details. Many underachieving children have no clue how to study effectively. They have never learned how to identify important information, remember key facts, budget study time, or anticipate what is likely to be asked on the next test.

A continual battle to survive academically can exact a terrible toll on children's self-confidence, expectations, attitude, effort, behavior, and pride. (This battle can also obviously generate overwhelming concern, stress, and anxiety for the parents of these youngsters!) To protect themselves, struggling children often begin to avoid challenges. Their defense mechanisms offer only an illusory protection. Rather than provide a shield against feelings of inadequacy, their counterproductive behaviors simply guarantee continued marginal performance and a continued deterioration of self-confidence. Children enmeshed in an underachievement loop, of course, do not recognize this obvious irony. Convinced, either consciously or unconsciously, that effort is futile, they choose the path of least resistance: they deny, blame, rationalize, resist, complain, give up, turn off, and shut down.

Achieving youngsters respond very differently to obstacles and challenges. They establish personal performance goals and develop strategies for attaining their goals. They persevere despite setbacks. They figure out how to neutralize or avoid obstacles. They are motivated because they believe they can prevail and because they enjoy the payoffs their efforts produce.

If you have concluded that you cannot necessarily count on your child's school to correct his or her academic problems, you are not alone. Each year tens of thousands of parents come to this painful realization. In many cases, schools do not even provide help for children with significant learning problems. Those students with subtle or nonspecific problems typically fall through the cracks. Left to fend for themselves, they flail and flounder while their parents watch helplessly. That their untreated minor problems often become academically and emotionally debilitating is an unpleasant reality that many poorly funded school districts choose to overlook.

Whether your child has subtle, nonspecific learning deficits or significant, specific learning disabilities (or "learning differences"), you do not have to stand ineffectual on the sideline watching your child suffer. You do not have to feel frustrated, powerless, and demoralized. This book, the distillation of more than twenty-five years of experience treating more than 12,000 underachieving youngsters, will show you step-by-step how you can help your child succeed in school.

By becoming better informed and understanding the educational and psychological issues that affect your child's schoolwork, you can play a direct and proactive role in assuring that your child develops his or her full academic and intellectual potential. You will be able to identify deficits, resolve problems, respond to crises, evaluate options, monitor progress, assess programs, and communicate effectively with school personnel. Because you understand the issues and know the jargon, you will be able to ask penetrating, incisive questions that require meaningful, substantive answers from teachers, school psychologists, counselors, and resource specialists. If conflicts, inequities, or disputes with school officials occur, you will be able to serve effectively as your child's advocate. You will "know the ropes," and you will know precisely what is mandated by federal law. You will also know if your child's school is in compliance with these laws. This informed parental activism sends an unequivocal message to the educational system: "My child deserves a first-rate education, and I am here to see that he gets it. I promise to be reasonable and do my share at home. I insist that you also be reasonable and do your share in school."

HOW TO USE THIS BOOK

Designed as a reference guide, *Improving Your Child's Schoolwork* incorporates a format similar to that of an encyclopedia or dictionary. This format allows you to look up issues quickly and within a few minutes to have an overview of your child's problem. Key symptoms, behaviors, attitudes, issues, and academic deficits are succinctly described and then followed by a wide range of practical, easy-to-implement techniques that address the specific deficits. These techniques have been used successfully to help thousands of underachieving children during the last twenty-five years at the Developmental Learning Center in San Jose, California.

Ideally, your child's academic problems can be solved in school. To facilitate this, each entry includes specific suggestions and strategies for enlisting the help of your child's teacher. Each entry also outlines practical methods for helping your child at home and for supplementing school-provided learning assistance. The objective is not to transform you into a teacher or educational therapist, but, rather, to show how you can participate productively in the process of helping your child improve her schoolwork. *You do not need to be a trained teacher to use these strategies.* The only requirements are that you be concerned about your child's learning progress and willing to assist in a constructive, supportive, patient, and loving way.

Certain learning difficulties, of course, do not lend themselves to easy or quick solutions. Problems such as attention deficit disorder (difficulty concentrating), dyslexia (letter and number reversals), spelling problems, and chronic self-sabotaging behaviors are complex and often involve overlapping educational, physiological, and psychological factors. Checklists have been included under certain entries to help you, your child, and your child's teacher identify the specific underlying deficits that may be causing academic problems. Although the identified deficits may not necessarily lend themselves to easy solutions or quick fixes, there are positive, practical steps you can take to assist your child. While children with significant learning problems may require the assistance of trained professionals, these children often make greater progress when provided with effective supplemental assistance, support, and guidance at home.

You do not need to read this book from cover to cover. Use it as you would a dictionary. Look up a specific problem or issue and experiment with the suggested strategies. If you want more information, examine the many cross-referenced entries. Select a strategy consistent with your parenting style and temperament. If your first choice does not work, try another.

HOW TO HELP YOUR CHILD

The following guidelines will facilitate the process of providing learning assistance. Take the time to read through them *before* beginning to work with your child:

• Your child will be more receptive and do better work when you communicate optimism and positive expectations, when you are supportive and patient, and when you affirm his or her progress.

• Be creative and intentionally make the time you spend with your child as interesting and engaging as possible. Having fun is not only permissible, it's ideal! Encourage your child's active involvement in the skill-enhancement process. Use examples and analogies your child can understand and appreciate. (For example: "If you were playing a video and ten alien spaceships attack you and you destroy half of them, how many would be left? Now if you destroyed fifty percent of the remaining ships, how many would be left?" "If your team needs to gain eight yards for a touchdown and on the first down the fullback carried the ball for twenty-five percent of the distance, how many yards would you still need to gain for the touchdown.")

• Keep the sessions relatively short. Your child's attention span is shorter than yours. As a general rule, sessions with younger children (grades 1–3) should last no longer than ten to fifteen minutes, unless, of course, you and your child are having so much fun that neither of you want to quit! Children in grades 4–6 can generally be expected to work for fifteen to twenty minutes at a time. Children in junior and senior high school should be able to work for twenty-five to thirty-five minutes without a break.

• Provide reasonably spaced breaks when your child is becoming mentally fatigued. Children who are struggling with schoolwork will tire more quickly than those who find the work easy.

• If your child is becoming fatigued, frustrated, and/or resistant, stop for the day even though she has not achieved your objective and is still confused. To plow ahead is certain to trigger counterproductive resentment and overt or covert oppositional behavior.

• If your child is highly resistant to your help, and you cannot elicit cooperation, consider hiring an educational therapist or private tutor. Some children may also require counseling, especially if they have very negative or phobic associations with school.

• Actively involve your child in the learning assistance process. Discuss his or her academic or behavioral problems and the objectives of your interactive sessions in simple, concrete, and understandable terms. Urge your child to participate in the goal-setting process. Engage cooperation and active involvement in a far more effective strategy rather than attempting to impose your own academic agenda or timetable.

• Have realistic expectations. You cannot reasonably expect a child who is reading two years below grade level to catch up in three months.

• Set aside a specific time for the assistance sessions. Consult with your child about this timetable. Although you do not have to work with your child *every* evening, you both should agree that the sessions should take place, for example, between 7:00 and 7:30 P.M. If your child has a specific problem with his homework (e.g., he's confused about what a participle is), you can, of course, provide "crisis intervention." Be succinct. Children who want a quick "fix" to a minor problem resent long-winded, comprehensive explanations, even if *you* believe they would benefit from such a comprehensive explanation. You might inquire at some point if he would like *some* help. If you attempt to spend three hours helping him, don't be surprised if he

actively or passively resists your offer of help in the future.

WHAT TO EXPECT FROM YOUR CHILD

Some problems can be resolved relatively quickly. Others may require months or even years of educational assistance. Even highly trained and competent educational therapists often have difficulty predicting how much time will be required to remedy learning problems.

If your child has several learning deficits, you must decide whether it would be strategic to work on these issues concurrently or whether it would be preferable to establish priorities. A child who has both handwriting and spelling problems could certainly work on correcting both problems at the same time. In some cases, however, it makes more sense to work exclusively on one deficit before beginning to work on another. Consult with your child's teacher and trust your intuition. Do not be afraid to change your strategy if your judgment call was wrong and the plan is not working.

You should always match the remediation strategy you select with your child's age, skill level, emotional maturity, and attitude. Note that the suggested corrective strategies for junior and senior high school students have been combined because classes at this level have the same format (i.e., individual subjects are taught in forty to sixty minute periods by different teachers who spend less time with their students than do elementary school teachers). Although the remedial suggestions are combined, you should calibrate the difficulty of the activities to your child's current ability and skills. Seventh graders generally have a shorter attention span than tenth graders. There are, however, exceptions. A tenth grader with a long history of learning problems may be resistant to help and may have developed an elaborate system of psychological defense mechanisms to insulate himself from failure, frustration, and feelings of inadequacy. His attention span may actually be shorter than a seventh grader's. If you encounter resistance, you may need to limit the duration and frequency of the assistance sessions and make creative adjustments in your expectations, approach, and techniques. You may also need to seek professional help.

A Proactive Response to Real Problems

Many parents and educators are becoming increasingly alarmed about the quality of American education. This alarm is legitimate and justifiable. Every day the media bombards us with depressing stories about the deterioration in our children's academic skills. Well, you no longer need to be a passive spectator who must watch from the sidelines as your child struggles in school and becomes increasingly frustrated and demoralized. This book is designed to help you assume a significant and constructive role in helping your child remove the barriers impeding his or her progress and success in school. *Improving Your Child's Schoolwork* will provide you with the information and practical tools you need to get your child back on track and functioning at an academic level commensurate with his or her true potential.

Note about Codes Used in This Book

The suggested corrective strategies within each entry are sometimes preceded by the code ES or J/HS. ES means the strategy applies to elementary school students. J/HS means the strategy applies to junior high and high school students. A strategy without a code applies to all students, regardless of their grade level.

Anger and Frustration

Frustration is a natural response to mistakes, setbacks, and unyielding problems. When minor problems trigger rage or depression in a child, these excessive reactions signal unresolved emotional and self-esteem issues that are defeating the child's coping mechanisms. Children who cannot handle their anger and frustration are at risk for becoming emotionally and academically dysfunctional.

The effects of chronic frustration and anger are cumulative and psychologically corrosive. Children who (consciously or unconsciously) conclude that their situation is hopeless may compensate for feelings of inadequacy and incompetence by becoming withdrawn, defensive, irresponsible, aggressive, or academically immobilized. As defeats and real or imagined humiliations take their cumulative toll, the self-confidence of these struggling children inexorably erodes and pain begins to warp their perceptions about themselves and their abilities.

Some children respond to setbacks immediately and openly express their upset and frustration. They either resolve the problem, put it aside, or move on to the next challenge. Other children warehouse anger and frustration, and their feelings implode. In time, the walls of the containment structure start to leak or crumble, and the suppressed emotions detonate in rage, seep out in the form of teasing, sarcasm, or cruelty, or implode in the form of depression.

The conscientious student who becomes moderately upset and frustrated upon receiving a poor test grade is reacting quite normally. If his self-esteem and confidence are secure, he can cope with the setback. He will analyze the situation ("I studied the wrong information."), make appropriate tactical adjustments ("I'll study for the next test with a friend who gets good grades, and we'll make up practice test questions."), and tell himself he will do better next time (see Bouncing Back from Setbacks and Learning from Mistakes; Smart Thinking). If, however, he continues to do poorly on tests despite his best efforts, he's likely to become discouraged and demoralized and be tempted to give up. Although he may continue to go through the motions of studying, his motivation, effort, and expectations of success will diminish. To hide feelings of ineptness and cope with frustration, he may acquire an elaborate set of counterproductive compensatory behaviors (see Psychological Problems and Psychological Overlay).

The spectrum of behaviors that children use to express anger is broad. One child may act out, become the class clown, or focus energy exclusively in areas where he can excel such as sports or art. Another child may retreat into a shell or become aggressive and hostile. A third child may cry, throw temper tantrums, contravene his parents' rules, or tease his little brother unmercifully. The anger these children feel may quickly subside, or it may continue for hours.

For some children, an explosion of fury can be cathartic and reduce stress and anxiety. As steam escapes, the dome of the volcano recedes. After a brief cooling-off period, these children are ready to move ahead. If these youngsters, however, experience a seemingly endless series of setbacks, and the source of their difficulties is not identified and resolved, pressure will build, and the volcano will once again rumble ominously.

The underlying issues responsible for a child's anger must be addressed and resolved, or this pattern of building frustration followed by explosive anger could persist indefinitely. Children enmeshed in this cycle are often described as having a short fuse, a nasty temper, or a volatile personality. Because they cannot control their anger, they often make flawed, impulsive decisions that later could cost them their marriages, jobs, and friendships. A chronically volatile child is clearly at risk for ultimately becoming entangled in the penal system.

Frustration and anger do not always explode. When these emotions implode, children may become withdrawn, depressed, and emotionally isolated. Some children who have imploding anger may daydream or escape into a fantasy world that provides a peaceful oasis, while others may fantasize about violence. (Video games clearly create a context for these violent fantasies.) Some children express their frustration and unhappiness through passive aggression (i.e., striking out at others in camouflaged ways). They may sabotage themselves, thwart their parents, or become overtly or covertly resistant. Children who regularly repress anger can become so adept at denying and hiding their feelings that even mental health professionals may not recognize the extent of their inner turmoil (see Behavior and Attitude; Psychological Problems and Psychological Overlay).

Intense emotions can be frightening and difficult for children to acknowledge. Most unhappy children are not aware when they are hiding or running from disturbing feelings. Perceiving themselves as "bad," they will often disown the unpleasant troubling emotions. Their guilt can be especially intense when they're consciously or unconsciously angry at their parents (see Guilt).

A child's chronic anger rarely disappears of its own accord. Although it may assume different forms as the child matures—hitting, bullying, self-sabotage, vandalism, sadism, violent fantasies, stealing, cutting school, lying—the anger will continue to manifest in one way or another until the feelings and causative factors have been identified, examined, and resolved. The sooner the child receives help in identifying the underlying feelings, the lower the risk of lasting psychological scarring.

The chronically angry child who expresses emotions explosively (as rage, cruelty, rebelliousness, violence) or implosively (as depression, sarcasm, self-defeating behavior, passive resistance) desperately requires counseling or psychotherapy. The goal of therapy is to help the child make peace with himself, his parents, and the world around him. As he achieves greater insight and self-acceptance, the need to deny, disown, camouflage, or hide his innermost feelings will be less compelling. Family, school, and social problems can then be productively addressed and resolved.

Learning problems can be a primary source of frustration and anger. The child who must struggle intensely to read or do math, who is continually thwarted academically and embarrassed by bad grades, and who is repeatedly reprimanded or punished cannot help but feel upset and angry. If this no-win situation persists, the child's sense of despair will grow and his coping behavior will become increasingly defensive, nonadaptive, and, perhaps, self-sabotaging. Children who don't like themselves will act in ways that reinforce their negative self-perception. They may flagrantly break the rules, associate with counter-culture youngsters, dress in ways that set them apart from the mainstream, and become increasingly alienated from their families (see Behavior and Attitude; Self-Esteem and Self-Confidence).

Family problems can also be a major source of frustration and anger. The dysfunctional family whose interaction is characterized by poor communication, poorly defined values, resentment, double messages, manipulation, inconsistently enforced rules, unrealistic expectations, and sibling rivalry will often produce dysfunctional children.

In some instances, anger and frustration may be attributable to overlapping conditions. The child who is depressed because of a personal trauma (such as the loss of a parent) or a dysfunctional family situation (continual vitriolic arguments at home) may also have dyslexia. To treat the learning problem without addressing the psychological issues will be ineffectual. To treat the family issues without addressing the dyslexia will also be ineffectual. Resolving this child's problems requires both psychological and academic intervention (see Learning Disabilities).

Although chronic frustration can cause emotional damage, some types of frustration serve a positive function. Challenges, problems, and limited frustration can motivate children to mobilize their emotional and intellectual resources. Learning how to cope with frustration, solve problems, and prevail over challenges is vital to the development of self-esteem (see Bouncing Back from Setbacks and Learning from Mistakes; Self-Esteem and Self-Confidence). A key distinction, however, must be made between occasional "positive" frustration that mobilizes a child's resources and continual "negative" frustration that generates feelings of hopelessness and despair.

Corrective Strategies

In School

1.   If your child's teacher informs you that he is experiencing frustration and is angry or hostile in school, you and the teacher must make every effort to identify the sources of the frustration and brainstorm ways to reduce the unhappiness and stress. If he cannot complete his assignments because his skills are inadequate, he should be provided with learning assistance. The quantity and difficulty level of his assignments should also be modified until his skills improve and he can complete the assigned work successfully. Discuss with the teacher whether reducing the workload or providing supplemental out-of-school tutorial support would be advisable.

2.   If your child is having social problems in school that trigger anger and frustration, explore how he might better handle teasing or rejection. Encourage him to be aware of and eliminate those specific behaviors that alienate him from other children, such as "telling" on other youngsters or acting silly. Also urge him to develop talents that would improve his self-confidence, such as karate or gymnastics. Enrolling him in after-school programs that encourage the development of confidence-building talents can be instrumental in reducing frustration and non-adaptive social behaviors.

3.   If your child is frustrated because of academic difficulties, ask the teacher to identify his specific learning deficits and work with the teacher and your child to create a practical strategy for systematically resolving these deficits. Components of this strategy may include: an assessment by the child study team (an in-class observation and performance review by school personnel for the purpose of determining whether a comprehensive evaluation is appropriate), a diagnostic assessment by the school psychologist, assistance from the resource specialist, placement in a resource program or special day class (a full-time learning assistance program), and/or private educational therapy. Refer to relevant entries in this book for specific methods for correcting the identified learning deficits.

4.   If you or the teacher observe explosive rage or depression and are concerned about your child's mental health, request an evaluation by the school psychologist. If symptoms of an emotional problem are detected, ask for a referral to a mental health professional (psychiatrist, psychologist, licensed social worker, or marriage, family, and child counselor). Some enlightened school districts have social workers and therapists on staff or on call. Chronic anger and frustration caused by learning problems (see Psychological Problems and Psychological Overlay), family problems, or

psychological trauma cannot be disregarded. If left untreated, exploding or imploding anger can cause permanent psychological damage and can cause the child to become emotionally, academically, and vocationally dysfunctional.

At Home

1.   Note the specific behaviors that concern your child's teacher. Select appropriate issues to examine with your child. If the list is extensive, prioritize the list and address problems sequentially. Pointing out all the deficiencies and attempting to address them at once would be overwhelming and counterproductive. For example, you might say: "When I met with your teacher today, she told me that you're hitting other children. This concerns me. Tell me what you think might be causing the problem." Allow time for your child to respond. If the child is unable to answer, ask questions to help him identify his underlying feelings and to help him examine alternatives for expressing these feelings:

- Could the fact that you're having a hard time with reading be causing you to get frustrated and angry?
- How could this problem of becoming frustrated and angry and then hitting other children be solved?
- Do you think a tutor could help with your reading?
- What could you do when you sense yourself become angry or frustrated?
- Could you talk to the teacher about what's upsetting you?
- Could you hang on to your anger until you get home and discuss the situation and your feelings with me?

- Would it help to hang a punching bag in the garage that you could hit to let off steam?
- If you feel you're about to hit or tease someone, could you walk away and take time to get yourself under control?
- Could you count slowly in your head to fifteen before responding?
- Would it help to have someone beside your parents or teacher to talk to about what's upsetting you? (If your child seems receptive to the idea, explain that this is what a counselor does. Her job is to listen to a child's problems and help him and parents work things out. She doesn't take sides.)
- Let's make a list of things you could do when you're feeling upset.
- Let's identify what's making you upset.
- What could you do about it?

Helping your child identify his feelings and explore options for handling strong emotions is the critical first step in helping him deal with chronic anger and frustration.

2.   Consult a mental health professional if you conclude that you cannot identify the source of the problems or resolve the issues causing frustration and anger. Admitting that your child or your family requires counseling is not an admission of inadequacy, but is a testimony to your honesty, concern, and rational thinking. Responsible parents admit when they need help in solving their child's problem or their family's problem. Irresponsible parents either put their head in the sand and naively hope that the problems will magically disappear, or they plow ahead mindlessly using methods and interventions that have already clearly proven to be ineffectual.

Attention Deficit Disorder

Children who have difficulty filtering out distractions, staying on track, inhibiting impulses, focusing their attention, and controlling their bodies rarely function in school at a level commensurate with their potential. For many years, physicians, psychologists, and educators described these children as *hyperactive* when they manifested chronic, frenetic, and often purposeless activity, because it was believed that their inattentiveness was caused by their hyperactivity. Extensive observations of distractible children have revealed, however, that this cause and effect explanation was flawed. Although most hyperactive children are indeed inattentive, all inattentive children are *not* necessarily hyperactive. The terms *attention deficit hyperactivity disorder* (*ADHD*) and *attention deficit disorder without hyperactivity* (*ADD*) were created to underscore this important distinction and to permit a more precise diagnosis.

ADD and ADHD occur when the brain is not regulating itself efficiently. The conditions are usually associated with a perceptual dysfunction (the inefficient processing of sensory data) and are often compounded by specific learning disabilities[1] (see Learning Disabilities). In some cases, ADD or ADHD can undermine academic performance in all subjects. It is also possible, however, for the conditions to manifest themselves exclusively in one or two specific areas. For

example, a child may be able to concentrate when doing math but may be inattentive when studying spelling or history.

It is estimated that from 2 to 4 percent of all children have ADHD. This translates into approximately two million hyperactive children in American classrooms at any given time. Although estimates about the size of the nonhyperactive ADD population vary depending on the diagnostic criteria, many additional millions of children clearly fall into this category.

The counterproductive behaviors associated with ADD and ADHD include impulsivity, inattention to details (see Attention to Detail), disorganization (see Disorganization), improperly recorded assignments (see Incomplete Assignments), missed deadlines (see Time Management), and sloppy, incomplete, inaccurate work. These nonadaptive behaviors can undermine the academic performance of students with specific learning disabilities as well as students with good academic skills.

Concentration deficits can be especially problematic when children are required to do work they find uninteresting or difficult. Keeping a distractible, impulsive child on task while he completes a page of "boring" math problems or diagrams sentences can be a nightmare for a teacher in the classroom and for a parent monitoring homework. Ironically, many parents report that their ADD child cannot sustain attention for more than a few moments when doing schoolwork, but can concentrate for hours

---

1. Some educators and parents prefer to use the term "learning differences" because they believe this term is less stigmatizing to the child.

when building a model airplane or playing a video game. This selective capacity to concentrate suggests that high interest activities can sometimes offset the effects of ADD.

ADD children generally have difficulty handling challenging, repetitive, or detail-oriented academic tasks that demand sustained effort, self-discipline, and focused concentration. The traditional "prescription" for dealing with ADD in the classroom is to impose additional structure and external control and to create an environment with few distractions. A teacher might, for example, place the highly distractible child near her desk or designate a "quiet place" where the child is sent when he becomes excessively hyperactive or unmanageable.

Children with concentration deficits often function best in an environment where external stimulation and distractions are controlled and where there are clearly defined behavior guidelines and performance standards, immediate feedback, affirmation for improved behavior, and individualized teaching strategies. This solution, however, is not necessarily ideal for all ADD students. Some chronically inattentive youngsters drift off and become even more distracted when deprived of stimulation. These children, who do better in an interactive, creative classroom that is not tightly controlled, are often very bright. They pay attention because their brains are actively and creatively engaged. Conversely, they become inattentive when they're required to do repetitive, mindless work. The realities of the classroom, however, dictate that bright, capable children must also be able to handle tedious assignments. They must develop the capacity to regulate themselves, focus, attend to details, and stay on task even under less-than-ideal conditions. Those who don't acquire this capacity are on a collision course with the educational system.

Chronic inattentiveness and hyperactivity generally create stress for everyone affected by the behavior. In a class of thirty students, each child should theoretically receive approximately 3 percent of the teacher's time and energy. A hyperactive or highly distractible child who demands 10 percent of the teacher's energy undermines this equation. Teachers who must continually monitor and control ADD or ADHD students find themselves reluctantly thrust into the role of police officers. Realizing they're depriving other students of their fair share of instructional time, these teachers may become frustrated, resentful, demoralized, impatient, and weary.

Because ADD children often act out in class, fidget, distract other students, disregard instructions, and "forget" to do assigned work, they usually receive a great deal of negative attention. This continual disapproval can erode self-confidence, and cause children to become demoralized and possibly conclude they are "bad." Such children frequently acquire a pattern of counterproductive behaviors consistent with this negative self-perception.

Limited funds, inadequate teacher training, too few trained specialists, insufficient parental support and involvement, and a production line mentality have forced some school districts to latch onto simplistic solutions to the problems of ADD and ADHD. When students with concentration problems are unable to conform to demands and standards that may be reasonable for other children, they are often isolated, punished, resented, denigrated, disregarded, or targeted for drug therapy.

Research published in the *New England Journal of Medicine* (November, 1990) has pinpointed a brain abnormality that could explain why children develop ADD and ADHD. The report indicates that the brains of hyperactive adults (50 percent of hyperactive children become hyperactive adults!) use 8 percent less glucose than normal. (Glucose is the brain's main source of energy.) The research suggests that hyperactivity results when specific regions of the brain that control attention, handwriting, motor coordination, and inhibited responses function improperly. These findings, in tandem with previous research that found approximately 30 percent of all children with ADHD have at least one parent with ADHD, confirm that hyperactivity is genetically and biologically based and pave the way for development of a precise diagnostic test for ADHD. Genetic research is advancing, and new treatment protocols may be imminent.[2]

Some physicians who treat ADD and ADHD children regularly prescribe stimulants or antihistamines such as Dexedrine, Ritalin, Cylert, or Benadryl to control the symptoms. (For complex neurological reasons, stimulants can have a calming effect on many children with ADD and ADHD.) Although these drugs have demonstrated effectiveness in treating concentration disorders and neurologically based learning disabilities, some professionals are concerned about the potential long-term physical and emotional consequences of extended use of attention-focusing medication and particulary about possible depression after children stop using the drug, as well as sleeplessness, inhibited growth, reduced appetite, accelerated heart rate, and drug dependency. In rebuttal, other physicians argue that drugs such as Ritalin have been used safely and effectively for over twenty years with no conclusive, documented serious side effects. (A drug program that focuses on neurotransmitter functions is now being used by some physicians to treat ADD. Doctors using this protocol claim that ADD and ADHD are linked to an imbalance in cerebral hormone levels and that antidepressants drugs such as Norpramin, Epramin, Prozac, and Desyrel act for more extended time periods and do not produce many of the negative side effects of stimulants and antihistamines. Parents considering drug therapy should question their child's pediatrician, neurologist, or psychiatrist closely about the pluses and minuses of the recommended treatment. If their concerns are not allayed, parents should seek a second opinion and/or explore alternative strategies for helping their child (some suggestions follow).

Although hyperactivity usually diminishes with the onset of puberty, distractibility and impulsivity may persist in less obvious forms. A teenager (or adult) may no longer appear overtly hyperactive, but may still have difficulty staying on track, following instructions, maintaining interest, remaining motivated, completing projects, and filtering out distractions. Unless the underlying perceptual processing problems and focusing deficits are addressed and resolved, ADD and ADHD children will often continue to struggle in junior high school and high school. These focusing and impulse control deficits could also erect monumental barriers to vocational achievement.

There are other ways besides medication to treat ADD and ADHD. Externally imposed structure, clearly defined behavior guidelines and performance standards, behavior modification techniques, relaxation techniques, counseling, a diet that eliminates food additives, creative and intellectually stimulating teaching strategies, highly disciplined athletic training, and consistent and firm parenting and teaching have proven beneficial in helping ADD and ADHD children control their impulsivity and inhibit their inattentiveness and distractibility.

Another technique for improving the self-regulation of children with ADD and ADHD incorporates EEG biofeedback. This method (which is also called neurofeedback or brainwave training) employs a computer to teach the child's brain how to produce specific brainwaves that are associated with concentration, relaxation, and cooperative behavior. Clinicians using these training methods contend that biofeedback significantly reduces hyperactivity and distractibility and generates more consistent, flexible, and controlled behavior. Extensive clinical trials and numerous studies appear to verify the effectiveness of the treatment.

The neurofeedback method for treating ADD and ADHD typically involves having a child play

2. One of the most recent genetic advances into understanding the causal biological factors responsible for ADHD involves the discovery of a specific gene that appears to be associated with hyperactivity. This gene regulates the action of the powerful neurotransmitter dopamine. Research at University of Chicago indicates that when a genetic marker is associated with this gene (or mutations of the gene), there is greater susceptibility to ADHD. These new findings could permit physicians to spot susceptible youngsters at birth and could lead to earlier intervention, better parent-coping strategies, and new treatment protocols.

video games while electrodes are attached to his head. The child's brainwaves are monitored by a computer that provides immediate feedback. The computer teaches the child how to regulate his brainwaves so that he actually uses his mind (and not an electronic joystick) to control the game. When the child achieves desirable brainwave bands, the game continues and goes faster. Less desirable bands inhibit the game. As the child's brain responds to the computer's feedback, enhanced brainwave regulation occurs. Cognitive performance (i.e., the ability to learn), concentration, and self-control improve while impulsivity, distractibility, irritability, and oppositional behavior descrease. Clinicians using the method report that some clients who receive the training are able to reduce or eliminate medication, and research appears to document that the positive gains tend to be maintained over time.

Corrective Strategies

In School

1.   (Elementary School, ES) If your child is manifesting ADD behaviors, consult with her teacher. (She's undoubtedly already aware of the problem!) If she concurs that your child is struggling to pay attention and keep his body under control, discuss the matter with the school psychologist and your pediatrician. If the concentration deficits and hyperactivity also involve specific learning disabilities, your child should be tested to determine if she qualifies for learning assistance (see Parents' Rights).

2.   (ES) A well-conceived behavior modification strategy can be an important teacher resource for controlling ADD students. Children who are expected to modify their behavior must be helped to identify specific problem areas, taught methods for achieving clearly defined objectives, and given incentives for making changes (see the Daily Self-Control Checklist). You, the teacher, and your child have a vested interest in working together to solve the problem. Once your child gains greater control, everyone's life will be easier. Daily feedback is vital. Ask the teacher to fill out the checklist to provide information about how well your child was able to focus. Tell the teacher it will require only a few moments to complete at the end of the day.

DAILY SELF-CONTROL CHECKLIST

Code: *1 = difficult   2 = average   3 = good   4 = excellent*

	MON.	TUES.	WED.	THURS.	FRI.
You paid attention in class.					
You didn't disturb other students.					
You worked independently.					
You completed your assignments.					
You handed your work in on time.					
You followed instructions.					
Your work was neat.					
Your work was complete.					

Encourage your child to aim for a minimum daily score. This target score can be raised as she develops more self-control and self-discipline. The teacher could establish a symbolic reward such as a gold star for achieving daily and weekly targets. You can reinforce this incentive system by providing additional incentives for good behavior at home. Suggest to the teacher that she provide a great deal of verbal encouragement and acknowledgment for improvement. Affirmation for effort and progress, clearly communicated positive expectations, and patience are vital. The ultimate goal is for your child to make the transition from working diligently for extrinsic payoffs (gold stars, free time, reduced homework, and so on) to working for the intrinsic satisfaction of doing a good job.

3.   (ES) An alternative to the daily checklist is to provide your child with more immediate feedback. Positive and negative reinforcement is the cornerstone of behavior modification. With younger children (grades K to 4), the teacher might affix a wide piece of masking tape to the upper corner of your child's desk. A "sad face" should be drawn on the top left-hand side of the tape and a "happy face" should be on the top right hand side of the tape, thus creating two columns. When the teacher is conscious of your child paying attention and getting work done, she could signal your child with a raised index finger. Your child would then put a check in the "happy face" column. When she's distracted or inattentive, the teacher could call her name and signal her with two fingers. She would then put a check in the "sad face" column. You and the teacher should encourage your child to aim for a specific number of "happy face" checks each day (or period). A reward for improvement should be established in school and at home (for example, a minimum of ten "happy face" checks in one day can be used for an extra half hour of TV or an ice-cream cone).

The target score should be realistic and the expectations reasonable. Never take away earned points for poor performance. When you first begin using a systematic behavior modification program, you may discover that your highly distractible or hyperactive child is capable of earning only one or two checks each day. Encourage her to raise the target score in small increments, and praise her for even small gains. Your goal is to reinforce positive behavior and to help your child discover and appreciate that with sufficient desire she's actually capable of controlling herself.

Rewards should not be confused with bribes. A reward (or reinforcement) is an acknowledgment for effort and positive performance, while a bribe is an instrument of manipulation that demeans the person who accepts it. Just as paychecks, praise from a boss, promotions, and bonuses motivate adult rewards, treats, toys, and excursions are equally motivating rewards for children. Do not hesitate to use extrinsic rewards as incentives until your child is motivated to do a first-rate job for her own intrinsic satisfaction (see Behavior and Attitude; Effort and Motivation; Goals).

Be prepared for periodic "bad days." Even though your child's self-control may be improving, a wide range of stimuli could set her off and cause a temporary regression in her capacity to control herself, focus her attention, and stay on task. Don't be discouraged. If it becomes apparent that the behavior modification program is not working, discuss the situation with your child's pediatrician and explore alternative strategies.

At Home

1.   If you suspect that your child has ADD, have him evaluated. Behavioral scales such as the Conners Scale or the Attention Deficit Disorder Evaluation Scale can be highly accurate diagnostic tools. Consult your child's pediatrician or school psychologist for more information about these scales. A computer-based test called the TOVA (Test of Variables of Attention) is also highly reliable.

2.   (ES) Enroll your child in an athletic program that stresses self-discipline and control. This should preferably be an individual as

opposed to a group sport. Gymnastics, karate, judo, tennis, and swimming are ideal.

3.   Establish reasonable homework periods during which there will be no interruptions. Encourage your child to concentrate intensely for these agreed-upon time segments. For younger children (grades 1 to 5), these segments initially might last for five minutes of sustained effort followed by a short break. Gradually increase the periods to ten minutes. The goal is to condition your child in much the same way that an athlete is conditioned to develop endurance. Structure, practice, and repetition are essential. Establish a point system to reward your child when she attains the targeted goal for the day. Remember to praise your child for all progress. ("I'm so pleased with your self-control today! I'm very proud of you.") Provide honest feedback and express positive expectations when your child has a bad day. ("You had some difficulty focusing today in school. I bet tomorrow will be a better day. Remind yourself that you can control your attention, and be willing to work at it. You have a choice about whether to concentrate or not concentrate.")

4.   When your child realizes (or you inform her) that she's becoming agitated or distracted, use relaxation techniques to help control the inattentiveness and hyperactivity. At first, you will need to provide feedback about behavior (see Monitoring Homework). You might say: "You're becoming overactive (or inattentive). Do you realize that you've gotten out of your chair seven times and dropped your pencil four times during the last three minutes? This is interfering with your concentration on your homework. I'd like you to close your eyes and take a slow, deep breath. Take another breath, keeping your eyes

closed. Now take another." (Don't have her do this more than three or four times or she might hyperventilate.) "I want you now to do three more math problems calmly without getting up or dropping your pencil. If you sense you're becoming distracted, do the breathing technique again." By providing nondemeaning feedback ("Jen, I can see you're not paying attention right now."), helping your child recognize counterproductive behavior without causing embarrassment, and encouraging her to relax and become "centered," you (and the teacher if she also uses this method in class) can orient your child toward taking more responsibility for her behavior. You'll know the technique is working when she begins to use it without having to be told that she's out of control.

5.   (ES) Select games such as Junior Scrabble, chess, pickup sticks, and computer video games that you and your child can play together to improve her concentration skills. Choose games that your child would enjoy and make the sessions fun. Establish a specific time for playing them and know when it's time to quit for the day. Your goal is to develop your child's concentration skills in increments. If the games involve competition, give your child a handicap. For example, you might say: "I've had sixteen years of education, and you have had four years. I will give you a handicap of ten points for every additional year of education I have had. Let's do the math together and figure out your handicap." When your child reaches the point where she prefers to play the game with friends or siblings, by all means urge her to do so. Affirm her for improving her concentration span. Once she realizes that she can control her attention and focus for sustained periods, her self-concept will begin to change, and this will reinforce continued positive behavioral changes.

Attention to Detail

Successful students pay attention to important details. They carefully proofread their reports to find spelling and grammar mistakes. They recheck their math problems to make sure they subtracted when they were supposed to subtract. They rewrite their essays to make them legible, accurate, and neat. They take pride in their work, and they covet and take pride in the payoffs they derive when they do a first-rate job. The rewards may be a good grade, a compliment from their teachers, or affirmation from their parents.

Children who do not pay attention to details are at the other end of the achievement spectrum. Because their primary objective is to complete the work as quickly as possible, the quality of their performance and the outcome are of secondary importance. The effect of their failure to proofread essays or check over math computations is predictable: a potential A or B paper receives a C-, a D, or an F.

Inattention to details is habit-forming. Once the behaviors and attitude become entrenched, they could errect barriers to achievement that might persist into adulthood (see Behavior and Attitude). Self-monitoring demands attention, time, and effort. Children who are in the habit of not paying attention to details are rarely willing to make this investment. Checking over an assignment requires too much work. This attitude is usually associated with other counterproductive traits. Children who do not pay attention to details

- are passive learners
- do not establish personal goals
- do not establish personal performance standards
- are not motivated by the payoffs for diligence
- have not internalized the basic principles of cause and effect (see Disregarding Consequences)

Children who are cavalier about important details rarely link their choice not to check their work carefully with the predictable consequence of this decision: a lower grade. When their parents or teachers point this out, chronically careless students typically disregard the warning or deny they have a problem. This attitude guarantees marginal performance and a defeatist attitude. Before long, these youngsters become resigned to mistakes and sloppy work as their "fate in life." To protect themselves from feeling inadequate, they might rationalize, "I can't spell no matter what I do!" "The teacher is unfair." "I can read what I write! That's what counts." "I don't care!"

Chronic inattentiveness to details is often associated with ADD (see Attention Deficit Disorder). Because children with concentration problems have poor impulse control and struggle to stay on task, filter out distractions, and monitor themselves, they characteristically rush through projects. The result is substandard work replete with mistakes.

Most children who habitually disregard important details can be taught to be more attentive. You must be prepared, however, for resistance. Like their adult counterparts, your child may be very reluctant to relinquish entrenched habits.

Corrective Strategies

In School

1.   (Elementary School, ES) If your child is not paying attention to details, ask her teacher to

in whose subjects your child is having difficulty. (If your child is in junior high school or high school and has teachers for each subject, it may be practical to have the school counselor distribute the checklists.) Explain to your child why you are requesting this information: "If you're going to improve your schoolwork and your grades, you need to know what the problem areas are. This

---

DAILY PERFORMANCE

Work Completed	_____	*Work Not Completed*	_____
Work Neat	_____	*Work Sloppy*	_____
Spelling Correct	_____	*Spelling Mistakes*	_____
Good Handwriting	_____	*Poor Handwriting*	_____

---

specify what is being neglected. Ask him if he would be willing to provide daily feedback. You might want to have the above Daily Performance rubber stamp made up at an office supply store. The teacher could stamp each assignment and pinpoint specific problems and accomplishments for one month. (This technique is not recommended for older students as such a stamp would cause embarrassment and probably trigger resentment.)

By indicating accomplishments as well as deficits, the teacher will provide your child with positive feedback. Your child needs to know when she's deficient, but she also needs to know when she's succeeding. Positive reinforcement is generally far more effective than negative reinforcement in stimulating effort and productive changes in behavior.

2.   To identify the specific details your child is overlooking or neglecting, ask your child's teacher(s) to complete the Attention to Details Checklist. (Make as many copies as you need.) Ask the teacher(s) to complete the same checklist one month later so that you can assess if your child is making progress. Ask only those teachers

checklist will provide this information, and we can then discuss a plan for making improvements."

ATTENTION TO DETAILS CHECKLIST

	YES	NO
This Student:		
Submits neat work.	_____	_____
Adequately proofreads assignments.	_____	_____
Writes legibly.	_____	_____
Hands in assigned work.	_____	_____
Hands in complete assignments.	_____	_____
Hands in assignments on time.	_____	_____
Follows instructions carefully.	_____	_____
Avoids careless mistakes.	_____	_____

At Home

1.   (ES) Use the teacher's daily feedback on the stamp to create a reward system, perhaps giving

points for each accomplishment. Your child might use the points to get a desired toy or perhaps a trophy. Do not subtract points for negative checks. Resist the temptation to lecture or sermonize. Help your child figure out why the teacher found problem areas. Identify with your child specific sloppy sections or spelling mistakes. Brainstorm together how these errors might be avoided on the next assignment. Show her how to proofread and edit. Make the sessions short.

2.   Brainstorm with your child how she could correct deficiencies on the checklist. Develop a plan with specific behavior and performance goals. She might create her own checklist for each assignment including categories such as "read twice," "check spelling," and so on. When your child is convinced her work is legible, she would check the appropriate column. Have her do the same after carefully proofreading the assignment. You might agree that initially you will check over the work. Once you see that your child is taking responsibility for the details, you will no longer need to monitor the work.

3.   (ES) Write a simple paragraph with basic, easy-to-identify spelling, grammar, and punctuation errors. Make a game of finding the errors, and encourage your child to locate as many mistakes as possible on her own. Then write a paragraph that's sloppy and hard to read. Examine the work with your child, brainstorm how to improve the legibility, and then rewrite the paragraph together. Perhaps you could write one sentence,

and your child could write the next. Keep the sessions short. Use your discretion in determining when to discontinue this process. Some children will make significant improvement in only five sessions. Others will require extended help. Remember to make these interactive exercises fun!

4.   (ES) Follow the same procedure with math problems. Make computational mistakes and let your child find them. Then intentionally do sloppy work. Actively involve your child in the process of attending to the details. When your child demonstrates that she is focusing on the details and is able to find her own mistakes, move on.

5.   (Junior High/High School, J/HS) Suggest to your child that she write as many assignments as possible on a computer. Show her how to use the spell check feature. If your word processing program does not have a grammar check, find out if you can supplement or upgrade your current program (see Grammar).

6.   (J/HS) Ask your child if she would be willing to critique and correct something you have written quickly. It could be a business letter you dashed off without careful editing. (Make sure you've "unintentionally overlooked" some obvious grammar, spelling, and syntax mistakes.) Discuss with your child the negative consequences of sending out the uncorrected letter to a business or professional associate or customer. Don't give a lecture or sermon! Discuss the issues matter-of-factly. Make the session short.

Atypical Learning Problems

Some learning deficits puzzle parents, teachers, resource specialists, and school psychologists. Everyone recognizes that a child is not learning efficiently, but no one may understand why. Unfortunately, children with hard-to-identify academic problems often slip through the safety net and receive little or no help. Schools generally reserve their assistance programs for students with specific learning deficits, and those children with subtle, nonspecific, or intermittent learning deficits are rarely provided with assistance. These struggling children with enigmatic problems are often described as being unmotivated or lacking in ability. Those who are intelligent but who are clearly not working up their full potential are labeled underachievers (see Underachievement).

Schools that prioritize educational problems according to seriousness may rationalize the denial of educational assistance to children with atypical learning problems, especially in an era when many school districts are woefully underfunded. The practice is analogous to battlefield triage where doctors are forced to treat only the most gravely wounded and must send the "walking wounded" back to the front lines. Unfortunately, the "minor" wounds often become infected and may ulitimately prove incapacitating.

Perplexed teachers who cannot define the source of a child's learning problems may be tempted to attribute the difficulties to immaturity, irresponsibility, laziness, or a negative attitude. These explanations are convenient, but they are often simplistic, inadequate, and misleading. Although counterproductive behaviors undoubtedly contribute to poor academic performance, the behaviors are often symptoms of underlying problems that must be diagnosed and remedied.

The term immaturity is especially misleading. Relatively few children who struggle in school are actually developmentally or physically immature. Labeling a child immature is often the teacher's way of saying "I don't really know what's wrong. I just know this student is doing marginal work and is capable of doing better. Maybe he's not ready to settle down and learn."

Parents and teachers may erroneously conclude that children with elusive problems are intellectually deficient. Unfortunately, these children often arrive at the same conclusion. Some students with atypical learning problems may on their own intuitively figure out how to overcome or compensate for their learning deficits, but many others become academically defeated and psychologically scarred by their painful school experiences. These youngsters may continue to perform below their potential throughout their education and, in many cases, throughout their lives. Children who become convinced by repeated negative experiences that effort is futile will be very tempted to turn off and shut down academically. To protect themselves emotionally, they will often acquire a set of psychological coping behaviors that include procrastination, irresponsibility, and laziness. These defense mechanisms only magnify their learning deficits (see Psychological Problems and Psychological Overlay). To deflect their parents' and teachers' high expectations and insulate themselves from frustration, disappointment, and feelings of incompetence, some children simply give up; some direct their attention and energy to pursuits at which they can succeed and may focus on sports or social relationships as surrogates for academic achievement; some will spend hours cerebrally anesthetized in front of the TV; others will experiment with drugs.

The inherent difficulty in identifying and treating atypical learning problems is compounded by another perplexing phenomenon. Some children with atypical learning problems do well in certain subjects and poorly in others. In second grade, a child may excel in math and struggle in reading. The following year, he may do well in reading and struggle in math. In high school, he may pay attention and be conscientious in history class but be distracted and unmotivated in science class. He may be inspired by his art teacher and work diligently and be unresponsive to his English teacher and not submit his assignments. He may study diligently during the first semester and shut down during the second half of the year. Such erratic performance patterns can perplex and test the patience and fortitude of even the most concerned and dedicated parents and teachers.

Because schools generally reserve their assistance programs for students with specific learning deficits, the resources for diagnosing and treating students with minimal, nonspecific, hard-to-identify, and nonacademically debilitating learning problems are quite limited. These children usually fall through the cracks.

Identifying nonspecific learning problems involves a degree of subjectivity. A school psychologist who relies exclusively on standardized tests and is locked into narrow diagnostic criteria (a minimum of two years below grade level, a significant discrepancy between subsections on the IQ test, or a significant discrepancy between standardized test performance and classroom performance) may overlook, disregard, or misdiagnose atypical learning patterns (see IQ Test Scores;

Performance on Standardized Tests). Children who aren't working up to their potential but who deviate only slightly from established test performance norms generally slip through the diagnostic screen. To assess these children properly, professionals must examine complex, overlapping factors that may include family dynamics, peer pressures, individual learning styles, teaching methods, perceptual decoding deficits, focusing deficits, and psychological issues. Many school districts would consider this comprehensive examination a luxury that they are unable to fund.

Once the underlying issues causing the child to function poorly or inconsistently in school are identified, the next challenge is to provide meaningful learning assistance. The appropriate intervention for a particular child might involve teaching him how to regulate and discipline himself (see Attention Deficit Disorder), organize his ideas (see Critical Thinking; Disorganization), budget his time (see Time Management), prepare for exams (see Preparing for Tests), recall information (see Memorizing Information), or write cogent reports (see Language Arts).

Not remedying hard-to-define learning deficits increases the risk that your child will continue to struggle and underachieve. The academic, psychological, and long-range vocational consequences can be disastrous. If you believe your child has atypical learning problems and diagnostic and remedial assistance is not available at school, seek help outside of school. Disregarding or minimizing the danger signals could lead to a tragic waste of human potential.

Corrective Strategies

In School

1.   If you suspect that your child has an atypical learning problem, request an evaluation by the school psychologist. If he doesn't qualify for testing (see Parents' Rights) or learning assistance, consider consulting a private diagnostician or educational therapist.

2.   If you believe that your child is struggling because he lacks effective study skills, request

that he be provided with assistance in this area (see Study Skills).

3.   If your child's teacher(s) can identify specific academic deficit areas, brainstorm together how the deficiencies might be resolved. Supplemental materials in spelling, reading, math, vocabulary, or in specific subject areas such as history or biology could be provided for use at home. Inquire if your child might benefit from a tutor and, if so, ask the teacher to refer you to one who is creative, skillful, and motivating.

4.   (Elementary School, ES) Inquire if it's feasible to create incentives in school for your child to improve his work, such as extra-credit projects. Perhaps the teacher could create a weekly award for the student who has made the most improvement. This system would permit struggling students to be acknowledged and affirmed for their effort, progress, and accomplishments (see Parent–Teacher Conferences).

At Home

1.   Encourage your child to establish realistic goals for improving work in specific subject areas (see Goals). For example, he might establish the short-term goal of improving his performance on weekly spelling tests. Also urge him to establish long-term goals such as raising his Spanish semester grade from a C- to a B-. One key to effective, motivational goal-setting is to involve your child actively in the process of establishing meaningful personal goals. You may want to "sweeten the pot" and increase his motivation by proposing incentives. For example, you might offer a camping trip or new skis as rewards for achieving a targeted grade on the next report card. These incentives are not bribes. They are rewards for work well done. Clearly, the ultimate goal is for these extrinsic payoffs to be supplanted by intrinsic payoffs: deriving personal pride and satisfaction from doing a first-rate job, being acknowledged for progress, being rewarded with a good grade, and receiving affirmation from parents, teachers, and peers (see Goals).

2.   Ask your child for his ideas about how he could improve his school performance, produce more accurate work, and prepare more effectively for tests (See Preparing for Tests). You might want to use the DIBS Problem-Solving Method to define the problems, identify the underlying issues, brainstorm possible solutions, and select a strategy to try out (see page 190 for a comprehensive description of the DIBS Method).

3.   If your child doesn't qualify for learning assistance in school and you cannot provide appropriate help at home, consider hiring a qualified tutor. If your child requires specialized help or intensive study skills instruction, consider enrolling your child at a private learning center or hiring a first-rate, highly trained educational therapist. Ask the teacher or principal for a referral. The person you select should be skilled in working with children who have atypical or puzzling learning problems and should be enthusiastic, creative, affirming, and motivating.

4.   Praise your child enthusiastically for improvements in attitude and performance. ("I'm very proud of you! You're getting much better at checking over your math homework and finding errors.") Communicate unequivocally your conviction that he can overcome the problems that are holding him back in school.

Auditory Discrimination

Being able to identify and differentiate accurately the sounds that letters and groups of letters produce is fundamental to learning to read and spell phonetically. The process of distinguishing or decoding spoken and written letters and sounds is called *auditory discrimination*.

Children are first taught basic auditory discrimination skills in kindergarten and first grade. In a phonetically oriented reading program, students are expected to break words down into phonetic fragments or *phonemes* (called *word, attack,* or *sounding-out*) and to blend the sounds together (see Phonics). The ability to discriminate sounds auditorily is central to the word attack/blending process. A child must be able to hear the difference between the sounds *a* and *o*, *fla* and *plo*, and *t* and *p* if he is to read words such as *flap* and *plot*.

Auditory discrimination skills are not only vital to reading, they are also essential to spelling; when spelling, children usually use three overlapping perceptual processing skills: auditory discrimination, auditory memory, and visual memory. Most good spellers rely primarily on visual memory and "see" the letters of words in their mind. Auditory discrimination can also be a very important resource for spelling, especially when a child is unfamiliar with the word and the word is phonetic (follows prescribed pronunciation rules). The child who cannot distinguish between the short *i* in the word *pig* and the short *e* in the word *peg* will often have spelling problems.

Children identified as having significant auditory discrimination deficits will require assistance from a resource specialist, educational therapist, or speech pathologist. These specialists can employ a wide range of highly effective remedial methods to help students overcome auditory discrimination problems. If the discrimination problems are severe, the student's hearing should be tested by a pediatrician or licensed audiologist to determine if the deficits are attributable to a hearing impairment. Most children who struggle to discriminate sounds, however, do not have a hearing loss. They can actually hear the sounds, but for complex neurological reasons they have difficulty decoding the auditory input.

The *sight method* has been another widely used system for teaching students to read. In the United States, the popularity of reading techniques is cyclical. The phonetic approach may be in vogue for a while, and then the sight method will be reintroduced with perhaps minor modifications. Finally, a "revolutionary" new method will be developed and sold to schools. In time, this method will be abandoned, and the cycle starts again. The net gains in reading scores generally remain the same, irrespective of what method is used. A positive explanation for this educational phenomenon is that the recycling of methods reflects the sincere effort by educators and publishers to improve reading instruction. A negative explanation is that textbook publishers want to sell new books and "churn" reading methods for the same reason that unscrupulous stockbrokers churn accounts and suggest unnecessary sales and purchases to generate more commissions.

The sight method de-emphasizes phonics and auditory decoding and sequentially introduces entire words to students. The level of difficulty of these words is carefully controlled and linked to the grade level of the students. Students learn to read through repeated exposure and practice, without having to sound out the words. The sight method is generally effective with children who have good visual memory and no underlying reading or learning disabilities. Children with reading problems, however, usually do better in a phonics-oriented program. Although the instructional pendulum periodically swings from the sight method to the phonics method, most schools are now teaching children to read phonetically or are using the new "whole language approach" (see Nonphonetic Words; Phonics).

Corrective Strategies

In School

1.   If you suspect that your child has an auditory discrimination deficit, request that she be evaluated by the school psychologist, speech therapist, or resource specialist. Many excellent tests can quickly pinpoint deficiencies. An especially effective and comprehensive test is called the LAC Test, published by Developmental Learning Materials.

2.   If deficits are identified, request that your child be provided with remedial assistance from a resource specialist, speech therapist, or reading specialist. In some schools, teachers and volunteer parents have been trained in the Lindemood Auditory Discrimination in Depth Program (also referred to as the A.D.D. Program). This systematic and comprehensive program has proven very effective.

At Home

1.   (Elementary School, ES) Go to a teacher supply house and ask about tapes, books, computer software, and games that teach auditory dis-

crimination skills. An extensive range of materials is available, and publishers are continually adding new materials. (Refer also to the Resource List at the end of this book.)

2.   (ES) Write all of the consonants on a sheet of paper and practice pronouncing with your child the name of the letter and the sound the letter makes. (If your child is very young or is having a hard time discriminating sounds, use only one sound each time you work together.) To help your child discriminate the consonants, carefully enunciate (exaggerate if your child is struggling) a selected word that begins with the consonants you're teaching (for example, *top*). Have your child underline the consonants she hears. Select your sample words in advance.

After practicing all of the beginning consonants (not in one session!), select a word with a consonant in the middle (for example, *sitting*). Ask your child to identify the beginning and the middle consonant. Then have her identify the final consonant in selected words (for example, *big*). Later, have your child identify beginning, middle, and ending consonants in words. Make the activity fun! Make the session a game. You might give points for each correct answer. Keep track of the points and encourage her to improve her score each time you play. Repeat the activity over several weeks. Know when to quit for the day. Stop if you find yourself losing patience or becoming frustrated. You may have to go over the same sound for several days before your child masters it. A child with significant auditory discrimination problems cannot reasonably be expected to master a number of sounds in one day. Be patient and be prepared for plateaus and occasional regression. Spend time watching *Sesame Street* with your child. Pay special attention to the sounds they introduce and reinforce for the day. (This recommendation is primarily for younger children, because older children may consider *Sesame Street* demeaning. Be sensitive and respectful of their feelings. If you cannot convince them of the value of the activity, abandon the idea.) Reinforce the sound or sounds introduced each day, using some of the show's highly creative ideas. You could also put plastic alphabet letters in a hat and have your child pick a letter, and then try to think of as many words as she can that have that letter (or sound) in it. Many of the materials that can be purchased in a teacher supply store or bookstore will suggest other games and activities you can play with your child that will help her learn to discriminate sounds. If you conclude you cannot work easily with your child, consider hiring a well-trained tutor or enrolling your child in a specialized learning center.

3.   (ES) Following the same procedure outlined above, write the five vowels on a sheet of paper. Say a single-syllable phonetic word (for example, *peg*, *top*, *pin*) and have your child write down the vowel sound she hears in the middle of the word. Once she becomes proficient at identifying the five vowel sounds, begin using multisyllable words (for example, *hanging*) and have her write down both of the vowel sounds she hears. Make this a game, and make it fun by giving her points for correct answers. Keep track of your child's score each time you play and encourage her to improve her score the next time. Be careful not to lose your patience if she struggles or has difficulty identifying a sound you thought she had already learned. When she has mastered these sounds, progress to identifying vowel/consonant sound combinations (such as *en*, *un*, *in*, *an*) and follow the same procedure.

Auditory Memory

Students are constantly bombarded with verbal information. They must remember their teachers' instructions about how to format an English book report, fill out a test answer sheet, and solve an algebraic equation. They must remember which science exercises to complete in class and which pages in their history text to read for homework. They must recall the definitions of vocabulary words and the teacher's clues about what will be covered on the next Spanish test. For reasons that cannot be easily explained, some children have difficulty with auditory memory tasks. These children are at a significant disadvantage in school. If their memory deficits are chronic, their performance in every subject area could be undermined.

The negative effects of poor auditory memory are not limited to the classroom. If your child is struggling to remember what he is told in school, he will probably also have difficulty remembering what you tell him at home. You might ask him to set the table, feed the dog, and bring in the newspaper. He may appear to be listening, but thirty minutes later you discover that the chores have not been done. Your child's explanation is usually quite simple: "I forgot."

Students with auditory recall and auditory sequencing deficits (remembering information in the proper order) usually receive a great deal of negative feedback from perplexed and frustrated teachers and parents. (Some of these children may also have concentration problems—see Attention Deficit Disorder.) Because they do not know how to compensate effectively for their memory deficits, they may seem confused, disoriented, and absentminded. Memory lapses may lead parents and teachers to conclude erroneously that they are disinterested, inattentive, resistant, and/or lacking in intelligence.

The most obvious way for children to compensate for their poor auditory recall is to write down important information (see Notetaking; Recording Assignments). Students who can think strategically will recognize the practical benefits of this solution and avail themselves of it (see Smart Thinking). Some students, however, overcompensate and try to write down everything, and in their attempt to "get it down on paper," they may not actually listen to what they are told (see Listening in Class). This will undermine their comprehension.

Even students with good auditory memory skills must record assignments and instructions. Ironically, children with the greatest need to record information are usually the most resistant to doing so. They are either too lazy to make the effort, or they insist on deluding themselves that they will remember. The consequences are inevitable: they omit important details, forget to do assignments, fail to follow instructions, submit incomplete work, and miss deadlines (see Following Verbal Instructions).

Youngsters with short or long-term auditory memory deficits are at a particular disadvantage when they have teachers who do a great deal of lecturing. These children understandably experience insecurity and anxiety whenever they're required to follow and recall instructions and explanations. Stress magnifies their frustration, demoralization, and diminished self-confidence. By the age of eight, many bright and potentially capable children with severe auditory memory problems have already concluded they're inept. This conclusion can have tragic academic and vocational consequences.

With systematic training and sufficient practice, most children can significantly improve their auditory recall skills. They can acquire a range of memory "tricks" that utilize other sensory modalities to compensate for their memory deficits. A child given verbal instructions could compensate for his memory deficits by visualizing the steps as opposed to trying to hear and remember them by sound. (Specific strategies are described below.) As children improve listening and auditory recall skills, they will acquire more confidence. This, in turn, will positively alter their mindset about their listening and retention capabilities.

Corrective Strategies

In School

1.   If you believe your child has an auditory memory problem, discuss your concerns with the teacher. If he concurs that there is a problem, request that your child be tested by the school psychologist or resource specialist. Highly reliable tests can quickly confirm if a short or long-term memory problem exists.

2.   If diagnostic testing reveals an auditory memory deficiency, request that the resource specialist provide your child with special assistance. If this request is denied because your child's problems are not deemed sufficiently serious, you may need to become assertive (see Parents' Rights). For teaching materials commonly used in resource programs to develop auditory memory skills, see the Resource List at the back of this book.

3.   (Elementary School, ES) Request that the teacher initial an assignment sheet each day to confirm that your child has properly recorded the information (see Recording Assignments). The teacher might also periodically check to make sure the child understands and remembers instructions for completing in-class assignments. The teacher might ask your child to repeat instructions from time to time, thus serving notice that he must pay attention and remember directions. This should be done diplomatically to prevent embarrassment, especially if your child has chronic memory problems. It serves no purpose for your child to feel ridiculed or harassed. As your child's memory skills improve, such monitoring can be phased out.

4.   If your child's memory deficits are compounded by concentration problems, refer to the suggestions and strategies listed under Attention Deficit Disorder. Also see suggestions under Following Verbal Directions.

At Home

1.   When giving instructions to your child at home, initially limit the amount of information you're asking him to remember. You might begin with two or three tasks. (Too many instructions can cause a child with auditory memory problems to go into meltdown!) Ask your child to repeat the instructions and then close his eyes and see himself doing the tasks in the proper sequence: setting the table, placing the food in the dog's bowl, and taking out the trash. Encouraging your child to make a visual picture of auditory information will help him compensate for auditory memory deficits (see Memorizing Information; Visual Memory).

2.   Play auditory memory games around the dinner table. One person says a number (initially two or three digits) and the person sitting next to him says the number in reverse order. Encourage your child to close his eyes and see the number in his mind, perhaps in his favorite color. The person then asks the first person to repeat the number in the original order. Build to three, then four, numbers. Later, build to as many numbers as possible. Remember to make the interaction a

game. Siblings are not permitted to tease (or put down) each other. Follow the same procedure with the names of objects (hat, needle, plum, hairbrush). Have your child make a mental picture and then repeat the objects in reverse order. If reversing the order is at first too difficult, have him repeat the original order. Control the level of difficulty until his skills and confidence improve. Make up variations of the game using sounds or clapping patterns (two fast beats, four slow beats, three fast beats). This will develop auditory memory skills and auditory sequencing skills. Your objective is to set your child up to win and help him overcome negative associations with his capacity to recall what he has heard.

3.   Urge your child to make up acronyms to help him remember verbal information (for example, SOHCAHTOA: sine = opposite over hypotenuse / cosine = adjacent over hypotenuse / tangent = opposite over adjacent). Making up rhymes and simple songs can also help him retain information ("Go to the store for eggs and bread. Get some milk and cheese instead. When you get home, the dog must be fed and take the cat off of the bed.")

4.   Encourage your child to record homework assignments and teacher's instructions on paper (see Recording Assignments and Following Verbal Instructions).

5.   (ES) Go to your local teacher supply store or bookstore and ask for books, software, and games designed specifically to develop auditory memory skills.

Behavior and Attitude

Children who are not clear about their family's rules for acceptable and unacceptable behavior are invariably confused and unhappy. The absence of clearly defined and consistent external structure and control prevents these youngsters from developing clearly defined internal structure and control. This capacity to self-regulate is a requisite to acquiring self-confidence, self-sufficiency, and self-esteem (see Expectations and Performance Guidelines).

When children lack a frame of reference for what is permissible and what is not, they inevitably have difficulty conforming to society's value system. Because they're unclear about the difference between right and wrong and haven't internalized limits, they never complete the normal testing phase of two- and three-year-olds. Those who remain unsure of the boundaries may express their confusion by becoming disrespectful, unruly, manipulative, or delinquent. Others may manifest their uncertainty by continually breaking the rules and then denying their responsibility for the consequences. They may conveniently rationalize their actions by blaming others for their problems, transgressions, mistakes, and setbacks. They may act out in class, cut school, and constantly challenge the "system" and all authority figures. They may become bullies, liars, sneaks, or con artists. In extreme cases, they may cheat, steal, become violent, or take drugs.

Children who haven't imprinted their family's standards, values, and guidelines usually have great difficulty relating to basic cause-and-effect principles and are frequently oblivious to the predictable negative consequences of their actions and attitude. Some don't do their homework. Some take unnecessary risks. Some take great pleasure in disregarding or purposely contravening the feelings and wishes of others (see Disregarding Consequences). Although they may manifest great bravado, these youngsters are typically insecure, resistant, defiant, unmotivated, and unwilling to establish personal goals and meet reasonable performance standards.

During the first eight years of a child's life, the nuclear family is not intended to be a model of democracy. Children must be told when to go to bed, when to turn off the television, and when to stop making noise. They must be taught socially acceptable manners and be trained to consider other people's feelings. They must be taught to be respectful of their parents and teachers and to live by their family's and their society's rules. Fair, reasonable, and consistently applied guidelines provide them with security, values, and a moral foundation that will help them handle effectively life's challenges, problems, setbacks, and opportunities.

Your child must understand unequivocally that you expect him to do homework, make the best possible effort, keep commitments, complete projects, submit assignments on time, do chores, attend to important details, and use his head when confronting danger. He must understand that you expect him to act honorably and treat others with respect and consideration. Clearly communicate the value you place on acquiring a first-rate education and the academic and social skills needed to succeed in life. If he fails to assimilate your guidelines, values, and rules, how can you realistically expect him to reject the drugs offered him, resist the temptation to cheat on a test, or refuse to drive with someone who is intoxicated?[1] As your child matures and demonstrates he has internalized the family's rules, standards, and values, he'll discover that he will be rewarded with greater freedom. By demonstrating responsibility and a knowledge of the difference between right and wrong and between smart and not smart, he'll earn more control over his own life. This incremental empowerment is a vital requisite to preparing your child to become a self-sufficient, independent, responsible adult.

Corrective Strategies

In School

1.   If the teacher has indicated on report cards that your child is having difficulty conforming to the rules of behavior or academic guidelines, request a conference to acquire as much specific information about his behavior and attitude as possible. Make note of the teacher's concerns. Unless you believe the teacher is unfair or unreasonable, do not attempt to excuse your child's behavior. Brainstorm how the unacceptable behaviors might be modified. If your child is manifesting a great many counterproductive behaviors, prioritize the list, as it will be impossible to correct all of the problems at once. Ask for suggestions about how you might modify your parenting strategy. Also explore changes that might be made in the classroom. For example, if your child tells you the teacher is embarrassing him in class or continually reprimanding him, and if you believe your child is reacting by misbehaving, discuss how this situation might be altered. Could the teacher make an effort to find

something positive and compliment your child? (Children usually respond better to positive feedback than to negative feedback!) Ask the teacher if he believes your child would benefit from individual or family therapy. (You don't necessarily have to follow the recommendation.) By convincing the teacher that you appreciate the difficulties your child's behavior might create in the classroom and expressing a sincere desire to help solve the problem, you will enlist his active support.

2.   Ask the teacher if your child's unacceptable behavior may be due to frustration because he cannot do the assigned work or due to feelings of inadequacy and demoralization. If your child has learning problems or study skills deficits, inquire about his eligibility for resource programs. (Refer to relevant entries in this book for the specific symptoms of learning disabilities and strategies for correcting these problems.) If you conclude that your child should be tested by the school psychologist to identify the underlying factors that may be causing counterproductive behaviors and/or learning difficulties, request a diagnostic evaluation (see Parents' Rights).

3.   Ask if the school counselor, vice principal, or principal should be also involved in counseling and monitoring your child. If your child is disruptive or fighting with other children, he may need someone with extensive counseling experience to help him examine his actions and clearly define the school rules and behavior guidelines. Ideally, this involvement by the school administration will not be exclusively punitive.

At Home

1.   Create a checklist of specific behaviors you want your child to improve (see model page 12). Focus initially on one to three behaviors you would like your child to modify. Ask the teacher to evaluate your child each day in such areas as paying attention, following instructions, or handing in assignments on time. Have the teacher use a simple code: 0 = poor; 1 = fair; 2 = good; 3 = excellent. The process should take no more

---

1. See my book *The Life-Smart Kid* (Prima Publishing, 1995) for more about teaching children to make wise choices.

than two minutes and will provide you with daily feedback. Initial the checklist each evening so the teacher knows you've seen it. Explain succinctly to your child why you're setting up this system and why school rules such as paying attention, raising your hand, and following directions are as important as at-home rules such as telling the truth, completing chores, being cooperative, and brushing teeth. With your child's active participation, establish a system for rewarding improvements in behavior. Reward systems usually work better than punishment systems (although punishment may be appropriate in certain situations). Rely on your judgment. The ultimate goal is for your child to behave for intrinsic rewards such as pride and satisfaction, and not for extrinsic rewards. Behavior modification requires time and patience. As a general rule, the more insight and awareness your child has about his behavior and its impact on oth-

ers, the more receptive he'll be to making positive changes.[2] And the more actively you involve your child in the process of establishing personal behavioral goals, the more successful the process will be. (For additional ideas, see the DIBS Method desribed on page 190).

2.   If your child will not accept reasonable behavior guidelines despite your best efforts and continues to break the rules at home and in school, consult a trained mental health professional. Request a referral from your pediatrician, school principal, or school psychologist.

---

2. Behavior modification "purists" would argue it isn't necessary for children to understand the underlying issues causing their negative behavior and all that matters is that child's counterproductive behavior is modififed. The long-term benefit of this "who cares about what's causing the problem, let's just eliminate the behaviors" approach is debatable.

Bouncing Back from Setbacks and Learning from Mistakes

Mistakes and setbacks are inescapable facts of life, and children must learn to overcome them if they are to survive and prevail in a competitive, demanding world. Those who don't develop the ability to analyze challenges, problems, and miscues, who cannot figure out how to make tactical adjustments, who lack emotional resiliency, and who are unable to bounce back from life's defeats are destined to suffer greatly.

Successful students share several key traits. They have a compelling need to understand the issues, to pit their talents against the obstacles and challenges they encounter, to learn from their mistakes, and to make things work. To an achieving, self-confident child with healthy self-esteem, a setback is an invitation to a wrestling match. Convinced she deserves to prevail in the battle and driven by ego (a positive sense of self and one's own power), she perseveres until she succeeds or becomes absolutely convinced the problem is indeed insoluble (see Effort and Motivation; Goals; Smart Thinking).

In contrast, the nonachieving child, when faced with a setback, typically lacks self-confidence, effective problem-solving skills, and emotional resiliency. Rather than seek a pragmatic alternative plan to get the job done, the child either plows ahead mindlessly and repeats the same mistakes or simply gives up whenever she experiences a defeat. Repeated setbacks take a cumulative psychological toll, and the child will become increasingly frustrated, demoralized, insecure, and fragile. Convinced that effort is futile and failure inevitable, the child will probably shut down. (See Anger and Frustration; Fear of Failure/Success/Competition; Psychological Problems and Psychological Overlay).

A child's confidence in her ability to handle predicaments effectively is a direct reflection of her life experiences. Children who overcome obstacles and survive occasional failures, disappointments, and rejections acquire faith in themselves. Repeated failure and defeats, on the other hand, will erode this self-confidence and trigger anxiety, frustration, depression, anger, and counterproductive, self-protecting behavior.

Fearful of exposing themselves to additional failure, children who have been chronically unsuccessful in school usually try to distance themselves from situations that might expose their real or imagined inadequacies. By running away, they can avoid the stress of having to confront and prevail over obstacles, challenges, and problems that from their vantage point seem monumental and insurmountable (see Learned Helplessness). They may blame others, procrastinate, manipulate, act irresponsibly, become withdrawn, or feel sorry for themselves. Although on the surface they may appear lazy, resistant, and unmotivated, beneath the surface they are driven by fear, insecurity, frustration, feelings of incompetence and futility, and a powerful instinct to protect themselves. From their vantage point, the outcome seems inevitable: if they continue trying, they will fail again.

Every child of normal intelligence can be systematically taught how to analyze problems, link errors in judgment with the outcome, identify consistencies and inconsistencies, find common denominators, and deal with setbacks (see Critical Thinking; Problem Solving; Smart Thinking). Teaching children these skills is every bit as vital as teaching them how to read, write, and do math.

The child who continues to be crushed by mistakes and setbacks is waving a red flag. If he doesn't respond to your best efforts to help (see suggestions below) and you suspect that psychological or family problems may be overwhelming his coping skills, it is vital that you provide him with professional counseling.

Corrective Strategies

In School

1.   If you observe that your child lacks emotional resiliency and is not applying appropriate problem-solving skills to setbacks and reversals, ask the teacher if she has observed the same behaviors in class. If so, explore strategies for helping your child modify his response patterns. For example, if he does poorly on a math test, have him analyze the test problems with you and help him identify specific difficulties. Did the errors involve "silly" computational mistakes or did he not know how to solve the problems? Was he nervous? Did he forget his number facts? Did he forget how to solve algebraic equations? Encourage him to develop a practical strategy for improving his performance on the next test. For example, design a simple checklist that he's completed his homework and checked it over for careless mistakes (see Incomplete Assignments; Monitoring Homework; Study Skills). Perhaps he might do some simple relaxation techniques before taking a test. The goal is to show your child how he can avoid making many common mistakes and how to respond strategically to setbacks when they occur. Once he becomes convinced that he can handle glitches and learn from setbacks, his self-confidence cannot help but improve (see Smart Thinking for other methods that encourage more strategic planning and problem solving).

2.   Ask your child's teacher if other students are also having trouble handling setbacks and mistakes. If she says yes, ask if she would be willing to incorporate into the curriculum procedures designed to improve the students' analytical problem-solving skills. The class might be given a copy of a test that received a poor grade. (This should not be a student's actual test, but rather a test the teacher has intentionally sabotaged for the purposes of illustration.) The class (or small cooperative learning groups) could analyze why the student did poorly and explore specific ways to improve his study strategy for the next test. The problem-solving template that appears below provides a practical step-by-step format for analyzing mistakes.

PROCEDURES FOR LEARNING FROM MISTAKES

- *Define the obvious.* ("I didn't accurately identify the information that would be covered on the test, and I made careless mistakes.")
- *Identify the mistake.* ("I didn't make a checklist of important information I needed to learn.")
- *Investigate.* ("What specific study skills techniques might I use in preparing for the next test?")
- *Explore corrective options.* ("I'll need to allow enough time to learn the important information, and I'll need to figure out a system for memorizing key facts.")
- *Look for the common denominator.* ("If the teacher usually gives this type of test, and my study strategy hasn't worked so far, I need to make adjustments.")

Students must practice analytical problem-solving procedures many times before they master the method and make it an integral part of their responses to problems, challenges, and reversals.

---

3.   If you would like more specific input from the teacher, ask him to complete the two checklists that follow.

At Home

1.   If you've observed your child having difficulty handling setbacks and mistakes, the following checklists will help you identify specific counterproductive behavior patterns.

LEARNING FROM MISTAKES CHECKLIST

	YES	NO
My child (or student):		
Becomes very discouraged when she makes a mistake.	____	____
Is afraid of making mistakes.	____	____
Tends to give up if she makes a mistake.	____	____
Makes the same mistake repeatedly.	____	____
Fails to examine her mistakes.	____	____
Does not perceive the common denominators that run through her mistakes.	____	____
Resists admitting that she has made a mistake.	____	____
Demonstrates deficient judgment.	____	____
Is very defensive about mistakes.	____	____
Is unwilling to discuss mistakes with me.	____	____
Blames others for his mistakes.	____	____

BOUNCING BACK FROM SETBACKS CHECKLIST

	YES	NO
My child (or student):		
Gets very discouraged when he encounters a setback.	____	____
Is tempted to give up when he fails at something.	____	____
Tries to avoid things that are difficult.	____	____
Is convinced he is dumb when he has a setback.	____	____
Regrets having tried something when he doesn't do well.	____	____
Believes people think less of him if they know he has failed at something.	____	____
Doesn't like to admit that he has had a setback.	____	____
Wants to run away and hide after a failure.	____	____
Quits when doing something that becomes too difficult.	____	____
Is unwilling to ask for help.	____	____
Gets so frustrated when he encounters difficulty that he can no longer work efficiently.	____	____
Becomes defensive when he must ask for help.	____	____

2. Use the DIBS Problem-Solving Method described on page 190 to analyze the issues identified on the checklist that are causing your child to respond counterproductively to setbacks and mistakes. If your child's nonadaptive response patterns persist, consult a mental health professional. Chronic challenge-avoidance tendencies, phobias, insecurity, demoralization, frustration, and exploding or imploding anger can cause serious psychological damage and erect major academic and vocational barriers. The underlying problems must be addressed and resolved if you want to prevent self-sabotaging behavior patterns from becoming entrenched.

Communicating with the School

How involved parents should become in their child's education is controversial. Some teachers and school districts welcome active parental participation in the educational process. Others consider this involvement an intrusion, especially when parents presume to find fault with the system and the status quo. Although parents have traditionally been encouraged to participate in organizations such as the PTA, their participation is typically restricted to sponsoring paper drives, helping out on the playground, or chaperoning field trips. The welcome mat is usually withdrawn when parents attempt to question educational policies, methodology, objectives, and priorities, or teachers' and administrators' salaries and qualifications. The notable exception occurs in "open" schools where parents are expected to assist in the classroom and interact with the professional staff. Teachers and administrators opposed to parental involvement in the day-to-day affairs of the classroom generally justify their resistance with the same arguments that physicians might offer in discouraging laypeople from becoming involved in the day-to-day affairs of the local community hospital. They argue that nonprofessionals are unqualified. This elitism is a common by-product of highly specialized training. Experts, be they physicians or educators, tend to acquire an inflated sense of their skills, autonomy, and prerogatives, and they may convince themselves that those who have not been trained professionally cannot possibly understand the complex issues central to their work.

School personnel who construe inquiries as criticism, suggestions as threats, or requests for help as exploitive are insecure, lazy, arrogant, and/or incompetent. Something is wrong when reasonable requests for information, flexibility, or justifiable special treatment are greeted with resistance and resentment. Providing information and responding to questions is a basic responsibility of educators. Those who forget this obligation do a disservice to their profession and their students.

The argument that most parents lack the expertise to develop a curriculum or to critique educational objectives fails to acknowledge the value and legitimacy of their questions, perceptions, and insights. Competent teachers and administrators are usually delighted when parents want to take an active role in monitoring their child and want to be kept apprised of what is happening in class. They realize that when parents understand the issues, provide support at home, and have realistic expectations, the school's job becomes easier.

You don't have to be a professional educator to sense intuitively when a teacher or a school is not meeting your child's needs. You have a right to communicate with the school authorities. You are also justified in expecting that teachers and school administrators will examine any issues you raise, even if your perceptions prove inaccurate or your concerns prove unwarranted.

The option to become actively involved in your child's educational process is, of course, predicated on your being reasonable and rational. Your right to be consulted, request information, examine issues, and make suggestions is not an unrestricted license to interfere in the operation of the classroom nor is it a license to make unfair and excessive demands on the teacher's time.

By monitoring your child's progress, clearly expressing your concerns, asking pentrating questions, requesting incisive answers, discussing the merits and possible shortcomings of particular programs, and requesting that teachers and administrators clarify their educational objectives, you serve notice that your child is not the only one being held accountable for a good performance. The educational establishment is also accountable. When you, as a member of the local community, request cogent answers to your reasonable concerns and exert pressure on your childs's school to improve the quality of its "educational product," you perform a vital function. Your proactive, constructive participation significantly increases the likelihood that your child will receive a first-rate education.

The first step in becoming involved in your child's education is to talk with your child's teacher. If you are dissatisfied with her response to your concerns or request for information, you have several options:

- You can resign yourself and accept the status quo.

- You can discusss your concerns with the principal.

- You can request that your child be placed in another class.

- You can seek private educational therapy or tutoring.

- You can discuss your concerns with the superintendent.

- You can exercise your right of due process and request a hearing if you feel your child's federally mandated rights are being violated (see Parents' Rights).

- You can address your concerns to the school board.

- You can enroll your child in a private school.

The need to become actively engaged in monitoring your child's education is more urgent if you are convinced that the teacher's attitude or methods are causing your child to suffer academically or psychologically. Whether it is lack of direction, structure, discipline, or standards in your child's class, you have a responsibility to discuss these matters with the teacher. Realize, however, that if you become hostile, confrontational, accusatory, unreasonable, irrational, adversarial, argumentative, arrogant, or intransigent, you will likely meet with resistance and resentment. It is far more strategic to present your concerns diplomatically, to be sensitive to the teacher's feelings, and to acknowledge the challenges she faces (for example, she may have a large percentage of non-English-speaking students or students with widely divergent skills). Teachers who feel they are being unfairly attacked often become preoccupied with defending themselves and tend to resist making changes in their modus operandi.

You, your child's teacher, and the school administration have a shared objective: to help your child become skilled, productive, self-sufficient, and self-confident. This goal becomes attainable when everyone is willing to work together.

Corrective Strategies

In School

1. If you and your child's teacher are having difficulty discussing or resolving legitimate issues relating to your child's education, diplomatically express your concerns. You might say: "I sense that we may be having some communication problems. I need to identify problem areas so that I can figure out how to provide appropriate support for my child. You are a vital source of information. If positive changes are to occur, we have to be able to work together." If the teacher is overly sensitive or defensive, you might say: "I'm not here to criticize you or to make your job more difficult. My objective is to find solutions to

problems and to help my child remove the obstacles blocking academic success. Your observations and suggestions are invaluable to me."

2.   The more specifically you can identify deficits and develop corrective strategies, the better. You might say to the teacher: "You said that my child procrastinates and is unmotivated. What can we do to help him stop these counter-productive behaviors, and what specifically should I be doing to help him?" (To get specific feedback about your child's possible deficits, refer to the Student Evalutaion Checklists on pages **128–130**.) "Would a behavior modification checklist be effective in getting him on track? The checklist would keep me informed about his daily performance and behavior. How could we set up this system in your class, and how could I set up a parallel system at home?"

At Home

1.   The information your child's teacher provides about his classroom performance, effort, behavior, and attitude can be used as a catalyst for discussion and problem solving at home. If the teacher tells you that your child is not submitting assignments on time, you might say: "Your teacher is concerned about your late assignments. She says your last book report, for example, was handed in two days late. Let's take a look at how you could solve this problem . . ." (For additional suggestions, see Disorganization; Goals; Inadequate study Time; Incomplete Assignments; Planning Ahead; Smart Thinkging; Time Management.)

2.   If your child is not making an adequate effort in school, let him know that you will be in close communication with the teacher. Realizing that you "mean business" about being responsible and conscientious and that you are going to monitor behavior can be a powerful deterrent to counterproductive behavior (see Behavior and Attitude, and Expectations and Performance Guidelines).

3.   If you conclude that you cannot communicate successfully with your child's teacher, request that a mediator be invited to participate in your next conference. You might suggest the principal, vice principal, school psychologist, school counselor, or resource specialist. (See Conferencing with School Officials, and Parent-Teacher Conferences).

Conferencing with School Officials

When parents feel thwarted in their attempts to communicate with their child's teacher or resource specialist (see Communicating with the School; Parent-Teacher Conferences) or when they cannot allay their concerns about their child's academic progress, they have two options: they can resign themselves to the situation or they can shift into a more aggressive, proactive mode.

Parents who choose the second option should make an appointment to discuss their concerns with the vice principal, principal, counselor, and/or school psychologist. If they are still dissatisfied, they should request a meeting with the superintendent.

Legitimate topics for discussion with school administrators include educational goals, teaching methodology, classroom discipline, grading criteria, friction between a child and the teacher, friction between the parent and the teacher, and homework assignments. If parents conclude that their child has learning problems and is being damaged in school, they are justified in requesting:

• reasonable instructional accommodations to their child's learning weaknesses and strengths (such as an individualized instructional strategy).

• reasonable modifications in the quantity and difficulty level of in-class work and homework assignments.

• reasonable accommodations when administering tests (for example, allowing the child more time to complete tests or "downloading" test

questions so the child with learning disabilities and seriously deficient academic skills will not become demoralized).

Parents are also justified in exploring with school administrators:

• the rationale for refusing to administer a diagnostic test to a child who is struggling academically

• the rationale for refusing to place an academically deficient child in a resource program

• the rationale for wanting a child to repeat a grade, enter or leave a resource program, or be transferred to another class or "magnet" school.

You have a compelling obligation to serve as your child's advocate, especially when you feel your child's educational needs are not being met by the classroom teacher or the educational system. You may be reluctant to go "over the teacher's head," but doing so is reasonable if this can help spare your child from unnecessary pain and suffering.

Parents who experience anxiety when they contemplate conferencing with school officials may have imprinted negative associations about confrontations with authority figures. They may recall being sent to the office when they misbehaved in school. Although they are now adults, they may still have misgivings about dealing with a school principal or counselor. The antidote for these apprehensions is for parents to remind themselves that their taxes pay the salaries of school officials and that they have a responsibility to represent their child's best interests when problems arise in school.

Anxiety about dealing with school officials may also be linked to the tendency by educators to use technical jargon. Terms such as *attention deficit disorder, dyslexia, auditory discrimination,* and *visual memory* can be incomprehensible and intimidating to an uninitiated parent. (All of these terms are defined in this book.) In fairness, it should be noted that this specialized vocabulary and jargon serve the legitimate function of permitting educators to discuss complex issues with precision. However, when educational jargon is wittingly or unwittingly used to exclude parents from understanding matters that are vital to a child's welfare, this technical language becomes an impediment to communication. Professionals who intentionally employ jargon as a smoke screen or to deflect dissent are either insecure or incompetent and deserve to be challenged.

Any capable educator should be able to explain your child's educational problems and academic issues in terms that you can understand. If you're confused about the meaning of a standardized achievement test score or about diagnostic terminology, do not hesitate to ask for clarification (see Performance on Standardized Tests; Understanding Diagnostic Test Results). If you are still confused, ask for further clarification. Admitting that you are not familiar with technical jargon or that you do not understand a test score is not an admission of ignorance. You have a legal right to all educational information that pertains to your child, and you have the right to insist that this information be explained in language you can comprehend.

Conferences with school officials are most productive when the participants are reasonable, nonadversarial, nonstrident, and committed to working together. Avoiding conflict is clearly in everyone's best interest. Presenting your position, expressing doubts, and communicating disapproval without triggering defensiveness and

resistance can be a monumental test of your diplomatic skills.

Federal law requires that your child's school provide learning assistance if her needs can be clearly documented and if she meets the defined qualification criteria (see Parents' Rights). If your child's school refuses to provide learning assistance because of stringent entrance requirements or limited resources, you may agree to a less-than-ideal compromise (such as the teacher trying to provide extra help for your child before class), or you may decide to do battle with the school system. Acceptance of a compromise does not mean passively acquiescing to an incompetent teacher, an inadequate program, or an inflexible and insensitive bureaucracy. If you believe that your school district is in noncompliance with federal and state law, it may be in your child's best interest to become confrontational. The law clearly mandates avenues for filing a protest and guarantees due process for resolving disputes (see Parents' Rights).

If you cannot procure the help your child needs within the public school system, seek help outside the system. Tutoring, educational therapy, counseling, or private schooling may be your only recourse. Unfortunately, these can be expensive.

Request periodic conferences (every four to six months) with school officials to discuss concerns and problems, evaluate progress, and develop strategies. Be reasonable. Do not make unrealistic or excessive demands on the time of teachers or administrators or you will undoubtedly meet with resistance and resentment. Use your judgment as to what is reasonable and what is unreasonable.

Corrective Strategies

In School

1.   The guiding principle in conferencing successfully with the school administration is to ask focused questions and address specific issues.

Problems must be accurately identified before they can be solved. The Student Evaluation Form for elementary school children (pages 128–129) and for junior and senior high school students (pages 129–130) will identify specific deficits and can help you establish priorities in the learning assistance program.

You may want to use the DIBS Method (page 190) when preparing for these meetings or during the meetings. The method can be a powerful problem-solving resource (see Problem Solving).

2.   Request clarification if you are confused about any issues raised during the meeting. Your child's future is at stake, so continue to ask questions until you are satisfied.

3.   If it would be beneficial, request that the teacher and resource specialist participate in a conference with the principal or other school personnel. This request is reasonable even if you've already met with these people at the IEP (Individual Educational Program) or PPT (Pupil/Parent/Teacher) meeting.

4.   Have your child attend the meeting with the principal, school psychologist, and/or counselor if everyone agrees such participation is appropriate. Students obviously should not be there when sensitive issues regarding their performance, IQ, or emotional state are being discussed. Examine these matters with your child at home or with school personnel after a clear strategy has been determined.

At Home

1.   Prepare for conferences with school officials by thinking about important issues in advance and making a list of questions you want to ask. Review recent test scores, report card grades and comments, and written or oral communication with your child's teacher. If the teacher or resource specialist has completed an evaluation form, identify the deficits that concern you and discuss them during the conference.

2.   Discuss with your child at home the issues that were examined during the conference. Follow your instincts about what subjects are appropriate to discuss. Gear the discussion to your child's developmental maturity and use understandable language, examples, and metaphors. For example, you might say: "I met with the principal today and we discussed your behavior on the playground. Do you have any ideas about what her concerns are? Well, you seem to be getting into fights with other kids. I'm curious if you're angry at these children. . . . Do you have any ideas about how to solve the problem? This is a solution the teacher and I came up with . . ."

3.   Brainstorm with your child about how she might contribute to resolving identified academic, social, or behavior problems. Use the DIBS system. For more ideas about how to involve your child actively in the problem-solving process, consult *The Life-Smart Kid* (see the Resource List at back of this book).

Critical Thinking

Mastery of higher level academic course material requires that children be able to use their intelligence and get to the heart of an issue or a concept. This higher level or *critical thinking* demands that students be able to:

- Analyze information
- Identify and understand key ideas
- Ask penetrating questions
- Apply reason and logic
- Consider the pluses and minuses of events and decisions
- Question the validity of assumptions
- Identify contradictions, inconsistencies, and deceptions
- See matters from different perspectives
- Relate new information to previously learned information
- Evaluate issues, ideas, arguments, and contentions qualitatively
- Perceive underlying fallacies and flaws

These capabilities are certainly linked to intelligence, but critical thinking is also a skill that can be systematically developed, improved, and refined with good coaching and practice. Teachers and parents are directly responsible for helping children master this skill.

American schools have traditionally been preoccupied with teaching children academic skills and pouring information into their heads. In many American classrooms, students are required to memorize and regurgitate chemical formulas, historical dates, Spanish verb conjugations, and vocabulary definitions. This approach might produce *quantitative learning*, but it does not guarantee *qualitative learning*. Most students quickly forget, or never bother to learn, information and data they perceive as irrelevant. Even information that is relevant and important may be quickly forgotten, as most physicians and attorneys would attest two months after passing their licensing exams.

During the last thirty years, critical intelligence has been largely ignored by primary and secondary schools. The effects of this neglect are abundantly clear. Each day thousands of cerebrally anesthetized youngsters make flawed decisions about drugs, sex, and violence that lead to drug and alcohol addiction, car accidents, unwanted babies, sexually transmitted diseases, suicide, gang killings, and prison time.

A renaissance in teaching critical thinking in American schools is taking place. More and more teachers have integrated analytical thinking components in their curricula and are training their students to question, reason, and apply logic (see Logic). They are showing children how to use intelligence to expose important issues that lie beneath the surface in much the same way that a surgeon uses a scalpel. The goal is for students to use this intellectual scalpel deftly, not only in school, but also in their personal lives. The child who thinks critically carefully considers in advance the potential consequences of accepting a dare, hitchhiking, getting into a stranger's car, driving while intoxicated, or experimenting with drugs or casual sex. He will also learn to think twice before unquestioningly accepting the words of a salesman, a demagogue, or a bigot. (see Smart Thinking).

Some educators consider the recently introduced critical thinking components in textbooks and curricula quite innovative. These educators have forgotten that Socrates, Aristotle, and Plato were training students to reason and think logically and critically more than three thousand years ago.

Children face frightening perils today. Those who don't know how to assess temptations and problems analytically, evaluate their choices, and consider carefully the repercussions and implications of their actions are at risk (see Disregarding Consequences). Many of these youngsters will become tragic victims of their own mindlessness.

Encouraging children to "stretch" and develop better thinking skills is clearly one of the basic objectives of the educational process. For children with intellectual limitations, however, critical thinking will be challenging. These children will have more difficulty understanding issues and concepts. To demand that they comprehend more than they are capable of understanding can trigger stress and cause psychological damage. Children struggling to grasp concepts, relationships, and abstract meanings should be tested to determine their capacity to understand (see IQ Test Scores). Although expectations should be high and all children should be encouraged to develop their full intellectual potential, these expectations must also be reasonable.

It is unrealistic to expect the teacher to assume the entire responsibility for teaching your child how to think critically. The intellectual environment you create at home is a crucial component in the equation. By urging your child to reason and think analytically, you significantly increase the likelihood that he will develop an ability to ask astute, incisive questions and make reasonable, logical assessments and choices.

Corrective Strategies

In School

1.   If your child has difficulty applying critical thinking skills, request the teacher to assign supplemental in-class or homework materials designed to improve these skills. The teacher might be willing to provide your child with extra help after school or before class. Classroom materials specifically designed to develop critical thinking skills are included in the Resource List at the back of this book.

2.   If your child is struggling with critical thinking skills and is in a learning assistance program, diplomatically suggest to the resource specialist that she devote time to working with your child on critical thinking materials. The resource specialist may believe that your child's basic skills deficits must be remedied before higher-level critical thinking skills can be taught. This position is sound as long as there is a commitment to incorporate critical thinking skills into the remedial strategy at the appropriate time. The materials in the Resource List at the back of this book can be used creatively to teach both reading and critical thinking skills concurrently.

At Home

1.   To develop your child's critical thinking skills, urge him to pay more attention to what is happening in his own world and in the world at large. The starting point is to emphasize the basic "thinking questions"—how, why, and what. At the dinner table you might ask: "How do you think the problem of the homeless might be solved?" The child studying American history might be asked: "Why do you think religious freedom was so important to the Founding Fathers?" "What is the link between religious freedom and the concept of 'separation of church and state?'" These interactive sessions produce another valuable payoff: your child's communication skills will improve. When you discuss topics in the news, encourage your child to recognize that events can be seen from another point of

view. A person living in Rio de Janeiro might perceive the issue of ecology differently than a person living in Omaha.

2.   If your child is struggling with critical thinking, ask his teacher if she can recommend a workbook that could be used at home. Perhaps she could provide you with extra critical thinking worksheets that you and your child could do together. Ask her to suggest how best to monitor your child and how to respond to wrong answers or confusion. Extra assignments should not require more than ten to fifteen minutes of additional homework per evening. Work together and make the sessions enjoyable. Overloading your child would be perceived as a punishment. Be patient and supportive if your child struggles.

3.   If you observe your child having great difficulty acquiring critical thinking skills or if you lose your patience working with him, consider hiring a tutor. Red flags that signal a significant critical thinking problem include chronically poor logic and reasoning, confusion, frustration, and resistance. Select a tutor with whom your child can establish rapport, ideally someone who has had experience teaching critical thinking skills. Ask your child's teacher for a recommendation. If your child continues to struggle despite your best efforts and the tutor's best efforts, request that the school psychologist administer an intelligence test.

4.   Read with your child. Use school textbooks, newspaper articles, or library books. Select material within your child's reading "comfort zone." If you're unsure of your child's reading level, ask the teacher. (If your child is capable of understanding material that she cannot yet read, read it to her. See Reading Aloud.) As you read together, ask questions. Do not, however, become a question machine. A continual stream of questions will make the experience unpleasant and cause your child to become resistant. Be creative and make the process enjoyable and stimulating. For example, if the article is about nuclear energy, you might ask, "What are the dangers? How might you be affected by a nuclear accident?" After modeling how to ask questions, urge your child to ask you questions. Make these sessions short (no more than ten to fifteen minutes). Be patient! Developing critical thinking skills takes time. If you communicate exasperation or disappointment, your child will become demoralized and this will trigger resentment and active or passive resistance.

5.   Look for materials or games at your local teacher supply store that are expressly designed to develop children's critical thinking skills. Select materials appropriate to your child's age and reading level. Materials you might want to examine are included in the Resource List at the back of this book.

Disorganization

The chronically disorganized child is on a collision course with his teachers, his parents, and the educational system. Energy that should be devoted to studying and learning is dissipated looking for misplaced materials and struggling to meet deadlines. Because the disorganized child "spins his wheels" with little or no forward momentum, he rarely achieves in school at a level commensurate with his true ability.

Several key traits differentiate organized students from their less organized classmates. Children with good organizational skills:

- Establish goals and priorities.
- Plan ahead.
- Budget time effectively and meet deadlines.
- Develop an effective system for recording assignments and checking them off when completed.
- Have the materials they need to do their work (paper, pens, textbooks, notebooks, pencils, dictionary, and so on).
- Keep their desks and study areas neat.
- Have designated places where they store their school-related materials and supplies.

The poorly organized child must be constantly reminded to straighten his room, put away his toys, make his bed, put dirty clothes in the hamper, and clear the mess off his desk. To insulate himself from repeated barrages of negative feedback, he will probably tune out his parents' predictable admonitions.

Realizing that chronic disorganization can cause monumental problems for your child throughout his life, you will probably feel a compelling responsibility to intervene. Unfortunately, the traditional parental methods of intervention—lectures, bribes, and punishment—are rarely successful and usually trigger active or passive resistance. Youngsters with the most urgent need to alter their behavior are often the most unwilling to change and the most oblivious to the effects of the chaos they create in their environment (see Disregarding Consequences; Smart Thinking).

Children enmeshed in counterproductive behavior are generally quite resistant to changing their habits. The most effective antidote is to help them realize that organization will make their lives easier and that the payoffs for the new orderliness are superior to the payoffs for their old behaviors. The key to defusing resistance is to create a "let's work together on solving this problem" context in which you and your child experiment with organizational strategies and systematically practice the fundamentals of good organization. By involving your child actively in making up the new rules, you increase the likelihood that he'll be cooperative and use the procedures. Show your child how to organize his notebook and desk and how to budget his study time (see Time Management). Encourage him to apply these methods every day until they become a habit. Then diplomatically monitor and affirm his progress until he demonstrates mastery of the skills. (See corrective strategies that follow.)

You will know your child has made a break-through when he voluntarily begins to organize specific areas of his life. Creating a system for organizing his baseball cards, for example, is a good first step. You cannot realistically expect your child to transform overnight. He may make progress then plateau or even regress. Such blips in the learning curve are frustrating, and you must be patient, supportive, and consistent during the behavior modification process. Once he becomes convinced that order will create more free time to do what he wants to do and allow him to achieve at a level previously beyond his reach, he will be more receptive to becoming organized.

At Home

1. Teaching your disorganized child how to create order in his life is a far more effective strategy than lecturing or punishing him. The following guidelines will facilitate making this strategy work:

• Define the objective of your interactive activity. ("Let's spend a few minutes making your desk more organized so that you can do your homework more efficiently.")

• Demonstrate the value of organization with relevant examples. ("Let's do a flow chart that

---

DAILY ORGANIZATIONAL CHECKLIST

Code: 1 = poor   2 = fair   3 = good   4 = excellent

	MON.	TUES.	WED.	THURS.	FRI.
Desk is neat.	_____	_____	_____	_____	_____
In-class assignments are neat.	_____	_____	_____	_____	_____
Work handed in on time.	_____	_____	_____	_____	_____
Notebook is neat.	_____	_____	_____	_____	_____
Homework assignments recorded.	_____	_____	_____	_____	_____

Corrective Strategies

In School

1. (Elementary School, ES) If your child is chronically disorganized in school, ask the teacher to help you identify specific deficit areas, using the preceding checklist. Add to and modify the checklist so that it includes your child's particular deficits.

Brainstorm with the teacher how you might work together to reorient the counterproductive behaviors. Ask the teacher to affirm your child when his performance begins to improve. Keep track of the points your child receives each day and apply them to earning a prize or reward.

outlines the steps you'll need to take to finish this history project." See Planning Ahead.)

• Model how to use study materials more efficiently. ("Let's see how you can organize this material for your term paper and put it on index cards. Then you can develop a practical filing system for keeping track of what you are doing.")

• Provide clear "how to" guidelines. ("Let's write down the steps for doing this research report in an order that makes sense." See Priorities.)

• Provide repeated opportunities for practice and application. Monitor your child to make sure he is using the techniques you have developed together.

• Be patient, affirm progress, and be supportive when there are plateaus or temporary regressions. ("Your system for organizing your notes and quotations for your term paper looks great! You're getting the hang of it.")

2.   Find a disorganized area in your house (the attic, garage, workshop, or your own closet or desk. Develop a reorganization strategy with your child and then implement the plan together. Urge your child to help you to organize a commonly shared area of the home (not his own room). By sharing this task you can defuse resistance. A family project for designing and building closet shelves or organizing the garage, for instance, demonstrates basic organizational principles in very concrete terms. Encourage your child to contribute his ideas during the design

and planning stages. Hands-on participation in the actual construction stage is vital and teaches your child to make concrete (as opposed to abstract) associations with sound organizational principles. Once you have modeled how to reorganize, work together to develop a plan for reorganizing your child's closet. You may need to buy or build a shoe organizer or a box for toys or sports equipment. Make the project fun and resist any temptation to lecture or sermonize about the value of organization.

3.   (ES) Set up a point/reward system at home that acknowledges your child when his desk, room, notebook, backpack, assignment sheet, and homework are neat and organized. To keep track of points, you might use a format similar to that of the Daily Organization Checklist (see page 40). Combine points earned in school for good organization with those earned at home and follow through with a well-earned reward.

Disregarding Consequences

Some youngsters chronically fail to consider the implications of their actions. Either they are oblivious to basic cause-and-effect principles or they consciously or unconsciously choose to disregard them. Because their thinking is so rooted in the present and the immediate, they do not plan ahead or consider potential risks. These children can pay a heavy price for their subsequent mistakes, indiscretions, and flawed decisions. Their repeated, predictable miscues frequently place them in conflict with parents and teachers, and, in some cases, with the judicial system.

Children who think strategically have integrated cause-and-effect principles into their decision-making process. They know how to analyze problems, learn from mistakes and setbacks, define goals, consider options, develop fallback positions, and formulate pragmatic strategies for attaining their objectives (see Bouncing Back from Setbacks and Learning from Mistakes; Smart Thinking). A child who is in the habit of thinking about consequences would repair a loose wheel on a skateboard before having an accident. In contrast, the child who is oblivious to consequences would have to fall repeatedly and injure himself before he might take the time to fix the loose wheel.

Mastery of cause-and-effect principles is a requisite to success in school. Students who carefully apply these principles weigh the implications of a decision to study or not study, to cheat or not cheat, or to take drugs or not take drugs. Their future-oriented thinking reduces the likelihood of repeated crash landings and contrasts with the present-oriented thinking of children who are impulsive and demand immediate gratification.

Some parents naively assume that their child will naturally learn cause-and-effect principles because they themselves naturally assimilated these principles. These parents may not even remember how they learned to link their actions with the potential implications of those actions. If they took the time to examine their own behavior, they would probably discover that they were strongly influenced by the behavior of their parents or older siblings. They may have also had the good fortune to have have been strongly influenced by a special teacher, coach, relative, or friend. To assume that your child will be as observant, perceptive, responsive, or fortunate as you were is risky. Your child may be very intelligent, but she may not be as strategic as you are (see Smart Thinking). She may not intuitively connect her failure to proofread a book report carefully with the spelling and syntax errors that caused her grade to be lowered. This cause-and-effect link may be obvious to you and her teachers, but she may not recognize it on her own.

Unfortunately, many capable children think and act impulsively, irresponsibly, and mindlessly. They misbehave in class, submit incomplete or sloppy assignments, and spend inadequate time studying. They can't figure out how to record homework assignments efficiently, manage time effectively, or write an organized term paper. Because they are not well attuned to the effects of their decisions and actions, they perform below their potential and are often labeled under-achievers (see Study Skills; Underachievement). Their poor performance in school obscures their true talents and undermines self-confidence. As success appears increasingly unattainable, these students often lower their expectations and then perform congruently with these diminished expectations. Once this happens, a pattern of underachievement may become integrated into their self-concept.

Reprimands, lectures, and sermons are rarely effective in helping children make the connection between inadequate effort and poor performance. Rather than motivate children to change their behavior, continual negative feedback elicits resistance and resentment. The more effective alternative is to teach children how to make more astute decisions and to train them to ask key questions such as: "What's going on here?" "What are my options?" "What are the possible consequences of my choices?" This analytical questioning process must be practiced until it becomes a reflex.

Fortunately, children who are not in the habit of applying cause-and-effect principles can be systematically trained to do so. Unless they receive this instruction, they are at risk for making nonjudicious choices throughout their life. Epidemic substance abuse, teenage pregnancy, gang killings, and tens of thousands of high school dropouts each year attest to the catastrophic effects of our society's failure to teach children to think about the potential implications and repercussions of their actions and attitudes. Children who arrive at life's critical junctures and fail to consider carefully the effects of their choices are at serious risk. If a pattern of mindlessness becomes entrenched, these children could emotionally or physically self-destruct.

Corrective Strategies

In School

1. If your child is continually getting into trouble or repeatedly making errors in judgment, it's likely that she has a marginal understanding of cause-and-effect principles. Ask your child's teacher to complete the following Cause and Effect Checklist so that specific thinking deficits can be pinpointed.

CAUSE AND EFFECT CHECKLIST

	YES	NO
This child:		
Leaves projects and assignments until the last minute.		
Does not allow sufficient time to complete projects.		
Is disorganized.		
Acts impulsively and without thinking.		
Does not plan ahead.		
Makes nonjudicious choices.		
Is chronically forgetful.		
Repeats the same mistakes.		
Resists assistance.		
Rarely establishes short-term or long-term goals.		
Has little sense of purpose.		
Gives up easily.		
Avoids responsibility.		
Tends to blame others for problems.		
Does not weigh potential danger or risks.		
Does not change behavior even when reprimanded or punished.		
Appears satisfied to do a second-rate job.		

---

2. Discuss ideas with the teacher for helping your child learn and understand cause-and-effect principles. Focus initially on one or two specific deficit areas identified on the checklist. For example, if your child chronically struggles to find her assignments or complete homework, you might help her develop a plan for organizing her notebook and desk (see Disorganization). If she's in elementary school, the teacher might be willing to monitor her to make sure she is using the organizational system. You, in turn, will need to monitor her at home, being careful not to make your child overly dependent on supervision and help (see Learned Helplessness).

3. (Elementary School, ES) Talk with the teacher about integrating cause and effect activities into the curriculum so that the entire class could practice and apply the principles. Some scenarios follow that could be used for class discussions on cause and effect:

- You forget to bring your homework to school.
  EFFECT: _____

- You don't chain your bicycle to a tree at the park.
  EFFECT: _____

- You receive a poor grade on your science report.
  CAUSE: _____

- You win an award for the most improvement in school.
  CAUSE: _____

If students are to develop heightened awareness of the consequences of their decisions and actions, they must practice anticipating possible and probable effects and deducing possible and probable causes. The process of listing as many as possible to reinforce the cause-and-effect link can be fun for everyone.[1]

1. See my elementary/junior high school workbook *Study Smart, Think Smart* (Center for Applied Research in Education, Prentice Hall, 1993) and *The Life-Smart Kid* (Prima Publishing, 1995) for more information and hands-on activities and exercises.

4. (Junior High/High School, J/HS) You might diplomatically suggest to school administrators that they urge teachers in the upper grades to spend time in the classroom discussing choices and consequences. A history teacher should not assume that all of his students know how much time and planning are required to do a first-rate report. Nor can he assume that his students realize the implications of not allocating sufficient time for taking notes, writing a first draft, editing, writing a second draft, proofreading, and properly formatting footnotes. Teachers who value strategic thinking skills must be willing to devote sufficient instructional time to teaching students the nuts and bolts of the analytical thinking and planning process.

At Home

1. Parents have the primary responsibility to teach their children cause-and-effect principles. Preaching and delivering sermons are usually ineffectual and trigger active or passive resistance, so you must find creative ways to actively involve your child in thinking about what is happening to her and around her. Events described in the newspaper or on TV can be excellent catalysts for discussion. You might explore the reasons why reservoirs become polluted or examine the causes of acid rain. You might discuss factors that contribute to the greenhouse effect or to the destruction of rain forests. You might explore the effects of raising the gasoline tax or of no-fault insurance. You might also examine the consequences of not submitting work on time.

2. (ES) Make up simple cause-and-effect scenarios and go over them with your child. For example:

- Your friend decides to steal something from the supermarket.
  EFFECT: _____

- A child throws rocks at moving cars.
  EFFECT: _____

- You get a D on your math homework.
  CAUSE: _____

- A teenager gets arrested on the freeway.

  CAUSE: _____

There are obviously several "correct" responses. Encourage your child to think up as many causes and effects as possible. Make the sessions enjoyable. Be patient if she has difficulty. Your child is in the process of learning how to make logical connections.

3. Use cause-and-effect principles to examine real problems your child is having. You might ask: "What behaviors might have caused your teacher to get upset with you?" "What could you do to change her attitude about you?" "If your goal is to do better on the next spelling test, what specific steps could you take?" "What specific steps could you take to reduce the risk of not doing a first-rate job on your term paper?"

Distractions while Studying

Parents and teachers with traditional attitudes about education generally have strong opinions about how children should study. Citing their own experiences as students, they argue that noise, distractions, and interruptions undermine effort and performance and contend that children are able to study most effectively in a quiet environment.

These traditional attitudes set the stage for repeated parent-child confrontations. The adults want the TV and stereo off, nonessential phone calls eliminated, and breaks kept to an absolute minimum. Children argue that TV, music, and breaks for phone calls and snacks do not negatively affect their ability to study.

Many parents and teachers will be surprised to learn that some respected educators support the children's position. After analyzing the performance of students who study with the radio or TV playing and comparing their work with that of students who study without environmental distractions, they have found no significant differences. One authority has coined the term "Walkman Learner" and maintains that many children in modern society have become so acclimated to loud rock music, pulsating videos, and blaring TVs that they may actually study and learn best under these conditions.

It may be true that some children can study effectively with distractions, but keep in mind that students with chronic concentration deficits are highly susceptible to environmental conditions.

These youngsters struggle to stay on task even under the most controlled conditions and often become academically dysfunctional when there are diversions (see Attention Deficit Disorder).

If your child has difficulty concentrating, studies inefficiently, and performs below her potential because of distractions, you have three options:

- You can assert your parental prerogative and autocratically insist that your child turn off the TV or stereo.

- You can nag, lecture, admonish, threaten, and/or punish.

- You can objectively analyze the situation, help your child understand the issues, and show her how to create a study environment that is more conducive to efficient learning.

The autocratic response—insisting that your child turn off the TV or stereo—is often ineffective and can trigger bitterness, hurt feelings, and showdowns. Children who are forced into compliance usually feel victimized and tend to become resentful, defensive, and openly or passively resistant. If they believe they are being treated unfairly, they may retaliate by intentionally sabotaging themselves. These youngsters can become so enmeshed in resisting their parents' authority that they either do not recognize, or choose to deny, that their behavior is hurting them as well as their parents (see Anger and Frustration; Behavior and Attitude; Disregarding

Consequences; Expectations and Performance Guidelines; Monitoring Homework; Negative Attitude toward School).

Because many children tend to dismiss their parents' sermons and lectures about the need for good study habits, these well-intentioned admonitions are frequently ineffectual. The alternative is to assess your child's schoolwork objectively and decide if parental intervention is required. If your child does her homework under less than ideal conditions but, nevertheless, gets good grades, she can certainly make a persuasive argument for being permitted to study in her own way. If, however, her grades indicate she's not working up to her potential, it is justifiable for you and your child to develop reasonable study guidelines. Rather than resort to a heavy-handed, autocratic imposition of rules, it would probably be more effective to take a "let's figure out how you might improve your grades" approach (see Problem Solving). This process requires more parenting skills, but it usually elicits less resistance (see the DIBS Method on p. **190**). If the cooperative approach doesn't work, you may have no choice but to impose study rules autocratically.

Corrective Strategies
In School

1. Some teachers run a "tighter ship" than others. Students are not allowed to talk to each other in class or get up from their seats without permission. Other teachers prefer a less structured, more interactive classroom and value cooperative learning. Many students thrive in this more relaxed learning environment; others have difficulty filtering out the associated distractions. If you believe your child cannot handle excess stimulation or distractions, diplomatically discuss your concerns with the teacher. Be aware, however, that although a highly structured classroom may be best for your child, it's not necessarily best for all students. One solution might be to transfer your child to a more structured, traditional classroom. If this is not feasible, ask the teacher to help your child adjust to the realities of her teaching style and classroom format. Don't expect the teacher to completely change her modus operandi to suit your child, but she may agree to make some accommodations. Your child's desk, for instance, might be placed closer to her desk. The teacher might also develop some simple signals to alert your child when she's becoming distracted (for more specific corrective strategies, see Attention Deficit Disorder; Working Independently).

At Home

1. Children with concentration problems who discover they can improve their grades and the quality of their schoolwork by reducing the distractions in their study environment are generally more receptive to making changes than those who are lectured. Discuss with your child in a nonconfrontational manner how distractions and concentration problems are linked. Brainstorm how she might reduce distractions when she studies (see the DIBS Method, p. **190**). For example, she might eliminate incoming and outgoing telephone calls during study periods (see Study Breaks; Time Management). Showing your child how to reengineer her environment will not resolve chronic attention deficit disorder, but it can help her figure out some of the logical "do's and don'ts" of efficient studying.

2. Involve your child in an experiment to determine if distractions are undermining school performance. Have her record her most recent grades. Then ask her to make up a list of specific distractions she agrees to eliminate for three weeks. Each day, have her use the checklist following (or her own checklist of selected distractions) to record that she successfully eliminated these distractions when studying. After three weeks, compare her new grades with those she

STUDY ENVIRONMENT CHECKLIST

	MON.	TUES.	WED.	THURS.	FRI.
No TV or music while studying.	_____	_____	_____	_____	_____
Telephone calls only during breaks.	_____	_____	_____	_____	_____
Concentrated study sessions of twenty minutes without taking a break.[1]	_____	_____	_____	_____	_____
Two breaks of no more than fifteen minutes.	_____	_____	_____	_____	_____

1. The duration of study sessions for highly distractible younger children might initially be five minutes at a time and then slowly increased to ten, fifteen, and ultimately twenty mintues (or longer!).

received before making the changes (see Study Skills).

If your child's performance in school improves after the experiment, discuss the obvious payoffs for limiting distractions when studying. Create a reward system that acknowledges improvements and encourages continued use of the system. The goal is for her to control her study environment voluntarily because the rewards of doing a first-rate job are enjoyable and worth the effort.

Dyslexia

Dyslexia means different things to different people. Some educators use the term to describe any type of serious reading problem, others use it to describe a specific type of reading dysfunction characterized by letter reversals (*b/d, q/g*), number reversals (*3/ ε ,7/ ⌐*), upside down letters and numbers (*b/q, 6/9*), word reversals (*saw/was*), letter, word, and syllable transpositions and omissions. (Although letter and number reversals are quite common in kindergarten, parents should become concerned if the reversals persist beyond the fourth month of first grade.)

The process of reading is a grueling, emotionally draining nightmare for students who see letters, words, and numbers backward. Asking a seriously dyslexic youngster to read is the equivalent of asking a child to play baseball with her hands tied behind her back. The continual battle to make sense out of words that dance, wiggle, and tumble across the page corrodes the child's self-esteem and self-confidence and leaves behind profound feelings of inadequacy, hopelessness, and embarrassment.

To protect themselves psychologically, many demoralized dyslexic children become phobic about reading and develop elaborate ego-protecting behaviors. Their defense mechanisms range from laziness, irresponsibility, procrastination, acting out, and manipulation to truancy and drugs. Although these behaviors ironically call attention to the very deficits the children are attempting to camouflage, the children are too enmeshed in their academic survival drama to recognize this irony.

The reasons why children reverse letters and numbers are complex and not fully understood. The most common theories include:

- right/left confusion (directionality deficits)
- poor ocular muscle control of horizontal movement of eyes across the printed line
- difficulty with convergence (getting both eyes to focus together when reading)
- disequilibrium (poor sense of balance)
- neurological dysfunction (inefficient sensory processing)
- cranial misalignment (a controversial theory promulgated by some chiropractors)

Although there is no consensus about the causes of dyslexia, specialists generally agree that the condition is genetically based. Dyslexia may affect several members of the same family as well as family members from previous generations. Experts also agree that although dyslexia is linked to the neurological processing of sensory data, the condition rarely involves measurable organic brain damage.

Considerable progress is being made in understanding and identifying the neurological factors that cause dyslexia, the specific area in the brain where decoding dysfunctions occur, and the specific genetic anomalies responsible for the condition. Methods for treating dyslexia include:

- perceptual training (teaching children how to focus and process sensory data more efficiently)

- visual tracking exercises (workbooks, handouts, and other remedial materials)

- eye muscle training (practiced by specialists in developmental optometry)

- kinesthetic/neurological imprinting (incorporated in the Slingerland and Orton-Gillingham methods)

- colored lenses (used to treat a condition called *scotopic dyslexia* in which letters run together or "fall" off the page)

- visualization methods (see Auditory Discrimination; Spelling Problems)

- drug therapy (Ritalin, Dexadrine, and others)

- motion sickness medication (see *A Solution to the Riddle of Dyslexia* by Harold Levinson, M.D., in Resource List at the back of the book)

- cranial adjustments (a controversal chiropractic technique)

Dyslexic children may respond positively to a wide range of remedial techniques. Most resource and reading specialists focus on developing children's visual discrimination skills (seeing the difference between letters such as *b* and *d*) and improving visual tracking skills (effectiveness with which the eyes move from left to right across the printed line). The fact that dyslexic children can respond positively to radically different remedial methods strongly suggests that rapport with the teacher and the *halo effect* must be factored into any attempt to substantiate the efficacy of a particular remedial technique. The *halo effect* (also referred to as the *Hawthorne effect*) acknowledges that some improvement may be attributed simply to the extra attention and may not necessarily reflect the efficacy of a particular intervention method. A child's skills may improve because he likes his tutor and wants to please her and/or because he's receiving affirmation, encouragement, and individualized help.

Motivation is a key factor in the successful remediation of learning problems. Children who make progress and become convinced that they can prevail over their reading deficiencies will be far more willing to work diligently and will make more progress than children who are defeated and demoralized.

Certain remediation methods may also prove more successful with some children than with others. Well-trained and perceptive educational therapists who possess a wide range of remedial resources often combine different methods until they discover the most effective remedial prescription for a particular child.

Significant breakthroughs in treating dyslexic children have occurred during the last twenty years. More effective instructional methods and better-trained teachers now make it possible for children with serious reading deficits to overcome or compensate successfully for their dyslexia. Despite these improvements in instructional methodology, many school districts still provide only marginal assistance for dyslexic students. In many instances, these districts require children to be at least two years below grade level to qualify for remedial help—even though there is compelling evidence that early diagnosis and intervention can prevent devastating psychological damage and lowered self-esteem. When deprived of meaningful help, stymied, frustrated, and discouraged children often conclude that their problems are insoluble and that they are hopelessly inadequate and defective. To prevent this unnecessary tragedy, parents must become their dyslexic child's advocate. They must find help either within the system or outside of it, and they must insist that this help be provided before the window of opportunity slams shut and their child becomes demoralized, turns off to reading, loses academic self-confidence, and shuts down in school.

Corrective Strategies

In School

1.   The primary symptoms of dyslexia usually become apparent in first grade. Chronic decod-

ing (sensory processing) problems are red flags. Children who manifest such deficits (for example, reversals and inaccuracies when reading or doing math) should be diagnostically tested by the school psychologist. If your school district insists that students be at least two years below grade level to qualify for help, be persistent and, if necessary, aggressive in requesting an evaluation. Federal law 94-124 stipulates that children with learning problems be tested (see Parents' Rights). It is critical that your child be provided with learning assistance from a resource or reading specialist before irreparable educational and self-concept damage occurs.

2. If your child is identified as dyslexic, inquire if the school has a resource specialist trained in the Orton-Gillinghan or Slingerland Methods. The Lindemood Auditory Discrimination In-Depth Program has also proven effective in helping some dyslexic children. Materials available to resource specialists specifically designed to improve visual discrimination (seeing the difference between letters) and decoding are included in the Resource List at the back of this book.

At Home

1. Patience is vital when you attempt to help a dyslexic child. Youngsters who struggle to decode written words are usually reading phobic, highly sensitive, and emotionally vulnerable. Anticipate resistance when you provide reading assistance. Children who have painful associations with reading often make every effort to avoid reading and are reluctant to expose deficiencies to their parents. Be sensitive to your child's feelings and be creative. Make reading a positive experience. Select high interest stories to read with your child. Have you child sit next to you and encourage her to try to follow along as you read. Your goal is to improve your child's skills and help her realize that reading can be a pleasurable experience.

Improving Your Child's Reading Skills

• Ask the teacher what your child's reading level is and choose books that are slightly below her comfort reading level. (The teacher, reading specialist or resource specialist, or local librarian can also recommend appropriate books.)

• Read a line to your child slowly, and then ask her to read the same line. Be patient when she struggles. You may need to read the line several times before she feels comfortable reading the line aloud. Your goal is to improve your child's reading confidence. By modeling how to read the words accurately, you are setting her up to succeed.

• As your child's reading improves, experiment with reading two lines aloud before asking her to read. The objective is to progress to reading an entire paragraph or page before she reads it. At some point, she will acquire the skills that will allow her to read to you without you having to read the material first.

• Gently point out if she reads (or writes) a *b* as a *d*, or a *p* as a *q*, and so on.

• Ask your child if the teacher or resource specialist has taught her methods for recognizing the difference between commonly reversed letters. (For example, she could make two fists. The knuckles of the right hand should touch the knuckles of the left. She should then point the right and left thumbs up. The left hand is always the *b* and the right is always the *d*. Kinesthetic association can help children recognize the differences between the two letters.

• Do not communicate displeasure or disappointment when your child makes errors. These errors occur because her brain is not decoding the letter symbols properly, not because she is lazy or resistant. Affirm and praise her for even meager progress. Remember, she has to work harder than other children to decipher words accurately.

• Make the process of reading fun. Be aware when your child is becoming tired and be prepared to quit for the day, even if you haven't covered as much ground as you would have liked.

• Be enthusiastic and express confidence in your child's ability to prevail over these reading problems.

• Expect temporary plateaus and regressions. These setbacks are common with dyslexic children.

• Avoid unwittingly creating stress and anxiety.

• Affirm your child repeatedly. Your goal is to alter negative associations with reading and build self-confidence. Children thrive on praise!

2.   (Junior High/High School, J/HS) Teenage dyslexic students who have been badly scarred by their reading experiences in school are often resistant to reading aloud with their parents. You may be able to defuse this resistance by explaining the rationale for reading together. If your child is unwilling to work with you, propose that she work with a tutor, preferably a specialist who can teach methods for tracking words more proficiently. With practice your child will become more proficient, and her sensitivity and resistance to learning should diminish.

Effort and Motivation

Goal setting, motivation, effort, and achievement are directly linked. The motivated child establishes meaningful personal targets he believes will provide immediate or long-term gratification. He then plots trajectories that intersect with these goals. His short-term objective might be a hit in the next baseball game or an A on the next spelling test. His long-term objective might be an A in English on his report card, a part in the school play, a varsity football letter, a car, or a college scholarship. Because the goals are important, the child is willing to work diligently to achieve them. He will prioritize his efforts, make sacrifices, be critical of his own performance, and strive to improve and excel (see Goals; Priorities).

The value that any child attaches to a specific goal is affected by a complex mix of family, personality, social, peer, and mass media influences. During early formative years, children are continually observing and cataloguing the values, standards, and expectations of their parents, siblings, friends, and teachers. Their evolving value system, attitudes, and work ethic are inevitably influenced by this ongoing process of storing experiences and impressions (see Behavior and Attitude; Expectations and Performance Guidelines).

A child's level of effort and motivation may also reflect inherited personality traits. Certain behaviors once believed to be exclusively shaped by environmental forces have now been linked at least in part to genetic and hormonal factors. Research by Jerome Kagan, a developmental psychologist at Harvard University, has shown that chronically shy children, for example, have an elevated level of the hormone cortisol in their saliva. Although both cortisol and adrenaline are typically secreted in response to fear, some timid, inhibited children appear to have a constantly elevated cortisol level. This anomaly can even be measured in newborn infants. Given these breakthroughs in metabolic and genetic research, it is possible that someday scientists may identify the specific genetic and hormonal predispositions that affect behavior such as effort and motivation.

Intelligence, academic skills, study skills, and strategic thinking skills must also be factored into the motivation equation (see IQ Test Scores; Smart Thinking; Study Skills.) Children are usually motivated and conscientious when they believe they possess the ability to achieve their objectives. Those who have good skills and self-confidence are typically willing to accept challenges, establish goals, risk occasional setbacks, work diligently, and persevere (see Atypical Learning Problems; Bouncing Back from Setbacks and Learning from Mistakes; Learning Disabilities; Underachievement). In contrast, emotionally fragile children who struggle in school and repeatedly fail are understandably predisposed to shut down, become irresponsible, lazy, and unwilling to accept challenges and risk potentially ego-bruising defeats (see Fear of Failure/Success/Competition; Self-Esteem and Self-Confidence).

If your child seems lazy and unmotivated, the most effective means for reorienting a child from counterproductive behavior to productive behavior is to develop a method for communicating family values, expressing concerns, defining problem areas, teaching achievement-oriented skills, modeling productive behavior, affirming progress, and conveying positive expectations. Guidelines will facilitate this process:

• Express clearly and unequivocally your position on effort and motivation. ("Going to school and getting a good education are your job. I expect you to do the best you can.")

• Resist preaching. ("When I was in school, I studied until midnight.")

• Encourage and model honest communication and feedback. ("I'm pleased with how hard you worked on this assignment. If you spend some extra time learning the irregular verb conjugations, you may get a better grade on the next test.")

• Be consistent. ("We agreed that you would finish your homework before you telephone your friends. Please keep that agreement.")

• Be patient. ("I know that you'll ultimately prevail over this problem.")

• Be reasonable. ("I want you to work conscientiously, but I also want you to set time aside for having fun.")

• Urge your child to establish short-term and long-term goals. ("What grade are you aiming for on the history midterm, and what grade do you want in the course?")

• If necessary, help your child develop a practical plan and timetable for attaining goals. ("Let's look at what you need to do to complete this term successfully and make a flowchart of required tasks.")

• Acknowledge and affirm success and progress. ("You did a great job on the book report!")

• Be sensitive. ("It's easy to get discouraged when you've studied so hard, and you receive a lower grade than you expected.")

• Express love and positive expectations. ("I am proud of you, and I am convinced you will achieve what you want in life.")

Children who continually sabotage themselves by refusing to work and who resist their parents' best efforts to get them on track require professional counseling. To ignore underlying problems that are responsible for counterproductive attitudes and actions increases the risk of academic and emotional shutdown. Psychological problems rarely disappear on their own. Responsible parents admit when they cannot deal with a problem and recognize that professional help is the wisest investment they can make in their child's future (see Psychological Problems and Psychological Overlay).

Corrective Strategies

In School

1.   Discuss concerns about your child's unacceptable work ethic with his teacher and/or school counselor. Ask for suggestions about how you might work together to improve motivation and effort. Also ask if the teacher feels your child has the requisite skills to do the assigned work. If his skills are deficient, it's imperative that learning assistance be provided, either in school or privately. It is not reasonable to expect your child to be motivated if he is convinced that he cannot possibly succeed.

2.   It is vital that you and the teacher pinpoint factors that might be impeding your child academically and undermining his willingness to establish goals and work diligently. Refer to specific entries in this book for other suggestions and use the checklists that are designed to help you identify underlying problems. If, for example, your child has problems with reading comprehension, phonics, spelling, vocabulary, or auditory memory, these learning deficits must be addressed before you and the teacher can reasonably expect a great deal of effort and motivation from him. Your child must feel he has a chance to succeed before he will show a willingness to sustain effort

and to take the risks inherent in defining personal goals and working toward attaining these goals.

3.   If your child lacks the academic skills to do the assigned classwork or homework, ask his teacher to lower temporarily the difficulty level and reduce the quantity of assignments until he has a chance to catch up. Children who feel that effort is futile will invariably become demoralized and unmotivated.

At Home

1.   Discuss concerns about effort and motivation with your child. Ask for theories about this unwillingness to establish personal goals and work diligently (refer to the DIBS Method on page **190**). Don't be surprised if your child resists acknowledging the problem and denies that he's "coasting." Help define factors that could be undermining effort and motivation. These factors may include learning problems, study skills deficits, or family issues. Once you identify the sources of your child's poor motivation, either unilaterally or, ideally, cooperatively develop a practical strategy for resolving the underlying

deficits. This plan might involve tutoring, educational therapy, and/or counseling. Explore ways in which the agreed upon plan can be monitored without triggering resentment. Be careful not to preach or lecture.

2.   If specific learning or study skills deficits are causing your child to resist working diligently, refer to relevant entries in this book for suggestions about how to correct these problems. (See Student Evaluation Checklist, pages **128–130**.) It may be advisable for you to work with your child on goal setting, planning, disorganization, problem solving, study skills, or time management.

3.   Resisting work and acting lazy can be weapons that an angry child might use consciously or unconsciously to express unhappiness, hostility, or depression. If you observe that your child is chronically angry at you or his teacher, and you don't know how to help him defuse this anger, provide professional counseling. Unless he examines and resolves his negative feelings, he may become habituated to sabotaging himself and making the minimum possible effort. These counterproductive behaviors could persist throughout life.

 # Essay Tests

When students take essay tests, they must demonstrate that they understand important concepts and have retained key information. They must also demonstrate that they can tie relevant information together cohesively. They must be able to organize their thoughts, present facts to support their position, and express ideas cogently and persuasively.

A typical high school essay test in a history course might instruct students to discuss the factors that led to the civil rights movement in the 1960s. Students may have twenty minutes to pull together all the relevant information they know. Although facts are important, knowing a great many facts does not guarantee a good grade. Students must select information that clearly documents their insight and understanding of the subject, and they must cull, distill, and shape the data into a well-crafted essay. If they are strategic (see Smart Thinking), they will probably take a few moments at the start of the test to make a mental or written "thumbnail" outline of the key information they want to include in the essay. Ideally, they will begin the essay with a powerful topic sentence, write neatly, spell accurately, tie information together, express ideas succinctly and sequentially, and make points convincingly.

There are two basic formats for writing an essay. The most common is called the *deductive method*. A student using this format makes a general overview statement in the opening or topic sentence, such as: "Two hundred years of oppression, prejudice, and discrimination made the civil rights movement of the 1960s inevitable." The essay would then describe historical events and sociological conditions that contributed to the movement and include data to substantiate opinions and document knowledge. In the concluding paragraph, the student would tie the information together and concisely summarize his position.

The deductive method is best visualized as a triangle or pyramid with the introductory topic sentence at the top point of the triangle and substantiating data in expanding layers below the tip. The concluding sentence, which encapsulates the information presented in the essay, is the base of the triangle.

An alternative to the deductive method of writing an essay is called the *inductive method*. The student using this format presents information and supporting data and carefully leads the reader to the main point in the concluding sentence or paragraph. The first sentence of the essay might be: "Blacks were initially brought to this country as slaves during the early colonial period." After presenting relevant information that describes sociological conditions and historical issues, the essay might conclude by stating, "It was inevitable, given centuries of oppression, prejudice, discrimination, and widespread denial of basic rights and freedoms, that American blacks would ultimately demand equality in school, on the job, in housing, and at the ballot box. They would no longer tolerate second-class citizenship. Their demand for basic civil rights, which were constitutionally guaranteed, finally exploded in the 1960s and dramatically changed the course of American history and the values of American society."

The inductive method is best visualized as an inverted triangle. Information is stacked in descending layers that lead to a logical conclusion. The conclusion, expressed in the final sentence or paragraph, is the inverted point of the triangle. Although inductive essays can be very persuasive, they require advance planning, organization, and expressive language skills (see Language Arts). For this reason, most students choose the deductive model when taking an essay exam.

Another method for writing essays incorporates a *dialectic* format, which involves stating and documenting a well-reasoned position on a subject (the thesis), stating and documenting a contrasting position (the antithesis), and blending the best components of both positions into a balanced conclusion (the synthesis). The Hegelian dialectic format (named for the philosopher Hegel) is used extensively in European countries. The method can be highly persuasive, but students require extensive practice before they can use the format effectively.

Practice, feedback, constructive criticism, encouragement, and patience are vital components in the learning process that ultimately produces good essay writing skills. Because expository writing and analytical thinking skills improve slowly and incrementally, mastery requires systematic instruction, incisive feedback, and constructive criticism (see Language Arts). Students must write hundreds of essays and reports before they can reasonably be expected to express themselves effectively in a timed essay exam. Even children with natural writing talent require practice and feedback and must make a concentrated, sustained effort to develop and refine expressive language skills.

Students in elementary and junior high school who have taken only multiple choice, short answer, and true/false tests may become overwhelmed and demoralized in high school when they encounter teachers who give essay exams.

Memorizing facts, circling the correct answer, writing True or False, or responding to a test question with one or two words does not prepare children for the rigors of having to organize, distill, and communicate what they know about a subject in a two- or three-page essay.

Some educators contend that multiple choice tests adequately measure information retention and comprehension and that such tests are easier to grade and less subjective than essay exams. There is a high price to pay for this convenience. The exclusive use of multiple choice tests to measure data retention and comprehension deprives students of a vital opportunity to master the mechanics of written expressive language. These skills are fundamental to a complete education. The widespread practice of depriving children of the opportunity to develop their thinking and expressive language skills has had a catastrophic impact on American education. The effects are eloquently and incisively described in Allan Bloom's book *The Closing of the American Mind*.

Corrective Strategies

In School

1.   (Elementary School, ES) Although there are teachers who believe that elementary school students cannot reasonably be expected to take essay exams, most fourth graders can learn to write cogent and effective essays, assuming they have been systematically taught how to condense information and express their ideas sequentially. If you believe your child's school has an inadequate language arts program, discuss your concerns with the teacher. You may need to involve the principal in these discussions and enlist his or her support in your campaign to upgrade the program at your child's school (see Language Arts). Many enlightened elementary schools have introduced innovative writing programs that have produced documented, dramatic improvement in students' written expressive language skills (see the Resource List at the back of the book).

2.   (Junior High/High School, J/HS) If you believe your child's teachers are not giving enough

essay exams, diplomatically express your concerns. Be prepared for resistance from teachers who have developed their own teaching and testing style and who may construe your suggestions as meddlesome. These teachers may reject your suggestion without considering the logic of your position. Some teachers may not give essay exams because they believe that multiple choice, short answer, or true/false tests are better testing instruments. They may also reject the idea of giving more essay tests because the tests require considerably more time to grade. (In fairness, it should be pointed out that a high school teacher could have more than 120 essay tests to grade each week if he teaches four classes a day and gives an essay exam to all of his students each week. This assumes that he doesn't have a reader to assist him.) If you believe that your child should have more opportunities to develop and refine her essay-writing skills, and the teacher does not concur, discuss your concerns with the department chairman and/or the principal. Even if they agree with you, they may not be able to require a tenured teacher to change his testing philosophy. Effecting major changes in educational philosophy at the local school level usually requires a concerted effort by a significant number of concerned parents. The superintendent, and perhaps the school board, may need to be actively engaged in this process of altering a clearly unacceptable status quo situation.

At Home

For specific suggestions for improving your child's essay writing skills, see Language Arts.

Evaluating Special Education Programs

Most parents of children who are struggling in school are delighted if their child qualifies for learning assistance. They realize that individualized help from a resource specialist is an ideal means to make certain their child gets the remedial help he requires.

There are two types of learning assistance programs: the self-contained program ("special day class"), where children spend most or all of the school day, and a resource program ("RSP class"), where children spend only a portion of the day. Children in special day classes generally have more severe learning handicaps and lack the requisite skills to keep up with a regular class. Children in RSP programs generally have less debilitating learning problems and can usually keep up with their class if provided with forty-five to sixty minutes of learning assistance each day. During the remainder of the day, these children are mainstreamed back into regular classrooms.

Not all parents are receptive to learning assistance programs. Some fear that if their child is officially classified as learning disabled or learning different, the child will be permanently stigmatized. Other parents fear that their child will be embarrassed when asked to leave the classroom each day to work with the resource specialist. They may also fear that their child will miss important classwork while participating in a pullout program. These misgivings may be justified. Children in RSP programs often do, in fact, miss important work and are often held responsible for making up this work. Many students in well-intentioned learning assistance programs often find themselves in a "Catch 22" situation: they require remedial assistance, but while they are out of the classroom receiving help, they fall further and further behind.

Classroom teachers who are flexible and understanding about missed classwork can significantly reduce the stress on students. The work, however, must somehow be made up, and this can pose a monumental challenge to even compassionate teachers. To address this problem, some schools now send their RSP teachers and teacher aides into the regular classroom to provide on-site remedial assistance. There's a potential disadvantage to this strategy: focusing primarily on helping children complete daily classwork takes valuable time away from remedying the underlying learning deficits.

Many parents of children assigned to special day classes have other concerns. They may fear that their children will never learn the skills requisite for successful reintegration into the mainstream. These parents may also be apprehensive about negative behaviors and attitudes that may be prevalent in classes comprised of children with histories of serious learning problems. Teasing, taunting, and social rejection by other students are another consideration. Social ostracism can be traumatic for special education students. Although these children may have perfectly normal IQs, they may be rejected socially by mainstream students because they are considered different, "strange," or retarded. This stigma may cause students to resist placement in special programs.[1]

Before deciding whether to accept the recommendations of school authorities and placing your child in a special program, you must understand the issues and take time to observe and evaluate the proposed remedial program (see Individual Educational Program [IEP]). If you do agree to have your child participate, it is vital that you monitor his progress and periodically assess the program. Conferences with the resource specialist or special day class teacher are essential (see Parent-Teacher Conferences). These meetings do not always have to be face-to-face; telephone contact and progress checklists are often sufficient. Periodically requesting updates is justifiable, but be reasonable: checking in with the teacher every two months is usually sufficient.

Remedial programs rarely follow a precise, predictable timetable. Some children improve quickly and dramatically, but most students make slower progress. The learning curve may rise steadily, or have peaks and valleys. Be realistic when assessing the efficacy of your child's program. Serious problems typically take longer to resolve, even if your child is enrolled in a first-rate program. Your child may show improvement for several months and then plateau or even regress. Individual students may also respond differently to the same remedial program. Despite occasional temporary setbacks, you are justified to expect improvement after a reasonable period of time. Reexamine the learning assistance program if you conclude your child is not meeting agreed-upon goals established in the IEP or if you conclude that the goals are insufficient to allow your child ultimately to be reintegrated successfully into mainstream classes. Discuss any concerns with the resource specialist.

You have a fundamental right to request clarification about why the RSP program or special day class is not achieving the educational goals

defined during the IEP conference. You cannot afford to allow years to pass before asking for an incisive explanation about the lack of meaningful progress. If the explanations prove unacceptable, you have a legitimate right to insist that the remedial program be objectively evaluated and, if necessary, revised (see Parents' Rights).

Corrective Strategies

In School

1.   Periodically request that the teacher and resource specialist evaluate your child. Use the Student Evaluation Checklists (pages 128–129 for elementary students and pages 129–130 for junior and senior high students) to provide substantive information to help focus parent-teacher conferences on specific issues. Strategies for correcting your child's deficits should be evaluated and adjusted if necessary. Ask for recommendations about how to help your child at home. If you cannot work successfully with your child in a tutorial capacity, inform the teacher and inquire whether hiring a tutor or educational therapist is advisable. Ask for guidelines about how much help you should provide and how much homework your child should be expected to do. This discusssion is vital if you feel your child is doing too much or too little homework. (Refer to appropriate suggested corrective strategies under specific relevant entries in this book.)

2.   Make a list of concerns you want to explore during your next conference, IEP meeting, or PPT (Pupil/Parent/Teacher) meeting. This conference ought to examine substantive issues, so be prepared to ask penetrating (but nonantagonistic) questions. Don't be overwhelmed or intimidated by the professionals in attendance. If you don't understand the jargon, ask for clarification. Your understanding of the issues and support of the remedial program will have a direct impact on your child's progress. (See Communicating with the School; Conferencing with School Officials.)

---

1. In a well-run school, teasing and taunting of students with special academic and physical needs are simply not tolerated.

At Home

1.   Discuss progress and problem areas that need to be addressed with your child. Decide which issues discussed during the parent-teacher conference are appropriate to examine with your child. You may need to simplify issues or withhold certain information. Trust your intuition. A simple explanation about the learning assistance strategy or about changes in your procedures for providing help or supervision at home may be sufficient for younger children. Older children may require a more comprehensive explanation. Use examples your child can relate to and understand. (For example, "Do you remember how your Liittle League coach had you practice your swing for hours? Well, according to your teacher, you are going to have to do more practice to learn the parts of speech.") To help your child overcome learning problems:

- inform him about the issues
- involve him in the process of establishing specific academic objectives (see Goals)
- encourage him to take an active role in the program
- keep him apprised of his progress and problem areas, and acknowledge and affirm him for progress.

2.   Periodically review the objectives of the learning assistance program with your child. Explore strategies for achieving goals and examine problem areas. Engage your child in brainstorming solutions and developing a plan to attain his goals (see Smart Thinking). Discuss homework, study habits, and schedules. If your child becomes overly dependent on you, explore solutions to this problem with him (see Learned Helplessness; Monitoring Homework).

Expectations and Performance Guidelines

Determining reasonable academic performance standards and expectations for struggling students can be a challenge. Parents and teachers want youngsters to stretch, for it is only by reaching for goals slightly beyond their grasp that children motivate themselves, develop character and determination, attain coveted payoffs, build self-confidence, develop to their full potential, and experience the exhilaration, pride, and satisfaction derived from a job well done.

The expectations and standards that parents and teachers establish for a child must be reasonable and based on a realistic assessment of the child's ability and skills. When parents and teachers wittingly or unwittingly make excessive and unreasonable demands, they can cause debilitating emotional stress and undermine the child's self-confidence. Expectations are a double-edged sword. If too little is expected, the child will usually perform commensurately with these lowered expectations. Conversely, if too much is expected, the child becomes anxious, frustrated, and demoralized.

Defining any child's potential capabilities is risky, because so many factors can affect school performance and achievement. These factors include inherited and acquired personality traits, temperament, intellectual ability, family and peer influences, culture, educational opportunities, and role models. Given this complex mix of variables, it is clearly easier to assess a child's demonstrated ability (based on classroom performance and standardized test scores) than it is to assess accurately her true potential ability. Too many issues (for example, attention deficit disorder, emotional problems, and a host of other unknowns) can skew supposedly reliable and objective evaluations of intelligence and potential (see IQ Test Scores).

Establishing realistic expectations and standards for children is more difficult in the case of those who have learning deficiencies. Making challenges and academic demands reasonable and fair requires a careful and insightful assessment of all available data on the child. To conclude on the basis of an IQ test score, standardized achievement scores, and/or classroom performance that a struggling child lacks ability can be erroneous and unfair. Unfortunately, such erroneous conclusions are far too common. Every day bright, potentially capable children are written off by teachers, administrators, and school psychologists, and their unique abilities are discounted. Many of these children then perform consistently with these flawed assessments (see Behavior and Attitude; Effort and Motivation).

If you are wrestling with the challenge of how to establish reasonable performance guidelines for a child with learning problems, ask several key questions:

• Can we realistically expect our child to do what is asked in class and for homework? ("If our child is reading two years below grade level, can we reasonably require her to complete all the assigned homework? Should we ask the teacher to make adjustments in the quantity and difficulty of these assignments?" See Monitoring Homework.)

• Are our child's learning, focusing, and self-confidence deficits skewing her performance on an IQ test and undermining her schoolwork? ("How can we get an accurate assessment of our child's true intellectual potential if she appears incapable of focusing for more than 45 seconds at a time?" See Attention Deficit Disorder.)

• Is our child unmotivated because she anticipates failure or fears competition or even success? ("Is our child unwilling to work diligently because she's convinced that effort is futile?" See Fear of Failure/Success/Competition; Negative Attitude toward School.)

• Has our child acquired a set of psychological coping mechanisms to deal with frustration, poor self-confidence, low self-esteem, and negative expectations? ("Is our child misbehaving, acting irresponsibly, and procrastinating because she lacks self-esteem and she doesn't feel she deserves success?" See Anger and Frustration; Psychological Problems and Psychological Overlay.)

• Does our child appear lazy and irresponsible because underlying learning problems make it difficult for her to sustain effort, meet expectations, and achieve at a level commensurate with her ability? ("Is our child phobic about academic challenges because of a lack of the skills required to do these tasks?" See Atypical Learning Problems; Learning Disabilities; Underachievement.)

• What is our role in defining academic performance expectations and standards for our child? ("Should we accept the school's assessment of our child's problems and ability or should we also factor an independent assessment into our educational planning and performance expectations and standards?" See Understanding Diagnostic Test Results; Communicating with the School.)

Children are programmed by nature to learn. When they shut down academically, this behavior is invariably linked to underlying issues that must be identified and addressed. Parents who conclude their child is not working up to potential must figure out how to rectify this situation. The alternative is to allow the child to tread water in school for twelve years. If a clear pattern of underachievement is evident, a comprehensive evaluation of the child's skills, learning efficiency, and intellectual ability is vital. Test results, however, must be cautiously and judiciously interpreted, as scores may be skewed by the factors cited above.

Expectations and performance guidelines must be carefully calibrated to be challenging and demanding, but also realistic and reasonable. This determination requires insight and an informed judgment call based on test scores, class performance, and parental intuition.

Corrective Strategies

In School

1.   If you're uncertain about what constitutes realistic expectations and performance guidelines for your child, request a conference with your child's teacher or teachers. Ask for an assessment of her current skill level as determined by standardized test scores, classwork, and homework (see Performance on Standardized Tests). Use this information to establish reasonable, realistic, and challenging performance standards (for example, neatness, maximum number of acceptable errors, deadlines, amount of homework, and so on. See Conferencing with School Officials; Goals; Study Skills; Time Management.) If your child's skills are very deficient, discuss reasonable and appropriate modifications in the quantity and difficulty level of the assignments. Put work that meets the teacher's expectations into a folder. You might select a math homework assignment or English essay your child has submitted that conforms to an agreed-upon standard for legibility or accuracy. Refer to this folder when you and your child are in disagreement about the standards.

2.   If you believe your child is working below her potential, and she hasn't been adequately evaluated for learning problems, request that the

child study team and/or school psychologist do so. (See Parents' Rights). Be cautious about accepting professional pronouncements about your child's potential. If these are inaccurate and you accept them at face value, you will lower your expectations. Your child will then lower her own expectations and may never actualize her full potential.

3. If your child is in a resource program, explore how you might work with the resource specialist to establish challenging but fair performance guidelines. Involve your child in the process of setting the guidelines. Her active participation significantly enhances the likelihood that she will attain the standard.

At Home

1. Discuss the teacher's performance guidelines and expectations with your child. Examine strategies that will allow your child to achieve this level of performance. For example, she might carefully proofread each assignment two times before submitting it. Or she might use the spell-check function on the typewriter or computer to find spelling errors.

2. Place examples of acceptable work in folders or plastic sleeves. When your child's work does not meet this standard, show them to her and say: "This is what I know you are capable of doing. Please redo this work so it is as legible as the sample. I want you to take pride in your work and get into the habit of doing the best job you're capable of doing.

3. Write out (with your child's active participation) general performance guidelines for homework and place them near her desk or study area. These might include: completing assignments on time; writing legibly; checking carefully for spelling, grammar, syntax, or math errors; submitting work on time; maintaining a study schedule and recording all assignments. Urge your child to go through the checklist before submitting each assignment.

4. Without preaching or self-aggrandizement, share with your child how you establish demanding performance standards for yourself when doing a project at home or at work. Discuss in concrete terms how you establish a challenging goal and define the specific steps you must take to attain the goal and do a first-rate job.

5. Do nonacademic projects with your child at home. These might involve building or planning something together. Model how to define the objective, develop a strategy, establish a performance and quality standard (such as a smooth, unblemished finish on the table you're reconditioning), and intentionally incorporate this performance standard in the planning and execution of the project.

Fear of Failure/Success/Competition

When faced with danger, a child's brain triggers an involuntary neurological, hormonal, psychological, and behavioral chain reaction. The child may respond to the perceived threat by running, by fighting, or by neutralizing the danger. However he responds, he will instinctively attempt to protect himself from harm. This is the quintessential survival function of fear.

Fear warns children not to climb on dangerous rocks, not to jump from a bridge into water of unknown depth, not to get into a stranger's car, and not to ride in a car with someone who is drunk. Fear, however, is not always an ally. When it is excessive, inappropriate, or irrational, it can distort a child's perceptions and judgment and can cause the child to become emotionally and academically debilitated.

The demoralized child who has repeatedly experienced pain in school and who lacks self-confidence and emotional resiliency is especially vulnerable to fear. If he believes his situation is hopeless, he is at risk for becoming phobic about school and for running away from any challenging situation that might cause additional suffering or frustration. He may retreat into a "circle the wagons" stance and refuse to venture outside the perimeter of his psychological defenses, or he may charge ahead mindlessly and continue to repeat the same mistakes.

Once children become convinced that effort is futile and failure preordained, they usually resort to a pattern of self-protecting compensatory behaviors that include laziness, procrastination, re-sistance to help, irresponsibility, manipulation, denial, blaming, cheating, lying, or codependency. Some children act out aggressively. Others become timid and withdrawn and may shut down. The list of nonadaptive behaviors attributable to fear, poor self-esteem, and insecurity is extensive, and these behaviors invariably impede effective problem solving (see Anger and Frustration; Behavior and Performance Guidelines; Bouncing Back from Setbacks and Learning from Mistakes; Disregarding Consequences; Effort and Motivation; Negative Attitude toward School).

In contrast, children with healthy self-esteem, good academic skills, self-confidence, and a successful track record of dealing with problems respond with confidence to challenges. They have faith in themselves and their abilities because their life experiences and achievements have confirmed their talents. They enjoy competition and believe they can win. They also believe they deserve to win. They take reasonable risks, commit the requisite time and effort to attain their goals, and revel in the pride their accomplishments generate. When they do experience a setback, they possess the confidence and emotional resiliency to bounce back. After analyzing the presenting difficulty and the underlying causal factors, they will try again using a more effective strategy. If, however, they conclude the problem is insoluble or the challenge is not worth the effort, they will move on to something else (see Critical Thinking;

Goals; Planning Ahead; Self-Esteem and Self-Confidence; Smart Thinking).

Insecure, academically deficient children are often preoccupied with protecting themselves from failure, and many of these children are traumatized by the fear of failing again. These youngsters perceive each new challenge as potential defeat and respond to each glitch as confirmation of inferiority. To cope with fear, they often capitulate *before* they have a chance to fail, unconsciously rationalizing that they haven't really failed because they haven't really tried.

Ironically, a struggling child who is accustomed to marginal achievement may become so habituated to doing poorly in school that the idea of success may actually be frightening. Marginal performance may provide a familiar sense of identity and security, and the child may perceive success as scary, uncharted territory. Increasingly accustomed to limited achievement, the child may become convinced that he does not deserve to succeed.

Ensconced in a comfort zone where relatively little is expected of him, the insecure, fearful child may passively or aggressively resist leaving the safety of the refuge. To achieve would require him to revise his assessment of his own abilities and potential. Such a drastic revision in self-concept can seem threatening and unsettling and trigger anxiety once he begins to succeed. His relationship with his parents and teachers would undoubtedly change. Instead of accepting D's or C's, they might start expecting B's or even A's and be less willing to offer help and accept excuses (see Learned Helplessness). Meeting the new standards would also require more effort and work. He might even face the prospect of being rejected by the nonachieving peers with whom he identifies, and he would have no guarantee that the achieving students would accept him.

With assistance and guidance, most children can conquer fear of failure, success, or competition. Your role is to orchestrate repeated opportunities for your child to succeed, affirm his accomplishments, build his self-confidence, and provide the academic and study skills needed to prevail academically. If your child's fears are profound and are linked to psychological issues, seek help from a mental health professional. Hoping that chronic fear will disappear on its own is unrealistic. Not to provide help could be a tragic miscalculation with catastrophic emotional, social, academic, and career implications.

Corrective Strategies

At School

1.   (Elementary School, ES) If you believe your child's ability to function in school is being undermined by excessive fear, discuss your concerns with the teacher. Do not automatically assume that he's afraid of failing. He may actually be afraid of succeeding. Consider whether your child has become so habituated to a marginal performance comfort zone that he's unwilling to change old attitudes and behavior. Consider also whether he is afraid of succeeding because he perceives himself as being unworthy of success.

2.   Take a close look at your child's behavior. Identify his specific strengths and deficiencies. Observe his responses to setbacks. Identify his desired payoffs. Does he act like a clown to get attention? Does he act helpless to elicit assistance (see Learned Helplessness)? Does he intentionally try to elicit sympathy and concern? What triggers his anxiety and stress?

3.   Once you and the teacher have assessed the possible underlying sources of your child's fears, brainstorm how you might both orchestrate successful experiences for him. For example, if he's struggling in spelling, you might use new strategies for helping him study for his spelling test. The teacher might also agree to reduce the number of words he's required to learn. Suggest that she intentionally acknowledge and affirm him for even relatively minor successes. Acknowledgment may initially trigger discomfort, especially if your child has become habituated to negative feedback and comments. A child's fear of failure,

competition, or success is not easily overcome, nor are entrenched habits easily changed. The goal is to reorient your child so that he begins to derive pleasure and pride from positive rather than negative payoffs. This reorientation process requires insight and patience.

4.   Ideally, your child's self-concept will begin to undergo a transformation, and his self-confidence and motivation to succeed will improve commensurately. If, however, his fears are chronic and persistent, your child will require professional counseling (see Psychological Problems and Psychological Overlay).

At Home

1.   Encourage your child to examine the situations that frighten him. If he has difficulty identifying or discussing the specifics, you might say: "Let me tell you some situations that frighten me. When I was in school I was afraid to try out for plays because I was certain I would forget my lines. The fear of having people laugh at me if I flubbed my lines was terrifying. Somehow, I was persuaded by my dad to give it a try despite my fears. I only made one small mistake, and no one laughed. I can still remember how proud I felt when everyone in the audience applauded at the end of the performance, and I couldn't wait to try out for another play. I've noticed that you often give up on challenges at the last minute. For example, you've told me you want to drop out of your karate class, even though you're making good progress. Let's list the reasons why a person might be tempted to give up on something before completing the job. Then let's list the possible consequences. I'll start with the first reason. The person is afraid that his work will not please his teacher. The consequences he fears are that he might get upset or his parents might be angry when they see his grade. Now you give a reason for giving up and a possible consequence." Using the third person (he or she) may provide emotional distance and be less threatening to your child.

2.   Be patient as you attempt to draw out your child's feelings. This may be a very challenging exercise for him, as most children do not think consciously about their fears. Being asked to identify underlying issues may be threatening and emotionally unsettling. Don't make negative judgments about your child's responses. If he says that the teacher would get mad at him, you might reply: "How could you deal with this?" Your objective is to encourage your child to begin looking at his fears so that he can "process" them and overcome them.

3.   Resist the temptation to try to solve your child's problems. Give him something to think about, and allow him time to ponder and consider his options. For example, you might say: "If the teacher did get upset with the child's work, what could the child do? Could he talk to her about it? What might he say? Could his parents help in any way?" Be prepared for "I don't know." Your objective is to plant seeds, encourage analytical and strategic thinking, and elicit the expression of feeling. At this point, you might make a transition to one of your child's fears and say: "You've told me you're afraid when you have to read aloud in front of the class. Let's list the reasons why you're frightened . . ."

4.   Don't expect immediate insight or resolution of the issue. Processing fear usually takes time. Assistance from a trained mental health professional will be necessary if your child is unresponsive and unable to examine and resolve his fears, especially if these fears are emotionally debilitating (see Self-Esteem and Self-Confidence).

5.   Be patient. Altering the dynamics of your child's attitude and imprinted emotional and behavioral responses to fear of failure, success, or competition is a slow process. Your child needs time to become comfortable with a new modus operandi. Once you and the teacher identify the underlying issues, make incremental changes in your parenting style, standards, and guidelines. You don't want to overwhelm your child, have unreasonable expectations or an unrealistic

timetable, and produce unnecessary anxiety. Gradually begin to provide less help with homework (see Learned Helplessness). Encourage him to take karate, swimming, or tennis lessons. This could be especially valuable if he has poor coordination or lack of confidence. Don't let him quit the karate class when it begins to get more difficult; to do so would be tantamount to setting him up for another self-confidence-eroding failure. Prior to beginning the class, insist on at least a six-month trial before he decides whether or not to continue the program.

Following Verbal Directions

During a typical school day, students are expected to respond efficiently to a constant barrage of verbal instructions. A teacher might instruct them to turn to page 43 in their history textbook, read unit 1, complete exercises 1 through 7 at the end of chapter 3, skip a line between answers, use a pen, answer with complete sentences, and hand in their work at the end of class. Some children assimilate these instructions effortlessly. Others struggle to make sense of even the most basic verbal directions (see Auditory Memory).

Children who have difficulty following verbal instructions are in a constant state of confusion. Because their classwork and homework rarely conform to the teachers' guidelines, their grades inevitably suffer. To keep up, they must constantly ask the teacher for clarification or somehow figure out through observation what their classmates are doing. In desperation, they may ask other students for help and possibly get into trouble for talking in class. As their frustration and feelings of incompetence increase, their behavior, self-confidence, and attitude will often deteriorate. Those who are repeatedly reprimanded for not paying attention will probably conclude the situation is hopeless and simply shut down whenever verbal directions are given. From their vantage point, there can be only one explanation for their ineptitude: they are dumb.

Difficulty processing oral directions can usually be attributed to deficits in one or more of the following areas:

- Auditory memory
- Auditory sequencing (remembering information in the proper order)
- Concentration (see Attention Deficit Disorder)
- Impulsivity (see Attention Deficit Disorder)

On the surface, chronically poor listeners may appear uninvolved, unmotivated, and apathetic, but their seeming indifference is a coping mechanism. These children are usually on the receiving end of a great deal of negative feedback. While they struggle to make sense out of what their teachers are saying, they see their classmates effortlessly following the instructions. Negative comments, poor grades, embarrassment, and frustration will confirm feelings of inadequacy and inevitably take a frightful toll on self-esteem.

Before your child can realistically be expected to improve his ability to follow instructions, he must be taught specific techniques that will help him process, remember, and respond to verbal input more effectively. Systematic instruction, practice, and carefully orchestrated successes are requisites to breaking the cycle of poor performance, frustration, demoralization, negative expectations, and deteriorating self-confidence.

Corrective Strategies

In School

1. If you observe your child having difficulty following verbal directions and the teacher

concurs, request an evaluation by the school psychologist or resource specialist. Tests should indicate if there are any short-term or long-term auditory memory or auditory sequencing deficits. If deficits are revealed, specific remedial methods and materials can be used to develop your child's skills in these critical areas (see Corrective Strategies under Auditory Memory). If you suspect that your child may have a hearing loss, have his hearing tested by his pediatrician or by an audiologist.

2.   (Elementary School, ES) Ask your child's teacher if he would be willing to give him instructions in smaller "chunks" and monitor him more closely to make sure he has understood the directions. This should be done diplomatically to avoid embarrassment. As your child's listening skills improve, the teacher can begin to phase out this monitoring procedure.

3.   (Junior High/High School, J/HS) Because junior and senior high school teachers see so many students each day, it is difficult for them to supervise children as closely as elementary school teachers. If your child indicates he is having difficulty following directions and instructions, discuss the issue with the teachers or school counselor. (Many teachers assume students should be able to follow verbal instructions by the time they reach seventh grade, and they may attribute a student's difficulty to irresponsibility.) Request that the teachers monitor your child more closely (without embarrassing him) to make sure that he has understood the directions and has recorded his assignments accurately. (Many teachers deal with this problem by handing out written weekly assignments. If your child's teacher does not, diplomatically explore the possibility of him doing so.)

4.   If your child is having difficulty following verbal directions because of Attention Deficit Disorder, refer to Corrective Strategies in that listing.

At Home

1.   (ES) Practice is essential if your child is to improve his ability to follow verbal instructions. If your child is resistant to your help, the best way to defuse this resistance is to make the process of improving listening skills fun. For example, create a game in which something is hidden (a little inexpensive toy or a cookie) and give your child explicit instructions on how to find the prize. Start out with two or three directions. Increase the complexity as your child's skills improve. Have your child close his eyes and picture going into the living room and picking up the couch cushion on the far left. This visualizing process reinforces the auditory process and is especially effective when children have intrinsically weak auditory skills. To reinforce auditory memory, ask your child to repeat the instructions before doing them. Explain that by forming visual pictures in his mind, he will be able to remember better what he hears.

2.   When giving your child a series of instructions ("Please set the table, feed the dog, and bring in the garbage pail."), encourage your child to follow the visualization procedure described above. Have him form a visual picture in his mind of what you have asked him to do and then have him repeat the instructions.

3.   (ES) Play Simon Says around the dinner table. ("Simon says cut your chicken into twelve pieces, put your fork down for five seconds, eat a forkful of peas, put your fork down, and then eat a piece of chicken.") Have your child make a visual picture, repeat the instructions, and then follow them. Then have your child give you a series of instructions.

Following Written Directions

A child spends a significant portion of a typical school day responding to instructions written on the chalkboard, in textbooks, on handouts, and in workbooks. The youngster who has difficulty understanding and following written directions faces an uphill struggle that will be reflected in his grades.

Relatively few children intentionally or capriciously disregard instructions. Some do not pay attention to what they are doing (see Attention Deficit Disorder). Others are confused because they cannot decipher, understand, remember, and/or apply what they read. They typically do the wrong assignment, format a report improperly, or misinterpret directions on a test. The effects of these mistakes become increasingly problematic as students progress into the upper grades.

Children who observe their classmates effortlessly following written instructions and working efficiently while they themselves are in a continual state of confusion are at risk for becoming frustrated and demoralized. If the situation persists, they will probably conclude that they're hopelessly inept. To protect themselves psychologically, these youngsters often resort to an elaborate system of coping behaviors that includes procrastination, irresponsibility, and resistance.

The first step in helping a child learn how to follow written instructions more efficiently is to identify specific factors responsible for the problem. Observations by parents and teachers and diagnostic assessment by the school psychologist or resource specialist should help pinpoint underlying deficits (see Parents' Rights). Once the causal factors are known, a systematic and effective remedial strategy can be designed and implemented.

Difficulty following written instructions can usually be attributed to one or more of the following causal factors:

- Visual decoding deficits (see Dyslexia)
- Reading comprehension deficits (see page 207)
- Difficulty working independently (see page 277)
- Distractibility (see Attention Deficit Disorder)
- Visual memory deficits (see page 271)
- Visual sequencing deficits (remembering written information in the proper order, see Visual Memory)
- Impulsivity (see Attention Deficit Disorder)
- Anxiety (see Self-Esteem and Self-Confidence)

Begin the process of helping your child learn to follow written instructions more effectively by showing her how to break instructions into small chunks. Once she learns this basic "divide and conquer" procedure (see suggestions that follow) and begins to identify sequentially the specific bits of information in a series of directions, she'll assimilate directions more efficiently. Her anxiety and chronic confusion will dissipate, and her confidence in her ability to understand directions will increase.

The next step in helping her deal with written directions is to teach her how to form either a visual picture or auditory soundtrack in her mind about what she's being asked to do. By showing her how to use this visual or auditory map as a guide through each step of the instructions, you can help her make the decoding task less awesome and intimidating. Encourage your child to choose a representational system that capitalizes on her preferred learning modality: if she's a visual or kinesthetic learner, she should create and visualize a picture of the information in her mind; if she's an auditory learner she should create and hear a soundtrack. Once she masters basic practical information assimilation/comprehension/recall "tricks," her ability to understand written instructions will improve dramatically.

Corrective Strategies

In School

1.   If your child is struggling with written instructions, discuss the issue with her teacher. Request that she be evaluated by the school psychologist or resource specialist (see Parents' Rights). Once the underlying deficits have been identified, the resource specialist can develop an assistance program (assuming the student qualifies for the resource program). For specific corrective strategies for use in class and at home, refer to entries relevant to her particular deficit and to the Resource List at the back of this book.

2.   Ask your child's teacher to monitor her to make certain she has understood the directions for assignments. Because elementary school personnel teach fewer students each day than teachers in the upper grades, they're generally more willing to provide this individualized supervision. You might elicit cooperation from the teacher by explaining your concerns and your desire to improve your child's ability to follow directions. The school counselor might also become involved in the monitoring process. The ultimate goal is to remove this safety net. Until her skills improve, however, supervision is vital.

At Home

1.   If your child is evaluated by the school psychologist or resource specialist and specific deficits are identified (such as dyslexia or attention deficit disorder), refer to corrective strategies listed under these entries. Your own observations will also guide you in targeting areas to work on at home.

2.   Monitor your child closely to make certain she has understood the directions for doing her homework or for preparing for tests. Ask her to read the instructions and explain to you what she's being asked to do (see Monitoring Homework; Recording Assignments; Working Independently). Suggest that she close her eyes and visualize herself following each chunk of information. For example, she should see herself turning to the exercises at the end of the unit, formatting her paper with her name on the top line near the left margin line, and writing her answers in complete sentences (each sentence contains a subject and verb). As instructed, she should see herself skipping a line between each answer. These visual pictures should be vivid, detailed, and precise. If your child's preferred learning modality is auditory (see Auditory Discrimination and Auditory Memory), have her use words to describe each step. If she is a kinesthetic/tactile learner, have her draw a map or visual representation of the steps. As her decoding skills and self-confidence improve, these procedures may be phased out (or retained, if desired).

3.   Be gentle and patient if your child is confused. If her problem is caused by a visual decoding problem (see Dyslexia), she may be expending so much energy deciphering the actual words in the instructions that she has little left to devote to understanding what the words mean. Once she has read the material with your

assistance, discuss the instructions and help her with the "chunking process." Be affirming and positive. If your child feels you are continually judging her or that you are disappointed in her, she will be reluctant to accept your help. As her skills improve, you can begin to remove this monitoring/support system incrementally (see Learned Helplessness).

4.   If your child doesn't qualify for help in school and/or is not responding as quickly as you would like, consider hiring a well-trained tutor or educational therapist, or consider enrolling your child in a private learning center. The teacher resource specialist, school psychologist, or your pediatrician should be able to refer you to a qualified specialist or agency.

 Goals

Successful students grasp the fundamental cause-and-effect principles that link the establishment of personal goals with achievement. They may not think consciously about this connection at all times, but their focused effort, astute choices, and strategic behaviors and attitudes attest to the fact that goal setting is an integral part of their modus operandi.

A goal-directed child might decide he wants an A on his math test, a part in the next school play, a hit in the next inning, or a music scholarship to a first-rate university. Like a guided missile, he plots his trajectory and relentlessly closes in on his target. He may not be the most brilliant student in the class, but he typically ranks among the highest achievers.

Several key traits distinguish goal-oriented students:

• They select their objective. ("I want an A on the book report.")

• They identify the barriers that stand in the way. ("To get an A, I have to reduce my spelling errors.")

• They consider their options and develop a practical strategy. ("I'll allow extra time to proofread my report carefully.")

• They learn from mistakes. ("Even when I proofread carefully, I still miss some spelling errors. I have to figure out a better plan for dealing with this problem.")

• They anticipate potential problems, make adjustments, and establish contingency plans. ("I'll ask John to proofread my paper, and I'll offer to proofread his. As an extra safeguard, I'll use the spell-check on my computer.")

Goal-directed children thrive on challenges. They enjoy pushing themselves beyond their limits. They want to run a faster fifty-yard dash, speak French fluently, and win the school science award. They are motivated and conscientious because they have faith in their ability to prevail over the challenges they create for themselves. Their faith rests on a foundation of positive life experiences. Their accomplishments generate pride, self-confidence, and the desire for more success. This achievement loop naturally recycles itself. Once these children attain an objective, they quickly establish a new goal.

There are obvious advantages to encouraging your child to become goal-directed but there are also potential dangers. You may unwittingly place your child at emotional risk if you:

• Impose your own achievement agenda on your child

• Overtly or covertly pressure your child to actualize your own thwarted ambitions (for example, to become a physician or a concert pianist)

• Encourage your child to aspire to goals incongruent with his interests, needs, personality, and talents

Goals are a double-edged sword. If they mesh with a child's talents, interests, and desires, they can provide inspiration and motivation. If they do not mesh, they can trigger emotionally destructive stress, guilt, anger, and depression.

Intensely goal-directed children face other dangers. Those who are unrealistic about their abilities or who seek specific goals primarily to please or appease their parents will probably not achieve their objectives. If they fail repeatedly, these failures can trigger frustration, demoralization, despair, and damaged self-confidence. Some children unconsciously orchestrate failure by sabotaging themselves because they feel unworthy of success or have a need to punish themselves. Defeats will further undermine already tenuous self-esteem and self-confidence and could trigger depression, hostility, and socially nonadaptive behavior (see Anger and Frustration; Psychological Problems and Psychological Overlay; Self-Esteem and Self-Confidence). Children manifesting chronic self-sabotaging behavior desperately require psychological counseling.

Society's materialism creates additional hazards. Goal-oriented children may fall into the trap of equating achievement and monetary rewards with happiness. Success and wealth may enhance self-confidence, but they do not guarantee self-esteem. This irony is apparent when one examines the personal lives of many ostensibly successful actors, rock stars, and business tycoons. The "achievement equals happiness" illusion underscores a paradox and a conundrum: achievement may not necessarily produce happiness, but chronic nonachievement almost invariably produces unhappiness.

As a parent, you face a monumental challenge. You must help your child realize that goals and achievement are important, and, at the same time, help him realize that his value as a person is not exclusively contingent on what he achieves. This insight can prevent subsequent disillusionment, and, perhaps, an emotionally devastating midlife crisis forty years down the road.

To attain his goals, your child must learn how to plan (see Planning Ahead). Some children intuitively figure out how to create a practical strategy for achieving their objectives and require little formal instruction in strategic thinking. Most children, however, must be shown how to get from point A to point C. You cannot assume that if your child declares he wants an A in science, he knows how to make this happen. If he has not had a successful academic track record, he will need to be taught how to establish specific short-term goals (A's on quizzes and weekly tests) that will help him attain his long-term goal (an A in the course) . He will need to be taught how to prioritize, manage study time, take notes, recall information, check over daily homework assignments, anticipate what is likely to be asked on tests, and write a term paper (see Essay Tests; Language Arts; Notetaking; Preparing for Tests; Priorities; Smart Thinking).

Your child does not need to know at the age of ten, or even at the age of eighteen, what he wants to do with the rest of his life. Relatively few ten-year-olds who profess that they want to become professional basketball players, ballerinas, or airline pilots actually attain these objectives. These transitory goals, however, serve a vital purpose. They provide your child with a sense of direction and produce an appreciation for the cause-and-effect principles that link focused effort and self-actualization.

Corrective Strategies

In School

1.   (Elementary School, ES) During your next parent-teacher conference, discuss the value of encouraging students to establish specific short- and long-term goals in each subject. You might diplomatically suggest that at the beginning of the semester students write their targeted semester grades on pieces of paper that are then sealed in envelopes. These envelopes could be placed in a "time capsule." (The letters, of course, would

be private.) The teacher might also discuss her grading criteria for giving students an A, B, or C. She might brainstorm with the class methods for meeting these standards and the entire class could create strategies for achieving a targeted grade. Students would then know precisely what they need to do to attain their goal. The students could include in their time-capsule envelope their personal strategy for achieving their objectives. After report cards have been issued, the teacher could open the time capsules and return each students' unopened letter. A class discussion about strategies and goals could then be initiated. Students should not be pressured to reveal in front of their classmates their grades or goals and whether or not they attained their objectives.

2.   (Junior High/High School, J/HS) Students in junior and senior high school should also be encouraged by their teachers to record their personal grade goals for each semester. Ideally, the teacher will devote time to explaining her grading criteria and show students strategies for attaining their target grades. She might also examine with the class the average amount of homework and study time necessary to achieve a particular grade (such as, an A in a high school history course typically requires approximately forty minutes of quality study and homework time each day). Practical techniques for helping junior and senior high school students establish academic and career goals and master time management are described in the school editions of *Study Smart, Think Smart* and *Getting Smarter*. See the resource list at the back of the book.

At Home

1.   At the beginning of the school year, make it a family tradition to establish personal nonacademic goals for the year. These goals might include getting a minimum of 100 points during the basketball season, advancing to the intermediate ski runs, or earning a brown belt in karate. You could use the following format to record these goals. The activity would take on more meaning if you also listed your own short- and

long-term goals, demonstrating how you use the goal-setting process to achieve your personal and vocational goals.

GOALS

Long-Term Goals

1. _____

2. _____

Short-Term Goals

1. _____

2. _____

Medium-Range Goals

1. _____

2. _____

---

2.   Follow the procedure described above for establishing academic goals. At the beginning of each semester, have your child indicate target semester grade goals for each subject. Then examine his strategy for achieving his objective. If appropriate, help him integrate a study schedule and a task completion checklist into the strategy. Place the target grades in an envelope and at the end of semester, see how close your child came to achieving his goals. You might want to establish a reward system if it is obvious that your child will have to stretch to achieve his goals. Suggest that he tape a copy of the target grades near his desk.

If your child does not achieve his goals, discuss in a nonemotionally charged and nonjudgmental way what might have gone wrong and what obstacles were encountered that weren't anticipated. Brainstorm possible adjustments in his study strategy (see the DIBS method on page 190). For more specific ideas, see Corrective Strategies under Planning Ahead; Priorities; Recording Assignments; Smart Thinking; Time Management.

 Grades

Teachers have many responsibilities, including establishing performance standards and evaluating the quality of their students' work. The teacher's requirements, guidelines, deadlines, verbal and written criticism, and assessments are an initiation for students into the real world where rewards and advancement will be determined by effort and performance.

Grades are a rite of passage that prepare children for the harsh realities of the life they will face as adults in a highly competitive society. In many respects, the grading procedure is a paradigm for the survival of the fittest phenomenon. Youngsters who can adapt successfully to teachers' demands and performance criteria will excel in the academic arena and usually have less difficulty adjusting to the stress and rigors of adulthood. Successful students recognize, accept, and adjust to the facts of life: they must study conscientiously and efficiently, complete work on time, write legibly, attend to important details, identify and recall key information, understand key concepts, and effectively use the skills they've been taught. They realize that they will be judged not only on the quality of the work they produce, but also on their attitude, effort, and behavior. These insights will serve them well not only in school, but also when they subsequently begin their careers. (See Attention to Details; Behavior and Attitude; Disregarding Consequences; Effort and Motivation; Smart Thinking).

Although grades may provide children with important feedback about their performance and prepare them for handling society's demands, the grading procedure is fraught with potential danger. Children who lack the ability or skills to meet teachers' standards and expectations can be psychologically damaged. Those who continually receive poor grades and negative feedback will invariably suffer damage to their self-confidence (see Learning Disabilities). If they conclude they cannot succeed academically, they will become demoralized and overwhelmed by feelings of frustration and a sense of futility. At this juncture, these children have four options:

- Persist and continue to work conscientiously.

- Lower expectations and resign themselves to marginal performance.

- Give up, shut down, or go through the motions of being educated and, in the process, acquire a range of counterproductive, self-defeating psychological defense mechanisms.

- Orient their emotional and physical energies toward alternative, nonacademic pursuits.

Most struggling, demoralized children select the third or fourth option. Some actually throw in the academic towel in first grade! Acquiescing to their "incompetence," they perform commensurately with the negative feedback to which they have become habituated. Unless there is meaningful intervention in the form of educational therapy and/or counseling, they may feel their fate is all but sealed and they could remain marginal performers throughout their lives (see Expectations and Performance Guidelines; Negative Attitude toward School; Self-Esteem and Self-Confidence; Underachievement.)

The dangers of the academic evaluation process notwithstanding, grades are a functional assessment tool that reflects the teacher's objective and subjective assessment of students' skill mastery and work. A teacher's grading criteria may be narrow or broad, fair or unfair. One teacher may give a student good grades because he is well behaved and personable or because he diligently completes reams of assigned handouts. She may give another student with equivalent skills lower grades because he does not conform to her behavior, attitude, or performance standards. A student may be negatively evaluated because he hands in sloppy, incomplete, or late work or because he spends hours drawing and neglects to proofread his history report or finish his math problems. Confronted with these behaviors, the teacher can certainly justify giving the child poor grades (see Effort and Motivation).

Other factors that can have a negative impact on your child's grades include: learning disabilities, study skills deficits, family problems, emotional problems, uninspiring teaching, drugs, and negative peer pressure. Children with learning deficits, those who are depressed, angry, or in conflict with their family, and those who consciously or unconsciously sabotage their schoolwork will require professional assistance before their grades can realistically be expected to improve (see Psychological Problems and Psychological Overlay and other relevant entries in this book).

Teacher-designed tests are the foundation of the grading process. These tests are typically criterion referenced (the questions are linked to material contained in your child's textbooks or presented in class). In grading these tests, teachers often use both objective and subjective criteria. An essay test is objectively evaluated on the basis of the quantity and relevance of the included information and subjectively evaluated on the basis of the child's ability to organize information effectively and persuasively express ideas in written language (see Essay Tests; Language Arts).

Some educators consider the annually administered, standardized (nationally normed) achievement tests to be a more objective measure of students' skills (see Understanding Diagnostic Test Results). The lack of statistical objectivity in teacher-designed tests, however, does not diminish their validity in measuring skill mastery.

Most teachers are required by their districts to cover designated material in the curriculum, but they are generally given latitude in choosing their priorities and teaching methodology. When developing lesson plans and performance standards, one teacher may emphasize writing skills, and another may emphasize reading comprehension, handwriting, and spelling. Selection of course content, teaching methods, and grading criteria reflects the teacher's training, educational philosophy, and classroom experience. If tests are properly designed and fair, they should provide valid and important information about students' skill proficiency.

Unless you have evidence to the contrary, you can generally assume that the grading criteria used by your child's teacher are fair. Poor grades are red flags that indicate an academic problem that must be addressed. Additional warning bells should go off when poor grades are accompanied by low scores on standardized tests. If your child is doing poorly in class, on standardized tests, and on teacher-designed tests, request that the school psychologist evaluate your child diagnostically to determine if he has a learning disability (see Parents' Rights).

In an ideal educational system, every teacher would be highly skilled, open-minded, unbiased, organized, affirming, reasonable, dedicated, motivating, and sensitive. Some children may be fortunate to be in an excellent school and have superb teachers, but ideal educational systems are rare. The realities of a classroom with thirty children of divergent backgrounds and skills is not always congruent with the theories taught in graduate schools of education. Although many teachers are indeed outstanding, dedicated, and inspirational, others are, at best, marginally competent. They may be insensitive and biased, or they may not have had a creative thought or taught a dynamic lesson in twenty-five years.

Your child must be able to "produce" in school despite any shortcomings the teachers might have, just as someday he must be able to produce at work for a less-than-perfect boss. The grading process may not always be fair and the teaching may not always be superb, but these are facts of life your child must learn to handle. Other hard facts:

- Your child's work will be continually evaluated.

- Grades will reflect how well your child is able to adjust to each teacher's guidelines and standards.

- Grades in upper level courses will profoundly affect future academic and vocational choices and opportunities.

- The system is designed to judge your child's skills, and (unfortunately!) not those of the teacher.[1]

Every child can be taught practical strategies for improving his grades. The subsequent rewards—achievement, pride, personal satisfaction, and acknowledgment—are addictive. Children with good academic skills, a winning game plan, and a successful track record in school will be motivated and self-confident and they will strive to excel with little or no parental prompting (see Study Skills).

Conversely, children with poor academic skills, a losing game plan, and an unsuccessful track record in school will be unmotivated and lacking in self-confidence. These students must

be targeted for help. Their specific deficits must be identified and a meaningful remedial plan implemented.

Corrective Strategies

In School

1.   The first step in helping your child improve his grades is to identify specific problems. Communicating with the teacher is vital (see Parent-Teacher Conferences). The objective of the conference is to examine deficits, understand the grading criteria, and develop, with your child's active participation, a plan for improving performance. The teacher may make specific suggestions, ranging from spending additional time studying to checking assignments more carefully for mistakes before submitting them. The teacher may also be willing to provide extra help before or after class.

If your child's poor grades are the result of negative attitude and behavior, help him identify the causal factors (for example, not handing in assignments or writing illegibly). If his study skills are deficient, explore with the teacher a plan for helping him improve his skills. You may also need to consider hiring a private qualified tutor or educational therapist. For specific remediation suggestions, refer to relevant entries in this book.

2.   If you feel your child's teacher is using unfair or biased criteria for evaluating your child, diplomatically express your concerns. The teacher may be able to explain and justify her criteria. You will elicit far more cooperation if you are nonadversarial, reasonable, and sensitive to the challenges the teacher faces. Your objective is to resolve problems. Being confrontive or making the teacher "wrong" is nonstrategic and counterproductive. People who feel attacked stop listening and spend most of their energy defending themselves. If you remain convinced that the teacher's criteria are flawed and cannot resolve the issue, request a conference with the principal (see Communicating with the School; Conferencing with School Officials).

---

1. Most teachers are evaluated before given tenure, and once they receive tenure, are rarely held accountable for their performance. The educational system usually provides for dismissal, censure, or peer criticism only in cases of egregious incompetence or malfeasance.

3.   If you or the teacher suspect your child has a learning disability, request diagnostic testing. He may qualify for help from the resource specialist. Be persistent, if need be, in requesting an assessment, especially if the school does not consider the problems sufficiently serious compared to those of other struggling students. This is irrelevant. If your child has learning deficits, these deficiencies must be addressed, irrespective of any other students' more serious problems (see Parents' Rights).

At Home

1.   Help your child establish specific short-term goals. Ask him to indicate what grades he is aiming for on spelling tests, math tests, book reports, and so on. Start with an immediate goal: the grade he wants on his next homework assignment (see Effort and Motivation; Goals; Priorities; Motivation).

2.   Have your child establish specific long term-goals: what grades he wants in each subject on the next report card. (The form on this page can be used to record these goals.) Develop (with your child's active participation) a practical strategy for attaining the stated objectives (see Planning Ahead; Smart Thinking). Periodically review the goals to determine if the plan is working and if scheduling adjustments need to be made. Be careful not to dictate what grades you want your child to target. Encourage your child to stretch, but don't suggest unrealistic objectives (see Expectations and Performance Guidelines). A child getting a D in math is probably setting himself up for a defeat if he aims for an A on the next report card. If he insists, have him complete a second form. Explain that the grades on the second form should represent an acceptable fallback position in the event he doesn't achieve his first choice. Although you want to encourage him to strive for the A, you also want to help him understand that raising a D to an A usually requires more than one semester. (See Goals, for a more comprehensive description of how to help your child utilize long- and short-term goal-setting strategies.)

3.   Help your child develop a study strategy that will allow him to achieve his objectives. Specific (and realistic) amounts of study time should be allocated for each subject and a daily study schedule should be developed. (See Time Management for methods for creating a study plan.) Periodically check to see that the teacher's instructions are being followed.

DESIRED GRADES

Elementary School

SUBJECT	MOST RECENT REPORT CARD GRADES	GRADES DESIRED NEXT REPORT CARD
Reading	_____	_____
Spelling	_____	_____
Math	_____	_____
Social Studies	_____	_____
Science	_____	_____

Junior and Senior High School

SUBJECT	MOST RECENT REPORT CARD GRADES	GRADES DESIRED NEXT REPORT CARD
English	_____	_____
Math	_____	_____
Science	_____	_____
History	_____	_____

---

4.   Set up regular meetings with your child to evaluate his progress and problems. Keep the tone of the discussion upbeat. If you assume the role of grand inquisitor, you are certain to trigger resentment, resistance, and defensiveness. Your objective is to gather information about what's happening in school and engage your child actively in the problem-solving process. The context that you intentionally create for this discus-

sion should be one of working together. You might say: "We need to meet on a regular basis to examine how things are going in school. We can see if you're on target for attaining your goals. If there are problems, you may need to reexamine your goals and adjust your study schedule. We can work together on this. Once things are going well, the conferences will no longer be necessary. Let's look at a checklist that will help you pinpoint issues that can affect your schoolwork."

5.   Ask your child's teacher to complete the following Teacher Evaluation checklist. (Make copies if your child has more than one teacher.) Diplomatically compare the teacher's perceptions with those of your child. If there are discrepancies, you might say: "Your teacher indicates that you're handing in your assignments late, and you are not coming in for extra help. How could you convince her that you're being responsible about your homework?" (See the DIBS Problem-Solving Method, page 190.)[2]

SELF-EVALUATION CHECKLIST

	YES	NO
I aim for a specific grade in each subject.	____	____
I aim for a specific grade on each test, report, or project.	____	____
If I am having difficulty in a subject, I ask the teacher for help.	____	____
I attempt to identify and understand specific reasons why I'm having difficulty.	____	____
If I need extra help, I inform you about the problem.	____	____
I spend sufficient time studying and doing homework.	____	____
I record my assignments and hand them in on time.	____	____
I pay attention in class.	____	____
I hand in neat and legible assignments.	____	____
I take the time to proofread my work carefully to correct spelling and grammar mistakes.	____	____
I use a study schedule.	____	____
I have the materials that I need to do my work.	____	____
I feel I am doing the best job I can.	____	____

TEACHER EVALUATION

	YES	NO
This student:		
Asks for help when having difficulty.	____	____
Appears to spend sufficient time studying and doing homework.	____	____
Pays attention in class.	____	____
Hands in assignments on time.	____	____
Hands in neat, legible work.	____	____
Proofreads work carefully to correct spelling, grammar, and computational mistakes.	____	____
Brings to class the materials needed to do work.	____	____

6.   If your child continues to receive poor grades despite his best efforts to establish and attain agreed-upon goals, plan, manage time, and study efficiently, he may require special assistance. If he does not qualify for help in school, consider hiring a tutor or educational therapist or enrolling in a private study skills program.

2. Refer to *The Life-Smart Kid* for effective communication strategies and to *Study Smart*, *Think Smart* and *Getting Smarter* for specific study skills techniques (see resource list at back of this book).

Grammar

All languages are bound by rules that regulate the mechanics of spoken and written speech. These rules are called grammar.

Children start to assimilate the conventions of English grammar during infancy. As they listen to their parents speak, they begin, at a genetically predetermined developmental stage, to mimic sounds, words, intonations, and grammatical constructions. They then begin to associate the sounds, words, and phrases with meaning. During the early stage of language development, the process of mastering the rules of language is relatively painless. Children are motivated to learn how to communicate more effectively for a compelling reason: they want to make themselves and their needs understood.

By the time children enter kindergarten, they have already learned a great deal about grammar. They may not be able to cite the rule for subject/verb agreement, but most children know that the boy *goes*, and the boys *go*, and they will apply these accepted conventions when communicating (unless their subculture uses other conventions). By listening and mimicking, children naturally figure out how to use adjectives and adverbs properly in most circumstances. They learn to speak in past, present perfect, and future tenses. They may not know how to identify or define participles, but they use them effortlessly in everyday speech.

For many children, the process of assimilating grammar becomes less natural and more painful when the learning arena shifts from the informal context of home to the more formal context of the classroom. Here children are often required to memorize the rules of grammar and practice these rules ad nauseam. Most children perceive these rote procedures as another boring, irrelevant academic chore intentionally created by adults to make kids' lives miserable.

The "memorize the rules" approach has endured despite ample evidence that it "turns kids off" and often fails to achieve its stated objective. Teachers committed to the memorization method usually direct their students to "fill in the blanks" in textbook exercises, workbooks, or handouts. For most youngsters, the rules are at best only remotely related to the language they speak at home and with friends. That many of these students find grammar complex, mysterious, and impenetrable and actively or passively resist such repetitive, mind-numbing exercises should surprise no one. Although a persuasive argument can be made for systematically teaching young children the rules of grammar, an equally persuasive argument can certainly be made for teaching grammar dynamically and creatively so that the rules and their application appear relevant and practical to children.

Grammar deficiencies manifest themselves in four areas:

- Difficulty using grammar correctly in reports and essays (run-on sentences, nonparallel construction, mixed tenses, and others)

- Difficulty speaking with grammatically correct language

- Difficulty identifying parts of speech

- Difficulty citing the rules

To help your child overcome difficulties with grammar, first identify the specific deficits. The next step is to teach practical techniques for checking over what she says and writes so she can begin to eliminate mistakes. When you hear or see a specific grammatical error (like, "I like to eat ice cream and playing baseball"), examine the appropriate rule for correct usage (parallel construction) and practice together. To reinforce mastery, apply the rule to other examples ("He likes to go to movies and build things in his workshop"). Use this technique selectively. If you continually correct every grammatical mistake, your child will probably become resentful and begin to tune out what you say. Also, take time to show your child how much grammar she already knows. Without consciously thinking about it, she probably uses parallel tense in most contexts. She knows that it is correct to say, "While I was watching the movie, I ate popcorn," and that it is incorrect to say, "While I was watching the movie, I eats popcorn."

Helping your child master the rules of grammar can actually be fun if you make the process creative and relevant. (If you need to brush up your own grammar, consult *The Goof-Proofer* by Stephen Manhard, Collier Books, 1985.) Hire a tutor who is imaginative and dynamic if you feel you lack the skills, inclination, or patience to help your child.

Corrective Strategies

At School

1.   To identify your child's specific grammatical deficits, ask the teacher to complete the Grammar Checklist.

2.   If deficits are noted, request supplemental materials from the teacher that reinforce the grammar concepts your child does not understand. Ideally, these materials should be relevant and interesting. To have your child repetitively go over grammar exercises and handouts that have already proven ineffective, boring, or irrelevant will do little good, especially if your child has negative associations with learning grammar. Materials you might request from the teacher or

resource specialist are included in the Resource List at the back of this book.

GRAMMAR CHECKLIST

	YES	NO
This student:		
Recognizes subject-verb agreement.	_____	_____
Avoids run-on sentences.	_____	_____
Uses parallel constructions when writing.[1]	_____	_____
Uses tenses properly when writing.	_____	_____
Writes in complete sentences.	_____	_____
Knows the parts of speech.	_____	_____
Uses punctuation correctly.	_____	_____
Uses adverbs and adjectives correctly.[2]	_____	_____
Uses pronouns correctly.[3]	_____	_____
Avoids dangling or misplaced modifiers.[4]	_____	_____
Uses transitive and intransitive verbs correctly.[5]	_____	_____

---

1. *Incorrect:* She is singing, dancing, and likes to have a good time. *Correct:* She is singing, dancing, and having a good time. (Parallel construction)

2. *Incorrect:* She feels good. *Correct:* She is good. (Predicate adjective modifies subject.) She feels well, or she is well. (Adverb modifies verb.)

3. *Incorrect:* It is between she and I. *Correct:* It is between her and me. (Object of preposition)

4. *Incorrect:* We learned that Pearl Buck wrote the book in English class. *Correct:* We learned in English class that Pearl Buck wrote the book. (Nondangling modifier)

5. *Incorrect:* I want to lay down. *Correct:* I want to lie down. (Intransitive verb.) I want to lay it down. (Transitive verb)

At Home

1.   Compose a short essay with glaring grammatical mistakes. (Example: "How he go to the store is him business. What I wants were candy quick.") Play at finding the mistakes together. Gear your expectations to your child's grade level. The skills of elementary school students will obviously be less developed than those of high school students. Later, have your child try to find mistakes on her own in longer paragraphs that contain grammatical errors. Give a point for each mistake. Explain why "they wants" is incorrect (subject/verb agreement) and give other examples of this type of grammatical error. For fun, have her write paragraphs that contain intentional grammatical mistakes. Then have her find the mistakes, cite the reason or rule, and correct the mistake. Give points for each error she identifies and each rule she can cite. These points can be applied to earning a desired reward. Consult *The Goof-Proofer* for verification.

2.   After completing the process described above, have your child check over her own reports and essays to see if she can correct the mistakes her teacher has identified. Urge her to experiment with different grammatical constructions for communicating her ideas more effectively. If your child is willing, rewrite the essay together. The tone you establish during these interactive sessions is vital. Be creative and make the sessions enjoyable. Stop if your child becomes fatigued, distracted, or resistant. The duration of the sessions should depend on the age and maturity of your child. Be patient if she makes a mistake even if you have gone over the particular rule several times. Do not express disappointment. Positive feedback for even small gains is a far more effective teaching tool than a continual stream of negative feedback and criticism. Remind yourself that children usually require several exposures before they achieve mastery.

 Guilt

When children do poorly in school, they are vulnerable to a range of painful emotions that include frustration, embarrassment, shame, discouragement, feelings of inadequacy, demoralization, defensiveness, and insecurity. These feelings are often compounded by conscious or unconscious anger at being in a no-win situation and by conscious or unconscious guilt about being unable to fulfill the expectations of their teachers and parents. (See Anger and Frustration; Expectations and Performance Guidelines; Fear of Failure/Success/Competition.)

Children with academic problems are often so enmeshed in the daily struggle to survive in school, that they lose perspective on their problems and have difficulty identifying and handling the underlying issues and feelings. Many will attempt to flee from the pain, fear, shame, anger, and guilt by denying they have a school problem or by blaming others for their situation.

Ironically, the anger and resentment some struggling children feel toward their parents and teachers for making "unfair" demands often triggers even more guilt. Most youngsters are conditioned from early childhood to believe that it is disrespectful and wrong to express anger openly to parents and teachers. Frustrated, angry children are in a double bind. If their anger explodes and they throw tantrums, talk back, fight, bully, or act rebellious, they will get into trouble and be punished. If their anger implodes, they'll either become depressed or express their hostility passively in the form of self-sabotaging behavior, manipulation, resistance, sarcasm, teasing, devi-

ousness, whining, and belittling others. Children do not consciously choose to explode or implode. Their unconscious mind decides how to deal with their underlying feelings.

Openly expressed anger toward authority figures usually assumes the form of defiance. This behavior is guaranteed to elicit reprimands and punishment that, in turn, will trigger resentment as well as additional anger and guilt. If the causal issues responsible for these emotions are not identified and addressed, delinquency, antisocial behavior, depression, or violence often result.

When children repress or disown unpleasant emotions, they usually repress other emotions at the same time. This sublimation of feelings can have profoundly negative psychological consequences. Children who are unconsciously compelled to disavow their emotions cannot possibly like or respect themselves. To cope with their lack of self-esteem, they often acquire a pattern of counterproductive behaviors that include procrastination, irresponsibility, lack of effort, and, in extreme cases, truancy, delinquency, alcoholism, drug abuse, and even suicide. These self-defeating and self-destructive behaviors, of course, call attention to the very problems and inadequacies the children are attempting to camouflage, but children rarely recognize this irony (see Effort and Motivation; Psychological Problems and Psychological Overlay; Self-Esteem and Self-Confidence).

Some children who repress their anger and guilt are noncommunicative, withdrawn, and nonresponsive. Others retreat into a fantasy world or become obsessed with one or two interests such as Dungeons and Dragons or video games. They may appear to be coping with their learning problems and feelings, but beneath the calm surface of appearances is often a powder keg of powerful feeling and the ever-present danger that the keg will suddenly explode and spew shrapnel. It often requires a well-qualified and perceptive mental health professional to recognize the danger signals.

Guilt should not be confused with remorse. Remorse has socially redeeming value. A child who steals, lies, or cheats might feel bad, struggle with his conscience, and remorsefully decide never to repeat the act. Unlike healthy remorse, the guilt that is often associated with learning problems has no redeeming value. This insidious emotion invariably distorts a child's perceptions, undermines his reasoning powers, erodes his self-confidence, erects barriers to identifying and resolving the underlying issues, reduces motivation and productivity, impedes communication, and causes emotional damage (see Behavior and Attitude; Negative Attitude toward School).

Parents who intentionally use guilt to modify their child's behavior or improve his performance are building a ticking time bomb. Those who denigrate their child, continually express disappointment, or compare the child to other more successful children or siblings will not only succeed in generating anger and guilt, they will also succeed in undermining their child's self-esteem, triggering defensiveness and nonadaptive behaviors, and eliciting seething resentment and alienation. This ill-conceived behavior management strategy will produce a dysfunctional child and a dysfunctional family.

Parents must be clear about their primary objectives: to help their child acquire vital academic skills and to build self-confidence. Realizing that guilt can immobilize a child, wise parents do everything in their power to shield him from this insidious emotion. They establish realistic, fair, and consistent expectations and performance guidelines (see Expectations and Performance Guidelines). They intentionally orchestrate re-peated opportunities for success both in and outside of school. They communicate openly and empathetically and provide ongoing emotional support by acknowledging and affirming improvement (see Atypical Learning Problems; Effort and Motivation; Learning Disabilities; Underachievement.)

Just as guilt can distort a child's perspective, it can also distort the parents' perspective. Admitting that a child has a problem can be especially threatening to parents who have difficulty accepting imperfections. Some parents consciously or unconsciously fear they are genetically responsible for the child's learning problems or that they may have done something to damage their child's learning capacity (such as smoking or drinking during pregnancy). This fear can cause profound feelings of guilt. Rather than deal with the problem, they may try to protect themselves emotionally by denying their child has a problem, despite irrefutable evidence to the contrary, or they may attempt to deflect their guilt by blaming the teacher or the school system. Other parents may try to rectify their child's learning problem by exerting excessive pressure on him to "get better" and become more diligent. This pressure will invariably trigger stress, anxiety, and a range of defensive, counterproductive responses from the child.

Parents who feel in some way responsible for their child's problems may also attempt to assuage their guilt by expecting very little from the child or by serving as an on-call tutor, surrogate teacher, forever vigilant monitor, and/or constant defender (see Behavior and Performance Guidelines; Learned Helplessness; Monitoring Homework). Ironically, parents who objectively conclude their child can do the work on his own and refuse to be manipulated into providing help may also feel guilty. Despite their intellectual insight, they may feel on an emotional level that they are being cruel and insensitive to their child. This guilt-driven conclusion is, of course, erroneous.

Denial-oriented parents frequently give lip service and marginal support to those providing help for their child. They may go through the motions of being supportive and then impulsively decide to withdraw their child from a valuable learning assistance or counseling program. Others may look for a scapegoat if there is not immediate and dramatic improvement. They may blame the child's lack of progress on the incompetence of the resource specialist, the teacher, the school, or the educational system. Sensing his parents' lack of commitment, the child will also lack commitment. Parents who react this way have unwittingly set their child up to fail.

When parents respond to their guilt feelings with excessive concern that undermines their judgment, they invariably impede the remediation process. For example, a mother may volunteer to help in the classroom. On the surface, there is nothing wrong with this offer. If, however, the mother's real agenda is to monitor her child's performance more closely, the strategy may backfire, and her child may feel like he's under a microscope and become anxious, resentful, or dependent on his mother's constant supervision. Although concerned parents may recognize intellectually that their anxiety is contributing to their child's stress, their irrational guilt feelings may prevent them from allowing their child to own his problems and from trusting those who are providing help.

When guilt causes parents to think and act irrationally, parent/school personnel communication barriers are likely to occur. For example, the school psychologist may recommend that a child with specific learning disabilities be enrolled in a resource program. The child's parents may reject this recommendation and justify their position by arguing that enrolling their child in the program would cause the child to feel embarrassed when leaving the classroom for the resource room or that their child would be permanently stigmatized as handicapped (see Communicating with the School; Conferencing with School Officials; Individual Educational Program). This guilt-distorted reasoning does not serve the child and interferes with vital remediation. Any concerns about the short-term disadvantages of possible embarrassment or labeling are clearly offset by the advantages of having the child's learning problems identified, treated, and remedied.

At any given time, perhaps eight million students in the United States are struggling in school. This represents the potential for eight million frustrated, demoralized, angry, guilt-ridden children and sixteen million frustrated, demoralized, angry, guilt-ridden parents. Parents can choose to feel guilty, or they can choose to respond constructively and proactively. Smart parents select the constructive, proactive option. They identify the problems and do everything in their power to help their child overcome these problems.

Corrective Strategies

In School

1.   If you feel your child is embarrassed by learning deficits and that this is causing frustration, demoralization, shame, anger, and guilt, discuss your concerns with the teacher or resource specialist. If your child's not receiving learning assistance, request an evaluation by the school psychologist (see Parents' Rights). Examine with the teacher not only how your child's learning deficits might be resolved, but also how to provide protection from embarrassment. If you believe the teacher may be causing your child to feel guilty about any deficits (saying things like, "You'd do a lot better in school, young man, if you would just remember what I tell you!"), communicate your concern that this approach is counterproductive and could be emotionally damaging. Although you don't want to defend your child's misbehavior, you have a compelling responsibility to protect him from a teacher who is insensitive to the underlying problems. As you wrestle with how best to respond to your child's problems and needs, consider the child's best interests. Are you continually coming to the rescue? Are you rationalizing his deficits and defending him when he doesn't need to be defended? Are you encouraging him to be helpless? (See Learned Helplessness.) Are you providing legitimate and necessary help designed to insulate him

from unnecessary frustration, pain, and demoralization? There is no absolute formula for determining the correct strategy. Your job is to acquire the necessary information from school personnel that will allow you to make an informed decision. If appropriate, consult with your pediatrician or an independent counselor. Based upon this data, you must then make a well-informed and intuitive judgment call. If you and the teacher cannot agree on an acceptable strategy, request that the principal or assistant principal participate in the discussions.

2.   If you believe your child is compensating for learning deficits by misbehaving in school, explore appropriate in-class and at-home behavior modification strategies with the teacher and/or school counselor (see Behavior and Performance Guidelines).

At Home

1.   If you feel guilty because you believe you're in some way responsible for your child's learning difficulties or because you are constantly angry at your child, do some introspection of your own. If you cannot resolve the issues on your own, seek a qualified counselor or therapist to help you examine your feelings and fears. It is easy to lose perspective when you are deeply enmeshed in a problem. Admitting that you need help testifies to your concern, integrity, and responsibility.

2.   If you believe your child feels guilty because he thinks he is disappointing you or because he is frustrated and angry at you or his teacher, encourage him to examine these feelings, identify problem areas, and develop a practical plan for resolving the issues (see DIBS Method, page **190**; Anger and Frustration). If you cannot make inroads into the problem, request a referral to an educational therapist or mental health professional (family therapist, social worker, psychiatrist, or psychologist). Guilt is an insidious emotion. It is imperative that you provide help before serious emotional damage occurs. If damage has already occurred and your child is manifesting red-flag symptoms, getting help is all the more urgent (see Psychological Danger Signals Checklist). In most cases, the damage can be repaired. You cannot simply hope that the problems will go away of their own accord. Emotional problems can, like cancer, quickly metastasize if not properly identified and skillfully treated.

Handwriting (Dysgraphia)

Teachers are obligated to read their students' work, and they are usually very unhappy when assignments are illegible and sloppy. Difficulty in any of the following areas can cause poor handwriting: fine-motor control, spatial awareness, copying, concentration, and attitude. The child who chronically submits hard-to-read assignments may be struggling with one or more of these problems at the same time.[1]

Fine-motor control deficits interfere with children's ability to regulate their fingers as they grasp and move a pencil, pen, or chalk. When a child's fingers are "uncooperative," letters and numbers are invariably misshapen and uneven.

Spatial awareness deficits signal that children are having problems recognizing proportions. Individual letters and the spaces between letters and words are not uniform. These spatial deficits can also create major problems for students when they attempt to line up number columns while adding, subtracting, dividing, and multiplying.

Near-point deficits can cause children to make mistakes when they copy words and numbers written in textbooks or on assignment sheets. Children with *far-point deficits* make mistakes when copying words and numbers written on the chalkboard.

Chronic concentration deficits can also contribute to poor handwriting. Children who are oblivious to details (see Attention to Details) often forget to indent, cross *t*'s, space letters properly, write on the line, and dot their *i*'s. They frequently "slap down" their work on the paper without caring if anyone can actually read it (see Attention Deficit Disorder).

Attitude must also be factored into the poor handwriting equation. Children who have received continual criticism about their handwriting often conclude they're incapable of writing legibly and become resigned to doing sloppy work. Having accepted their "fate," they may not be willing to invest the extra effort required to improve the legibility of their work.

Many children who are capable of writing neatly and legibly also submit substandard work. Many have become lazy and have not assimilated a basic cause-and-effect principle: sloppy work produces lower grades. Unless this cavalier attitude about writing legibly changes, the proclivity to do sloppy work might become an entrenched habit that could plague them throughout life (see Attention to Details; Disregard of Consequences).

The first step in helping your child correct a handwriting problem is to identify the specific sources of the illegibility. If deficient fine-motor control is the cause, a resource specialist or

---

1. The term *dysgraphia* may be used to describe chronic handwriting deficits. Educational techniques for remedying this condition include intensive fine-motor and visual perception instruction. Children with dysgraphia must be systematically trained to control the fine-motor muscles of their hands, perceive visual relationships and proportions more accurately, and integrate their visual-motor and fine-motor coordination skills. This specialized training is usually implemented by a resource specialist, educational therapist, or occupational therapist.

private educational specialist can use specific remedial techniques to improve this skill. If a near-point or far-point copying difficulty is the source, an evaluation by an ophthalmologist or optometrist is advisable. Developmental optometrists can teach your child eye-muscle training techniques that have proven effective in correcting visually based copying, reading, and word tracking deficits (such as seeing letters, numbers, and words accurately and in the proper sequence; see Inaccurate Copying).

Handwriting deficits that are attributable to distractibility, impulsiveness, and concentration problems can be especially challenging to resolve (see Attention Deficit Disorder). The child with ADD who writes illegibly will clearly need to make a more intensive effort to control her hand when writing. She will also need extra feedback, encouragement, and practice. A qualified resource specialist, private tutor, or educational therapist can provide specialized instruction that can help the ADD child overcome or compensate for handwriting deficits. Attention-focusing drugs such as Ritalin or Dexadrine have also proven successful in improving the legibility of children's handwriting.

Identifying the causal factors responsible for your child's handwriting problems and implementing a systematic corrective strategy are only two components in the process of helping her write more legibly. You must also establish reasonable standards and performance guidelines (see Behavior and Performance Guidelines) and engage your child actively in working toward attaining specific improvement goals (see Goals). Positive expectations, acknowledgment for effort, praise for achievement, and patience are powerful confidence builders and motivators. You must guide your child to the realization that she can improve her handwriting if she's willing to make the requisite effort.

Corrective Strategies
In School

1.   (Elementary School, ES) Ask the teacher if your child's handwriting problems or sloppy work might be caused by poor fine-motor con-

trol, poor spatial awareness, attention deficit disorder, and/or copying deficits. If she suspects one or more of these underlying issues may be responsible, request that she assign materials your child could use in class or at home to remedy the deficits. Specific materials that focus on correcting handwriting problems are also included in the Resource List at the back of this book.

2.   If you or the teacher suspect that underlying perceptual deficits in the areas of fine-motor control, spatial awareness, near- and far-point copying, or concentration are contributing to your child's handwriting problem, request an evaluation by the school psychologist or resource specialist (see Parents' Rights).

At Home

1.   (ES) Tell your child that you would like to do some experiments together. As a pretest, have her carefully copy every letter of the alphabet in upper and lower case. Younger children should print, and older children should use cursive. This exercise will reveal which letters are difficult for your child to form.

2.   (ES) Now ask your child to copy a paragraph in her very best handwriting. Remind her to space her letters carefully and to use capitals and periods. Do not tell her now why you are asking her to do this. Allow her to take as much time as she needs. When she has finished, acknowledge her for her effort. If she is struggling with any of the deficits described above, her work will probably be far from perfect. This sample will serve as a baseline of your child's careful work without a time limit and a starting point for making improvement.

3.   (ES) Have your child copy another paragraph as quickly as she can. Stop her after two minutes. This sample provides a baseline of your child's fast work. Fast work is rarely as neat as slow, careful work; nevertheless, your child must be able to write legibly when writing an essay on a timed test in school. This sample also represents a baseline of your child's hurried work and a starting point for making improvement.

4. (ES) Place the carefully copied paragraph (see #2 above) in a plastic sleeve that you can purchase at an office supply store. Explain that this good, clear sample will serve as a new standard for homework assignments. Whenever written work is below this standard, take out the paragraph and simply say, "You have shown me that you are capable of doing work as good as this. I would like the assignment you just did to be as neat and legible. Please redo the assignment using this paragraph as your standard." Be careful not to sound harsh, punitive, or disappointed. Also be careful not to imply that you've tricked her, as this will obviously elicit resentment. Be matter of fact and express your conviction that she can equal or excel the standard. Enthusiastically acknowledge and affirm her when she does. By actively engaging her in the process, encouraging effort, and demonstrating that the standard is attainable, you can help her take pride in her work and motivate her to stretch toward a higher standard.

5. (ES) Place the quickly copied sample in another plastic sleeve. Your child needs to be in the habit of writing more carefully and meticulously, you also want her to be able to write legibly when she is under pressure to write quickly. In junior high and high school, she will be required to take notes during lectures, and she must be able to read her own work. Ideally, the practice she gets learning to write meticulously will have a positive impact on her speed writing. Her writing may not be as neat as when she writes slowly, but it should be somewhat more legible than before. Once her handwriting begins to show significant progress, you might want to play some dictation games in which you intentionally pressure her to write down something you are saying to her. Tell her to write as quickly and legibly as she can. Compare her current performance with the original sample of her speed writing that you placed in a plastic sleeve. If you see improvement in the legibility, acknowledge and praise her for the gains she has made.

6. (ES) Copy a sentence in neat legible handwriting. Have your child trace over your sentence several times. Then have her copy the sentence in her best handwriting. If your child is in elementary school, have her use graph paper ($1/2$-inch boxes) to help with spacing and letter proportions. (This paper is available in teacher supply stores.) If your child is having difficulty lining up columns of numbers when doing math, graph paper will help. Create a model for properly aligned, legible addition, subtraction, and/or multiplication problems. Have your child trace over your numbers and then copy the problems on graph paper. As she shows improvement, she can begin to use graph paper with $1/4$-inch boxes. Make the sessions short and nonstressful. Communicate positive expectations. Children respond far better to praise than they do to negative comments. Be patient. Do not expect miracles overnight.

7. (ES) Every few months have your child recopy the original paragraph (see #2 above). Acknowledge her for any progress she makes in being less sloppy and writing more legibly. You might want to establish a reward for improvement, such as a toy or an excursion to an amusement park. (This is not a bribe, but an incentive!) Insert the new sample in the plastic sleeve. This will become the new standard. In time, this procedure should no longer be necessary.

8. (Junior High/High School, J/HS) Copy a short paragraph very carefully. Then copy the same paragraph quickly and intentionally make the paragraph illegible. Show your child the illegible sample and ask her to read it. Tell her to pretend she's a teacher. Have her circle in red the words she cannot read because they are illegible. Ask her what grade she would give a report or an essay answer on a test that is written with this quality handwriting. Now show her the legible sample. Identify the specific handwriting components that make something legible (slant and size of the letters, spacing, margins, crossouts, and care taken). In a nonaccusatory way, examine with your child some previously submitted assignments. Ask her to pinpoint illegible words or sentences. Brainstorm how she might develop a plan for improving her handwriting and legibility

(see the DIBS Method on page 190). Encourage her to establish specific performance goals.

9.   Make copies of the following Handwriting Checklist. Ask your child to complete the checklist before handing in each assignment and staple the checklist to it. Examine the assignment and discuss with your child whether or not you concur with her assessment. Have her remove the checklist before submitting her assignments, unless, of course, the teacher would also like to see the self-assessment.

10.   (ES) Review handwriting development materials at your local teacher supply store to use with your child at home.

HANDWRITING CHECKLIST

	YES	NO
I have carefully recopied my rough draft.	_____	_____
I have done the best I can to make my work neat and legible.	_____	_____
I have paid attention to the size and slant of my letters.	_____	_____
I have followed my teacher's directions (indented paragraphs, skipped a line after title, etc.).	_____	_____

Identifying Important Information

Each day in school, children are assaulted with prodigious amounts of information. Because they cannot realistically be expected to recall everything they are taught, they must develop the ability to sort through the plethora of facts, rules, formulas, procedures, concepts, and definitions and identify what is truly important. This targeting ability is especially vital in high school and college. Children who have difficulty identifying what is important and prioritizing what they must learn and remember can easily become overwhelmed by the continual barrage of information being presented in upper-level classes. To get good grades, your child must not only be able to identify what she consider important but also what her teacher considers important. The ability to create a ladder of importance is integral to effective studying (see Priorities; Study Skills).

Successful students are pragmatic. They are alert to the types of information their teacher emphasizes in class and on tests. Does the history teacher want students to remember the date when Fort Sumter was attacked, or does he want them to be able to discuss the social, political, and economic conditions responsible for the American Revolution? The ability to distinguish concepts and ideas from details and facts and to recognize the teacher's hierarchy of what is important to learn is standard operating procedure for achieving students. These youngsters may not always be aware they are psyching out their teachers, but their grades testify to the effectiveness of their study radar and focused study skills. They figure out what they need to do to win in school, and then systematically implement a strategy to do so.

Some educators may argue that children should not be encouraged to devote their intellectual energy to "psyching out" their teachers. This argument is as naive as suggesting that a football quarterback should not be encouraged to anticipate how the opposition's defense is likely to react on the field. Goal-oriented, cause-and-effect thinking is fundamental to achievement in school, in the sports arena, on the job, and in life. Strategic thinking does not preclude having a quest for knowledge, an inquisitive mind, or a genuine enthusiasm for learning (see Smart Thinking). When your child thinks strategically, she is intentionally using her intellectual ability pragmatically. She wants to get the job done efficiently and reap the rewards of her efforts with a minimum of pain and suffering.

Recognizing that there is an infinite amount of data to assimilate and a finite amount of time and energy available to do so, tactical students accommodate themselves to reality. They use time effectively, distinguish what is important, relate what they are currently learning to what they have already learned, anticipate what is likely to be asked on tests, and develop individualized methods for retaining key information (see Auditory Memory; Preparing for Tests; Visual Memory).

Corrective Strategies

In School

1.   If your child is struggling to identify the important information in her textbooks, ask her teacher if she might have a reading comprehension problem. Review your child's performance on standardized reading tests. If her scores are below grade level, request supplemental remedial materials to use at home to improve her skills (see Reading Comprehension, for specific assistance strategies, and the Resource List at the back of this book). If her comprehension is more than one year below grade level, request that an evaluation by the Child Study Team,[1] the school psychologist, or the resource specialist to identify the underlying learning deficits (see Parents' Rights). An "item analysis" of your child's answers on a standardized reading test can also be used to identify her specific comprehension problems (see Reading Comprehension, for an explanation of this procedure).

2.   If your child is having difficulty identifying important verbal information in class, ask for a diagnostic evaluation to determine if she has auditory memory, auditory sequencing, or concentration deficits (see Attention Deficit Disorder; Auditory Memory; Following Verbal Directions). If deficits are revealed, request specialized help from the resource specialist. An auditory acuity test administered by the school nurse, your pediatrician, or an audiologist may also be advisable to rule out the possibility of a hearing impairment.

3.   If you suspect other students in your child's class are having difficulty identifying important information, for reasons other than poor reading comprehension, diplomatically suggest that a

study skills component be integrated into the curriculum. Most children need to be taught systematically how to identify key information and take notes (see Notetaking).

At Home

1.   Select an article from a magazine or newspaper that you believe will be of interest to your child. Read it aloud to her and discuss it in general terms. Ask her if the article contains anything of interest or importance that should be remembered. Then reread the article paragraph by paragraph. Work together at picking out the key ideas or facts. Discuss why the information is important. Use a highlight pen to mark this information. As you go through each paragraph and select important facts, ask your child if the information is a detail or a main idea. Discuss the difference between the two. When you have finished, summarize what you remember from the article then ask your child to summarize what she remembers. You might leave out some information intentionally and then affirm your child for adding this data when she does her summary.

2.   After using the procedure described previously several times, change roles with your child and have her read the article to you. (This assumes, of course, that she has the skills to read the article. If not, ask the teacher to recommend high-interest material written at your child's skill level.) Encourage your child to play teacher and lead the discussion. Have her summarize the content of the article. Make a photocopy of the article. Each of you should then independently highlight the important information. Discuss the criteria you used for making your choices. Create a quiz from the material. This will help your child begin to think like a teacher. Urge her to use all of the techniques when studying. Refer to strategies under Reading Comprehension and Notetaking for additional methods for improving your child's ability to recognize key information.

---

1. Many school districts require that a team of in-school personnel review a child's test scores and make in-class observations to determine if a comprehensive diagnostic evaluation by the school psychologist is advisable.

Inaccurate Copying

The inability to copy accurately can undermine academic performance in every subject area. A child may know how to do a multiplication problem, but may write down the wrong answer because he copies a *6* instead of a *9*, or because he misaligns the columns (a *spatial orientation deficit*) and adds incorrectly. He may know how to spell the word *perform* but may transpose the letters and write *preform* when doing the final draft of his book report (a *visual tracking deficit*). He may not study for his history test because he wrote down that the test would be on Thursday when his teacher actually wrote Tuesday on the chalkboard (a *concentration* or *auditory processing deficit*).

Children copy inaccurately from their textbooks (*near-point copying*) and from the chalkboard (*far-point copying*) for diverse reasons. In some cases, the inaccuracies are attributable to fine-motor deficits. The muscles of the child's hand may have difficulty controlling the pencil, and as a consequence, the letters will be poorly formed and barely legible (see Handwriting). In other cases, the child's brain may perceive and decode visual symbols incorrectly, and these perceptual distortions will cause the child to make mistakes when copying. A *visual impairment* can also cause inaccuracies. The child who needs corrective lenses is going to make errors if he is not provided with glasses or refuses to wear them.

The first step in identifying the source of a copying problem is to have the child's eyes examined by an ophthalmologist or optometrist. If no organic visual impairment is detected (nearsight-edness, farsightedness, or astigmatism), further testing by a school psychologist, resource specialist, or developmental optometrist (see below) is the next step in the diagnostic process. (This procedure of ruling out what is *not* causing a problem to pinpoint the actual cause is called *differential diagnosis*.)

Some children copy imprecisely because they cannot perceive spatial relationships accurately or distinguish the nearground from the background. These children characteristically struggle to decode printed letters and symbols accurately and often do not perceive the difference between an *n* and an *m* or between *bed* and *bet*. These deficits are primary symptoms of a *perceptual dysfunction*.

Visual tracking difficulties (inefficient, jerky eye movements) can also cause inaccurate copying. The ocular motor muscles that control horizontal movement of the eyes as they move across the printed line must function efficiently if a child is to see letters and words accurately. Children with tracking deficits usually have problems differentiating letters such as *b/d* and *p/q* or numbers such as *6/9*. When copying, they may omit or transpose letters and words and flip words: *saw* is seen as *was* (see Dyslexia). *Convergence deficits* (the eyes do not work together) may also cause reading and copying inaccuracies.

Developmental optometrists are now using specific eye muscle training exercises to treat chronic tracking problems. Although some ophthalmologists dispute the value of these methods and argue that eye muscles cannot be trained, clinical and classroom observations generally substantiate claims that children with tracking problems can learn to read better after systematic visual training.

Concentration problems, impulsivity, and *inattention to detail* may also cause inaccurate copying (see Attention Deficit Disorder; Attention to Detail). Children who lack impulse control and who cannot focus on important details when they write are usually careless and inattentive to important information.

The child who chronically copies inaccurately and makes careless mistakes will need to work harder when writing. He must be trained to assess his work objectively and to take responsibility for finding and correcting mistakes. He must be taught to self-edit, become more vigilant, and tenaciously ferret out his errors. This extra effort will determine whether his work is first-rate or marginal.

Corrective Strategies

In School

1. If your child is making careless copying mistakes, ask the teacher to help identify possible causes for the inaccuracies. If the problem appears to be attributable to inattentiveness, see corrective strategies under Attention Deficit Disorder.

2. If you or the teacher suspect that perceptual processing problems (such as spatial, figure ground, and/or visual tracking deficits) are causing the inaccuracies, request that your child be evaluated by the school psychologist or resource specialist. See Dyslexia for specialized remedial materials that will help reduce copying errors. If your child appears to read and copy inaccurately because of visual tracking deficits, consider an evaluation by a developmental optometrist who specializes in treating visual dysfunctions. (The school should be able to make a referral.) If you suspect your child has a visual impairment have his vision tested.

At Home

1. (Elementary School, ES) Purchase wide-ruled paper at your local teacher supply store.

Have your child carefully copy a sentence from a favorite book. If there are mistakes, brainstorm together about how he might develop his own system for finding and correcting copying mistakes (see Handwriting).

2. (ES) Make a game out of finding mistakes. Intentionally make errors when you copy sentences and/or math problems and award your child a point for each error he can find. Show him how to align columns when adding, dividing, and multiplying, and have him practice copying the same sentences or problems. Award additional points for neatness. The points can be used for earning a prize or a special treat.

3. (Junior High/High School, J/HS) Brainstorm with your child a procedure for writing and copying more accurately. Suggest that he always assume that his work contains errors and that he be prepared to make an extra effort to find these errors. He will have to reread assignments carefully and search out the errors. Design a procedure for finding common errors, which might include the following steps:

- Read each assignment aloud two times and listen to the words to make sure they "sound" right.

- Check over every *d*, *b*, *p*, and *q* for accuracy.

- Look for any words that might be left out.

- Look for transposed numbers.

- Look up in the dictionary any word that doesn't "look" right.

- Make sure punctuation has been inserted.

- Check math to make sure numbers have been properly aligned.

Encourage your child to go through all these steps before submitting every assignment. Individualize the steps to address the errors he is prone to make. As an experiment, encourage him to use the procedure conscientiously for three weeks and see if his assignments are more accurate. He could use an acronym to help him remember the steps: SPORT-A (Spelling, Punctuation, Omissions, Reversals, Transpositions, Align).

Inadequate Study Time

No matter how bright students may be, they must spend time at home reviewing, practicing, and assimilating the information, skills, concepts, formulas, and procedures they are taught in class. Students unwilling to spend adequate time studying face predictable consequences: substandard work, poor grades, parental lectures, and the denial of privileges. Despite these foreseeable outcomes, many capable children continue to do the minimum studying possible.

If the homework battle has become an unpleasant ritual in your home, and recriminations, hurt feelings, threats, lectures, punishment, resentment, and resistance are the predictable elements in these showdowns, you have two options: continue on the same track, or take a step back from the conflict and analyze the situation objectively. Before you can realistically expect to eliminate the nightly showdowns, you will need to identify the reasons why your child is resistant to studying.

Chronic resistance can usually be linked to one or more of the following factors:

- Academic skills deficits
- Specific learning disabilities
- Inadequate appreciation of cause-and-effect principles (seeming obliviousness to the consequences of not doing homework)
- Poor study skills
- Failure to establish short-term and long-term goals
- Frustration

- Demoralization
- Laziness
- Procrastination
- Psychological problems (depression, anxiety, hostility, poor self-esteem, oppositional behavior, and others)
- Family problems
- Poor parent-child communication
- Negative associations with learning and negative expectations ("Why try? I'll fail anyway.")
- Negative peer influences

Lectures, threats, punishments, and sermons are seldom effective in reorienting poor study habits. A far more effective strategy for solving the problem is to determine if your child has the academic skills to do the assigned work. The first step in identifying underlying problems is to have a conference with your child's teacher, school counselor, and/or resource specialist and review scores on standardized achievement and diagnostic tests. (See Communicating with the School; Conferencing with School Officials; Parent-Teacher Conferences; Performance on Standardized Tests. Refer to the procedures described below for gathering and interpreting this data.)

Children with learning disabilities are often the most resistant to studying. For frustrated, academically defeated students, school is a painful ordeal. When the bell rings at three o'clock, they have had enough unpleasantness for one day. Spending precious free time studying is the last thing they want to do. (See Learning Disabilities; Underachievement; and other relevant entries for suggestions about how to help your child overcome learning problems and school phobias.)

Some children resist studying for another compelling reason: they don't know how to study. Disorganized students who haven't figured out how to record their assignments properly, establish goals or priorities, manage time efficiently, identify important information, or create a practical study plan derive little benefit from the time they spend studying. Once these youngsters conclude that studying produces no positive payoffs, they often shut down and become actively or passively resistant. (See Monitoring Homework; Planning Ahead; Recording Assignments; Study Skills; Time Management).

In some cases, children resist studying for no readily apparent reason. They have no identifiable learning or study skills deficits, and yet they show little desire to learn. Their inadequate motivation is a red flag that suggests underlying psychological, family, or peer group issues. If these children lack self-esteem and self-confidence, they may express negative feelings about themselves by intentionally orchestrating their own failures. Angry, frustrated, and demoralized youngsters who sabotage themselves by cutting class, chronically misbehaving, refusing to do the work, taking drugs, or becoming delinquent may use poor grades as a weapon against their parents. These children urgently require counseling (see Anger and Frustration; Fear of Failure/Success/Competition; Negative Attitude toward School; Psychological Problems and Psychological Overlay; Self-Esteem and Self-Confidence.)

Some children are unwilling to spend adequate time studying because of negative peer group pressures. Underachieving students with poor self-esteem often seek friends who share their values, experiences, attitudes, and behaviors. The negative energy of the peer group reinforces their alienation, defense mechanism, and nonadaptive behavior. Children who perceive themselves as nonachievers and who strongly identify with other nonachievers realize that they would have to seek new friends if they decided to achieve in school. The prospect of abandoning their comfort zone, redefining their self-image, and forming a new circle of friends can be very threatening. Because many children are quite reluctant to take this step, professional counseling may be required to help them examine the underlying issues and develop a healthier self-concept. As they begin to perceive themselves more positively and succeed academically, they will choose friends who also have positive feelings about themselves.

Parenting styles may also contribute to a child's poor attitude about studying. Parents who have been lax in asserting the family's position on such issues as effort, responsibility, commitment, and educational achievement must do some introspection. Although they may feel that they've clearly defined their position on the subject of diligence and conscientiousness, these parents may need to reassert unequivocally their commitment to a family work ethic. The starting point is to formulate fair, reasonable, and consistent guidelines (see Behavior and Attitude; Expectations and Performance Guidelines). Children are invariably confused by double messages. Knowing what the family rules, standards, and expectations are provides children with a sense of security. (Parents of children in counseling or psychotherapy should discuss appropriate parenting and behavior modification strategies with their child's therapist.)

The following logical steps can improve the likelihood that your child will be more willing to spend adequate time studying:

- Provide academic and study skills assistance, supervision, and emotional support.

- Establish clearly defined structure and reasonable (but challenging) standards and expectations.

- Be consistent.

- Communicate positive expectations.

- Carefully orchestrate victories.

- Provide effusive praise for improvement and progress.

All the above are vital components in the equation that transforms negative attitudes about school and studying into positive attitudes and improved performance. Success is addictive. Once your child begins to achieve in school, she'll be more willing to relinquish the mindset that homework and studying are cruel punishments intentionally designed by teachers to make her life miserable. This letting go of resistance signals that she's now ready to participate more actively and enthusiastically in the learning process.

Corrective Strategies
In School

1.   (Elementary School, ES) If you believe your child is not spending adequate time studying because she is unclear about how much work is required or expected, arrange a conference with her teacher. Your child should attend this conference. Ask the teacher to explain the homework requirements and grading criteria. Request that she explain to your child the amount of quality study and homework time she expects good students to spend each evening. Ideally, she will present a range of realistic guidelines. For example, she might indicate that to get an A in math, students need to spend on average a minimum of twenty minutes each evening (although this amount of time would not necessarily guarantee an A!). This clarification of the study guidelines would obviously be beneficial not only for your child, but also for the entire class. Do not assume that your child can figure out on her own how much homework she should do. Write down the teacher's guidelines in language your child can understand and have her sign the document. By signing, she acknowledges that she understands the standards and agrees to conform to them.

2.   If you feel your child's teacher is not devoting sufficient effort to showing students how to get organized, schedule and budget time, record assignments, and plan ahead, diplomatically express your concerns. These organizational activities could easily be integrated into the curriculum and the entire process might require only five or six hours of instruction.

At Home

1.   Help your child decide how much homework she needs to do on average each evening in each subject. To make this determination, get input from her teachers. (See step #1 above and refer to corrective strategies under Planning Ahead; Smart Thinking; and Time Management, for specific ways to schedule and utilize study time effectively.)

2.   If the teacher concurs that your child should spend more time studying, be prepared to monitor her more closely. Explain the reasons for this extra supervision and advise your child that the monitoring will cease when she demonstrates that she is spending adequate time doing homework and you get confirmation from the teacher that her effort and performance in school have improved. Keep your expectations realistic and in line with your child's skills. Communicate positive expectations and acknowledge and affirm improvements. (See Goals; Monitoring Homework; Planning Ahead; Preparing for Tests; Priorities; Procrastination; Time Management).

3.   If your child is failing to study adequately because of learning problems, academic deficiencies, or study skills deficits, it is vital that she be provided with learning assistance from the school resource specialist. Request that your child be referred for an evaluation by the Child Study Team and/or the school psychologist. (See Parents' Rights and relevant entries in this book for suggestions about how to handle specific learning deficits.)

4.   If you suspect your child is sabotaging herself because of unresolved family or psychological issues, seek professional counseling. Such behavior invariably becomes worse if not treated. Your pediatrician, the school psychologist, or your local mental health organization can refer you to a qualified mental health professional. (Sliding fee schedules are sometimes available to families with limited budgets.)

Incomplete Assignments

Teachers dislike incomplete assignments. They associate the practice with irresponsibility and usually express their disapproval with poor grades.

You have legitimate cause for concern if your child has acquired the habit of submitting incomplete work. The behavior has serious long-term implications. Your child must one day compete in a society that rewards effort, diligence, and responsibility with career advancement and higher compensation. This same society "rewards" substandard effort and performance with substandard pay and limited career options and advancement (see Behavior and Attitude). A pattern of submitting incomplete work is often attributable to one or more of the following factors:

- Academic deficits
- Poor assignment recording skills
- Lack of awareness or concern about consequences
- Difficulty following or remembering instructions
- Poor planning skills
- Poor organizational skills
- Inadequate motivation
- Poor time management skills
- Laziness and irresponsibility
- Procrastination
- Frustration and demoralization
- Confusion about family standards, performance guidelines, values, and expectations
- Psychological problems
- Family problems
- Negative peer influences

Poor academic skills and learning problems are the two most plausible explanations for incomplete assignments. Children who cannot do their assigned work and who are convinced they will get poor grades no matter how hard they try frequently develop poor work habits (see Atypical Learning Problems; Learning Disabilities; Underachievement). They may refuse to do their homework, or they may only complete the easy sections. Although this response is clearly escapist, the struggling child may consciously or unconsciously conclude that running away is the only solution to an intolerable situation.

Children who protect themselves from frustration by not completing their work either do not recognize, or choose to deny, an obvious irony: their self-sabotaging behavior calls attention to the very learning deficits they are trying to hide. Unless they receive help and develop more effective ways to handle challenges and frustration, the counterproductive behaviors will probably persist into adulthood (see Bouncing Back from Setbacks and Learning from Mistakes; Disregarding Consequences; Negative Attitude toward School).

When parents recognize that their child has acquired a pattern of chronic counterproductive behaviors, their natural instinct is to intervene and protect the child from the mistakes, defeats, and pain that usually result. Intervention in the form of threats, lectures, punishment, and showdowns is often ineffectual and typically triggers denial, defensiveness, resentment, anger, and active or passive resistance.

The following logical nine-step procedure offers a far more effective alternative to a frontal assault on the problem of incomplete assignments.

1. Determine if your child has academic deficiencies (see the Student Evaluation Checklists on pages 128–130).

2. Get help if you identify learning deficits. If your child has significant learning problems, request admission into the school resource program. He may also require tutoring or educational therapy to help him overcome his deficits and catch up with his class (see Parents' Rights).

3. Gear your expectations to a realistic assessment of your child's skills. If the work demands abilities your child does not yet possess, ask the teacher to adjust the assignments so that they are congruent with his current skill level. As his skills improve, the academic demands can be increased incrementally (see Expectations and Performance Guidelines).

4. Provide a carefully controlled amount of help and supervision (see Learned Helplessness).

5. If your child does not know how to study, you, the teacher, or a tutor will need to help him acquire practical study skills (see Monitoring Homework; Study Skills; and other relevant entries.)

6. Develop reasonable and consistent homework and performance guidelines and clearly assert the family's position on effort, commitment, and follow-through (see Behavior and Attitude; Expectations and Performance Guidelines).

7. Help your child establish specific academic goals for each subject (for example, a B in

history) and help him develop a practical, systematic strategy for attaining these goals (see Goals; Priorities; Smart Thinking).

8. Confirm that your child is using an effective system for recording assignments and deadlines (see Recording Assignments).

9. Help your child develop an effective study schedule that incorporates pragmatic planning and time management principles (see Planning Ahead; Study Breaks; Time Management).

Generally, a child's work ethic is directly linked to academic skills and self-confidence (see Effort and Motivation; Self-Esteem and Self-Confidence). If a child is floundering hopelessly and requires academic help, this assistance must be provided before you can realistically expect any changes in attitude, motivation, and diligence. Once he begins to receive better grades and starts to enjoy his success in school, he'll be far less likely to submit incomplete work. If, however, his learning deficits are addressed, and he still continues to act irresponsibly, you must be prepared to provide counseling. Depressed and/or angry children often resort to self-sabotaging behavior to express unhappiness, get attention, and punish concerned parents. These children require a talented mental health professional to help them examine underlying feelings and redirect self-defeating attitudes and actions (see Psychological Problems and Psychological Overlay).

Corrective Strategies

In School

1. If your child habitually submits incomplete work, ask the teacher if he possess the necessary academic skills to do his assignments properly. If she indicates that your child's skills are weak, request an evaluation by the Child Study Team, the school psychologist, or the resource specialist. If diagnostic tests confirm learning deficits, request remedial help (see Parents' Rights). The resource specialist may decide to focus on helping your

child with daily classwork and assignments or on improving basic skills (see Evaluating Special Education Programs; Mainstreaming and Special Day Classes). If the work demanded of your child in his mainstream classes is not reasonable, request modifications until he can catch up.

2.   If your child's incomplete work is attributable to poor planning, poor organization, or inadequate recording of assignments, discuss with the teacher the possibility of integrating into the curriculum a study skills segment that teaches these skills.

At Home

1.   If you conclude you haven't clearly communicated your position on diligence and responsibility, you may be tempted to assert aggressively a new set of demanding rules (see Expectations and Performance Guidelines). Assaulting your child with a radically different standard without first explaining calmly, and in understandable terms, the reasons for the new guidelines could overwhelm your child and trigger confusion, active or passive resistance, and resentment. It is far more strategic to explain why you are establishing new rules and to implement the guidelines in increments your child can more easily assimilate. Spell out the rewards for compliance and the consequences for noncompliance. Remember that positive reinforcement (praise for improvement) is generally more effective than negative reinforcement (criticism or punishment for transgressions). Consistency is essential. Equivocating about rules sends a confusing double message: "You better do this, but you don't have to if you really don't want to." The child on the receiving end of double messages rarely respects the rules and rarely respects his parents.

Once realistic guidelines are in place, clearly communicate that you expect conformity to the rules and standards. Insisting that your child complete work on time and in neat, legible handwriting is legitimate and reasonable, assuming he has the necessary academic, spatial, and fine-motor control skills to complete the work and write legibly (see Handwriting; Inaccurate Copying). Acceptance of a work ethic and reasonable performance standards at home is a requisite to

his ultimate acceptance of a work ethic in the more demanding and often harsher world that awaits him after school.

2.   Examine your child's homework assignment sheet to make certain that he's including essential instructions and information. Have him check off each assignment after completing it (or use the Project Completion Checklist below). Make sure he is bringing home the books and materials he needs to do the work. If he is not recording his assignments properly, patiently show him how to do so. Encourage him to use abbreviations (for example, *p. = page* and *ex. = exercise*), but make sure your child can read his abbreviations and that the shortcuts don't become confusing (see Recording Assignments).

3.   Encourage your child to use the following Project Completion Checklist. (Feel free to modify the checklist to your own purposes.)

PROJECT COMPLETION CHECKLIST

*I followed the instructions
for the assignment.*   _____

*I checked to make sure I completed
everything recorded on my
Homework Assignment Sheet.*   _____

I carefully checked over my work.   _____

*I put my completed homework where
I will be able to find it.*   _____

---

4.   If your child has academic deficits and doesn't qualify for assistance in school, consider hiring a tutor or educational therapist or enrolling him in a private learning assistance program. Make certain his specific deficits have been accurately identified. Your child may require intensive educational therapy, tutoring in a particular subject, a study skills program, or simply some short-term help with homework. The efficacy of the assistance program hinges on the accuracy of the diagnosis and the skills of the person providing the learning assistance.

Individual Educational Program (IEP)

Once a student has been referred by a Child Study Team (a panel of school personnel that examines the child's level of academic functioning) to the school psychologist for diagnostic testing and is identified as *learning disabled* (or *learning different*), his parents are asked to attend an IEP (Individualized Educational Program) conference. The purpose of this meeting is to pinpoint the child's specific learning deficits, discuss test results, propose a learning assistance strategy, and define remediation goals.

The composition of the IEP conference may vary from state to state and district to district. Usually the school psychologist, classroom teacher, resource or LH (learning handicap) specialist, principal (or vice principal), and school nurse attend the meeting. A speech therapist may also participate if the child has language or speech problems (see Speech Disorders). In some districts, an occupational therapist, physical therapist, social worker, or counselor may also attend the meeting if a child has physical or emotional problems that require specialized intervention. Parents have the option of inviting a private educational psychologist, clinical psychologist, psychiatrist, educational therapist, or tutor to present additional relevant information and, if necessary, to represent the interests of the child and family. In the event of disagreement, an independent consultant may also attend and serve as an advocate who evaluates the proposed learning assistance plan and debates legal issues involving compliance with local, state, and federal educational codes. Most IEP meetings, however, are nonadversarial, and relatively few parents feel the need to be represented by a consultant or advocate (see Parents' Rights).

If parents agree with the recommendations presented at the meeting, they are asked to sign the IEP document and formally authorize the implementation of the proposed learning assistance plan. In most states, an abbreviated IEP review is scheduled annually. At this meeting, current academic scores on standardized achievement tests (the most frequently administered test battery to determine students' skill levels is called the Woodcock Johnson) are examined and the remediation goals are redefined (see Understanding Diagnostic Test Results). A comprehensive reassessment of the child's progress is scheduled every three years. The results of this evaluation and an updating of academic goals are then examined at another formal IEP conference. At the end of this meeting, parents are again asked to sign the IEP document, assuming everyone agrees that the child would benefit for continued participation in the learning assistance or special day class program.

The IEP conference provides an invaluable opportunity for parents to ask questions, express concerns, and examine remedial strategies. The primary objective is to coordinate the efforts of the professionals working with the child, establish realistic educational targets, and provide focus and direction for the learning assistance program. Issues typically examined at the meeting include: homework guidelines, the amount of assistance that should be provided at home, techniques for monitoring homework, criteria for evaluating progress, responses to counterproductive behavior, and procedures for maintaining effective communication between parents and school personnel. If the parents conclude subsequent to the IEP conferences that their child's learning assistance program is not meeting its stated objectives, they need not wait until the next scheduled conference to express and examine their concerns with school personnel. Parents have the right to request an IEP review at any time.

Parents who feel intimidated by authority figures such as teachers, principals, or psychologists and those who are disconcerted by complex educational jargon may feel anxious about participating in their child's IEP (see Communicating with the School; Conferencing with School Officials). They may believe it would be presumptuous and inappropriate to question the test results, recommendations, or educational objectives presented by a team of highly trained professionals. With so many experts and specialists overseeing their child's needs, they may assume that everything must be under control. Unfortunately, these parents may be placing too much trust in a fallible system. Even competent, well-intentioned professionals can make mistakes in diagnosing and treating a child's learning problems, and these mistakes can produce serious and long-lasting academic and psychological consequences.

Although anxiety at the prospect of participating in an IEP meeting may be understandable, parents should not allow themselves to feel intimidated by the process. Informed and reasonable parental involvement in all aspects of the remediation program, and active parental support of the child's and the teacher's efforts, play a vital role in the ultimate success of the learning assistance program.

Parents who are dissatisfied with the information, conclusions, and/or recommendations they receive at their child's IEP conference have every

right to ask questions until they feel that the issues have been explained to their satisfaction and their concerns have been allayed. They also have every right to challenge (diplomatically, or, if necessary, aggressively) professionals who are inadequately prepared, ambiguous, use excessive jargon, gloss over issues, or are patronizing.

Your role during the IEP conference is to serve as your child's representative and to make certain that he receives the best help available. Your role is not to be a rubber stamp. You must serve notice—calmly, reasonably, and unequivocally—that you expect school personnel to do everything in their power to help your child attain the defined educational goals and that you expect alternative plans to be implemented if he does not respond as anticipated.

Participating actively in monitoring your child's learning assistance program and progress, however, does not translate into being obtrusive, hostile, or unreasonable. Although you have the right to expect improvement, you must also be realistic. Serious learning deficits usually resist quick fixes. Imposing an arbitrary and unrealistic remediation deadline is unfair to your child and his instructors. Your objectives, and ideally, those of the school, should be the following:

• To improve your child's academic skills to the point where he's functioning at or above grade level or at a realistic level commensurate with his intelligence.

• To improve your child's academic self-confidence (see Self-Esteem and Self-Confidence).

• To determine that your child is applying the skills being taught.

• To determine when your child is able to work independently and no longer needs the support of a learning assistance program.

The speed at which your child attains these objectives will vary depending upon the severity of his learning problems, the quality of the learning assistance program, the degree and quality of your active support of the remedial process, and the nature of your child's coping mechanisms (see Behavior and Attitude; Effort and Motivation; Expectations and Performance Guidelines; Psychological Problems and Psychological Overlay). Some children make quick and dramatic progress; others require extensive, extended learning assistance.

Trust your intuition about when it is appropriate to question the efficacy of the learning assistance program. If you conclude that your child is not making reasonable progress after a reasonable period of time, you have a responsibility to request that alternative strategies be explored. Examine your options, and, if appropriate, consider alternative programs in the private sector.

Corrective Strategies

In School

1.   Request a private conference with the school psychologist or principal if you question the validity of the diagnostic tests administered by the school psychologist, find that your child doesn't qualify for learning assistance despite obvious learning difficulties, or cannot resolve to your satisfaction key issues discussed in the IEP meeting. It may be appropriate to request that your child retake specific subsections of the test. If this request is denied, you may want to have your child privately tested. Although you shouldn't be afraid to "make waves," you should make every effort to communicate your concerns in a reasonable, nonhostile way. Your goal is to elicit cooperation. You do have legitimate rights, however, in the learning assistance equation, and you certainly have the right to express justifiable concerns! (See Parents' Rights).

2.   If you are perplexed by the test results or the proposed remediation strategy, or if you feel your questions and concerns have not been adequately addressed at the IEP, consider consulting a private educational psychologist or educational therapist. You may want to have this person rep-

resent you at the next IEP conference. Discuss the fees for this service in advance.

3.   You may request a conference with any or all of the school personnel involved in your child's case before the next regularly scheduled IEP conference. Realize, however, that teachers and other school personnel have many demands on their time and that there should be a valid reason for requesting this meeting. Asking for periodic updates from the teacher or resource specialist is both reasonable and legitimate. A quick, informal face to face or telephone conference is often sufficient.

4.   Make sure you and the school personnel agree about the amount of homework required from your child and the procedures for progress updates. You don't want to discover in April that your child has not been making an effort or submitting any work for six months.

At Home

1.   There may be aspects of the IEP recommendations and proposed remediation strategies that you can effectively reinforce at home. Reviewing spelling words or math facts may facilitate your child's progress, assuming you can work with your child without triggering resentment or resistance. Hire a tutor if you conclude you cannot implement appropriate corrective strategies.

2.   Once there is agreement about how much homework is reasonable each evening, help your child design a practical and effective study schedule that will allow him to complete his assignments and submit them when they are due (see Learned Helplessness; Monitoring Homework; Planning Ahead; Recording Assignments; Time Management). Monitor your child to make sure he's conscientiously doing what's expected (see Study Skills).

3.   Periodically review the IEP document. Make notes about which issues to discuss at the next scheduled meeting or at an "emergency" meeting.

Periodically ask the resource specialist or special day class teacher if the learning assistance plan is still on target. Compare previous IEP documents with the current one. If you feel that the goals are too optimistic or too pessimistic, express your concerns. By asking informed, penetrating questions, you serve notice that: you believe in reasonable accountability; you are committed to monitoring the program; and you are willing to do everything you can to help your child prevail over these learning problems. Be diplomatic and reasonable. Your goal is not to put the school staff on the defensive but to work cooperatively with them in resolving your child's learning deficits.

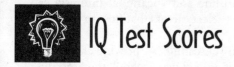# IQ Test Scores

Measuring intelligence can be a controversial procedure. The relatively recent critical attitude about IQ tests can be traced to the inherent difficulty in: 1) defining intelligence to everyone's satisfaction, 2) developing a testing instrument that is culturally and linguistically unbiased, and 3) creating a test that can accurately predict a child's potential to achieve in school and in life.

In theory, children with high IQs should get the best grades, attend the best colleges, enter the most glamorous, prestigious, and remunerative professions, and make the most significant contributions to society. Sometimes IQ scores do reliably predict subsequent achievement. In other cases, the tests fail miserably. Some children with high IQs do poorly in school or in their careers while other children with lower IQs can become highly successful students and major contributors to society. This phenomenon raises serious questions about the predictive value of IQ tests.

Children with identified high IQs who do not do well in school are generally described as *underachievers*. Because they fail to perform commensurately with their potential (as measured by IQ), these youngsters, who invariably perplex their parents, teachers, and, ultimately, their employers, are often accused of being lazy and unmotivated (see Underachievement).

Despite the relatively widespread use of IQ tests as diagnostic and prognostic tools, some professionals have charged that the tests are intrinsically flawed and highly biased against students from disadvantaged backgrounds. They argue that the scores can be skewed by cultural factors, language deficits, emotional problems, perceptual problems, hyperactivity, anxiety, poor rapport with the examiner, and inattentiveness. They also contend that the tests do not measure motivation, interpersonal skills, musical aptitude, leadership skills, or artistic talent, nor do they make provision for environmental stimulation and the quality of educational instruction. Because disproportionately large numbers of minority students have traditionally been placed in classes for the retarded as a result of low scores on IQ tests, IQ tests are now rarely, if ever, used by school districts as a primary criterion for special education placements of minority students.

Most educators would agree that the academic and vocational success formula is far more complex than the simplistic equation High IQ = High Achievement. Environmental, psychological, temperamental, and educational issues must be factored into any attempt to measure a child's potential to achieve. Clearly, culturally or environmentally biased components of the testing battery must be eliminated before an IQ test can be considered a reliable assessment and predictive instrument.

In spite of the limitations, flaws, and legitimate concerns about validity, IQ tests can provide a relatively objective, albeit imperfect, measurement of a child's level of intellectual functioning. Parents and educators, for instance, might consider the scores in determining fair and reasonable expectations and in establishing fair and reasonable performance standards and guidelines for a child (see Expectations and Performance Guidelines). If IQ test scores indicate that a child's intelligence is in the average to superior range, encouraging the child to reach for personally challenging goals and establishing fair but demanding standards at home and in school can be important catalysts for intellectual, academic, and character growth (see Behavior and Attitude). All children should be encouraged to "stretch" intellectually and develop their talents to the fullest, but if a child scores below average on an IQ test, this data should be factored into parents' expectations, especially if observations of performance by parents and teachers tend to confirm the accuracy of the data. Making unreasonable or excessive demands on a child with demonstrated intellectual limitations can cause stress, undermine self-esteem, and be emotionally damaging. On the other hand, making too few demands and discounting the child's potential can have an equally destructive effect. When establishing expectations, parents must make an honest and reasonable judgment call that relies heavily on intuition, objective observations, insight into their child, and a realistic assessment of the available testing data.

A significant discrepancy between your child's IQ test scores and achievement test scores suggest that learning, concentration, emotional, family, or environmental factors could be undermining her school performance. If this is the case, further diagnostic testing by the school psychologist or a private clinical or educational psychologist is essential. Bright children who consistently work below their potential usually require learning assistance and/or counseling.

IQ tests, in conjunction with other personality, aptitude, and vocational interest tests, can play an important role in career selection. Certain professions require higher-level abstract reasoning or analytical aptitude, while other careers require language or artistic aptitude. Obviously, the child who wants to become a physician must possess good scientific aptitude, and the child seeking a career in graphic arts must possess good artistic aptitude. Well-designed tests that measure aptitude and vocational interests can help children select careers that fit with their natural abilities.

Although IQ testing can provide clues about why a child is struggling in school, the procedure also poses risks. The test may not accurately measure the child's potential, or the test may measure certain abilities while disregarding others. If the measurement is flawed because of test design defects, anxiety, poor rapport with the examiner, or inattentiveness, the child may be inaccurately assessed. As a consequence, teachers and parents of a child identified as having below average intelligence may lower their expectations and unwittingly communicate a lack of faith in the child's ability and potential. The child may never be adequately challenged to develop her talents, and a tragic waste of potential may occur.

Two popular tests are generally used by psychologists to assess intelligence: the Weschler (the children's test is referred to as the Weschler Intelligence Scale for Children—WISC III) and the Stanford Binet. Today most school psychologists use the WISC III. (Other tests have recently been introduced but are not yet as widely used.) The format, tasks, and questions vary, but both tests evaluate the ability to analyze, perceive, associate, and recall. The number of correct answers is compared with scores attained by other students of similar background and age who have taken the same test. Statistical norms are established by administering the test to a broad population. The results are tabulated, and the number of correct answers on subsections of the test is compared to the norms and a statistically based score is derived. In determining a child's IQ, the examiner can use national or local norms. Local norms permit the examiner to compare children of similar socioeconomic backgrounds, which theoretically reduces cultural bias.

Some school districts place more emphasis on IQ tests than others, and many schools use the scores as the primary criterion for admitting children into enrichment and gifted programs.

Schools may also use the IQ scores in conjunction with achievement test scores as a rational for skipping students into a more advanced grade or an advanced placement course.

IQ test scores are also usually factored heavily into eligibility requirements for learning assistance programs. Psychologists consider a significant discrepancy between subscores on the WISC III Intelligence Test and discrepancies between above average IQ test scores and a child's achievement test scores (such as reading comprehension two years below grade level) and/or classroom performance (D's in reading) to be symptomatic of a learning disability.

Some educators and psychologists claim that parents can raise their child's IQ with systematic instruction, training, and stimulation. More traditional educators and psychologists argue that intelligence is inherited, genetically determined, and unalterable. Other psychologists believe that intelligence is 70 percent genetically determined and 30 percent environmentally determined. Although it may be true that a child's IQ cannot be significantly altered through instruction or highly focused stimulation, parents and teachers can certainly train children to use their inherited intelligence more efficiently, effectively, and pragmatically (see Critical Thinking; Smart Thinking).

By providing opportunities for intellectual growth, systematic guidance, and encouragement, you can help your child develop and significantly improve her applied thinking skills. Your efforts may not necessarily make your child more "intelligent," but they certainly will make your child *smarter*. Children who possess developed and enhanced strategic thinking skills and critical intelligence invariably do better in school and in life than those who coast along in cerebral neutral.

Corrective Strategies

See suggestions under Critical Thinking and Smart Thinking for specific strategies designed to develop your child's applied thinking skills. Your child's intelligence quotient (IQ) may not increase, but with systematic instruction, her smartness quotient (SQ) can be increased dramatically. Refer to my book *The Life-Smart Kid* (Prima, 1995) which describes comprehensive strategies for improving your child's ability to reason and think logically and rationally.

Keeping Up with the Class

The most plausible explanation for why children have difficulty keeping up with the class is the most obvious: deficient academic skills. Students with reading, math, or language arts deficits face major academic obstacles. These obstacles will appear all the more formidable to a struggling child whose classmates have above average skills. Because teachers raise their expectations and demands when the general ability and skill level of the class is high, academic pressure can cause a student with poor skills not only to fall further and further behind, but also to become increasingly demoralized. If the child concludes the situation is hopeless and effort is futile, academic and emotional shutdown is inevitable.

Unfortunately, many perplexed teachers describe students who cannot keep up with their class as immature. In reality most of these children are neither immature nor developmentally delayed, but, rather, have specific learning deficiencies that may never have been properly identified (see Atypical Learning Problems; Learning Disabilities; Underachievement). Labeling struggling students with puzzling problems as immature and recommending that they repeat the year is rarely an effective solution. Retaining these children is a stop-gap measure that may, at best, put off the "day of reckoning." Unless the underlying deficits are identified and remedied, these youngsters will most likely continue to struggle in school and remain at risk.

Other factors besides deficient academic skills can cause children to lag behind. These include: specific learning disabilities, poor study skills, poor time management skills, inattentiveness (see Attention Deficit Disorder), family or emotional problems (see Psychological Problems and Psychological Overlay), an inability to establish goals and priorities, a poorly developed appreciation for consequences (see Behavior and Attitude; Disregarding Consequences), and a general pattern of self-defeating behavior (see Distractions while Studying; Effort and Motivation; Fear of Failure/ Success/Competition; Incomplete Assignments; Negative Attitude toward School; Procrastination; Self-Esteem and Self-Confidence; Smart Thinking).

Pinpointing the academic and attitude deficits that are impeding your child's progress is essential if you're to help her catch up. To define these deficits, request specific and precise information from the teacher about the factors causing your child to struggle in school (see Student Evaluation Checklist on pages 128–130). If you suspect that your child has a learning disability (see Learning Disabilities), dyslexia (see Dyslexia), or other learning deficiencies, it's imperative that she be referred to the child study team and/or the school psychologist for diagnostic testing (see Parents' Rights).

Enlisting help from teachers can be more problematic when students are in the upper grades. Elementary school teachers teach approximately thirty students each day, while high school and junior high school teachers teach as many as 150, making them less able to monitor and nurture students who are not keeping up with the class. In most states elementary school teachers are also required to take at least one course in identifying and dealing with learning problems in order to be credentialed or certified. In many states, teachers in the upper grades are not required to take this course.

Most high school teachers are concerned primarily with teaching subject matter and have little time to identify the reasons for a student's academic problems. They generally write off students who do not work conscientiously, act responsibly, and keep commitments. Those who do not complete the assigned work and submit it on time are penalized with low grades. In defense of this "produce or suffer the consequences" practice, many high school teachers would argue: "It is not my job to hold a student's hand. If she wants my help, I'll give it willingly. Let her come and ask. And then let me see some real effort. If I don't see any effort, I will respond accordingly."

Economics makes any attempt to engineer a team effort to help a struggling student keep up with the class all the more problematic. Many school districts are under increasing budgetary pressure to scale down expenses. School counselors who should be monitoring and advising struggling students and their parents are often overworked and assigned more students to supervise than they can possibly handle. Some financially burdened districts have actually been forced to eliminate counselors altogether. As a result, many youngsters who desperately need guidance are slipping through the safety net and are being left to fend for themselves.

Another ironic situation compounds the plight of struggling students. Children whose skills are deficient and who go to the resource specialist for assistance miss a great deal of work while they are out of the classroom. Although the resource teacher might prefer to use remedial materials to correct the underlying learning deficits, she may be forced to spend time instead helping students complete classwork and homework. The net effect is little or no remediation of the deficits responsible for the students' academic difficulties.

Ironically, some classroom teachers resent the time struggling students spend away from class and punish these youngsters by holding them strictly accountable for everything covered in class while they were with the resource specialist.

The longer struggling children remain in a no-win situation, the greater the risk of frustration, demoralization, and shutdown. If your child is falling behind, it is imperative that you intervene, identify causal factors, provide emotional support, and help your child develop an effective strategy for getting back on track. To avoid academic and psychological damage, everyone (you, your child, the teacher, and the resource specialist) must be prepared to work together to develop and implement a practical and effective catch-up plan.

Corrective Strategies

In School

1.   To help pinpoint problem areas, ask your child's teacher to complete the following Teacher Evaluation Checklist, which describes common problem areas that can cause children to fall behind. Completing the checklist should require only a few minutes of the teacher's time. The information will provide you and your child with invaluable information about specific deficits and can guide you and your child in developing a successful catch-up plan. The checklist will also help the teacher pinpoint deficiencies that might be addressed in class or after school.

2.   Consult the teacher about how you can work together to help your child overcome pinpointed difficulties. If the teacher is not cooperative or supportive, discuss your concerns with the principal or vice principal. Also consider hiring a private tutor or educational therapist. If your child is having chronic problems and her skills are below grade level, request an evaluation by the school psychologist (see Parents' Rights). Also request supplemental materials your child might use in school or at home to correct specific problems. (Refer to Resource List at the end this book for additional recommended materials.)

TEACHER EVALUATION CHECKLIST

Code: 0 = Never 1 = Rarely 2 = Sometimes
3 = Often 4 = Always

This student:

Has difficulty keeping up with the class. _____

Has difficulty reading accurately. _____

Has difficulty with reading comprehension. _____

Has difficulty understanding math concepts. _____

Has difficulty with math computations. _____

Has difficulty with handwriting. _____

Has difficulty with written language arts. _____

Has difficulty concentrating. _____

Submits sloppy and/or illegible schoolwork. _____

Submits incomplete assignments. _____

Submits late assignments. _____

Procrastinates. _____

Is disorganized. _____

Is irresponsible. _____

Is forgetful. _____

Lacks pride in work. _____

Shows little motivation. _____

Avoids hard work. _____

Makes excuses for poor performance. _____

Avoids challenges. _____

Lacks self-confidence. _____

Becomes easily discouraged. _____

Abandons difficult projects. _____

Is easily frustrated. _____

Appears to be functioning below potential. _____

Misbehaves in class. _____

3.   (Elementary School, ES) Ask your child's teacher to complete the following Daily Performance Checklist at the end of each school day. This should require approximately two minutes of her time. The form will provide daily feedback about your child's work. Modify the checklist to include specific information you want to know about your child's performance. Initial the checklist each evening to indicate to the teacher that you have seen it. If your child is having difficulty completing assignments on time or writing neatly, have a conference with your child and the teacher, and explore possible solutions to the problem. (See Communicating with the School; Conferencing with School Officials; Parent–Teacher Conferences; Problem Solving). Involve your child in the problem-solving process (see the DIBS Method, page 190) and listen to her ideas and suggestions. She may know how to solve the problem once you help her focus on the key issues!

4.   Use the following checklists to identify problems and provide your child with feedback about her performance. Consider setting up a point system to reward her for attaining certain improvement goals. Each day, tabulate the total points earned. Make this an enjoyable ritual. Communicate enthusiasm, affirm progress, and express positive expectations, even if there are occasional regressions and plateaus. Establish rewards for achieving daily, weekly, monthly, and semester target scores in specific areas such as handwriting. By encouraging your child to reach for short-term and long-term objectives, you will help her become more goal-directed (see Goals), motivated (see Effort and Motivation), and self-confident (see Self-Esteem and Self-Confidence).

For additional ideas about how to help your child overcome any learning deficits indicated on this checklist, refer to the suggestions listed under specific entries in this book.

DAILY PERFORMANCE CHECKLIST

Code: 1 = Poor 2 = Fair 3 = Good 4 = Excellent

	MON.	TUES.	WED.	THURS.	FRI.
First and Second Grade:					
Reading					
Math					
Handwriting					
Listens in class					
Keeps up with the class					
Effort					
Behavior					
Completes in-class work					
Completes homework					
Submits homework on time					
Comments					
Parents' initials					

Third Grade and Above:

Subjects (Insert your child's subjects here—math, history, language arts, and so on.)

	MON.	TUES.	WED.	THURS.	FRI.
_____					
_____					
_____					
Completes in-class work					
Completes homework					
Submits homework on time					
Handwriting					
Listens in class					
Keeps up with the class					
Effort					
Behavior					
Comments					
Parents' initials					

5.   Verify that your child has the requisite academic skills to do the assigned classwork and homework. Standardized tests such as the Stanford Achievement Test, California Achievement Test, CTBS, and others given periodically in school can provide this information. If you do not understand what the scores mean, ask the teacher to explain them. (Also see Understanding Diagnostic Test Results.) If your child's skills are deficient, the difficulty level of the work being assigned or the quantity should be modified (see Completing Assignments; Expectations and Performance Guidelines). Academic demands can be slowly increased as your child's skills improve. If appropriate, request that the teacher or resource specialist provide extra assistance.

At Home

1.   Any areas marked 3 or 4 on the Teacher Evaluation Checklist (page 112) should be considered red flags and be examined with your child. Keep the tone and context for these sessions nonaccusatory and cooperative. The interaction should not feel like an inquisition. Your child may deny she has problems in the areas the teacher has identified. This is a common defense mechanism when children feel inadequate and threatened. Demoralized children often try to delude themselves that everything is okay. From their vantage point, denial is preferable to confronting painful issues. Your job is to communicate your conviction that the problems can and will be resolved and to assure your child that you are there to provide assistance.

2.   Help your child establish realistic academic goals in each subject, such as "complete and sub-mit on time all handouts for science chapters" or "get a minimum of 70 percent on all spelling tests." Discuss strategies for attaining these goals (see Goals; Smart Thinking). Consider creating incentives or rewards for achieving agreed-upon objectives (see Daily Performance Checklist, page 113). Perhaps your child could earn points toward a special toy. Once your child begins to succeed, extrinsic or external rewards should no longer be necessary and can be phased out. The intrinsic satisfaction of doing a good job and being proud of her accomplishments will be her motivation.

3.   If your child has specific academic deficits but doesn't qualify for special assistance, consider hiring a tutor or educational therapist or enrolling her in a private learning center.

4.   Communicate every day with your child about what's happening in school. Be careful, however, not to nag! Use the Daily Performance Checklist as a springboard for a nonthreatening discussion. Remember that lectures and recriminations typically fall on deaf ears. Threats and punishment should be used as a last resort as they usually trigger resentment and active or passive resistance. Praise, affirmation, sensitivity, and empathy are usually far more effective vehicles for modifying counterproductive behavior.

5.   Establish reasonable guidelines for the amount of homework expected each evening and help your child set up a study schedule (see Procrastination; Time Management). If appropriate, suggest an experiment that increases slightly the amount of homework done each evening in each subject. Do not propose this experiment if your child is already doing a great deal of homework.

Language Arts
Essays and Reports

To write effectively, a child must be able to find words that express his thoughts and feelings. Events, symbols, objects, and experiences in his environment are perceived through the five senses, and perceptions and impressions are translated by the brain into language. The neurological process of responding to sensory stimuli (such as the image of a kitten playing with a piece of string) is called *decoding*. The process of selecting language to express reactions (saying, for example, "That kitty is cute!") is called *encoding*. When your child says that he is sleepy or writes an essay describing his trip to the planetarium, his words indicate that the input from the experience has been decoded and output has been encoded.

When children communicate verbally, the decoding/encoding loop is usually spontaneous. A child hears his mother say, "Let's stop on the way home and pick up a pizza for dinner." He smiles, shakes his head affirmatively, and encodes his response: "Let's get the kind with the thick crust and extra pepperoni."

Verbal and written communication requires more intense and conscious effort when a child responds to complex stimuli (his reaction to a seeming betrayal by a friend) or expresses complex issues (his description of osmosis or his reactions to *Moby Dick* recorded in a book report).

The superior quality of the writing produced by some children suggests that they have probably inherited natural language aptitude. These youngsters have little difficulty mastering the mechanics of writing, learning good self-editing skills, acquiring a rich vocabulary, and developing a style and syntax (sentence structure) that are precise and aesthetically pleasing.

Researchers have been able to pinpoint specific the areas of the brain responsible for language. Research suggests that the structure and composition of these neurological regions have a direct impact on expressive language ability.

Some students struggle with basic writing skills because of intellectual limitations or neurological deficits. This population, however, is relatively small and certainly cannot be used to explain the epidemic of dismal writing skills that affects millions of students in the United States. The blame for this language arts crisis in American education must be shouldered by the educational system. Clearly, flawed instructional methodology and a tragic deemphasis on teaching effective writing skills are at the root of the problem.

With first-rate instruction, virtually every child of normal intelligence can be taught to write powerful sentences that communicate ideas and emotions clearly and effectively. Given sufficient practice and systematic feedback, students can be taught to produce cogent, well-crafted essays and reports. Each writing assignment provides an opportunity to develop and refine language arts skills, and each corrected essay provides an opportunity to analyze and learn from mistakes.

If children are to improve their writing skills, they must practice and their work must be corrected and critiqued. They must be apprised of errors, affirmed for progress, trained to be self-critical, and encouraged to search for ever more effective ways to communicate their ideas and insights. There are no shortcuts. Teachers must identify spelling, syntax, organization, and grammatical mistakes; analyze in class common errors (such as mixed tenses, dangling modifiers, and run-on sentences); model effective techniques for eliminating errors; teach practical methods for improving writing style (eliminating repetitive declarative sentences and redundancies, for example); and demonstrate efficient techniques for organizing and clarifying ideas. If this traditional procedure is circumvented, students' written communication skills will not improve.

Effective language arts instruction involves more than simply requiring students to insert the proper adverb, adjective, or verb tense into reams of mindless language arts handouts! Children—even those with natural writing talent—must be assigned daily writing activities, weekly essays, and monthly book reports.

Unfortunately, the tradition of assigning and correcting students' writing projects has become an anachronism in many schools throughout the United States. Some teachers no longer want to spend the time required to correct and critique their students' assignments. Those who are willing to grade assignments may actually be incapable of finding the mistakes, as the writing skills of many younger teachers are abysmal. This should come as no surprise. These teachers are themselves products of the same flawed educational system they are unwittingly perpetuating.

Children who conclude they are incapable of writing effectively often become phobic about writing. Consciously or unconsciously convinced that the situation is hopeless, they make minimal effort and minimal progress. Their negative mindset and expectations are often self-fulfilling.

The recipe for teaching children how to write effectively is quite basic. There are five requirements:

- A well-conceived language arts program
- An emphasis on writing skills in the curriculum

- An enthusiastic and competent teacher
- Adequate practice (regularly assigned essays, journals, diaries, book reports, and term papers)
- Meaningful criticism with an emphasis on training children to develop self-editing skills
- Parental support and, if necessary, parental monitoring[1]

The first clear indications of language arts deficits usually appear in third, fourth, and fifth grades. Chronically poor grammar and punctuation, sentence fragments, run-on sentences, poorly organized ideas, and unintelligible essays and creative stories are key danger signals (see the checklist on page 117). If your child has language arts deficits and they are not resolved, the deficits can produce monumental academic problems throughout school.

Fortunately, many effective and innovative methods for teaching language arts have been developed in the last decade, and there is no excuse for any school to have a poor writing skills program (specific programs are described below). Learning to write well should be one of a child's most enjoyable school experiences. If you have observed your child struggling and conclude that his language arts program is inadequate, express your concerns to his teacher or principal. You are your child's most important advocate. Your expectation that the educational system will teach him to communicate his ideas effectively in writing is legitimate! Communities that demand first-rate language arts programs in their schools get first-rate programs! In contrast, complacent communities can expect, at best, marginal programs.

---

1. Parents may need to verify that their child has completed his writing assignments according to the teacher's specifications, has carefully proofread the assignment several times, has corrected blatant errors, and is planning to submit the assignment on time. (See Expectations and Performance Guidelines; Monitoring Homework.)

Corrective Strategies

In School

1. To identify your child's specific language arts deficits, ask the teacher to complete the Language Arts Checklist below. Students in the lower grades will not yet have learned some of the skills that are described. Concern yourself only with skills relevant to your child's grade level. The teacher can indicate which skills have been taught and practiced.

LANGUAGE ARTS CHECKLIST

	YES	NO
This student:		
Uses capital letters when appropriate	_____	_____
Uses correct punctuation	_____	_____
Avoids sentence fragments (sentences without verbs)	_____	_____
Avoids run-on sentences (too many ideas included)	_____	_____
Uses proper subject/verb agreement ("The boy goes.")	_____	_____
Spells accurately	_____	_____
Writes neatly and legibly	_____	_____
Uses topic sentences correctly	_____	_____
Uses parallel tenses and constructions (does not mix tenses)	_____	_____
Presents ideas sequentially	_____	_____
Knows when to start new paragraphs	_____	_____
Can summarize in writing what has been read	_____	_____
Writes well-organized stories, essays, and reports	_____	_____
Can express ideas within a reasonable time frame	_____	_____
Can edit own work and find most grammatical and syntactical errors	_____	_____
Can write interesting, creative stories	_____	_____
Can identify parts of speech	_____	_____

2. If the teacher pinpoints specific deficiencies, ask for remedial materials that could help your child. Perhaps the teacher would help your child practice before or after class. Remedial materials to help improve language arts skills are included in the resource list at the back of the book.

3. (Elementary School, ES) Diplomatically ask which language arts program is being used in your child's class. If you believe the program may be deficient, check teacher supply stores and bookstores for alternatives you might recommend for review. Please note that high school English departments are usually not receptive to parents suggesting writing programs. This should not necessarily inhibit you, however, from making suggestions.

4. Talk to other parents. They may share your concerns about the quality of the language arts program at your child's school. If they agree that there may be a problem, discuss the issues with the teacher or principal. They might be willing to consider a different program. Your last resort is to complain directly to the superintendent or the school board.

At Home

1. For fun, co-author with your child letters to the editor of the local newspaper. You could also write letters to people featured in the news expressing your support or disapproval of what they are doing or saying.

2. Write an intentionally complex descriptive sentence (for example, "The man sat at the table and calmly sipped his coffee, and he seemed oblivious to the commotion that was exploding around him in the elegant restaurant on the Champs Elysee on a hot August day.") If you cannot create complex sentences, find some in books. (Many books written in the nineteenth century have a more complex and convoluted style.) Make a game of rewriting the sentences with your child. Produce as many alternatives as possible. ("Seemingly oblivious to the commotion exploding around him and the heat of the hot August day in the elegant restaurant on the Champs Elysee, the man calmly sipped his coffee.") Experiment with

breaking the sentence into two sentences. Discuss the merits of each alternative you create. Repeat this activity many times. Involve your child in creating the complex sentences and the alternatives. Make the activity fun. Your child is learning how to "massage" language!

3.   (ES) Co-author creative stories with your child. Suggest a title such as: *The Dragon Who Barked Like a Dog* or *Our Trip to Mars.* You might want to write the first sentence ("The little dragon knew there was something terribly wrong the first time he tried to roar like his father.") Have your child write sentence number two. Then you write sentence number three and so on. Later, as he becomes more confident, he may want to write most or all of the story. Make the process fun. Use discretion about correcting grammar and spelling. Being highly judgmental will trigger anxiety, defensiveness, and resistance. These stories don't have to be perfect. From time to time, diplomatically make suggestions such as: "I think this word is spelled . . ." or "Do you think we could play with this sentence and make it even more scary?" Encourage and affirm your child. Your goal is to create positive associations with writing. With sufficient practice, the quality of his stories will improve.

4.   Read over your child's school assignments. Make a mental note about spelling or grammatical errors. You might say: "I found five spelling errors. Let's see if you can find them." With younger children, you might want to give your child tokens for every mistake found, such as pennies placed in a jar to be traded in for a special prize each month. As an extra incentive, you might say: "If you can find the two run-on sentences, you get five pennies." (You must first, of course, show your child what a run-on sentence is!) You might give your child a ten penny bonus for an especially neat and legible assignment.

Language Disorders

A child is constantly bombarded in school with sensory stimuli in the form of spoken or written words, mathematical symbols, chemical formulas, pictures, events on the playground, and feelings of pain, joy, or hunger. Her brain must decode (decipher) this sensory data, retrieve relevant associated information from memory, and find the words to encode (communicate) accurately a wealth of ideas, emotions, information, and perceptions. Expressive language is the end-product of this complex neurological process (see Language Arts).

In most instances, the decoding-retrieval-encoding procedure is instantaneous and efficient. The teacher might ask your child to read a math word problem aloud and explain to the class how to solve the problem. If she can properly decode the words and symbols, understand the concepts, and do the required math calculations, but cannot intelligibly describe her problem-solving procedure to the other students, she may have an expressive language disorder. If, however, she can describe the procedure but cannot articulate the words properly, she probably has a speech disorder (see Speech Disorders).

Children with serious and chronic expressive language problems are generally described as *dysphasic* or *aphasic*. Although these two terms are often used synonymously, they should be differentiated. Children with aphasia have virtually no communication skills. Children with dysphasia are able to communicate but do so haltingly and have great difficulty finding the proper words to express their ideas. Both conditions require intensive speech therapy, and children manifesting symptoms of either condition are usually placed in special school programs.

Autism is another condition that can cause profound communication problems. This little-understood and perplexing disorder prevents children from establishing emotional bonds with the external world. Autistic children have great difficulty bonding emotionally and expressing their feelings in a form that others can understand. Their inability to communicate emotions, however, is distinct from the communication dysfunction associated with aphasia and dysphasia.

Any type of language disorder can erect formidable educational and emotional barriers. The child who cannot find the words to express her needs, ideas, and feelings will feel frustrated, demoralized, and isolated. Early intervention and specialized language therapy can significantly reduce this risk.

A wide spectrum of specific symptoms should alert you to a possible language disorder. The most obvious symptom is delayed language acquisition in young children. If the normal developmental progression from cooing to babbling to speaking isolated words does not occur, or if the progression is interrupted, consult your child's pediatrician. A kindergartner with a possible language disorder may not be able to say the names of the colors, the days of the week, or the months of the year. She may also be unable to count out loud or sing the words to the songs taught in class. (Please see the Language Disorders Inventory following for additional symptoms.)

Corrective Strategies

In School

1.   The Language Disorders Inventory identifies the primary symptoms of a language disorder. To complete the checklist, consult with your child's teacher and/or resource specialist. (Older children with language disorders have probably already been identified and have received assistance. This inventory, however, may be helpful to perplexed parents of teenagers with language problems who were not properly targeted for language assistance in elementary school.)

LANGUAGE DISORDERS INVENTORY

If this inventory indicates that your child has an expressive language disorder, request a speech and language evaluation by the school speech pathologist or the school psychologist (see Parents' Rights).

	YES	NO
Auditory Processing Deficits		
Difficulty paying attention to auditory stimuli	___	___
Difficulty discriminating sound versus no sound	___	___
Difficulty locating where sound is coming from	___	___
Difficulty discriminating different sounds	___	___
Difficulty distinguishing primary sounds from background sounds	___	___
Difficulty associating sounds with source of sounds	___	___
Difficulty filtering out extraneous sounds	___	___
Difficulty sequencing ideas	___	___
Oral reversals (saying emeny *instead of* enemy)	___	___
Circumlocutions (imprecise, roundabout communication, saying, "that place down there where they sell the thingamajig.")	___	___
Linguistic Processing Deficits		
Poor grammar	___	___
Wrong verb tenses	___	___
Use of only broad meaning of words	___	
Lack of understanding of subtle meanings or differences between words	___	
Difficulty understanding spatial prepositions (beside or beneath)	___	___
Difficulty understanding comparatives, opposites, and superlatives bigger/biggest, far/near, rough/smooth, fast/slow)	___	___
Cognitive (Thinking) Processing Deficits		
Difficulty following oral directions	___	
Difficulty expressing thoughts and information	___	___
Difficulty classifying	___	
Difficulty putting events in sequence or order	___	___
Difficulty making comparisons	___	___
Difficulty understanding or expressing the moral of a story	___	
Difficulty predicting the outcome of a story or event	___	___
Difficulty differentiating between fact and fiction	___	___
Difficulty remembering and expressing facts	___	
Evaluation Deficits		
Difficulty drawing conclusions ("Why did she need her gloves?")	___	___
Difficulty relating to cause and effect ("What would happen if he forgot to put gas in the car?")	___	___

Aphasia/Dysphasia

Difficulty making facial motor
movements to produce sound
(called dyspraxia)   _____   _____

Difficulty imitating sounds   _____   _____

Difficulty remembering words
(but can repeat them)   _____   _____

Difficulty formulating sentences
(but can use single words)   _____   _____

Difficulty naming common objects   _____   _____

Difficulty recalling a specific word _____   _____

Difficulty recognizing common
objects by touch   _____   _____

---

2.   If the school's evaluation indicates specific language deficits, carefully examine your options. Nonsevere problems can often be addressed by the speech pathologist at your child's local school. Most districts, however, place children with severe language disorders in special programs at magnet schools. These programs are usually under the aegis of the county and serve children from districts throughout the county.

3.   Make sure you understand the nature of your child's language problem. Consult appropriate reference books to learn more about the issues, symptoms, and remediation techniques. (Ask your local librarian or the school speech pathologist for the names of recommended books.) Periodically meet with your child's therapists and teachers to discuss the goals of the program, progress, and their criteria for monitoring improvement.

At Home

1.   Talk with your child! Provide nonstressful opportunities to practice communication skills. Your expectations should be geared to her skill level. Your child is struggling with a handicap, and you must demonstrate that you are sensitive to her struggle and committed to helping her prevail over the problem. Your patience, affirmation of her efforts, and emotional support are vital and will encourage her to develop more effective communication skills. If your child is struggling to express ideas in the proper sequence, help her draw a picture, "map," or flow chart that visually represents how the ideas are related. Encourage her to use the map as she orally describes the ideas in the sequence that she represented visually. Urging her to form visual pictures of what she wants to say can be a highly effective compensatory tool. Suggest that she experiment with closing her eyes and hearing what she wants to say before she says it. This *prevocalization* method may be very effective for children who learn best auditorily.

2.   Have your child dictate her ideas about smoking or children using drugs. Urge her to speak slowly. Draw a map or diagram that visually expresses what she is saying as she speaks (see mind maps under Reading Comprehension and Notetaking). Encourage her to make corrections in the map. Discuss the visual representation of her ideas and feelings and brainstorm how the content might be organized differently and how certain vocabulary words might enhance the communication.

3.   To reduce your child's anxiety and phobias about verbal communication, have her close her eyes and see herself calmly, effectively, and confidently communicating her ideas. Suggest that she take one or two deep breaths before beginning to talk. These visualization and relaxation techniques can significantly reduce her stress and fear.

4.   If your child does not appear to be responding to her language therapy program, consider supplemental private language therapy. Ask your pediatrician for a referral.

Learned Helplessness

A powerful instinct impels parents to protect their children when they face danger and to come to their aid when they are struggling. This mechanism serves a vital function during early childhood when youngsters are dependent, vulnerable, and incapable of assessing and responding appropriately to risks. Although children clearly require parental supervision, support, guidance, and assistance during the formative years, the extent of this nurturing must be calibrated to the child's developmental age: a four-year-old is certainly going to need more direction and reinforcement than a ten-year-old. A warning bell should go off, however, when maturing children remain overly reliant on their parents. Excessive dependence signals that the natural parental instinct to protect, albeit well-intentioned, is overindulgent and is preventing children from developing their own emotional and intellectual resources (see Self-Esteem and Self-Confidence). This dependency phenomenon is called *learned helplessness*.

A child with poor academic skills and little self-confidence is in jeopardy. If she concludes that her plaintive call for help invariably brings a concerned parent, teacher, or resource specialist to the rescue, she'll be very tempted to use this "hot line" whenever she experiences a setback or glitch. Her need for help may be legitimate, but the concern, attention, and strokes she is able to elicit may become the highest priority on her hidden agenda. This payoff may be more important to the child than getting the work done and succeeding in school.

Children are rarely aware on a conscious level that they are perpetuating their own helplessness. They telegraph their dependency through their behavior. Red-flag symptoms include chronic unjustified confusion, forgetfulness, sloppiness, procrastination, and irresponsibility. To elicit attention and nurturing, some children actually feign being dense, and, in extreme cases, affect mild retardation.

Continual "I can't do this" statements by the child or facial expressions that communicate insufficiency and desperation ("Rescue me, Mom!") are other indications that a child has learned to be helpless. Once she accepts her powerlessness, she'll become increasingly addicted to having her parents throw her a life preserver whenever she encounters even a minor setback. Her responses to challenges and a demeanor of inadequacy send a clear message: "Don't expect very much from me!" The typical ways in which she might manifest her dependency may include her demanding that her parents: 1) sit at her side whenever she does her homework, 2) remind her to study for tests, 3) organize her notebook, 4) verify her assignments, 5) help her write her book report, 6) manage her time, 7) put away her materials, and 8) check over her homework.

To preserve the parental 911 rescue service, some children may actually become very resistant to overcoming their academic problems. Others magnify their needs. Every demand, challenge, and setback becomes a major crisis that their parents must somehow solve for them. Helpless youngsters usually become quite skillful at manipulating their parents and teachers. Attempts to nudge them from their comfort zone and alter the status quo may trigger profound anxiety, insecurity, and resistance.

The most common verbal clue that parents may have unwittingly allowed themselves to become enmeshed in their child's helplessness is the use of the pronoun *we* and the possessive adjective *our*. When parents announce, "We have our math problems to do," or "We studied hard, but we still had difficulty on our last spelling test," the choice of words is more than an inadvertent slip of the tongue. These parents are sending a message to the child that dependency is acceptable when they should be signaling that the responsibility for the work belongs to the child, assuming the child has the requisite skills to do the work on her own (see Math; Monitoring Homework; Spelling Problems).

Parents may rationalize excessive support of their struggling child by arguing that the child cannot possibly survive without their help. Certainly, some children need extra help and guidance when they study their assigned spelling words or learn their multiplication tables. Providing this kind of assistance is very different from taking ownership of the child's responsibilities. While some parents are reluctantly coerced into the nightly homework ritual, others eagerly participate for complex psychological reasons that may include guilt (parents feel they are in some way responsible for the child's learning problems), inadequately defined ego boundaries (parents have difficulty delineating their own emotional needs from their child's), fear of separation (parents have an unconscious psychological need to keep their child dependent on them), and a host of other dysfunctional family issues.

Ironically, the most common excuse offered by excessively involved parents is usually quite accurate: "My child has learning problems and cannot complete the assigned work on her own." Without assistance, struggling children will fall further and further behind and become increasingly frustrated and demoralized (see Anger and Frustration; Self-Esteem and Self-Confidence). If given

too much assistance, however, these youngsters are at risk for becoming overly dependent. The paradox can cause parents great anguish. As there are no absolute guidelines for determining when to assist or resist and how much help to offer, parents must make an informed judgment call and base their degree of involvement on an accurate up-to-date assessment of their child's needs and skills, teacher feedback, test results, and intuition (see Working Independently).

If you believe you have become too enmeshed in helping your child and that she has become excessively reliant on you, you must make some difficult choices. Extracting yourself from the learned helplessness loop, incrementally withdrawing the security blanket, and resisting your child's manipulative "save me" behavior will undoubtedly cause stress and unhappiness not only for your child, but also for you. No parent wants to see their child suffer, even if the suffering might be self-induced or exaggerated. You must draw your resolve and strength from the realization that it is in your child's best interests to become increasingly more independent and self-sufficient. Unless she learns to rely on herself, she cannot possibly acquire self-esteem.

Children who are allowed to create excessive dependencies during the formative years often require someone to prop them up throughout their lives. Their sense of powerlessness can become so indelibly imprinted on their psyche that they may be continually compelled to seek emotionally destructive codependencies with surrogate parental figures.

Helplessness is an acquired mental state that is profoundly influenced by both verbalized and nonverbalized parental behavior. To build your child's self-confidence and to help her reformulate her perceptions about herself and her abilities, you must:

- Encourage her to reach for goals she can realistically attain.

- Control the difficulty of the challenges and increase the difficulty level in small increments.

- Gently but firmly resist her conscious or unconscious attempts to manipulate you into rescuing her each time she encounters a challenge, problem, or setback.

- Create repeated opportunities for her to succeed at tasks that do not require continual support or supervision.

- Help her discover that she can prevail over challenges and problems on her own.

- Slowly but firmly nudge her from her counterproductive comfort zone.

- Affirm and acknowledge progress and success.

- Express faith in her ability to deal with setbacks.

- Urge her to reach for goals slightly beyond her reach as her skills and confidence improve.

Although you certainly want to build your child's self-confidence by intentionally orchestrating repeated opportunities for her to experience success, you must also allow her to experience occasional setbacks. Children who do not learn to bounce back from setbacks and deal with frustration will have great difficulty handling life's challenges and prevailing in our demanding and highly competitive world (see Behavior and Attitude; Bouncing Back from Setbacks and Learning from Mistakes; Fear of Failure/Success/Competition).

The transformation of a helpless child into an independent child requires astute planning. You must challenge your child without allowing her to become discouraged, and you must establish realistic expectations and performance standards congruent with her skills and abilities (see Effort and Motivation; Expectations and Performance Guidelines; Keeping Up with the Class; Working Independently). While you cannot reasonably expect a dyslexic child to read without mistakes, you can insist (after reasonable modeling) that she do segments of her homework independently and that she submit her work on time, even if this results in errors! (See Incomplete Assignments.)

If she does not have the requisite skills to do the work, then provide a carefully controlled amount of help. You may also need to request that the teacher adjust the difficulty level of the assignments until your child can catch up.

Helping a highly dependent youngster become more self-reliant can be a long and arduous process. You must be willing to persevere. If the withdrawal of the security blanket causes profound anxiety and resistance, educational therapy coupled with family counseling or individual psychotherapy will be necessary.

Corrective Strategies

In School

1.   If you suspect that your child is capable of doing more than she believes she is capable of doing, or if you conclude that you have taken ownership of your child's problems, ask the teacher for an update on her current skills, behavior, and attitude. Determine what your child can realistically be expected to do on her own in class and at home (see Expectations and Performance Guidelines). Perhaps assignments could be simplified so that she can complete them with little or no help. If your child is in third grade and is reading two years below grade level, she requires extra help from her teacher, resource specialist, and you. The amount of help and the expectations for independent work must be geared to her skill level. Even if her skills are deficient, the self-directed work expected from her should be slowly increased, especially if you and her teacher believe she can do a particular assignment on her own and the correct procedure for doing so has been adequately explained and modeled. Each decision about how much assistance to provide requires an intuitive judgment call.

2.   (Elementary School, ES) Suggest to the teacher that she involve your child in establishing specific academic and independent work goals for herself (see Goals). The procedure of checking off each goal as it is achieved will make the goals more tangible and should increase her motiva-

tion. The teacher's acknowledgment of progress and successes are important components in the behavior modification equation.

At Home

1.   Discuss the issue of self-reliance with your child. Explain that you want her to become independent and self-sufficient. Be specific about how these objectives might be achieved. For example, you might tell her that if you believe she knows how to do her math homework, you will not provide help. If she is truly confused, review one or two problems, but insist that she do the rest on her own—even if she does some problems incorrectly or becomes frustrated (see Working Independently). It is important to explain why you are changing the rules of the game in terms she can understand. At first she may not be happy with the new rules, so it is crucial that she understand your reasons. To reduce her anxiety, withdraw support in stages.

2.   If your child has significant learning deficits and you conclude that you cannot help her without "buying into" her learned helplessness, consider hiring a professional tutor or educational therapist. Alert the tutor to your child's propensity to become dependent and urge him to use his best judgment about when it is appropriate to provide help and when to insist on independent work. Establish a goals check-off list for work completed independently at home. Entrenched resistance by your child to becoming more self-reliant should be assessed by a qualified mental health professional.

Learning Disabilities

Estimates about how many children have learning disabilities vary from 3 to 25 percent of the school population. This variance reflects the wide range of diagnostic criteria that may be used to define a learning disability and to identify struggling students. The lower percentage indicates highly selective criteria and includes only those children with specific and significant learning deficiencies. The higher percentage includes children with less severe and/or nonspecific learning problems (see Atypical Learning Problems; Underachievement).

The identification conundrum is further complicated by a wide range of often overlapping diagnostic labels that include: learning disability, learning different, dyslexia, decoding deficits, sensory-motor dysfunction, perceptual dysfunction, attention deficit disorder and attention deficit hyperactivity disorder, and minimal brain dysfunction. Despite the range of standards, terminology, and explanations about why children struggle, educators generally agree that early intervention is vital if academic and psychological damage are to be prevented.

In essence, a learning disability results when a condition (or set of conditions) prevents or impedes a child's sequential mastery of academic skills. In most cases, the learning disability (or more politically correct term *learning difference*) can be attributed to the inefficient processing of sensory information. The struggling child may have difficulty decoding (recognizing) auditory or visual data (letters and words), remembering written (visual) and spoken (auditory) information, paying attention, following instructions and sequencing data ("Open your textbook to chapter 3, read unit 1, and answer the questions on page 68."), comprehending what is read or said, and demonstrating mastery of course material on tests.

Although there is general consensus about the value of early diagnosis and treatment of learning problems, many school districts erect a formidable barrier to early intervention, insisting that students be a minimum of two years below grade level in reading or math to qualify for special help. As it's impossible for a child in kindergarten or first grade to be two years below grade level, younger students are often forced to flounder until their problems are deemed sufficiently debilitating to qualify for help. The academic and psychological consequences of this delay can be disastrous. Problems that might be quickly and painlessly remedied in first grade often become increasingly debilitating when the window of ideal treatment opportunity is disregarded.

Many school districts impose other highly selective diagnostic criteria for admission into special education programs. Some require a significant discrepancy in the subsection scores on an IQ test or a significant discrepancy between a child's IQ and scores on standardized achievement tests (nationally administered skills tests—see Performance on Standardized Tests; Understanding Diagnostic Test Results). The required IQ discrepancy may range from 20 points in one district to 26 points in another. Children with a low average IQ and poor academic skills are usually excluded from learning assistance because they are considered to be functioning at an academic level commensurate with their intelligence. This rationale could prevent dyslexic or chronically inattentive children with a low average IQ from receiving help. (Because many educators consider IQ tests culturally biased, the tests are generally no longer used to determine special education eligibility of minority students. See IQ Test Scores.)

Federal and state law stipulates that students manifesting symptoms of learning disabilities must be diagnostically tested (see Parents' Rights). Federal Law 94-142 also stipulates that if a learning disability is identified, the student must be provided with remedial help. This law, at least in theory, requires that every child suspected of having a learning disability must be referred to the school psychologist for testing. In practice, however, many gray area youngsters with subtle to moderate learning deficits are never tested. Students with atypical, intermittent, or enigmatic problems that are considered nonincapacitating are rarely admitted to resource programs. This exclusionary practice is not a callous conspiracy by insensitive school districts, but, rather, a classic example of misguided educational priorities and limited supply being overwhelmed by huge demand.

Too little money and too many children have produced a battlefield mentality where beleaguered school psychologists and administrators practice educational triage. The "seriously wounded" are helped and the "walking wounded" are sent back to the front line untreated. Unfortunately, the untreated "minor" wounds of the walking wounded frequently become "infected" and debilitating.

Because state and federally mandated guidelines are subjectively interpreted and selectively applied, the standards for admission to learning assistance programs vary greatly from state to state, district to district, and school to school. One school psychologist may be willing to bend the rules and admit a child with moderate prob-

lems into a remedial program, while another in a neighboring district may be unwilling or unable to bend because the program is full and there is a long list of children with more serious learning deficits waiting to be admitted.

It is popular today for educators, psychologists, reporters, columnists, and politicians to express alarm about "at risk" students. The statistics are indeed frightening. In some high schools, 50 percent of the students fail to graduate. Many youngsters are pushed through the system and educated in name only. Despite deplorable skills, an alarming number of semiliterate teenagers are awarded meaningless diplomas. Most of them discover after graduation that they cannot compete for decent jobs in a highly technological marketplace that seeks motivated, conscientious, goal-directed workers with good skills and efficient work habits.

The warning signals of a possible learning disability include:

- Letter and number reversals (common in kindergarten but more serious in first grade)
- Poor concentration
- Inaccurate reading with word and letter omissions and transpositions
- Poor reading comprehension
- Chronic math deficiencies
- Impulsiveness
- Overactivity
- Memory deficits
- Poor motor coordination
- Illegible handwriting
- Sloppiness
- Difficulty following written or verbal instruction

Inefficient decoding of sensory data is the common denominator in most of these problems. Children who struggle to decipher and recall written and spoken words and symbols are destined to suffer in school. Because their sensory input is garbled, their output (performance in class and on tests) is also garbled (see Language Arts). Parents who disregard their child's learning deficits in the hope that the problems will disappear of their own accord are placing their child at serious educational and psychological risk (see Psychological Problems and Psychological Overlay).

The need to become directly and actively involved in your child's education process is compelling, especially if you conclude that your child is being denied help or is not being adequately served by the learning assistance program. The prospect of becoming actively involved can be intimidating, especially if you are confused about technical jargon, unsure of your prerogatives, or uncertain about what steps to take. The more informed you are about the issues, the better prepared you will be to ask penetrating questions of the school personnel working with your child, critically evaluate your options, and make astute decisions. (See Communicating with the School; Conferencing with School Officials.)

Because the quality of learning assistance programs can vary significantly, you must be prepared to monitor your child's progress closely. One school may have a superb program while another in the same district or in a neighboring district may have an abysmal program.

A superior resource program will not only provide tutorial assistance, it will also address the underlying causes of a child's learning disability. A less adequate program will focus primarily on crisis intervention and helping children complete assigned classwork and homework. This "get the child through the day approach" rarely eliminates the source of a learning problem. At best, it teaches children how to cope and compensate. Schools committed to this approach tacitly assume that your child will never completely overcome his learning problems. If you are unwilling to accept this spoken or unspoken rationale, you must either become an activist who fights for better programs in your local school district, or be prepared to provide private learning assistance for your child. The alternative is to do nothing and allow your child to become increasingly frustrated and demoralized. A child on this track is likely to give up and shut down academically.

Corrective Strategies

In School

1.   (Elementary School, ES) To obtain specific information about your child's learning deficits, ask teacher(s) to complete the following Student Evaluation Checklist. The inventory describes many common symptoms of a learning disability. Your child need not manifest all, or even most, of the symptoms to be a candidate for remedial assistance. A significant pattern of "yes" responses is a warning signal that your child should be diagnostically evaluated by the school psychologist or by an independent diagnostician. (For more detailed and comprehensive information about learning problems, see *Learning Disabilities and Your Child* included in the resource list at the back of this book.)

STUDENT EVALUATION CHECKLIST

Elementary School Children

Academic	YES	NO
Poor reading comprehension	____	____
Difficulty with phonics	____	____
Reversals	____	____
Inaccurate reading	____	____
Difficulty with math computational skills (addition, etc.)	____	____
Poor handwriting	____	____
Inaccurate copying (from blackboard or at desk)	____	____
Difficulty understanding math concepts	____	____
Difficulty working independently	____	____
Sloppy work habits	____	____
Difficulty with spelling	____	____
Difficulty with written language arts (syntax, etc.)	____	____

Poor organizational skills _____ _____

Poor planning skills _____ _____

Incomplete projects _____ _____

Difficulty following verbal
instructions _____ _____

Difficulty following written
instructions _____ _____

Behavior

Short attention span _____ _____

Difficulty following directions _____ _____

Overactive _____ _____

Impulsive _____ _____

Fidgety _____ _____

Distractible _____ _____

Accident-prone _____ _____

Forgetful _____ _____

Daydreams _____ _____

Slow in completing tasks _____ _____

Excitable _____ _____

Unpredictable _____ _____

Disturbs other students _____ _____

Chronic procrastination _____ _____

Chronic irresponsibility _____ _____

Coordination

Gross-motor coordination
deficits (sports, etc.) _____ _____

Fine-motor coordination deficits
(drawing/handwriting, etc.) _____ _____

Clumsy _____ _____

Awkward _____ _____

Poor balance _____ _____

Right/left confusion _____ _____

Fear of physical activities
(climbing, sports etc.) _____ _____

Your level of concern about this student: (please circle)

EXTREME   MODERATE   MINIMAL   NONE

2.   (Junior High/High School, J/HS) To obtain information about junior or senior high school students, ask each teacher to complete the applicable sections on the following Student Evaluation Checklist. This inventory is less comprehensive and is formatted differently than the checklist for younger children because teachers in the upper grades have less opportunity to observe extensively the behaviors of their students.

STUDENT EVALUATION CHECKLIST
Junior High and High School
1 = Poor   2 = Fair   3 = Good   4 = Excellent   5 = Not Applicable
(ALL teachers please complete this section)

_____ General self-concept

_____ Effort

_____ Behavior

_____ Concentration

_____ Organization

_____ Completes assignments on time

_____ Works independently

_____ Keeps up with class

_____ Neatness

_____ Class participation

_____ Test performance

_____ Attitude

STUDENT EVALUATION CHECKLIST
Academic Performance
1 = Poor   2 = Fair   3 = Good   4 = Excellent   5 = Not Applicable
Please complete section pertaining to your subject.

ENGLISH/LANGUAGE ARTS:

____ *Correct grammar usage*	____ *Vocabulary*
____ *Punctuation*	____ *Comprehension*
____ *Spelling*	____ *Creative writing*
____ *Expository Writing*	____ *Term papers*

Most Recent Test Grade: ____
Most Recent Quarter Grade: ____

MATH:

Working at grade level?   YES ____   NO ____   *Approximate level:* _____

____ *Understands concepts*	____ *Computational skills*
____ *Applies concepts*	____ *Abstract reasoning*
____ *Accuracy*	____ *Recall*

Most Recent Test Grade: ____
Most Recent Quarter Grade: ____

HISTORY:	SCIENCE:
____ *Notetaking*	____ *Notetaking*
____ *Outlining*	____ *Outlining*
____ *Understands concepts*	____ *Understand concepts*
____ *Can identify key information*	____ *Can identify key information*
____ *Recall*	____ *Recall*
____ *Term papers and reports*	____ *Term papers and reports*
Most Recent Test Grade: ____	*Most Recent Test Grade:* ____
Most Recent Quarter Grade: ____	*Most Recent Quarter Grade:* ____

FOREIGN LANGUAGE:

____ *Vocabulary*	____ *Verb conjugations*
____ *Grammar rules*	____ *Declensions (Latin)*
____ *Conversation*	____ *Vocabulary gender*
____ *Completes assignments*	____ *Studies adequately*

Most Recent Test Grade: ____
Most Recent Quarter Grade: ____

ALL TEACHERS:

Your level of concern about this student's performance:
(please circle) EXTREME   MODERATE   MINIMAL   NONE

3. If deficits are indicated, discuss them with your child's teacher. A pattern of general deficiencies or a specific, severe deficit in one or more areas indicates that there should be an assessment by the school psychologist or by an independent educational psychologist (see Parents' Rights).

4. If you believe that your child's assistance program is weak or that your child is not improving after a reasonable period of time, you must intervene. Explore alternative remedial strategies with the resource specialist. You may want to hire a private tutor or educational therapist or enroll your child in a private learning assistance program. The alternative is to allow your child to fall further and further behind. Doing so could produce catastrophic consequences.

5. Refer to the table of contents and to specific entries for strategies and suggestions about how school personnel might be able to help your child in school.

At Home

1. Discuss problem areas identified on the preceding checklists with your child and brainstorm solutions to specific problems. Before doing so, refer to the appropriate entries in this book for ideas that you could explore together. For example, if your child is dyslexic or has attention deficit disorder, examine the suggestions that are offered under that entry with your child. If your child has several deficit areas, establish remediation priorities. You may decide to concentrate on math first and then work on vocabulary skills, or you may decide to work on several deficits concurrently.

2. After reviewing the Student Evaluation Checklist completed by your child's teacher(s), report cards, scores on standardized achievement tests, and notes from conferences with the teacher (and resources specialist), you may conclude that you cannot provide the required academic assistance at home. If the deficits are significant, you may decide that private tutoring or educational therapy is more appropriate. Ask your child's teacher, resource specialist, or pediatrician for a referral.

Listening in Class

Youngsters who can listen attentively and assimilate information when their teachers speak in class have a distinct advantage over those who are inattentive and nonresponsive. During the typical school day, students are bombarded with thousands of spoken words. Those who don't listen in class miss important instructions about how to complete an assignment or explanations that clarify a science concept or math procedure (see Following Verbal Directions). Because they haven't assimilated key verbal information, their work rarely conforms to the teacher's explicit directions and guidelines and is often incomplete and improperly done. Poor listeners typically do not follow along when classmates read aloud, and when it is their turn to read aloud, they cannot find their place. The effects of this nonadaptive behavior are predictable: a continual state of confusion, chronic inefficiency, and poor performance.

As children progress through school, the need for good listening skills increases dramatically. In most high schools, students can expect hours of lectures each week. Teachers who lecture usually justify the practice by arguing that they are preparing students for the realities of college where good notetaking skills are vital to academic survival. They expect students to record their pearls of wisdom and play back key information verbatim on tests. Few teachers would admit another primary motive for giving lectures: it is easier for them to read their own notes to their classes than to interact actively, creatively, and dynamically with their students.

Chronic listening problems may be attributed to several sources. Parents should first rule out, with diagnostic testing, an organic hearing impairment as a possible cause of their child's difficulty registering what is being said in the classroom. Some children have difficulty filtering out distractions and focusing because of attention deficit disorder. Others have auditory memory deficits and cannot retain what they hear. Children with auditory sequencing deficits have problems remembering verbal information in the proper sequence. These perceptually based conditions can undermine a child's ability to listen attentively (see Learning Disabilities).

A child's natural and preferred learning style can also affect her ability to decipher auditory information efficiently. The visual or kinesthetic learner is at a significant disadvantage if her teacher's preferred teaching modality is verbal. If she cannot accommodate successfully to the teaching style, she is at a serious disadvantage.

The child with poor listening skills who finds herself in a "verbally loaded" learning environment is at risk for becoming discouraged and demoralized. Unless the teacher is willing to make accommodations to each child's individual and preferred learning style (the ideal instructional methodology, but not necessarily the most realistic, given that there may be more than thirty other students in the class), your child must learn to accommodate herself to the less-than-perfect realities of the classroom. If she doesn't, her academic performance will suffer.

The poor listener must develop a system for disciplining herself. She must compensate by listening more attentively, learning to take effective notes from lectures, focusing when the teacher gives verbal instructions and communicates information, and recalling what the teacher has said. These pragmatic compensatory mechanisms are vital to her academic survival.

Corrective Strategies

In School

1. (Elementary School, ES) If you suspect your child is not listening in class, discuss your concerns with the teacher. The first step in identifying the source of the problem is to have your child's hearing tested by a pediatrician or audiologist. If there is no organic explanation (i.e., hearing loss) then you and the teacher need to brainstorm solutions to your child's auditory inattentiveness. Sometimes simply moving a child's desk closer to the teacher's desk can be an effective remedy. This proximity could allow the teacher to supervise your child more closely and provide immediate feedback when her mind is wandering.

2. (ES) If your child is in grades 1 to 3, you might suggest to the teacher that two wide strips of masking tape be affixed to the desk, one with a happy face at the top and one with a sad face. When the teacher observes your child listening attentively, she will use an agreed-upon signal and your child will make a check in the happy face column. When your child is not listening, the teacher will signal for a check in the sad face column. At the end of the day, the checks are totaled. You and your child might establish performance goals for each day (see parallel suggestions under Attention Deficit Disorder). There are two potential problems with this strategy: The teacher might not agree to make the extra effort to monitor and reinforce your child's behavior, and other children in the class may also want to participate in the behavior modification program. If the teacher is willing, she could use the happy face/sad face system with the entire class (see Goals).

3. Ask the teacher or counselor to monitor your child to make certain she's properly recording the day's assignments.

4. If your child is manifesting symptoms of attention deficit disorder, auditory memory, or auditory sequencing problems (for specific symptoms, see these entries), request an evaluation by the school psychologist, resource specialist, or speech and language specialist. If a deficit is confirmed, a wide range of effective remedial methods can be used. (Refer to corrective strategies for specific problems.) If your child qualifies for learning assistance, the resource specialist should also be able to monitor your child to make certain that critical verbal information communicated in class has been properly processed and understood. This supervision will require the close coordination of both teachers' efforts.

At Home

1. Discuss substantive, engaging subjects at the dinner table. Encourage your child to express her opinions and ideas, and to listen attentively to the ideas of others (see Auditory Memory). Perhaps you might ask your child (in a casual, nonthreatening way) to recap the points that have been made. (If appropriate, model how to recap information. Engage your child in a daily ritual of examining issues and events that affect her life to promote the development of good listening and verbal communication skills.

2. (ES) Play a game in which you give your child a series of verbal instructions directing her to a hidden treasure (see Following Verbal Directions). After giving the directions, ask your child to repeat them to you. Then have her follow the directions. ("I have hidden a spoon in the house. Follow my instructions precisely and you will be able to find it. Go into your bedroom. Make a quarter turn to the right. Go six steps forward, heel to toe. Make a quarter turn to the left and start searching.") Increase the complexity of the instructions in increments. (You may also need to demonstrate a quarter turn to the right and a heel-to-toe step.) Your goal is to improve your

child's listening skills, memory, and confidence. Set your child up to win. Be patient, and gear instructions to your child's age and ability. With practice, her auditory skills will improve and her negative mindset about poor listening capability should slowly dissipate.

3.   Encourage your child to close her eyes when listening to something complex so that she can form a visual picture in her mind about the content. If she does this in class, she (or you) should forewarn her teacher that she is not falling asleep, but is trying to form a mental picture of the information so she can understand and recall it. Other applications and a more complete description of this visual imprinting method are described under Spelling Problems.

4.   Do a project with your child that she would enjoy. Explain that the project is intended to be fun but that an important objective is to practice following instructions. Patiently give her a controlled amount of specific directions and ask her to repeat the directions before proceeding.

("Glue the green strip of paper in front of the drawing of the house and glue the gray paper walkway so that it leads to the front door. Then glue the fence around the house.") Select a project and give instructions geared to your child's age and interests. For example, do something relating to servicing or fixing a car when working with a teenager. Be prepared to repeat the instructions if your child needs to hear them again.

Be patient. As is the case in overcoming any deficit, the child with poor listening skills requires practice, patience, feedback, and affirmation for progress. The complexity of the instructions should be increased incrementally as your child demonstrates that her ability to decipher, understand, and remember verbal instructions is improving. From time to time, turn the tables and ask your child to give you a series of instructions that you will then follow. This systematic procedure of training your child to listen more intently reinforces a basic fact of life: she must listen attentively to develop the first-rate auditory skills that are essential for success in school.

Logic

Logic is a requisite to solving problems, understanding concepts, evaluating issues, making predictions, and communicating ideas effectively. Students who can capitalize on an ability to reason have a distinct advantage in school, especially in college-oriented and advanced placement classes. They also have a significant competitive advantage when taking exams for admission to college and graduate school. Because logic is a key component in many questions that appear on IQ tests, students with good reasoning skills usually receive the highest scores on these exams (see IQ Test Scores).

The workplace also rewards logical thinking. Employees who can analyze and solve problems effectively are eagerly sought, and their superior reasoning skills are considered important assets by their employers. Those who can think analytically, critically, and strategically are on an inside track to advancement (see Critical Thinking; Smart Thinking.)

On the most basic level, logic is linked to cause-and-effect principles (see Disregarding Consequences). The oft-cited anecdote about not touching a hot stove twice is a classic example of logic in action. Although many animals can make this cause-and-effect connection, human beings are unique in their ability to make logical associations from both direct and indirect experiences. They can read a book or hear a story about someone else touching a hot stove and draw conclusions, make predictions, and use their insights to guide their actions.

Logic is the foundation upon which critical thinking and inferential reasoning rests (see Reading Comprehension). Children who can apply logic continually use reasoning skills to probe, associate, and evaluate issues encountered not only in school, but also in their personal lives. The child who thinks logically might conclude from observations that: "Kids who are into drugs act weird, get bad grades, and get in trouble. I won't take drugs because I don't want to be like them." The child with good reasoning skills doesn't need to experience drugs firsthand to reject them. She can also use logic to assess situations when information can be inferred but is not necessarily stated: "My friends are taking raincoats and umbrellas to the football game. There must be a reason. Maybe they know something I don't know."

Although intelligence is clearly requisite to logical thinking and to problem solving, many highly intelligent children do not use their reasoning powers to full advantage and suffer setbacks they might otherwise have avoided. Failure to think logically and disregard of predictable consequences can cause them to function below their potential and, in some cases, to make egregious errors in judgment. It can also result in a chronic pattern of underachievement.

Youngsters who repeatedly miscalculate and show poor judgment often share two other distinguishing traits: They do not plan effectively, and they do not think strategically (see Smart Thinking). In cases of chronic self-sabotaging behavior, underlying psychological factors must also be considered. Children who continually "self-destruct" because their reasoning skills are flawed may require professional counseling.

Logic is the turbocharger in your child's intellectual propulsion system. Systematic "servicing" (in the form of instruction, modeling, practice, feedback, and affirmation) are vital if this turbocharger is to function at peak performance. Each time you encourage your child to analyze issues and problems encountered in everyday life and develop logical solutions, you help her refine her reasoning skills. These skills will serve her throughout her life.

The fact that logic and language are processed in the left hemisphere of the brain, and feelings, intuition, and artistic responses are processed in the right hemisphere has received a great deal of publicity in recent years. This phenomenon has encouraged some educators to differentiate logical *left-brain learners* from creative *right-brain learners*. Contending that our schools prioritize left-brain logic and language at the expense of right-brain artistic and creative functions, they maintain that the special talents of right-brain learners are often unacknowledged.

Although it is true that our educational system emphasizes left-brain skills, the currently popular left brain/right brain differentiation is misleading. No child is exclusively right-brained or left-brained. Children are continually using both hemispheres of the brain. The artistic child must be able to plan a project, and the child with scientific aptitude must be able to draw a diagram.

Logic *and* creative thinking can be developed and enhanced in virtually every child. Opportunities for developing reasoning skills and artistic and creative skills should be integral components of well-conceived and well-rounded educational program. Just as students with natural left-brain abilities should be encouraged and affirmed for their distinctive talents and accomplishments, so should students with natural right-brain talents be encouraged and affirmed for their distinctive talents and accomplishments. To develop their full range of intellectual, artistic, creative, and emotional resources, students ideally should be exposed to a learning environment that challenges and stimulates the right and left cerebral hemispheres of the brain. It is vital, however, that on-going, systematic training in logical thinking be an integral component of this curriculum.

Corrective Strategies

In School

1.   If your child is having difficulty thinking logically, talk with her teacher. Some questions you might ask:

- Does my child have difficulty making predictions?
- Does my child have difficulty perceiving how concepts and issues are related?
- Does my child have difficulty perceiving the progression of sequential ideas?
- Does my child have difficulty drawing reasonable conclusions and inferences from given information?
- Does my child use non sequiturs (conclusions or inferences which do not follow from the premises or evidence) when expressing ideas verbally or in writing?

Some teachers may have difficulty answering these questions because they are unaware that logic deficits and academic difficulties may be linked. If the teacher can't answer the questions, diplomatically suggest that she observe your child more closely and report back to you later. If she concludes that your child does appear to have difficulty with logic, request supplemental materials to use at home to improve her skills. Materials designed to improve logic are included in the Resource List at the back of this book.

At Home

1.   (Elementary School, ES) Create logic games to play with your child that encourage making reasonable associations and plausible responses to mind-teasers. Gear the difficulty and complexity

of your questions to your child's chronological, developmental, and intellectual age. You want your child to enjoy the process and to be able to answer your questions by stretching mentally. You don't want to demoralize your child by asking questions she cannot be expected to answer. Examples of reasonable logic questions for ten- to twelve-year-olds include:

• "Boy Scouts are taught how to make many different types of knots. What is the advantage of learning this skill? How many possible uses for knots can you think of? Why were different types of knots invented?"

• The light produced by the most powerful spotlight is not strong enough to reach the moon because the moon is 250,000 miles away. An extremely powerful laser beam, however, could conceivably reach the moon. Why do you think this might be possible?"

• Predict what would happen if atmospheric conditions caused all radio and TV transmission to break down for three days. List as many possible consequences as you can.

If creating your own logic games proves difficult, find out what is available at your local teacher supply store. To locate other materials and books at your child's developmental level that are designed to develop logical thinking, consult the librarian at your local library. Your local toy store may also have logic games. Your child's teacher or resource specialist may be able to recommend (and lend) materials to you. Also consult the Resource List at the back of this book.

2. See the cause-and-effect activities under Smart Thinking. These interactive exercises are designed to enhance logical thinking. For other logic development activities, see my book *The Life-Smart Kid* (see Resource List).

Mainstreaming and Special Day Classes

Federal law requires that students officially identified as *learning disabled* be assigned to special assistance programs (see Parents' Rights). These programs range from small, self-contained classes that students with serious learning problems attend for the entire day to part-time learning assistance programs that children with less severe learning problems attend for a portion of the day. When children participate in part-time resource programs (RSP classes) and attend regular classes for the remainder of the day, the procedure is called *mainstreaming*. Full-time programs are generally described as *special day classes*.

After a child is referred by the teacher or the Child Study Team to the school psychologist for diagnostic testing, an Individual Education Program (IEP) conference is scheduled to discuss test results, examine the child's academic deficits, and develop a plan for correcting identified problems. Factors that influence the recommendations made during the IEP include the severity of the child's learning problems, district resources, class availability, and the district's special education philosophy. Because student enrollment in RSP programs and special day classes is limited, each student, in theory, is provided with highly individualized, intensive remedial assistance.

Special day classes are intended to offer a safe haven where children with serious academic deficits can receive intensive academic assistance. Students who cannot meet the academic demands of the regular classroom are thus insulated from the embarrassment, frustration, and feelings of inadequacy that can demoralize them and undermine their self-confidence and motivation.

Segregating seriously learning disabled students who cannot do the assigned work in self-contained classes makes sense, but the practice also poses risks. At the junior and senior high school level, these classes are sometimes used as "warehouses" for teenagers with serious emotional and behavioral problems. Older students who have been enrolled in special day classes since elementary school and who haven't made a great deal of progress may become actively or passively resistant to correcting their learning problems. Their frustration, discouragement, and unresolved academic deficits often spawn a wide range of nonadaptive, ego-protecting, or oppositional behaviors. If other students in the class manifest the same behaviors, an anti-learning environment may develop. Students who were initially motivated to learn may begin to mimic the counterproductive behaviors and may soon become discouraged and unmotivated themselves.

Other potential risks associated with special day classes include:

• The program may be perceived by students to be demeaning and intellectually stultifying. (This perception may or may not be accurate.)

• The teacher may be inadequately trained, "burned out," unsupportive, and not empathetic. (Repetitive or boring activities are guaranteed to trigger resistance or apathy.)

• Students may not be sufficiently prodded to catch up. (Struggling students must be pushed out of their comfort zone if they are to make meaningful academic gains.)

• The curriculum may be poorly conceived. (Teachers and administrators who wittingly or unwittingly have a warehouse mindset about the function of special day classes do their students an injustice.)

• The class may not be homogeneous and may combine students with learning problems and those with emotional problems. (Children with emotional problems require counseling. Those with learning problems require educational therapy. There may be overlap in some cases, but a failure to delineate the underlying causal factors and address the distinct needs of the two populations is a disservice to struggling students.)

• Students may never be taught the vital academic and thinking skills they require for successful reintegration into the mainstream. (Creative, dynamic, and focused teaching strategies must be implemented by talented teachers, or students in special day classes will never overcome their deficits.)

• Children may be classified (and perceive themselves) as permanent "second-class" students with severely limited academic and vocational options despite having average to superior intelligence. (When students conclude from their own experiences and from the feedback they receive from adults that they are inadequate and that the situation is hopeless, they will give up and acquiesce to their "fate." Their negative expectations will become self-fulfilling.)

Some educators who are opposed to special day classes believe that any potential value derived from segregating seriously learning disabled students carries a huge price tag. They argue that monumental problems are inherent in attempting to reintegrate academically isolated youngsters into the educational mainstream. They also contend that students can become so dependent on the small teacher/student ratio that even after the learning problems have been ostensibly remedied, they still have great difficulty adjusting to the academic demands and psychological stresses of less nurturing and less individualized regular classes (see Learned Helplessness).

Special day classes can also produce social problems. Children in self-contained programs are often misunderstood (and may even be ridiculed) by the other students on campus. Their special status can cause segregated children to feel profoundly "defective." Some youngsters consider placement in special programs to be conclusive evidence that they are retarded. Once special day students become demoralized and shut down, the likelihood of their prevailing over their learning problems is significantly reduced.

Concern about the liabilities of self-contained programs has prompted most schools to mainstream as many students as possible. Students in pull-out resource programs spend a specified amount of time each day (in some cases every other day) with the resource teacher, reading specialist, and/or speech and language therapist. This specialist may focus either on remedying underlying learning deficits or helping students catch up and keep up with their classes. The resource specialist may choose to use specialized remedial materials or simply assist students with classwork. After the session, RSP students return to their regular classrooms. The severity of a child's learning problems and the specialist's availability will determine the frequency and duration of the pull-out sessions.

Ironically, children may be penalized for participating in an RSP program because they are held accountable for all classwork they miss while with the resource specialist. This creates a Catch-22 situation: students fall behind and are punished with poor grades if they do not receive assistance, and they may also be punished with poor grades for work missed while they are receiving remedial help.

Classroom teachers who consciously or unconsciously resent students being pulled out of class and who direct their resentment toward the students are myopic and "can't see the forest for the trees." Although their objective should be to help struggling children resolve their learning problems, these teachers are primarily intent on having every student in their class complete the assigned material. Requiring learning disabled students to finish a math worksheet assumes more importance than helping deficient students actually learn how to do the problems. Inflexible, insensitive teachers who lose sight of educational priorities cause unwarranted stress and embarrassment, they also cause struggling children to resist participating in the learning assistance program.

To resolve the Catch-22 situation, some school districts are sending their resource specialists and teacher aides into regular classrooms to provide on-site help. This practice eliminates the problem of pulling children out of mainstream classes, but the effectiveness of the approach has yet to be fully documented.

The value of any remedial program hinges on the skills, personality, and insight of the learning-handicap (LH) teacher (see Evaluating Special Education Programs). RSP programs and special day classes can be successful when those implementing these programs are talented, perceptive, affirming, creative, and motivating. With effective help, most children can make significant gains and acquire the skills and self-confidence they need to prevail in school. The challenge is to make certain they get into a first-rate program with a first-rate teacher.

Corrective Strategies

In School

1.   The objective of any remedial program is to help your child overcome his learning problems. If he's in a self-contained class, review the goals for the program, its teaching philosophy, instructional methods, and the projected time table for your child's reintegration into the mainstream.

Do not pressure the teacher into giving you an arbitrary and unrealistic target date for remedying your child's learning problems. You do not want your child mainstreamed before he is ready. On the other hand, you do want him to be reintegrated into regular classes when he is ready. You will need to monitor his progress and remain in touch with his LH or RSP teacher. In some cases, children with severe learning problems may need to remain in a self-contained program for their entire education.

2.   If your child is being mainstreamed, carefully review with the resource specialist and the classroom teacher the objectives of the remedial program. Examine the IEP document (see Individual Educational Program). Discuss how you might provide additional support at home and how you should monitor your child's work. Also discuss what criteria should be used to evaluate progress.

3.   If you believe that your child is being penalized for receiving out-of-class assistance, express your concerns to the teacher and the resource specialist. If you cannot resolve the problem, involve the principal in the discussion. Being intolerant about missed classwork can undermine the learning assistance program and defeat the goal of getting your child up to grade level and functioning efficiently and effectively in school (see Conferencing with School Officials).

At Home

1.   Monitor your child's progress carefully. Monitoring is vital whether he's in a self-contained classroom or a resource program.

2.   Once your child's learning deficits have been identified, you may want to provide additional help at home in specific areas. Refer to relevant entries for corrective strategies.

3.   If you are not satisfied with your child's progress in the RSP or self-contained class, consider hiring a tutor or educational therapist to provide supplemental assistance. As an alterna-

tive, consider enrolling your child in a private learning assistance program. Be realistic, however. Don't expect instantaneous progress, especially if your child has significant learning problems. Your child's progress in school may be slow, despite a first-rate learning assistance program in school and additional help after school. At some point, you must trust your intuition. If your child isn't making progress, do everything you can to identify the obstacles and locate the resources in your community that can help your child overcome these obstacles.

 Math

The starting point in correcting a child's math problem is to figure out where and why the child is "stuck." Is he struggling because he does not understand what fractions are (a *conceptual deficit*) or because he has difficulty performing specific mathematical operations such as subtraction or multiplication (a *computational* or *operational deficit*)? A child who has chronic math problems probably has deficiencies in both areas.

Assigning a confused child additional practice sheets or requiring him to recite multiplication tables ad nauseam will not resolve a conceptual problem. Even though the child must ultimately learn the multiplication tables by rote, drilling number facts without addressing his underlying confusion is at best a stopgap measure. In the long run, math mastery hinges on understanding the principles that govern how numbers work.

Math skills develop sequentially. Children must be able to multiply to solve division problems and understand part/whole relationships to solve fraction problems. Youngsters who do not comprehend basic concepts may be able to do some problems correctly, but they usually "hit a brick wall" at some point. They may forget how to do problems they had supposedly already mastered, or they may be unable to make the transition from arithmetic to algebra or geometry. Their conceptual deficits will invariably come back to haunt them as they proceed into upper level math courses.

In some cases, math deficiencies are linked to *perceptual decoding deficits*. Reversing number sequences (79 perceived or written as 97) or confusing the number 6 with 9 will invariably cause computational errors (see Dyslexia). The child who has difficulty copying numbers from his textbook (near-point copying) or from the chalkboard (far-point copying) or who, because of spatial problems (difficulty accurately perceiving visual input and forming background relationships) misaligns his columns when adding, subtracting, or dividing, is also going to make errors, even if he understands the underlying concepts (see Inaccurate Copying). Because of their visual perception and eye-hand coordination deficits, these children frequently make mistakes, even when using calculators to solve problems.

Children with concentration deficits are also at risk when they do math (see Attention Deficit Disorder). Inattentiveness to detail may cause them to disregard the minus sign and add when they should subtract. Children with ADD typically do poorly on homework assignments and tests where computational precision is required.

Most children of normal intelligence can master basic arithmetic. Although addition, subtraction, multiplication, and division involve aspects of rote memory, children who understand how numbers work have less difficulty learning their number facts and ultimately find higher level math less challenging than those who have simply memorized number facts without understanding the underlying concepts that govern the computational operations (see Auditory Memory; Memorizing Information; Visual Memory).

The widespread use of calculators by students in elementary, middle, and high school classrooms could, in some cases, mask serious math deficiencies. Although children in our technologically driven society must learn to use calculators and computers effectively, it is critical that they understand basic "number crunching" principles and be able to perform the computations manually if necessary. Those exclusively dependent on a calculator to solve math problems are at risk. If the calculator breaks down while they are taking a college entrance exam, they could be faced with a disaster.

Corrective Strategies

In School

1. If your child has math problems, request that a diagnostic math test be administered to identify specific deficits. This test should indicate whether the problem is computational or conceptual (or both). It should also reveal if your child is reversing or misaligning numbers when doing computations (see Dyslexia; Inaccurate Copying). The teacher or resource specialist can then employ teaching strategies specifically designed to remedy the identified deficits. For example, manipulatives (units such as pennies, cubes of different sizes, or popsicle sticks) can be used to help your child understand visually and kinesthetically how numbers function. Fraction tiles can be used by teachers to explain part-whole relationships. Any tactile and visual prop can be an invaluable resource for helping a child who is confused about basic math concepts. A method called "Touch Math" can also be very effective for teaching basic math concepts and operations.

2. The teacher's observations in class should provide important information about the origins and symptoms of your child's math problems. For example, your child may have difficulty adding numbers involving decimals, but may understand decimal concepts and how to add. If he makes "silly" computational mistakes when adding or forgets to insert the decimal point, he would ben-

efit from further directed practice. Extra homework that provides opportunities for practicing specific operations would probably be appropriate. If your child's problem is attributable to inattentiveness or sloppiness, you and the teacher may need to design a creative incentive program that encourages self-editing and rewards your child for neatness and accuracy (see Attention to Details). If your child is confused about how to add fractions or does not understand what decimals are, someone (ideally the teacher!) needs to teach the concepts more clearly. For materials designed to improve math skills, refer to the math section in the Resource List at the back of the book.

3. If your child is seriously deficient in math, he should be provided with learning assistance. In some cases, the classroom teacher may be able to offer help before or after class. If your child has serious or chronic math problems, he will need help from a trained resource specialist, highly competent tutor, or educational therapist who can identify his deficiencies and then systematically and sequentially remedy them. Math problems can be as debilitating as reading problems, and you must be your child's advocate if he is falling behind. Testing and remediation are essential (see Parents' Rights).

At Home

1. (Elementary School, ES) Behavior modification techniques can be effective in helping a child who understands concepts but makes silly mistakes because of inattentiveness. Set up a program that gives your child points for each problem he completes accurately and legibly. A prize, award, or even money could be the incentives. It may be sufficient to say simply: "These problems need to be recopied so that they are more legible. Let me show you how I would like them to look." Once he does a neat, legible set of problems, photocopy the page and put it in a plastic sleeve. When subsequent work is sloppy or illegible, show your child the facsimile in the sleeve and insist that the current work be just as neat and legible.

2.   (ES) If your child has computational problems, request that the teacher provide supplemental practice materials. If the class is working on long division, and your child has not mastered the multiplication tables, practice sheets should initially stress multiplication. If he doesn't understand the concept of multiplication, get your child extra help in this area. If you feel you can't explain math concepts to your child, ask the resource specialist or teacher to do so. Once the concepts are understood, flash cards can be used to drill multiplication facts. Make the sessions fun by creating games! ("Let's play Monopoly, but before anyone can throw the dice, he has to solve a math problem from this stack of cards.") You might also create incentives for your child ("Let's see how many of these problems you can get. You can earn a point for each correct answer. When you get twenty points, we can go out for an ice-cream cone.") Other incentives might involve long-range goals ("For each complete times table you can do, you'll receive five points toward the total number of points you need to win the radio-controlled car.") Points earned for math proficiency can be combined with points derived elsewhere, such as doing chores. Repeatedly praise your child's accomplishments. If your child is having an "off" day, stop! You can always come back to it later.

Ask your child's teacher for input about his current skill level and specific deficits. Begin with easy problems and concepts and progress systematically and sequentially to more complex problems. Rely on your judgment in determining if your child has mastered a particular operation or concept. Remember that children typically need several exposures to something they are taught for the first time and a great deal of practice before they truly learn it. Don't expect "closure" (complete mastery) after the first exposure. You want your child to have positive associations with math and with the time spent working with you. If you make the sessions painful or too long, your child will become resistant and resentful. If this happens, he'll derive little or no benefit from the process.

3.   (Junior High/High School, J/HS) Helping high school students with math problems can be challenging for many parents. You may have forgotten how to solve certain algebraic equations or how to prove theorems in geometry. Even if you are skillful in math, you may lack the patience or the skills to explain the concepts and operations to your child. If he cannot get help from the teacher or resource specialist, consider hiring a tutor. Ask the teacher to recommend someone qualified and effective.

4.   (ES) If you are uncomfortable making up your own math games, visit your local teacher supply store. Examine materials that address the deficits identified by the teacher (flash cards, number fact cards, workbooks, and videos, and so on). If you have difficulty working with your child in a tutorial capacity, ask about fun math games you could play together or computer software that focuses on the deficits. Make the sessions enjoyable. If your child struggles, provide emotional support and communicate positive expectations. Specific materials you may want to examine are included in the Resource List at the back of the book.

5.   Think of ways to integrate math into your family interactions. You might, for example, see who can add 977 and 341 the fastest—you are required to do the problem in your head and your child is allowed to use pencil and paper. Start with problems your child can easily do. If appropriate, give your child a handicap (you begin 5 seconds after he begins). You want him to win, so be patient and supportive if he makes a mistake. ("By next week, I bet you'll have no difficulty with these subtraction problems. You're getting better all the time, and with some more practice you'll be dynamite!") Your goal is not only to improve your child's skills, but also to reduce his anxieties and negative associations with math. You want to change his "I *can't* do math mindset" to an "I *can* do math mindset." As he improves, make the problems more difficult. You might say the remainder of a problem is *927* and he has to figure out any minuend and subtrahend that will produce that remainder. The simplest answer, of course would be *928 – 1*, but you could increase the difficulty by requiring that the minuend be at least five digits and the subtrahend at least four.

Memorizing Information

Our educational system has traditionally rewarded students who can recall prodigious amounts of oral and written data. Remembering information is a relatively easy task for some and excruciatingly painful and demoralizing for others.

The motivated child with poor memory skills may devote hours to studying math facts, vocabulary definitions, historic dates, spelling words, grammar rules, Spanish verb conjugations, chemical symbols, or biology phyla, only to discover at exam time that he cannot recall vital information. Because he does not realize that intelligence and good memory are not synonymous, he may simply conclude he is "dumb" (see IQ Test Scores).

A child with poor recall may be highly creative, intuitive, artistic, articulate, and/or analytical. He may struggle to recall math facts or memorize data that seems irrelevant, but he may be able to write excellent short stories or reason with penetrating logic. Such selective talents underscore the fact that intelligence is a multifaceted phenomenon. Unfortunately, many of the more creative manifestations of intelligence are rarely recognized, acknowledged, or affirmed in traditional schools. To survive in school, children must somehow learn to accommodate themselves to the values and priorities of the educational system. That this system often emphasizes memorization skills assimilated through the visual and auditory modalities and discounts other equally valuable talents assimilated through the kinesthetic and tactile modalities simply is accepted as a fact of academic life.[1]

The kinesthetic learner is at a particular disadvantage in schools that do not offer classes in art, mechanical drawing, drafting, or shop. He may be able to create a magnificent three-dimensional art project or take apart and reassemble an engine, but he may struggle to learn French vocabulary words, grammar rules, or any information that is not perceived as interesting or meaningful. In spite of superior mechanical, spatial, and artistic aptitude, this student will pay a high price for his difficulty in assimilating data in information-loaded courses (see Auditory Memory; Visual Memory). Frustration and feelings of inadequacy could permanently warp perceptions of his own talents and capabilities.

Teachers who base their assessment of a child's ability primarily on the retention of facts and information generally give A's to students who can do well on timed math tests, spell accurately, recall historical dates, and remember chemical

1. John Gardner, in his book *Frames of Mind*, describes a wide range of aptitudes and abilities not identified on traditional IQ tests. He contends that intelligence can manifest itself in interpersonal (social), musical, intrapersonal (self-knowledge), spatial (eye-hand coordination), artistic, or athletic talents. The book *In Their Own Way* by Thomas Armstrong extrapolates on Gardner's insights and argues that teachers have an obligation to individualize curricula so students can learn how to develop and utilize their natural abilities and be acknowledged for their distinctive talents and achievements (see Resource List at the back of this book).

formulas. Children with exceptional visual memory skills are often described as having "photographic memories" and are generally held in awe by teachers and classmates. The analogy is accurate. The child who learns how to take visual pictures when he studies, who can see words and numbers in his mind, and who can imprint the information in his memory transforms his eyes into a camera lens and his brain into a roll of film. When he needs to recall information for a test, all he has to do is scan the "photos" in his mind (see Grades; Spelling Problems; Visual Memory).

Because much of the information students are expected to learn and retain is written in their textbooks and notes, developing effective *visual memory* skills is usually a requisite to academic achievement. Youngsters must learn how to recall what they read irrespective of their own preferred learning modality. Although *auditory learners* (those who prefer to listen and imprint the sounds of what they are learning) and *kinesthetic learners* (those who learn and imprint through touch and the manipulation of objects) should be encouraged to utilize their natural learning style (see suggestions below), acquiring good visual memory skills will make study time less stressful and test-taking less traumatic.

With good instruction, ample practice, and systematic experimentation, virtually all children can significantly improve memorization skills. A new attitude ("I can get this!") will replace the defeatist attitude ("I'll never be able to get this!") Students who can accurately identify what they need to learn (see Identifying Important Information) and who can access effective memorization methods have a significant academic advantage over those who lack these vital academic survival skills.

Corrective Strategies

In School

1.   If your child is having difficulty memorizing information, ask the teacher for suggestions about how he might improve this skill. She may

be able to show you techniques that will facilitate memorizing number facts, vocabulary definitions, or grammar rules (see Auditory Memory; Visual Memory, and suggestions in "At Home" below).

2.   If your child has severe memory deficits, ask for an evaluation by the Child Study Team, the school psychologist, or the resource specialist. If significant visual or auditory memory deficits are revealed, request that learning assistance be provided in these deficit areas (see Individual Educational Program [IEP]; Parents' Rights).

At Home

1.   Try an experiment with your child. Select fifteen relatively difficult vocabulary words and their definitions. Your child should not be familiar with the definitions of these words. Group words randomly into three lists. On the first evening, have your child learn one list of words visually. Have him write out the definitions several times and study the material silently. Urge him to form mental pictures of what the words mean (for example, an image of a *vulnerable* person). Then give him a quiz. The next evening ask him to recite the definitions aloud. Encourage him to make an audio tape in his mind (for example, a *buoyant* cork floating as waves lap against it). Discuss the words and give your child a quiz. On the third night, have him dramatize the words and definitions from the third list. Have him act out the role of someone who is *parsimonious.* Ask your child which learning system seems best and compare the results of the quizzes.

Your child's preferred learning style may be visual, auditory, kinesthetic, or a combination of these three modalities. Urge him to use his preferred style when he has to study and memorize. Emphasize that learning is easier if he studies actively rather than passively. Explain with concrete examples what this means. You might make a distinction between someone who tries to learn to play baseball by watching another person play and someone who learns by actually playing the game. Encourage your child to get involved in what he is learning and to be highly creative when he studies and memorizes information. If he is an auditory learner, have him pretend he is a teacher and give a lecture to the class that contains information to memorize. By talking aloud, he can capitalize on his preferred learning modality. A kinesthetic learner might choose to spell out spelling words in modeling clay on a cookie tray, trace the words on fine sandpaper, or manipulate the letters from a Scrabble game. Urge creativity and inventiveness when studying and encourage your child to use the system that works best for him. Combining modalities is certainly acceptable. Your child may find it effective to form visual images and to reinforce mastery by also creating auditory associations.

2.   Explain to your child that certain types of information lend themselves to being learned visually. Being able to take a visual picture and see a fact or spelling word in your mind can be an important test-taking tool. For more ideas about how to develop your child's visual memory skills, see corrective strategies under Auditory Memory; Nonphonetic Words; Spelling Problems; Visual Memory; Vocabulary.

Monitoring Homework

The conscientious child who works independently and efficiently needs little supervision when doing homework. At the other end of the independence/efficiency spectrum is the child who chronically procrastinates, does the minimum possible, submits late, incomplete, and inaccurate assignments, and disregards the effects of his cavalier attitude and behavior. Such a child is a candidate for more intensive parental monitoring (see Behavior and Attitude; Disregarding Consequences; Effort and Motivation; Inadequate Study Time; Incomplete Assignments; Negative Attitude toward School; Procrastination; Time Management; Working Independently).

For obvious reasons, children with learning problems usually require more parental guidance and supervision than those with good academic skills. Frustrated, demoralized students are often tempted to avoid work that exacerbates their feelings of inadequacy. To defend themselves, struggling children may delude themselves that if they don't really try, they can't really fail. This conscious or unconscious rationalization makes their academic deficits all the more problematic (see Anger and Frustration; Bouncing Back from Setbacks and Learning from Mistakes; Fear of Failure/Success/Competition; Self-Esteem and Self-Confidence).

Poor study skills often make it imperative for parents to become actively involved in overseeing homework. The child who does not establish goals and priorities, plan ahead, record assignments, attend to details, take notes, follow instructions, identify and remember important information, and anticipate what the teacher is likely to ask on a test is waving a red flag. Without parental intervention and supervision, she will probably capsize academically (see Attention to Details; Goals; Inadequate Study Time; Memorizing Important Information; Planning Ahead, Recording Assignments; Study Skills; Time Management).

Children whose irresponsible homework behavior is linked to specific learning disabilities or study skills deficits require remedial assistance (see Learning Disabilities; Underachievement). Before you can reasonably expect your child to relinquish counterproductive behaviors and develop a more conscientious work ethic, you must make certain she has the requisite skills to do the assigned work. Ask the teacher for an update about your child's skills to make this determination. Once you have an accurate assessment your child must understand clearly and unequivocally your position on effort, responsibility, and commitment. She must also understand it's her job to learn (see Expectations and Performance Guidelines).

As your child begins to achieve and becomes more academically competent and confident, reduce the amount of supervision. Your goal is to help her be responsible, self-motivated, and diligent, not because you are standing over her shoulder and supervising her, but because she herself values the payoffs for doing a first-rate job: pride, acknowledgment, and success.

Monitoring your child's homework is essential if she is struggling academically and has acquired a pattern of counterproductive behaviors, but be aware that providing intensive supervision is not without risks. If your child feels she is being constantly scrutinized, she may become anxious, resentful, and resistant. She may also become emotionally and academically dependent on you. The risk of dependency increases if you take ownership of her academic problems and attempt to correct every mistake she makes. You must constantly make informed judgment calls as you weigh how much help to provide. Too much help can be as disadvantageous as too little (see Learned Helplessness). To determine the appropriate amount of assistance to provide, take into consideration your own intuitive impressions, as well as the teacher's assessment of your child's current skills (see Communicating with the School; Conferencing with School Officials).

Corrective Strategies

In School

1.   If you and the teacher believe your child has academic deficits, request a referral to the Child Study Team and a diagnostic evaluation by the school psychologist. If this evaluation reveals deficiencies, and your child clearly lacks the requisite skills to do her homework, insist that learning assistance be provided (see Parents' Rights). Request that assignments be modified so that she can complete them within a reasonable time frame and with a minimum amount of help and that work be graded flexibly until she can catch up with her class.

At Home

1.   To supervise your child effectively at home, you must have information about her strengths and weaknesses. Ask her teacher to complete the Student Evaluation Checklist (page 128). If it is clear that your child is deficient in a specific area such as reading comprehension or in several areas at the same time (handwriting, math, and spelling), discuss with the teacher how you can best help your child at home. Does she want you to correct the mistakes or simply make sure the work gets done? Does she want you to attempt to explain material that your child has not grasped in class? Does she want you to help your child write her book reports or simply proofread and edit them? Or does she prefer that you not supervise your child's assignments? It is vital that you examine these critical issues with the teacher. If she requests that you become actively involved in the monitoring process, ask her for suggestions about how best to do so. Develop a mutually acceptable homework intervention strategy and check in periodically so you can gauge the efficacy of your strategy. Let the teacher know if you have concerns about unwittingly encouraging your child to become helpless and excessively dependent on your supervision (see Learned Helplessness). Explore ways to avoid this. Discuss with the teacher any problems that arise. You might, for example, understand how to solve certain math problems using the methods taught in class. Share appropriate information and feedback from the teacher with your child.

2.   (Elementary School, ES) Ask the teacher to take a minute each day to fill out the following Daily Performance Checklist. This will tell you if your child is completing homework and studying adequately.

3.   (Junior High/High School, J/HS) Junior and senior high school teachers may feel that students in the upper grades should be responsible for completing and submitting their work and should not be monitored by parents. Therefore, they may not be willing to complete the Daily Performance Checklist. If you feel your child is not sufficiently responsible to work independently, discuss your concerns with your child's teachers or counselor, or, if appropriate, with the assistant principal. Ideally, they will be able to help you create an acceptable monitoring/feedback system. For more ideas, see suggestions under Disorganization; Distractions while Studying; Goals; Inadequate Study Time; Incomplete Assignments; Planning Ahead; Preparing for Tests; Priorities; Procrastination; Smart Thinking; Time Management; Working Independently.

DAILY PERFORMANCE CHECKLIST

Second Grade and Above

1 = Poor   2 = Fair   3 = Good   4 = Excellent

	MON.	TUES.	WED.	THURS.	FRI.
Completes assignments					
On Time					
Neatly					
Legible handwriting					
Keeps up with class					
Effort					
Behavior					
Comments					
Parents' initials					

4.   Using the Daily Performance Checklist, establish realistic daily performance goals and keep a weekly tally of points your child earns. She could work for a specific reward when the performance goal is achieved. Factor your child's academic skill level and learning deficits into the equation. If she has poor fine-motor or spatial skills, for example, you cannot reasonably expect her handwriting to improve immediately (see Handwriting).

Negative Attitude toward School

There is a direct cause-and-effect connection between a child's attitude about school and his acamedic success or failure track record. The child who achieves academically is likely to enjoy school. The child who receives poor grades and continual negative feedback is likely to become frustrated, anxious, and discouraged. That such a child often becomes highly resistant to learning and acquires a range of self-protecting, counterproductive behaviors is quite understandable (see Atypical Learning Problems; Bouncing Back from Setbacks and Learning from Mistakes; Effort and Motivation; Learning Disabilities; Psychological Problems and Psychological Overlay; Self-Esteem and Self-Confidence; Underachievement).

The child who dislikes school may suffer in silence, or may loudly proclaim his unhappiness to anyone who will listen. He may blame himself for poor performance and conclude he is "dumb," or blame others for his plight and feel victimized. The classic litany of rationalizations and complaints include: "The teacher is boring." "The work is stupid." "The teacher is unfair." "Why do I have to learn things I'll never use."

The fallout from learning problems can obviously trigger a great deal of unhappiness in school. When a child concludes he cannot do the assigned work, he will try to defend himself as best he can from feeling inept and worthless. He may procrastinate, refuse to complete homework, give up, or shut down. These self-sabotaging behaviors ("I don't care if the teacher gives me a bad grade for not handing in my homework!") call attention to the very weaknesses the child is attempting to hide, but the struggling child is usually so enmeshed in defensive tactics that he fails to realize this irony.

A negative attitude toward school may also be symptomatic of emotional or family problems. Troubled children rarely understand why they are unhappy or depressed, and they usually feel a compelling need to flee from unpleasant emotions such as anger, guilt, and fear. To justify their negativity, they often latch onto convenient scapegoats. They may blame their problems on an unfair teacher or dumb questions on a test. By denying responsibility for their behavior and performance, they attempt to deflect attention from themselves. By complaining and blaming, they vent frustration, unhappiness, anger, resentment, and inner turmoil. Other common coping mechanisms include self-sabotaging, manipulative, or oppositional behavior, and, in extreme cases, truancy and delinquency. Unhappy, demoralized children often gravitate socially to those who share their negativity, sense of futility, and alienation (see Peer Pressure). Self-sabotaging behaviors can be powerful passive-aggressive weapons in the hands of unhappy children, and these behaviors are guaranteed to make parents' lives miserable (see Anger and Frustration; Behavior and Attitude; Disregarding Consequences; Fear of Failure/Success/Competition; Guilt; Psychological Problems and Psychological Overlay; Self-Esteem and Self-Confidence).

Identifying the source of your child's unhappiness is the first step in reorienting negative attitudes. If he has learning problems, his specific underlying deficits must be identified and treated before you can realistically expect any attitude changes (see Learning Disabilities). Once your child begins to succeed in school, negative attitudes should change. As his self-confidence improves and expectations change, the need for self-protection by blaming or complaining will lessen (see Keeping Up with the Class; Monitoring Homework; Working Independently). If the negativity persists, however, consider it a red flag that suggests underlying emotional problems.

Children who are unhappy and negative because they are wrestling with emotional or family problems require counseling. If psychological issues are compounded by learning problems, learning assistance in school and/or private educational therapy outside of school may also be needed. In some cases, remedial help can be implemented concurrently with counseling. Extremely angry, resistant children who manifest chronic self-sabotaging behaviors often require counseling *before* they will cooperate with a learning assistance program.

Remedial assistance should not be considered a surrogate for counseling or psychotherapy when a child is profoundly anguished and distressed (see Psychological Problems and Psychological Overlay). Chronic unhappiness rarely disappears of its own accord. If the underlying emotional issues are not addressed, the child's attitude and school performance will continue to deteriorate. For this reason it is vital that appropriate psychological and educational support systems be established before the child shuts down academically and emotionally.

Corrective Strategies

In School

1.   Ask your child's teacher if your child's negative attitude about school might be linked to learning problems (see Student Evaluation Checklist in Learning Disorders, page 128). If she thinks that underlying skills deficits may be causing or contributing to the problem, request that your child be evaluated by the Child Study Team or school psychologist (see Parents' Rights). Help from the resource specialist will improve skills and self-confidence and this in turn should improve a negative attitude.

2.   If your child cannot do the class assignments or homework because of a skills deficit, ask the teacher to reduce the difficulty level and/or quantity of the work until your child can catch up. The child who believes the situation is hopeless is at risk for becoming discouraged, demoralized, and resistant (see Expectations and Performance Guidelines).

3.   Discuss concerns about your child's attitude with the school counselor, principal, or vice principal. He or she may have ideas about how to identify and address the issues responsible for your child's negativity.

At Home

1.   If your child has academic deficits and does not qualify for learning assistance in school, be prepared to provide help at home. Even if your child does qualify for help from the resource specialist, this may not be sufficient to guarantee success in class. Tutoring, educational therapy, or enrollment at a private learning center may be vital to changing negative attitudes about school. (See relevant entries in this book for suggestions about how to deal with specific learning deficits. To identify your child's possible deficits, refer to the Student Evaluation Checklists for elementary, junior high, and high school students in Learning Disabilities.)

2.   If you suspect your child's negative attitude toward school is linked to emotional or family issues, request a referral from the school psychologist or your pediatrician to a qualified mental health professional. Counseling should be provided before negative attitudes become en-

trenched and your child has established a pattern of self-sabotage in school (see Psychological Problems and Psychological Overlay for specific symptoms).

3. If your child's negative attitudes about school do not appear to be linked to underlying emotional problems, consider using the DIBS Problem-Solving Method (page 190) to help identify specific issues that may be causing a dislike of school. The method will also encourage active and creative involvement in the process of finding solutions to problems that are making your child unhappy.

Nonphonetic Words

Some children find it relatively easy to recognize and pronounce *nonphonetic* words (those that don't follow the "rules" of pronunciation) such as *should, drought, thought,* and *bough.* Others find the process of laboriously decoding these words to be a nightmare (see Phonics). Each time they encounter a previously learned word that does not follow phonetic rules, they struggle to make sense out of it. The inability to associate the visual appearance of a word with its pronunciation usually creates formidable barriers to reading fluency.

When children labor to read nonphonetic words, diagnostic tests usually reveal visual memory deficits (see Visual Memory). These deficits are frequently associated with chronic spelling problems (see Spelling Problems). Difficulty reading nonphonetic words may also be linked to other learning problems such as dyslexia and poor reading comprehension (see Atypical Learning Problems; Dyslexia; Learning Disabilities; Reading Aloud; Reading Comprehension; Slow Reading).

Nonphonetic words are often referred to as *sight words.* These "exception" words are quite common and can be traced to the unique oral evolution of the English language (see Spelling Problems). Pronunciation of the endings of words such as *through, bough,* and *although* was at one time identical. The pronunciation has changed over the centuries, but the spelling has remained as it was in the Middle Ages.

To read smoothly and effortlessly, students must learn to identify nonphonetic words *by sight.*

Innovative methods for teaching how to imprint these words using *visual recall loop* have proven highly effective. These methods are described below.

Corrective Strategies

In School

1.   (Elementary School, ES) If your child is not using the Dolch list (words grouped according to their level of difficulty; see Resource List), suggest that the teacher have him use the list to improve his recognition of nonphonetic words. The list incorporates many of the common words that children are expected to be able to read at each grade level. Your child might put five words from the list onto flash or index cards each day and memorize them. Techniques for memorizing the words are described below.

2.   Encourage your child to make a list of difficult nonphonetic words he encounters when reading. These words should also be placed on flash or index cards and studied using the visual imprinting method described below.

At Home

1.   To help your child access a highly effective technique for remembering sight words and developing visual memory skills, urge him to do some pretending. Tell him to imagine that his eyes are the lens of a camera and that his brain is a roll of film (see Memorizing Information;

Spelling Problems). With younger children it may help to have a camera on hand as a concrete model. Tell your child to take a "picture" of each difficult word when he reads. He should keep the "shutter" (his eyelids) open until he can see the word clearly in his mind. Once he understands how the technique works, have him write some difficult sight (nonphonetic) words on index cards, using colored pencils or felt pens. If he wishes, he can write the individual letters of each word in different colors. Color will provide an additional visual "handle" for the brain to register the appearance of the word. (Urge him to select colors he likes.) Have him hold (or tack) the card slightly above eye level. Tell him to place the word slightly to the right or the left of his nose. (He will probably have a preference.) Encourage him to experiment and determine which position produces the best results. Looking up and slightly to the right or left will help your child imprint the word, as the eyes naturally go up when information is being visually accessed and represented. Have him study the word until he thinks he knows it and has imprinted it on his brain (the roll of film). Then have him close his eyes and see if he can still "see" the word in the colors he has chosen. (Further illustration of this visual imprinting process can be found under

Spelling Problems.) If he can't, have him open his eyes and study the word again. Once he can see the word in his mind's eye, have him spell it aloud to you. Then have him write it. (In this instance, the purpose of the exercise is not necessarily to improve his spelling but to help visually imprint the spelling of nonphonetic words so that he can read the words quickly and effortlessly.)

Follow the preceding procedure for five to ten words and then give a review quiz. Urge your child to close his eyes and visualize the words when writing them. The same visual imprint method can be used to remember number facts (see Math), vocabulary definitions (see Vocabulary), historical dates, and chemical formulas (see Memorizing Information). Explain to your child that imprinting the data on the film will help him remember it. Some information, however, will fade if not reviewed, and he may have to do another "shoot." For example, he might visually imprint the word *perfidious* and its definition on his brain, but he may not recall it for more than a few days because it isn't a word he's likely to use very often. Once your child discovers how useful this photography technique can be when he is required to memorize vast amounts of visual data, he will voluntarily use his "camera" whenever it is to his advantage to do so.

Notetaking

Being able to take good notes is a requisite to school success. Students who cannot identify and record key information from textbooks, lectures, and class discussions will find themselves severely handicapped in upper level classes.

Some students figure out how to take good notes on their own, but most require systematic instruction and extensive practice. The general neglect of formal notetaking instruction in American schools can often be traced to a series of flawed assumptions and miscommunication. Many elementary school teachers assume that students will naturally figure out how to take notes. Others assume that students will be taught notetaking skills in junior high school.

Ironically, teachers in the upper grades generally have a different set of assumptions. They expect students entering seventh grade to know how to take notes and generally devote little or no time to teaching the skill. As a consequence, millions of children never master this vital learning and studying tool.

When taking notes, students must be able to extract, distill, and link important information they read in their textbooks or hear in class (see Auditory Memory; Identifying Important Information; Listening in Class; Visual Memory). The procedure also forces them to consider and evaluate what they are studying. Active involvement produces superior learning, enhanced comprehension, and improved retention (see Critical Thinking; Passive Learning; Memorizing Information; Study Skills).

Successful students realize that their notes will help them understand and remember what they are studying. Although notetaking initially requires extra time, the procedure can dramatically reduce the total amount of study time required to do a first-rate job. Instead of having to reread an entire chapter several times, they can simply review their notes (see Smart Thinking).

The nuts and bolts of good notetaking are not mysterious. Students must learn how to:

- Identify main ideas and details in textbook and lectures
- Understand information and concepts
- Record key data quickly using a consistent format
- Use notes effectively while preparing for tests

The ideal time to teach children notetaking and note utilization skills is in elementary school, before counterproductive study habits become entrenched and poor grades cause demoralization and lowered expectations (see Grades). When teachers begin teaching the notetaking process in fourth, fifth, or sixth grade, they provide students with an invaluable learning resource they will be able to use throughout their education (see Study Skills).

Because notetaking skills are often taught mechanically; it is common for students to develop negative associations with the procedure. Some teachers simply write notes on the chalkboard and require students to copy them. This may provide a model for "good" notetaking, but it can also be mind-numbing. By doing all the work and thinking, the teacher encourages passive thinking and passive learning. Students simply become scribes and quickly learn to dread the boring ordeal. Students who perceive notetaking as a useless exercise intentionally designed by their teachers to make their lives miserable usually become resistant to the procedure. This reaction is unfortunate, for notetaking doesn't have to be a boring or painful ordeal. By demonstrating how notetaking can be easily mastered and immediately used in preparing for the next history or science test, creative teachers can actually make the procedure relevant, interesting, and enjoyable.

Passive learners are usually the most resistant to spending the initial extra time and effort required to take good notes (see Negative Attitude toward School). Negatively conditioned by a poor academic track record, they often refuse to accept that any procedure that might involve additional work, even though the procedure could actually improve their grades, make their lives easier, and significantly reduce the amount of time required to study effectively (see Behavior and Attitude; Disregarding Consequences.)

Notetaking is only one component in a first-rate study plan. Students must also learn how to use their notes effectively. They must train themselves to ask questions about what they have written in their notebooks. They must connect important facts to underlying concepts and relate what they are currently learning to what they have already learned. Taking notes and reviewing them mindlessly does not constitute quality studying. Good students use notes as a springboard for delving into the substance of what they are studying and for organizing key material. This systematic, active-learning process enhances comprehension, recall, and mastery.

Notetaking should not be confused with *outlining*. Many children dislike outlining because the method appears contrived. Whereas outlining is a highly formatted and formulaic technique for organizing and recording information, note-taking is less structured. Both procedures can help children "digest" and retain information, and, in the appropriate contexts, both can be powerful study tools. Outlining can be especially useful in organizing information when preparing written reports and making oral presentations. As a general rule, notetaking should be taught before outlining.

Children who take good notes and use them effectively usually see a demonstrable improvement in their schoolwork (see Reading Comprehension). As they begin to recognize the connection between good grades and good notes and realize that notetaking will produce desirable payoffs, their resistance to spending the initial extra time usually disappears.

Corrective Strategies

In School

1. Ask your child's teacher if notetaking skills are being taught in class. If the skills are not being taught, diplomatically express your concerns and present reasons why you are convinced that this vital skill should be an integral part of the curriculum.

2. Discuss with the teacher the strategy you are using at home to help your child learn how to take and use notes effectively (described in the "At Home" section below). Ask for the teacher's feedback and suggestions about how to help your child achieve mastery.

At Home

1. Model for your child how to write a succinct pretend emergency telegram. For example: "Water pump broken Flagstaff. Two days fix. Send $250 overnight Flagstaff Hotel 123 Main Street." Create scenarios in which you and your child send telegrams with only the most important information included. Practice editing the telegram to eliminate superfluous words such as *a*, *an*, *the*. Explain that notetaking is like sending a telegram in which every words costs one dollar.

You want to include enough words to communicate clearly, but you also want to choose your words carefully and eliminate unnecessary, nonessential ones. Make the process of creating and editing the material fun. The subject matter can be serious or playful.

2.   To help your child acquire effective lecture notetaking skills, pretend you are a news broadcaster. Describe a current event (for example, a flood or a hurricane). Have your child apply the skills you have been practicing and write down only the key information that you communicate. Review your child's notes and discuss the reasons for including certain information and leaving out other information. Then have him use his notes and pretend to be the broadcaster. Don't be highly critical, especially in the beginning. Your child's skills will improve with practice. Make the sessions fun, short, and nonstressful. If your child enjoys the process, there will be less resistance and more willingness to try the new skills.

3.   Teach your child common notetaking abbreviations such as: *p. = page; ex. = exercise; w = with; thru = through.* Encourage him to use as many abbreviations as he can, but emphasize that he must be able to understand his own abbreviaitons. You might also have him practice a simplified form of speedwriting that leaves out most of the vowels (*"U mght also hv hm prctc a smplfd frm of spdwrtng tht lves out mst of th vwls."*). Explain that abbreviations save time when taking notes from a textbook and also help to quickly record key information from teachers' lectures. Demonstrate a format that will simplify his notes. If, for example, your child reads a section in a science textbook about lasers, the following notes might apply:

- *Lsers invntd 1954*
- *2 types: synthtc rby crstals & gas*
- *Rglr lght tumbls*
- *Lser lght strght lne*

Your child will need to practice notetaking and will need several exposures to the abbreviation method before he masters the procedure. Remember to make notetaking practice sessions fun and to praise your child repeatedly.

4.   Read a page in your child's textbook and model how you would take notes on the material. Explain your reasons for including and excluding specific content. Encourage your child to comment on your decisions and ask him why you included certain things and excluded others. He might want to include things you would exclude. Be affirming and open-minded. If your child's thinking is off base in certain cases, clearly explain why a particular fact might be important to record or disregard. Have your child take notes on the next page in the textbook. Discuss his choices, and be supportive. Acknowledge him for good decisions about what to include in his notes. Continue the activity with both of you independently taking notes on the third page of the unit. Then compare your respective efforts and discuss any major dissimilarities. Try to make the process interesting and stimulating. You want your child to perceive notetaking as a study resource and a means for improving retention of ideas and getting better grades. A series of positive associations with notetaking increases the likelihood that he'll use the procedure when he studies and that he'll not resent the initial extra time and effort required to record key information.

5.   An alternative to the standard notetaking method is called *mind-mapping* or *chunking.* This method encourages student to represent information graphically. Your child reads a section in the textbook and creates a *graphic picture* or a *word diagram* that represents what he remembers. (Examples of the mind-mapping method can be found under Reading Comprehension.) When the child rereads the material, the mind-map expands by adding more details. Urge your child to be creative. Artistic, playful embellishments are great, the more the better. You want your child to enjoy the process, be inventive, and have positive associations with the technique. Encourage the use of colored pens or pencils to make the process more enjoyable and artistic; it will also help your child retain a visual/mental picture of the information. If your child wishes, he may read the article a third time, and as he reads he can add still more details. Active, colorful, creative

involvement makes learning painless. It is perfectly acceptable to draw a picture of a laser, draw arrows, and put key information in small boxes.

Have your child "read" the finished mind-map and tell you all he has learned about lasers. Then have him put the mind-map aside and tell you all he can recall. Suggest that he try to see in his mind's eye a picture of the mind-map and the information he included in it. (For more about this visualization method, see Memorizing Information; Nonphonetic Words; Spelling Problems.) Verbalizing what he has just learned reinforces memory and allows your child to utilize the auditory modality to supplement the visual and kinesthetic modalities.

6.   Some children prefer the standard form of notetaking, while others prefer the mind-mapping method. Other children may prefer to alternate or use both systems concurrently. It is perfectly acceptable for your child to jury-rig his own system. If he is required to use the format the teacher uses, however, he should be prepared to accommodate himself creatively to the teacher's specific formatting instructions.

Parent–Teacher Conferences

Periodic conferences are vital links in the parent–teacher communication chain. When these meetings function as intended, they can provide you with important updates about your child's academic strengths and weaknesses and with vital information about her behavior, motivation, and effort. The meetings also serve as an early warning system. The teacher can alert you to specific problems such as letter and number reversals; poor reading comprehension; incomplete, late, or sloppy assignments; difficulty following instructions; concentration deficits; or inadequate studying. You and the teacher can then examine appropriate assistance strategies and coordinate your efforts in school and at home.

A good parent–teacher conference will inform you if your child is having difficulty in French because she is not memorizing her verb conjugations, if she is struggling in history because she is not taking good class notes, or if she is getting poor grades in English because she is not carefully proofreading her essays. Don't let these conferences focus only on deficiencies! Your child's talents and accomplishments must also be identified so that she can be rightfully acknowledged and affirmed for her achievements.

Unfortunately, many parent–teacher conferences are little more than a formality in which a great many nonsubstantive platitudes are exchanged. If this has been your experience and if you believe that your child's teacher has not provided precise, meaningful information or specific suggestions about how your child can resolve problems, you must take responsibility for focusing these conferences.

Because many classroom teachers receive little or no formal training in identifying learning deficiencies, they may be tempted to attribute your child's academic problems to misbehavior, laziness, immaturity, or a poor attitude. These explanations are usually inadequate and misleading. Relatively few children are truly developmentally or physically immature. Misbehavior, laziness, and a poor attitude are generally *symptoms* of a learning problem and not the source. These behavioral labels may seem convenient, but they are often simplistic and inaccurate. To use them to explain why a struggling child is inattentive and cannot concentrate, and why she seems unmotivated and unable to keep up with her class obscures the true causal factors. The misbehaving child who appears lazy and has a poor attitude may actually have a specific learning disability (see Attention Deficit Disorder; Auditory Memory; Dyslexia, or a host of other specific learning deficiencies). The implications of misdiagnosis of a child's underlying learning problems are often profound: critically important intervention and remediation may be delayed or never provided, and the child may be permanently damaged—educationally, emotionally, and vocationally.

General, amorphous descriptions of your child's behavior are of little value. Observations such as: "She's misbehaving," "She's not keeping up," "Her reading is poor," "She's creating a disturbance in class," or "She's having trouble with math" may be accurate and well intentioned, but they do little to help you identify and resolve the underlying issues. To get more information, you might respond to these statements as follows: "In what specific ways is she misbehaving? Why do you think she is manifesting these behaviors? Why is she not keeping up with the class? What specific reading deficits does she have? What does she do that creates a disturbance in the class? Is she having difficulty with math concepts or math computations? What can be done to address these problems?"

The more concrete the teacher's feedback, the more productive the conference will be. The child with a minor reading problem may require only short-term basic tutoring. The child with a serious reading problem will require more comprehensive learning assistance (see Learning Disabilities). You cannot afford to accept meaningless platitudes from the teacher. If you do not understand the underlying issues and if you cannot pinpoint your child's specific deficits, you will be unable to evaluate the situation intelligently, make astute choices, and be certain your child is receiving appropriate help.

Because you need information before you can help your child resolve her learning problems, be prepared to ask incisive questions. The teacher may not be able to answer all of your questions, but will realize by the nature of your penetrating queries that you expect him to monitor your child closely.

If a little knowledge is dangerous, no knowledge can be disastrous. Your goal is to contribute effectively to the remedial process. Poorly identified learning problems and skills deficits are a ticking time bomb. Deficits that may seem relatively benign during first or second grade can explode in third or fourth grade. The shrapnel from these explosions can cripple your child for life.

The efficacy of parent–teacher conferences is enhanced when you and the teacher are on the same wavelength. Putting a teacher on the defensive, implying that you are dissatisfied, or suggesting that he is handling the situation incompetently will create an adversarial situation not in your child's best interests. Make every effort to be reasonable, sensitive, and respectful. If communication breaks down, and differences cannot be resolved, confer with the principal or assistant principal (see Communicating with the School; Conferencing with School Officials). Should the disagreements prove irreconcilable, request that your child be placed in another class.

Corrective Strategies

In School

1. If you suspect that your child has learning problems, ask the teacher(s) to complete the Student Evaluation Checklists for elementary school students (page 128), or junior and senior high school students (page 129); (see Learning Disabilities). These checklists will help you identify deficit areas and provide precise feedback about how your child is functioning in the classroom. If your child is already in a special education program, a second form should be completed by the special education teacher. Once your child's deficits are identified, ask the teacher and/or resource specialist to assign appropriate remedial materials for in-class or at-home use. A tutor, educational therapist, or private learning center working with your child will also derive important information from this completed form. The information will give focus to the remedial program, facilitate the selection of teaching strategies, and encourage the establishment of reasonable, targeted improvement goals (see Learning Disabilities).

2. Once specific deficits have been identified, examine with the teacher relevant remedial strategies recommended in this book. Inquire whether he believes it is feasible to implement any of these corrective strategies. Ask for suggestions about alternative techniques to correct your child's learning deficits.

3. Use the Student Evaluation Checklists to focus subsequent parent–teacher conferences. You might say, "You indicated on the checklist

you completed three months ago that my daughter's handwriting is illegible. Have you seen any improvement?" Periodically (every six to nine months) ask the teacher to complete a follow-up evaluation. Use your best judgment about how frequently to request this update; some teachers become resentful if you make what they see as excessive demands. Teachers in junior and senior high school may consider it an imposition to be asked to complete these forms too frequently. These teachers often instruct as many as 150 students each day. Some consider themselves overworked and underpaid and are resistant to filling out forms and being asked to meet with parents on a too frequent basis. This mindset is unfortunate.

At Home

1.   Discuss the teacher's feedback with your child in terms she can understand. Use discretion about showing her the completed Student Evaluation Checklist. You may decide to give your child only selected information from the form. Ask the teacher if there is any objection to your sharing the information. (Ideally, there will be none.) The teacher's evaluation can provide important feedback for your child, especially if she's denying that she has problems in school. Brainstorm with your child how to resolve specific deficits that have been identified during the conference. For example, if your child is not concentrating in class, come up with some ideas together about how to take more personal responsibility for paying attention (see Attention Deficit Disorder). She might have valid ideas about how to improve her reading skills. Your child's active involvement is vital. See Smart Thinking for brainstorming strategies and relevant entries in this book for corrective strategies about how to resolve specific academic deficiencies and behavior problems.

Parents' Rights

The rights of children who require special educational services are mandated in the Education for All Handicapped Children Act of 1975 (PL 94-142) and later amendments. This law requires that schools:[1]

• Provide a free and appropriate public education to all handicapped children, which includes special education and related services to meet their unique educational needs.

• Provide handicapped children with an education in the least restrictive environment on the basis of individual needs.

• Guarantee to each handicapped child an unbiased, valid assessment in a mode of communication normally used by the child.

• Provide parents the opportunity to be involved in educational decisions concerning their child.

Each state supplements and amplifies PL 92-142 with their own educational codes, and counties and local school districts then superimpose their own local guidelines and policies. In California, for example, the state provides the following timeline for testing a child and developing an Individualized Educational Program.

PROCEDURE	DEADLINE FOR COMPLETION
Written Referral	*15 days*
Assessment Plan & Informed Consent	*At least 15 days*
Assessment Team Meeting	*50 days (not to include days in July and August)*
Development & Implementation of IEP*	*Immediately*
Review	*Annually or on Request*

* Individual Educational Program

State and local guidelines cannot in theory supersede federal statutes, but in reality local codes play a major role in determining how federal law is interpreted and implemented. Some states, counties, and districts apply Federal Law 94-162 quite "creatively"—which may have the effect of circumventing the intent of the law.

Parents who agree after diagnostic testing to enroll their child in a special education program may discover a disconcerting lack of consistent quality in the programs offered in different schools, districts, counties, and states. The program in one school may be excellent, while in another school in the same district or a neighboring district it may be woefully inadequate (see Evaluating Special Education Programs).

1. This information is derived from the "Child and Parental Rights in Special Education" manual published by the California State Department of Education.

Most school districts do not permit families to shop around for the best remedial services. Even though you may be convinced that a particular program or teacher in another district or even in another school within the same district might best serve your child's needs, districts generally discourage interdistrict and intradistrict transfers (enrolling a child in a school other than the one the child would normally attend). In most instances, children qualifying for special education are enrolled in either a resource (RSP) program or a self-contained LH (learning handicapped) class (also referred to as a special day class) at their local school. Some districts, however, may assign children with learning problems to special magnet schools.

You have a legitimate right to expect that your child will be provided with quality remedial assistance, and you have a compelling responsibility to speak out when the local program is inadequate, poorly conceived, or poorly taught. As is the case in most bureaucracies, "the squeaky wheel usually gets the grease." Unfortunately, the deficiencies in a school's special education program may not be easily remedied. This is especially true when districts are poorly funded, have an entrenched, threatened, and unenlightened administration, or are staffed by inadequately trained special education personnel.

If you are wrestling with whether to become embroiled in a confrontation with the school system, let your intuition be your guide. If your child's needs are not being met and if the classroom teacher, resource specialist, LH teacher, school psychologist, or principal cannot allay your concerns, the next step is to bring these issues to the attention of the district superintendent (see Communicating with the School; Conferencing with School Officials; Parent–Teacher Conferences). Balance any trepidation you might have about approaching this "luminary" with the realization that the superintendent is a public servant whose salary is paid with your taxes. Should the superintendent be unwilling to meet with you or should he or she be unwilling to make an honest effort to address the issues and find mutually acceptable solutions, you can then exercise your federally mandated rights and file a formal complaint, as described in Steps for Due Process, following.

If you believe your child is being unfairly denied special educational services, you may contest the decisions of the local school district. The U.S. Constitution and federal and state laws and regulations guarantee due process. You have the right to request a formal and impartial hearing to resolve disagreements about special education programs and services. The hearing process ensures that federal and state-mandated rules and time frames are followed. Local school districts are required to provide specific information about the hearing procedure.

Steps for Due Process

1.   Submit a written request to the Superintendent of Public instruction for a due process hearing. If both parties agree to mediation, the conference must be scheduled and completed within fifteen days of the date the hearing request is filed. The hearing officer mediating the disagreement must be from outside the local school district, and the hearing process must be completed within forty-five days, although exceptions are permitted if both parties agree. You can have access to any documents in your child's educational records, and you can be represented at the meeting by a private educational psychologist, educational therapist, mental health specialist, child advocate, or attorney who understands the academic issues and is familiar with the appropriate federal, state, and local codes. You can also refuse permission to place your child in any recommended program.

2.   If a school district refuses to participate in the hearing (this is unlikely) or if you disagree with the decision rendered, you may appeal to the court. This is obviously an expensive and time-consuming last resort.

3.   You can file a complaint with local or state superintendent that alleges that your child's

school is in noncompliance with federal and state law.

4. If you find yourself in conflict with your school district, request a copy of the district's *Parents' Rights Manual.* This manual, which districts are legally mandated to make available, will spell out the criteria for qualifying for diagnostic testing, the time frames for providing testing, the standards for admission to special education programs, and grievance protocols.

The decision to confront a local school district and create an adversarial situation should hinge on the urgency of your concerns. Your child's academic and vocational future and emotional well-being may hang in the balance. The prospect of confronting the school district may be unpleasant, but the alternative—reluctant acceptance of a flawed education program—could be disastrous for your child. You are your child's most important advocate, and you have the right to take a stand when a stand is clearly required.

Passive Learning

Passive learners may spend a great deal of time doing homework, but if they are not actively engaged in the educational process, they are simply going through the motions of studying. Ironically, some passive learners are actually quite conscientious and motivated. Their efforts, however, are typically scattered and nonproductive because they don't know how to study efficiently. Like cars on an icy road, they spin their wheels with little or no forward momentum.

Most passive learners are *not* conscientious and motivated and are resistant to learning, studying, and doing homework. Seeing little or no value in mastering new skills, their primary concern is to complete their work quickly and with a minimum amount of effort. For them, studying translates into little more than a mindless procedure of turning the pages of their textbooks. Mastery is simply not a priority in their lives.

Passive learners share certain characteristics. Unlike active, intellectually engaged classmates, complacent students lack the motivation to establish personal educational goals, identify challenges, hone academic skills, or knock down the barriers impeding their progress. The consequences of this apathetic mindset are marginal school achievement and poor grades. Their borderline academic track record further undermines their already tenuous self-confidence and motivation. Lacking pride, they typically submit incomplete, shoddy, or late work. Content to memorize facts without understanding the significance of the information, they have no interest (or lack the skills) to search beneath the surface for important underlying issues and concepts (see Critical Thinking; Reading Comprehension; Smart Thinking; Study Skills). Perfunctory, inefficient study habits and superficial learning inevitably impair comprehension, retention, and test performance.

Some children who might otherwise be active learners may become passive learners because of poor teaching. Students who are subjected to daily mind-numbing lectures and required to memorize and regurgitate facts ad nauseam often end up cerebrally anesthetized. An endless stream of seemingly meaningless handouts and repetitive drilling can dull the brain of even the most highly motivated child. Some children may continue to learn under these conditions; most will shut down and turn off (see Behavior and Attitude; Effort and Motivation).

Learning problems can also cause children to learn passively (see Atypical Learning Problems; Learning Disabilities; Underachievement). Struggling children often acquire a pattern of counterproductive behaviors as a defense against failure and feelings of frustration, inadequacy, and futility. Although some students with learning problems may continue to study diligently, many others simply give up. The likelihood of shutdown increases when underlying learning deficits are not properly diagnosed or are inadequately treated.

Students who feel overwhelmed by seemingly insurmountable obstacles have three options: they can grit their teeth and continue to plug away; they can express their frustration and anger by acting out; or they can withdraw into a shell and become academically uninvolved. By not investing themselves emotionally and intellectually in the learning process, they unconsciously rationalize that they are not really failing because they are not really trying.

The starting point in helping your child become an active learner is to identify why she is learning passively. If she has learning deficits, these must be diagnosed and treated, either in school or by a private educational therapist. If your child is not establishing personal performance goals, you must encourage her to work for realistic payoffs such as a B on her next spelling test (see Goals). You must also help her acquire the requisite planning and academic skills to achieve her objectives. If you suspect psychological or family issues are causing her to learn passively, have her evaluated by a competent mental health professional. The alternative is not to intervene and hope that the problem will go away. This path is fraught with grave risks and potentially disastrous academic and vocational consequences.

Your child must acquire effective study skills if she is to make the transition from passive to active learning. With systematic instruction, she can learn pragmatic methods that will actively engage her brain as she learns and studies. She can learn pragmatic methods for managing time, recording assignments, getting organized, meeting deadlines, asking incisive questions when she reads and studies, preparing for tests, identifying key information, remembering facts, and anticipating what is likely to be on an exam (see Memorizing Information; Notetaking; Reading Comprehension; Study Skills; and other relevant entries).

Most children enter kindergarten with a ravenous appetite to learn. They eagerly want to master new skills and acquire information about their world. Those who lose this natural enthusiasm are waving a red flag. Unless effective academic assistance is provided, a pattern of intellectual lethargy could persist throughout life and produce disastrous consequences.

Like unused muscles, unstimulated minds quickly atrophy. If your child seems unmotivated and unenthusiastic about learning, you have justification for concern and a compelling obligation to do everything in your power to stoke your child's intellectual furnace. The passive learner who is content to coast mindlessly through school will be content to coast mindlessly through life. If she is not coaxed from her comfort zone, her prospects for self-actualization are virtually nil.

Corrective Strategies

In School

1. Ask the teacher to evaluate your child's motivation, attitude, and performance. Can she do the required work? (If she can't, she should be tested by the school psychologist.) Does your child appear depressed, withdrawn, or insecure? (If she does, she should be evaluated by a mental health professional.) Does she cave in when she encounters a challenge? Does she give up when she experiences a setback or makes a mistake? Is she chronically lethargic or sleepy? (If she is, she should be examined by a physician.) Is she passive even when the material being taught is interesting? If your child is manifesting any symptoms of underlying educational or psychological problems that neither you nor the teacher feel competent to address, consult with the school psychologist, resource specialist, and your family physician. If appropriate, request that your child be diagnostically evaluated (see Bouncing Back from Setbacks and Learning from Mistakes; Learning Disabilities; Parents' Rights; Psychological Overlay and Psychological Problems; Self-Esteem and Self-Confidence).

2. The most basic antidote for passive learning is to stimulate students and engage them intellectually and emotionally. Creative, talented teachers encourage children to establish short-term and long-term goals. They show them how to plan, help them understand the rationale for learning today's lesson, and demonstrate the practical applications of the skills and information being taught. These are critical steps in the process of encouraging active learning. If your

child is learning passively, discuss your concerns with her teacher. Ask if he would be willing to work with your child (and ideally the entire class) on goal-setting and strategic planning. Diplomatically inquire if there are alternative methods the teacher could use to help your child (and other students) better appreciate the relevancy of the academic skills and information they are expected to learn. It would be nonstrategic and counterproductive to make the teacher feel that you blame him for your child's passivity. Your goal is to encourage the teacher to make your child's educational experiences as dynamic and stimulating as possible, not to make him defensive or cause him to dismiss you as an unreasonable, meddling parent.

At Home

1.   By intentionally creating opportunities to learn together, you will play a vital role in developing your child's enthusiasm for learning. An exploratory hike in the woods, a visit to the library to research a topic, a trip to a marsh to observe wildlife, an excursion to a planetarium or aquarium, or a discussion about current events at the dinner table are important catalysts in the equation that produces active thinking and learning. You want your child to sense your curiosity about life and share your enthusiasm for learning.

2.   Encourage your child to think about *what* she is learning and *why* she is being asked to learn certain material. Ask thought-provoking questions such as: "Why do you need to know how to do fraction problems? Let's look at a birthday cake. Would you prefer to eat $1/8$ of the cake or $1/5$? What are the advantages of knowing how to spell? How could we preserve this forest so that your children can also enjoy hiking through it?" Convey your own enthusiasm for life and learning. It is infectious!

3.   Determine your child's preferred learning modality (auditory, visual, or kinesthetic) and her preferred thinking mode (logic, feelings, concepts, information), and encourage her to employ her natural talents and preferences. Rely on your observations, the teacher's observations, and your

child's own perceptions about how she learns best. (See *In Their Own Way* by Thomas Armstrong and *Frames of Mind* by Howard Gardener for discussions of learning styles and preferences. See Resource List at the back of this book.) Make all the material that your child is being asked to learn as relevant and interesting as possible. For example, you might compare learning important historical dates with a quarterback learning the plays, a dancer learning steps, or a violinist learning scales. If your child likes sports, encourage her to compare learning important facts in her history class with learning key plays before a basketball game (for example, Constitution 1789/ articles 7/ amendments 22). Have her practice learning number facts or chemical formulas in the same way. If she is an auditory learner, have her pretend that she must give a speech that contains the information she needs to learn for her next science test. Have her practice giving the speech to an imaginary audience or to you. By hearing herself recite the information, she will be better able to·remember it. The goal after sufficient practice is for her to give the speech without looking at notes. This will indicate that she has understood and mastered the material. (See Auditory Memory; Identifying Important Information; Memorizing Information; Preparing for Tests; Visual Memory.)

4.   Share your own active thinking process with your child. Do projects together that involve research or planning, and have her participate actively in the investigation process. For example, involve your child in selecting a vacation destination and in planning what to do, where to stay, and how to get there (see Planning Ahead). Discuss the pluses and minuses of driving versus taking a plane or a train. Model how you critically evaluate options and choices, and encourage your child to do the same.

Ask questions about the material your child is studying ("Why did Lincoln want to prevent the South from seceding?") and urge her to ask questions of you and the teacher. After providing some guidance, have her search out answers to questions. Remember to affirm and acknowledge her enthusiastically for progress!

Peer Pressure

Children naturally gravitate to peer groups that share their attitudes, values, feelings, and life experiences. Athletes generally associate with other athletes. Students who enjoy acting or rock music pick friends who share the same aesthetic tastes. Successful students identify and socialize with other successful students. This principle applies to struggling children as well: They typically orient toward classmates also having difficulty in school.

A child's need for a peer group identity, comradeship, and acceptance and affirmation can be compelling. For an insecure child, the desire to seek like-minded friends and find refuge in a world that may be perceived as hostile is often consuming. The group may become the child's surrogate family, and he may look to them for the respect and encouragement he cannot find elsewhere. If your child is struggling, he may identify so intensely with his friends that he will vehemently resist any suggestion to disassociate himself from the group.

The collective energy of a peer group—whether positive or negative—affirms and reinforces the self-perceptions and values of its individual members. The negative effects of the group dynamic can be seen in the nonadaptive and self-deprecating behavior of some youngsters with serious learning problems who have been enrolled for years in special day classes. To protect themselves from feeling defective, these marginally performing students may band together to create their own social identity and isolate themselves from the mainstream. Shared negative school experiences, nonadaptive attitudes, learning deficits, low self-confidence, and psychological defense mechanisms bind them together. The peer group functions as a buffer and insulates the members from demands and expectations they are convinced they cannot possibly meet (see Evaluating Special Education Programs; Learning Disabilities; Negative Attitude toward School; Psychological Problems and Psychological Overlay).

When a peer group generates negative energy and attitudes, nonadaptive behaviors may become the standard for social acceptance by the group. Teenagers who have been in a no-win school situation for years may express frustration and anger by acting out, shutting down, resisting help, becoming demoralized, and/or acquiring a range of counterproductive social behaviors. In extreme cases, they may vent despair in destructiveness, drinking, drugs, vandalism, or theft (see Behavior and Attitude; Bouncing Back from Setbacks and Learning from Mistakes; Disregarding Consequences; Self-Esteem and Self-Confidence.)

Struggling students generally seek friends who share their life experiences, but there are exceptions. Some children who are not doing well in school remain motivated and choose academically successful friends. If, however, the gap between their performance and that of their achieving friends widens, it is possible these friendships will not endure. The contrast in performance levels may become so blatant and demoralizing that the marginally performing youngster may gravitate to other academically deficient students with whom they can more easily identify.

As children mature, their peer group's value system increasingly influences their own values. This is especially true when children are insecure, highly impressionable, and lacking in self-esteem (see Self-Esteem and Self-Confidence). Parents who perceive the potentially negative effect that a nonachieving peer group is having on their child and who want to counteract this negative energy may feel a compelling need to intervene. Unfortunately, direct attempts by parents to control a child's selection of friends can backfire and trigger resistance, resentment, and unpleasant showdowns. These unpleasant encounters may cause the reactive child to become even more enmeshed in the peer group.

If you are convinced that your child is manifesting poor judgment in selecting friends, the alternative to a family showdown is to seek guidance from a mental health professional. A well-trained counselor or therapist can help your child examine conscious and unconscious feelings about himself and his abilities. A mental health professional can also help your child examine counterproductive behaviors and attitudes and confront underlying issues that are influencing this choice of friends (see Anger and Frustration).

If learning or study skills deficits are undermining your child's school performance and self-confidence, the deficits must be identified and remedied (see Parents' Rights). As your child begins to feel better about himself and achieve academically, he'll choose friends who also have a positive self-image, and your concerns about the influence of the peer group will dissipate (see Fear of Success/Failure/Competition).

Corrective Strategies

In School

1.   If you are concerned about your child's choice of friends, talk to the school counselor or principal. Ask for ideas and suggestions about how you could handle the situation (see Communicating with the School; Conferencing with School Officials). If your child is getting into trouble because of association with particular children, intervention is urgent. Realize that the school has no authority to prevent your child from associating with other children on campus unless the group is considered to be a gang or is breaking the law, violating school codes, or causing disruptions. Ideally, your child's school will have in place a counseling program designed to help students examine and understand peer group dynamics. If such a resource does not exist, become proactive in encouraging the school district to establish an effective intervention program. The school has a vested interest in creating a positive learning environment, discouraging gang affiliations and antisocial behavior, helping students understand themselves and their actions.

At Home

1.   If you conclude that your child's peer group is exerting a negative influence and encouraging counterproductive behavior and attitudes, you must intervene. Deciding what situations you can handle effectively at home and what situations need to be addressed by a mental health professional demands a judgment call on your part. If your child refuses to look at the issues and the potential consequences of his actions and attitudes (see Disregarding Consequences) and is clearly on a collision course with reality, seek professional help.

If the situation is less urgent, experiment with the DIBS Method described on page 190. This method is designed to help your child examine problems and develop specific solutions to underlying issues that may be causing him to identify with a particular peer group. If you decide to consult a therapist, ask your pediatrician, family physician, or school psychologist for a referral.

Performance on Standardized Tests

Standardized tests are designed to determine your child's level of achievement in specific skill areas. To obtain comparative statistical data and establish national norms, the tests are administered to large numbers of children of the same age and at the same grade level throughout the country. This process is called *standardization*. Below is a facsimile of typical data produced by standardized achievement tests.

The Raw Scores represent the total number of correct answers that a hypothetical fourth grader had on the test. The Stanine Score is a statistical representation of the correct answers on a scale from 1 to 9 and indicates the child's performance relative to the other hundreds of thousands of children who took the exam. The Percentile score is another way of statistically ranking a child's performance relative to other children taking the test. In this hypothetical case, out of every 100 children of the same age and grade level taking the test, the child scored higher in reading comprehension than 45 children and lower than 53 children. (The 99th percentile is the highest statistical score that one can receive on a standardized test. A child who scores at the 50th percentile is considered to be approximately at grade level.) The tests usually also indicate how a child compares to children in the same geographical area. The norms on some tests are so specific that they can indicate how the scores of students attending a particular private school compare with those of other students attending other private schools (see Understanding Diagnostic Test Results).

The standardized testing procedure is currently being scrutinized by educators, for several reasons. Some believe that the tests do not adequately measure students' skills. Others argue that important academic skills are not being evaluated by the tests. Many educators also contend

FASCIMILE TEST RESULT REPORT

	RAW SCORE	STANINE SCORE	PERCENTILE GRADE	EQUIVALENCY
Reading comprehension	27	4	46	3.7
Vocabulary	32	5	48	3.9
Math concepts	37	6	54	4.3
Math computations	35	5	50	4.0

that administrators, parents, teachers, and the media place far too much importance on the test results. They point out that the performance ratings of principals and local, county, and state superintendents are often based primarily on their students' test performance. To improve scores, some school districts exert intense pressure on teachers to put the priority on teaching those skills that will be covered on the tests. In some cases, this pressure to "teach to the tests" and improve student scores is causing sound educational philosophy, academic objectives, and teaching procedures to be degraded.

Despite the limitations and potential misapplications of standardized tests, the comparative scores *do* provide valuable information that teachers, school psychologists, and resource specialists can use to identify students with deficient skills. The fourth grader who takes a standardized exam in the second month of fourth grade (4.2) and receives a score of 3.2 (third grade, second month) in reading comprehension is functioning one year below grade level. In theory, teachers and administrators would consider this score justification for targeting the child for learning assistance.

Tragically, one of the most valuable uses of standardized test scores—the identification of children requiring remedial help—is being subverted by fiscally troubled school districts. Although logic dictates that the learning deficits of a child testing one year below grade level should be diagnosed and remedied, many school districts myopically insist that students' skills must be more than two years below grade level before they will agree to provide learning assistance (see Individual Educational Program [IEP]; Learning Disabilities; Mainstreaming and Special Day Classes). As a consequence, children with less severe learning problems slip through gaping holes in the diagnostic screen and are forced to tread water through twelve years of school. These children are given help only when their problems become incapacitating. By this point the educational and psychological damage may already be

irreversible (see Atypical Learning Problems; Underachievement).

Children who score below the norm (usually below the 50th percentile) may have specific or nonspecific academic deficits that range from subtle to severe. These deficits may be attributable to poor teaching, learning problems, family problems, emotional problems, and/or cultural or environmental factors. Although a child's test performance can be skewed by test anxiety and distractibility (see Attention Deficit Disorder), the scores generally offer a relatively reliable profile of a child's skills. Children who test below grade level on standardized tests, receive poor grades on teacher-designed tests, and struggle in class are clearly prime candidates for more extensive diagnostic testing.

Current testing procedures may be inadequate and the way in which test scores are utilized may be flawed, but reality demands that children learn to accommodate themselves to the testing system. Students will be required to take standardized tests throughout their education. Those who want to go to college, win scholarships, enter selective training programs in the military, attend graduate school, pass professional and vocational licensing exams, and earn promotions must figure out how to get the best possible scores on these tests. Techniques for doing so are described in corrective strategies, following. Note that students with documented learning disabilities can apply to take untimed college entrance exams (SATs). Consult your child's school counselor for qualification criteria and procedures.

Corrective Strategies

In School

1.   If your child is scoring more than one year below grade level, request a diagnostic evaluation by the school psychologist or resource specialist. If your child doesn't qualify for learning assistance (see Parents' Rights), you may need to provide help at home. (Refer to Math; Reading

Comprehension; Spelling Problems; and other relevant entries for remedial strategies in each area). If you feel that you lack the skills or patience to provide tutorial assistance at home, consider hiring a tutor or educational therapist or enrolling your child at a private learning center.

2. If your child has difficulty with test taking because of concentration deficits, anxiety, or visual accuracy deficits, ask the teacher or resource specialist if your child could take some practice tests to improve her confidence and reduce any phobias, fears, or procedural problems she might have. If appropriate, she might take these practice tests at home.

3. Ask the teacher if she can use some obsolete tests to demonstrate methods for eliminating implausible multiple-choice answers. This procedure will reduce the odds of students selecting wrong answers. She could also teach students how to examine the multiple-choice answers *before* actually beginning to read the comprehension passage. This strategic procedure helps students focus on ferreting out the key information that test designers consider important. Providing students with opportunities to practice taking obsolete standardized tests familiarizes them with test-taking procedures and this test savvy can significantly reduce their anxiety. Discussing the correct answers as a class activity also allows struggling students to understand the analytical thinking process used by their more academically successful classmates.

At Home

1. If your child's scores on standardized tests are not consistent with her performance in class, test anxiety or test phobia could be the culprit. Some children tense up when taking tests (see Test Anxiety). Showing your child basic relaxation techniques could reduce the stress factor. Suggest that she close her eyes and visualize herself confidently taking the test and doing well on it. Urge her to imprint this image of success in her mind. This preview requires only

a few seconds and can significantly lessen the anticipatory panic some children experience while waiting for a test to be handed out. Also urge your child to close her eyes for several seconds and take two or three deep breaths before starting to answer questions. Deep breathing should help her relax and reduce anxiety. (A note of caution: explain to your child that more than two or three deep breaths could cause her to hyperventilate and become dizzy or even pass out.) You want your child to program herself with positive, as opposed to negative, expectations (see Self-Esteem and Self-Confidence). Refer to the Resource List at the back of this book for more suggestions.

2. Children with concentration problems usually have difficulty with standardized tests. If your child forgets to leave a blank line on her answer sheet when she cannot answer a question, she will incorrectly mark all subsequent answers. Her scores will also be skewed if she becomes distracted while taking the test. There are no quick fixes for concentration problems. Discuss with your child the value of concentrating while taking tests. Explain the importance of carefully matching the correct line on the answer sheet to the question being answered. Brainstorm together how she could discipline herself to focus on this important test-taking detail. Ask the teacher for a blank computer-scored answer sheet or make one up yourself to make the demonstration more relevant. The teacher might even be willing to give you a standardized test at your child's grade level that is no longer being used by the school district. Use this to practice the procedure for accurately filling out a test booklet or answer sheet. Demonstrate how placing one answer on the wrong line can cause all subsequent answers to be wrong. Then experiment with ways to make sure the answer sheet is marked accurately. Your child might, for instance, cover all but the line she is working on with her test booklet and move the edge down one line each time she answers a question. (See Attention Deficit Disorder and Attention to Details

for descriptions of the symptoms of concentration problems and suggestions about how to improve accuracy.)

3.   If your child has a tracking problem (reads inaccurately and loses her place), she will probably have a difficult time filling out answer sheets properly. Because her eyes move erratically, she could easily lose her place and be at a significant disadvantage when taking standardized tests and marking answer sheets. The practice procedure described above could be beneficial in helping her learn how to compensate for tracking problems (see Dyslexia; Inaccurate Copying).

 Phonics

During the last thirty-five years, educators and textbook publishers have debated the pluses and minuses of teaching children to read phonetically or by sight. The *phonics method* teaches children the sounds of individual letter and clumps of letters and has them use these sounds to decode words. Advocates of this approach contend that students who can learn and apply the rules and conventions that govern how letters and combinations of letters are pronounced possess an invaluable tool that they can use to read most words in the English language.

Proponents of the *sight approach* contend that many words in the English language do not conform to consistent phonetic rules (see Nonphonetic Words). Because of these exceptions, they maintain that reading should not be taught phonetically, but that students should be taught instead to recognize and link the entire word with its pronunciation. Arguing that the process of sounding out each word is cumbersome and reduces reading speed, they advocate carefully controlling the difficulty level of newly introduced words and providing ample practice so that mastery can be achieved. If this procedure is followed, they assert, children can quickly and easily learn to recognize most words by sight and achieve reading fluency.

The majority of children who have no underlying perceptual deficits can learn to read using either the phonetic or the sight method and can usually decipher and remember most words after a few exposures (see Atypical Learning Problems; Dyslexia; Learning Disabilities; Under-

achievement). Only extremely difficult words require extra effort. The majority of so-called *natural* readers rarely remember as adults how they were taught to read. Both the sight and phonetic approach are equally effective.

In contrast, poor readers never forget their struggle to decipher words. These children are typically found in the lowest reading groups in their classes; for them learning to read aloud is a nightmare. The embarrassment they experience every day in class may cause permanent emotional scars and trigger a profound aversion to reading that could persist throughout their lives. Because reading plays such a central role in academic success, many poor readers conclude erroneously they lack intelligence, despite the fact they may be as or more intelligent than classmates who can read effortlessly (see Reading Aloud).

The instructional pendulum currently appears to have swung back from the sight reading approach emphasized in many textbooks during the 1970s and early 1980s to a phonetic approach, and most elementary school reading programs now incorporate this method.[1] The phonics

---

1. Whole language has become quite popular in many school districts across the country. In this method, children do not receive formal, systematic reading or phonics instruction. Instead, reading is integrated into the science, math, history, and language components of the curriculum. Current research suggests, however, that this system is not as effective in teaching reading to learning disabled students as the more traditional phonics intructional method.

approach involves two steps: word attack and blending. Children "attack" (sound out) each phoneme and then link or blend the phoneme to subsequent phonemes.

Problems with phonics can usually be linked to specific decoding deficits in one or more of the following areas: visual tracking (seeing words accurately and perceiving syllables in the proper sequence), visual memory (remembering what is seen), auditory discrimination (hearing the difference between sounds), or auditory memory (remembering what is heard). These perceptual deficits, which are primary symptoms of a learning disability, can erect formidable obstacles for children no matter what reading method the teacher uses. Chronic reading inaccuracies involving letter, word, and number reversals, letter and word omissions, and transpositions are symptomatic of dyslexia. (See Auditory Memory; Dyslexia; Learning Disabilities; Visual Memory.)

As a rule, children with reading problems respond best to a phonetic approach. Because of the previously mentioned phonetic exceptions, however, these children must also learn to recognize many common words by sight (such as *two, could, lieutenant, rough, buoyant, thought, count, loud, laugh, colonel, although, bought, bough, though, caught,* and many others. See Spelling Problems).

Children with significant reading and decoding deficits often have difficulty learning to read whether they are taught with the phonetic or the sight method. Because of their struggle to decode words, they also often have difficulty comprehending the meaning of what they read (see Reading Comprehension). Fortunately, many innovative and highly effective remedial methodologies have been developed to help children with profound reading problems. These methods, which usually incorporate multisensory instruction, teach children how to utilize specific alternative sensory modalities (or a combination of learning modalities) to compensate for their deficits. The methods include Orton-Gillingham, Slingerland, neurological impress, neurolinguistic

programming, and the Lindamood Auditory Discrimination In-Depth Program. Talented, well-trained teachers, resource specialists, tutors, and educational therapists will experiment with different remedial approaches until they find one that works best for your child. (See Auditory Discrimination; Auditory Memory; Visual Memory.)

Corrective Strategies

In School

1.   (Elementary School, ES) Ask the teacher to alert you if she observes your child struggling with phonics. If he's having difficulty, ask if the teacher can provide additional help in, before, or after class. Also request supplemental materials for use at home. (Remedial classroom materials are included in the Resource List at the back of the book.)

2.   If the teacher indicates your child is having difficulty learning to read, request an evaluation by the school psychologist or resource specialist to determine if there is a perceptual dysfunction. If tests reveal auditory memory, auditory discrimination, visual memory, visual discrimination, visual tracking, word attack, and/or blending difficulties, request that the resource or reading specialist provide supplemental remedial assistance. (See Evaluating Special Education Programs; Mainstreaming and Special Day Classes; Parents' Rights.)

At Home

1.   (ES) Ask the teacher to indicate your child's current reading level and ask her (or the librarian) to suggest interesting books or materials that you might read together. Because you want your child to feel successful when reading and to acquire positive associations with the process, you should initially select books that are slightly below your child's "comfort" reading level. Read a sentence and then ask your child to read the same sentence, a modeling procedure designed to set your child up to read more successfully. Patiently help him sound out challenging words. Be

supportive and affirming. Use a pencil eraser or your finger to divide the word into syllables. (Your objective is for your child to learn to divide words into syllables without you.) Once your child can sound out the word, blending syllables together is next. Have him write difficult words on index cards for later review. (For visualization techniques to use in conjunction with flash cards, see Nonphonetic Words; Spelling Problems.)

2. (ES) Set up a system in which you give your child a point for each difficult word he can read aloud when you work together. The points could be applied to winning a reward such as a special toy or a trip to the zoo. For each word he can still read at the end of the week, he could receive bonus points. As his reading fluency develops, increase the number of sentences that you read before your child begins to read.

3. (ES) When it seems appropriate, experiment by not reading the sentences first. By no longer modeling how to read the sentences, you are, in effect, withdrawing a security blanket. Remove this blanket slowly and be especially sensitive if your child becomes anxious. As he progresses, slowly increase the difficulty of the reading material. Ask your child's teacher to reassess his reading level periodically. Don't be surprised if your child struggles with words you thought were already mastered. Children with reading problems frequently need many exposures to words before they achieve mastery. If you find yourself losing patience, quit for the day. If losing your patience is a chronic problem, consider hiring a tutor or enrolling your child in a private reading program. Communicating disappointment, anger, or frustration will only compound your child's negative associations with reading and further undermine his self-confidence. To admit that you cannot be your child's tutor is not an admission of failure as a parent! Rather, your realization makes a positive statement about your honesty and clarity. You recognize that your goal is to help your child become a better reader, and you also recognize that

becoming impatient works at cross-purposes with attaining this objective.

4. (ES) Ask the teacher to lend you a copy of the Dolch list, which contains words grouped according to grade level. With creativity, you and your child can make a game out of learning these words. For example, put the words on flash cards and award points for every word your child identifies. Or write a clue on the back of each card that tells where a small prize such as a cookie or a dime is located. Each time your child can read a word, turn over the card and help him read the clue. After he has enough clues, he can look for the prize. Another graded list you might find useful is the Key Word Inventory (see Resource List at back of book). You might also examine, at your teacher supply store or in catalogs, other supplemental remedial reading materials that focus on developing phonics skills; see Resource List.

5. (Junior High/High School, J/HS) A protracted academic struggle can cause teenagers with basic word attack, blending, and phonics problems to become very sensitive about their reading deficits. Because they feel inadequate and vulnerable, they may deny they have a problem despite overwhelming evidence to the contrary. Penetrating this defensive wall can be very challenging. Your child, however, might agree to let you help him read a popular teen or music magazine. You might offer to buy him a subscription to *Mad* or *Seventeen* or *Sports Illustrated* and, if he agrees, you could spend ten minutes each evening reading it together, using the techniques described above. Don't be surprised, however, if your teenager refuses your help. You cannot force him to accept assistance. Assure your child that help from you or a tutor will be available at any time. You may succeed in making him more receptive if you use examples (of famous athletes perhaps) that clearly demonstrate how practice can dramatically improve one's performance. Be patient, supportive, and affirming. Suggest that he make a list of difficult words and use the Dolch list or the Key Word Inventory to supplement that list.

6. If your child is enrolled in a remedial program, periodically meet with the resource specialist to coordinate efforts, assess progress, and identify problem areas. If your child does not qualify for help in school and you believe assistance is vital, assert your rights and insist on compliance with state and federal law (see Parents' Rights). If you believe your child requires more help than the school can provide, consider hiring a qualified tutor or educational therapist or enrolling in a private reading or learning disabilities center.

Planning Ahead

As children progress into the upper grades, academic success can hinge on their ability to plan and organize assignments effectively. They must be able to develop a practical strategy for writing a history term paper. They must allocate time for library research and for taking notes, and they must also factor in sufficient time to check footnotes, prepare a bibliography, write and edit a first draft, and write and proofread the final draft. If they are studying for an exam, they must budget time to reread the assigned units in their textbooks, review their notes, and answer practice test questions (see Disorganization; Goals; Grades, Inadequate Study Time; Preparing for Tests; Priorities; Procrastination; Recording Assignments; Study Skills; Time Management). No matter how bright and potentially capable they may be, students must be able to get the job done efficiently and effectively, or their grades will suffer.

Conscientious students face the same dilemmas their parents face: they must reconcile a seemingly infinite number of obligations with a limited amount of available time and energy. In addition to many academic responsibilities, students must allocate time for chores, paper routes, scout meetings, piano lessons, karate classes, gymnastics, part-time jobs, and/or after-school sports. Those who cannot handle these obligations are destined to "spin their wheels." The lack of forward momentum and the sense that they are losing the school battle often triggers stress, anxiety, demoralization, and possible academic shutdown. (See Behavior and Attitude; Effort and Motivation; Inadequate Study Time; Problem Solving; Smart Thinking; Time Management.)

Good students intentionally develop "task interception radar." Based upon past experience, they anticipate what they need to do to get the job done successfully, and plan accordingly. They establish goals and priorities (see Behavior and Performance Guidelines; Goals), create a study schedule, and develop a practical and efficient strategy for attaining stated objectives. This process requires focused effort, effective use of resources, and an appreciation for the principles of cause and effect. ("If I follow these logical steps, I can anticipate these consequences. If I don't follow these steps, I can anticipate these less pleasant consequences.") (See Disregarding Consequences.) Careful planning initially entails additional work, but good students recognize that the derived payoffs—good grades, pride, self-confidence, and, eventually, more free time—justify the extra effort.

Children who do not plan ahead are in continual crisis mode. They typically fail to finish homework and submit assignments late. They leave book reports to the last minute. They put off studying for tests until the night before. The predictable effects—poor grades, frustration, demoralization, and lowered expectations—invariably produce stress for everyone in the family (see Incomplete Assignments; Self-Esteem and Self-Confidence).

Learning good planning skills does not have to be painful, restrictive, boring, or even formal. An excursion to the beach may require little more than a simple written or mental checklist of things to do. Long-term projects involving many steps and components, such as writing a term paper, clearly require more careful planning. Through trial and error, strategic students discover that complex tasks are far easier to control when the required steps are written down and the target dates and check-off completion columns are created. They also realize that developing a flow chart and a daily schedule will facilitate their organization of these assignments.

Children who get into the habit of planning ahead apply the techniques automatically and unconsciously whenever they are faced with a project requiring careful, systematic preparation. Their strategic thinking, goal-directed effort, pragmatic prioritization of responsibilities, effective time management, and efficient organization can usually make long-term projects and challenges that initially seemed overwhelming quite manageable.

To help your child acquire good planning skills, you must provide a model for how to plan and repeated opportunities to apply and practice the techniques. Once your child realizes that good planning and organization will make life easier and permit her to attain her goals, she will voluntarily incorporate the procedures into her daily modus operandi. The payoffs she receives will be her incentive to continue using the procedures, and before long, good planning will become second nature.

Corrective Strategies

In School

1.   If you conclude that your child does not have good planning skills, ask if the teacher if he concurs. If you suspect other students in the class may also lack these important skills, you might diplomatically ask the teacher to incorporate planning activities into the curriculum. For example, all the students could learn how to systematically plan a field trip, class party, or community service project. Older students might develop an effective plan for studying for a science final exam or writing a term paper. This plan could be a cooperative effort in which the entire class participates. All students might then be encouraged to use the plan in preparing for the exam. To gauge the efficacy of the plan, each student could privately compare his or her test results with previous test results. (No pressure, of course, should be exerted on students to share their grades publically.)

At Home

1.   To help your child develop good planning skills, encourage the following:

• Apply planning skills to real-life situations. ("What steps must be taken to plan for the family picnic?")

• Experiment with different types of plans. ("When we build the dog house, let's make the project easier by developing a flow chart that lists the steps, a time schedule for each phase, a task sheet that indicates who is responsible for doing specific work, and a check-off list of completed tasks. This will help us organize and manage the project and work together more efficiently.")

• Analyze why certain plans are more successful than others. ("The plan for fixing your bike didn't work. What went wrong?)

• Incorporate planning into different contexts. ("What do we need to pack for the camping trip, and how can we load the gear most efficiently in the van?")

2.   Share with your child how you plan your own projects. For example, you might have a project at work that you must complete or a project at home that you want to do. Model the specific methods you would use to manage and

organize the work. If your style is to plan mentally, "map out" your thinking process on paper so your child can see what is involved. Discuss your reasoning and be receptive if your child offers ideas and suggestions. If the ideas are off target, explain patiently why you have reservations about a specific suggestion. Share and model your analytical thinking process without lecturing or being pedantic.

3.   For other corrective strategies to help improve your child's planning, time-management, goal setting, and organizational skills, refer to relevant entries in this book.

Preparing for Tests

Students must be able to prepare efficiently and effectively for tests if they want to achieve academic success. Those who possess this ability represent a relatively small and elite minority. The vast majority of students never acquire first-rate test preparation skills. Convinced by repeated negative experiences that they are destined to "bomb" tests, their expectations of disaster are often self-fulfilling. Poor test grades produce anxiety, frustration, demoralization, test phobias, and the loss of self-confidence, and these negative emotions, in turn, produce continued poor grades. This poor test performance/low self-confidence loop must be broken before you can expect your child to acheive in school and feel good about herself (see Bouncing Back from Setbacks and Learning from Mistakes; Fear of Failure/Success/Competition; Grades; Self-Esteem; Self-Confidence; Test Anxiety).

To prepare effectively for exams, your child must be taught how to identify important information. She must then be taught a practical system for comprehending and recalling this information. Finally, she must learn how to anticipate what questions the teacher is likely to ask on a test (see Auditory Memory; Identifying Important Information; Memorizing Information; Visual Memory). Strategic, test-wise students review previous tests and search for patterns and tendencies in the types of questions asked. They make note of their teachers' clues and comments in class. Using their "test-taking radar," they target what the teachers are likely to consider important and what they must learn in order to get a good grade. They actively and dynamically (not passively) involve themselves in the study process. They ask questions as they study. They take notes and carefully review those notes. Based upon the type of tests their teacher typically gives (essay, multiple choice, true/false, or short answer), they decide whether to focus on major issues or details. They make up practice tests, and if appropriate, they study with friends and ask each other questions (see Passive Learning; Smart Thinking; Study Skills).

Some educators recoil at the idea of encouraging students to "psych out" their teachers. This reaction is naive. Smart students always study strategically. The accuracy of their ability to anticipate the questions their teachers are likely to ask is a key characteristic that distinguishes these successful students from their less successful classmates (see Critical Thinking; Passive Learning).

Test-savvy students also figure out—through a process of trial and error—how they learn best and adjust study procedures to capitalize on a preferred or natural learning style. The strategic *visual learner* would draw diagrams, make flash cards, and create graphic mental pictures (see Visual Memory). The *kinesthetic* or *tactile learner* would intuitively design flow charts or use three-dimensional physical props, models, and other manipulatives. The *auditory learner* would probably recite information aloud or subvocalize the information so she can hear it resonate in her mind, or she might record key information with a cassette recorder and replay it until she registers the data (see Auditory Memory). This tactical utilization of natural abilities and preferred learning modalities becomes a powerful personalized learning tool that allows students to understand, "digest," and imprint vital information when preparing for tests.

The first step in helping your child develop more effective test preparation skills is to determine if she has any academic deficiencies. Learning disabilities, specific skills deficits (for example, poor reading comprehension), and inadequate study skills (poor notetaking or chronic disorganization) can undermine test preparation efficiency and test performance (see Atypical Learning Problems; Learning Disabilities; Reading Comprehension; Study Skills; Underachievement). If deficits exist, they must be addressed before you can reasonably expect your child to get good grades on tests.

Family and emotional problems can also undermine test performance. A depressed child or a child in conflict with her parents will usually have great difficulty concentrating and studying effectively. Counseling may be required to help her divest herself of the negative emotions that may be sabotaging her effort and test performance (see Psychological Problems and Psychological Overlay; Self-Esteem and Self-Confidence).[1]

If you conclude that your child has not been taught how to prepare properly for tests, you must help her acquire these vital skills. Your child's educational future and ultimate career options hinge on her learning how to study effectively, efficiently, and strategically.

Corrective Strategies

In School

1.   If you suspect a majority of students in your child's class do not know how to prepare ade-

quately for tests, diplomatically suggest to the teacher that a test preparation unit be integrated into the curriculum. The teacher might announce that a test will be given on a specific date and identify the material that will be covered (for example, chapter 3, units 1 to 3, in the science textbook.) The class could then brainstorm a strategy for how they could prepare for the test. After this discussion, the steps could be written on the chalkboard (read assigned material, take notes from textbook, review class notes, make up practice questions, and so on). Students would then write personal target grades for the test in their notebooks (These should not be announced publically). The class could create a priority list of study tasks that must be done and design a study schedule (see Planning Ahead; Time Management.)

Children could break up into small groups and study together (called *cooperative learning*). Ideally, these groups should comprise "good" students, "average" students, and "poor" students so better students could serve as models for less successful classmates. Students in each group should ask each other questions and make up a practice test. The groups might exchange their practice tests with other groups so that everyone has extra practice taking tests covering the assigned content. This procedure could be used by the class to prepare for several tests, thus reinforcing the methodology. The objective is for students to internalize a range of practical and effective study methods that can significantly enhance test performance.

At Home

1.   Ask your child what material in her textbook and notes she thinks will be covered on the next test. Review together her previous tests and examine (in a nonthreatening, nonaccusatory way) the types of errors she tends to make (factual, careless, computational, etc.). Be careful not to be highly critical of your child's deficiencies. Also be careful not to lecture, give a sermon, or extol your own abilities when you were a student.

---

1. The systematic procedure of ruling out potential causal factors as a way to pinpoint the actual source of the problem is called *differential diagnosis*.

Being judgmental will only trigger anger and resentment, and your child will probably actively or passively resist your efforts to help. Work together to make up a practice test that resembles the types of questions the teacher tends to ask (multiple choice, true/false, essay, or short answer). Obviously, in making up this test, you'll need to review with your child the assigned textbook material and the information in her notes.

Take turns asking each other questions. You want your child to be in the habit of anticipating the types of questions most likely to be encountered. If she cannot answer a particular question, look up the answer together. Be careful not to sound disappointed or create the impression that you are competing with her. Point out that even with systematic preparation, there is no guarantee that she'll "ace" the test. Your goal is to model effective test preparation techniques. If she doesn't get a good grade on the next test, analyze together what went wrong. Your child's ability to learn from miscues and rebound from glitches is vital to her developing emotional resiliency and analytical thinking skills (see Bouncing Back from Setbacks and Learning from Mistakes).

Once your child appears to have mastered basic test-preparation procedures, begin to withdraw your supportive role. You don't want your child to become overly dependent on your help (see Learned Helplessness).

2.   Encourage your child to make up practice tests whenever possible. Explain that by doing so, she'll begin to think like a teacher and this will help her prepare for the next test. The extra time will be well worth it. If she misjudges and does not anticipate correctly the teacher's questions, spend time analyzing the questions that surprised her and the teacher's possible rationale for including those particular questions. Also explore how she might better calibrate her test-taking radar to be better prepared for the next test.

3.   For additional corrective strategies to improve test-taking skills, refer to Disorganization, Essay Tests, Goals, Inadequate Study Time, Memorizing Information, Monitoring Homework, Notetaking, Planning Ahead, Priorities, Study Skills, Test Anxiety, Smart Thinking, and Time Management.

Priorities

Successful students realize that they must rank their school obligations in order of descending or ascending importance and urgency (see Goals; Planning Ahead). They may not always be consciously aware that they are creating a hierarchy, but they intuitively tackle things in order of priority when faced with a series of tasks that requires careful planning and execution.

The ability to establish priorities is a requisite to strategic planning, effective time management, and efficient study skills. Successful students define their long- and short-term goals, and their plan for achieving these goals incorporates a logical progression for doing the necessary interim steps (see Disorganization; Inadequate Study Time; Time Management). Because they realize that getting A's on their weekly Spanish quizzes will significantly improve the likelihood of getting an A in the course, they prioritize studying for quizzes over watching their favorite sit-coms (see Grades; Study Breaks; Study Skills). This clarity of purpose and the ability to create a tactical order for handling obligations can be as important as their academic skills in determining their grades.

The need to establish priorities often forces children to make difficult choices. Foregoing an afternoon of playing basketball or hanging out with one's friends in favor of studying for a biology exam demands sacrifices, self-discipline, and goal-directed focus. The child who is willing to suspend immediate gratification is assigning a higher value to the long-range payoff—a good grade on the test. This future-oriented thinking differentiates achieving children from underachieving or nonachieving children who can relate only to what's happening in the present (see Disregarding Consequences).

Prioritizing, planning, managing time, and establishing goals are intrinsically linked skills (see Goals; Planning Ahead; Time Management). Strategic youngsters know intuitively that these organizational skills are vital to attaining the payoffs they covet (see Smart Thinking). By creating a hierarchy and ordering tasks according to importance or urgency, they are able to direct and efficiently manage their physical, emotional, and intellectual energy. Less strategic children are often overwhelmed by challenging assignments and complex projects because they cannot develop a practical and sequential plan for doing the requisite tasks and for moving efficiently from point A to point B to point C (see Learned Helplessness; Planning Ahead; Problem Solving).

Being able to rank academic responsibilities is vital in upper level classes. A high school student may have a science term paper due in three weeks, a French midterm in three days, and math problems due the next day. If he doesn't know how to organize and schedule these tasks effectively, he will be unable to plan, establish realistic and motivational short-term and long-term goals, and manage his time well. Instead he will career haphazardly from assignment to assignment. The negative effects of such disjointed and unfocused effort are predictable: stress, inefficiency, wheel-spinning, demoralization, and marginal academic performance. These consequences can be avoided with intervention and proper instruction. Every child of normal intelligence can be quickly and painlessly taught how to rank responsibilities, establish priorities, and organize life more efficiently. The sooner your child is taught these nuts-and-bolts skills, the better.

Corrective Strategies

In School

1.   If you believe your child and his classmates have not been taught how to establish priorities (for example, ordering the steps involved in writing a term paper), discuss your concerns with his teacher(s). Elementary and junior high school teachers will probably be more receptive than high school teachers to the idea of taking valuable time away from basic academic instruction to teach prioritization skills. Perhaps if you diplomatically propose how the principles of prioritization could be integrated into content area instruction, upper grade teachers might be more willing to integrate this skill into their curriculum. For example, as a class activity, students might list the steps involved in writing a term paper and number the steps in order of priority or logical sequence. Students might also be asked to list reasons why the colonialists decided to break away from England, in order of importance or priority to the colonialists. This procedure would force them to think actively about the issues and lead, ideally, to a lively class discussion. Be aware that some high school teachers may consider your input unwanted and inappropriate, and may resent a parent suggesting how they should teach. Other teachers might argue that students should already know how to prioritize their work by the time they enter ninth grade. In theory this is true, but in reality many students

have never been systematically taught how to rank and order academic responsibilities.

2.   (Elementary School, ES) Your child's teacher could involve the entire class in planning a field trip or a class party. Children could brainstorm the necessary steps and make a list of tasks and responsibilities in logical order of priority. They could then transfer this information to a flow chart, a time table, and a task completion check-off list.

At Home

1.   (ES) Demonstrate for your child how establishing priorities can make life easier and actually free up time for other enjoyable pursuits. You might suggest planning a party together. Brainstorm the steps involved and the tasks that must be completed. List the food and party favors that he wants to purchase. Discuss when invitations need to be sent and who is responsible for buying, addressing, and mailing them. Have your child rank the tasks and purchases in order of priority, and examine the reasons for ranking each item. Address the issue of perishable and non-perishable food and when each item should be purchased. Have your child commit to completing certain tasks by specified dates once the list of priorities is established (see Goals; Planning Ahead; Time Management).

2.   Do imaginary prioritizing activities with your child. For example, create the following scenario: "Imagine that you're on a big yacht in the Caribbean and you hit a rock that rips a hole in the hull. The captain tells you the boat will sink in ten minutes. Let's list the equipment and survival gear you want to put quickly into the lifeboat. Number the list in the order of greatest importance or priority."

3.   Review the steps required to write a research report or term paper. Have your child list all of the steps and number them in a logical sequence. This order can vary somewhat. Prepar-

ing the bibliography might be the last step for some students. Other students might justifiably want to make this the next-to-the-last step. Library research, notetaking, and writing a first draft would obviously be at the top of the list, and final proofreading would obviously be done after the last draft is written.

4.   With your child's active participation, create a list of the steps required to get into college, make the Olympic hockey team, win an award at

the 4-H Club, or earn a black belt in karate. Have him number the steps in order of priority or importance. The goal of these activities is to make establishing priorities an ingrained habit that your child uses automatically when confronted with a challenge or complex problem.[1]

1. See *Getting Smarter; Study Smart, Think Smart; Smarter Kids;* and *The Life-Smart Kid* in Resource List at back of this book.

Problem Solving

Children must learn how to handle problems effectively if they are to become functional independent adults. A child who cannot cope with challenges, setbacks, mistakes, and occasional criticism, teasing, arguments with friends, or rejection is clearly vulnerable (see Self-Esteem and Self-Confidence).

Some children are intuitive problem solvers, but even analytical youngsters miscalculate and suffer setbacks from time to time. A critically important trait distinguishes these children from youngsters who become overwhelmed by reversals and mishaps: they can overcome most glitches because they have learned how to break problems down into manageable parts. Their mastery of this key divide-and-conquer principle allows them to avoid the wheel spinning characteristic of children who become exasperated and overwrought whenever they confront a complex or puzzling challenge (see Critical Thinking; Smart Thinking).

Observing a child with natural problem-solving skills can create a false impression. The child may appear to respond so effortlessly to the difficulty that she seems to be operating without a strategy. Functioning like a well-trained gymnast who reacts automatically and doesn't appear consciously aware of the complexity of her routine, the intuitive problem solver may not appear cognizant of her own systematic and logical analytical thinking process. She may take shortcuts and vary the procedure from time to time, but

careful analysis of her responses will reveal a classic six-step problem-solving procedure:

• Step 1: Define the problem or challenge. ("I've got to finish this term paper by December 6.")

• Step 2: Collect data. ("The assigned subject: 'Alternative Energy Sources'—is a broad subject. I'll have to do a lot of library research to write this paper. I'll do a computer search of all material written about the subject, select books and articles to review, and also incorporate information from several encyclopedias.")

• Step 3: Compare the data with what is already known. ("The term paper will follow the same guidelines I used for my history term paper last semester. I'll take notes on index cards, write down quotations and footnotes, organize the index cards, write a first draft, edit, write a final draft, proofread at least two times, and prepare a bibliography.")

• Step 4: Develop a plan that utilizes the data efficiently and effectively. ("The teacher described in the handout the steps she wants us to follow in formatting the term paper. I'll follow her procedure and check off each step as I complete it.")

• Step 5: Implement the plan. ("I'll begin my library research tomorrow. I'll complete the first draft by next Tuesday and the final draft by the following Thursday. It will be ready by the Friday due date.")

• Step 6: Determine if the plan will work and develop an alternative plan if it doesn't. ("If I fall behind schedule, I'll make adjustments. If I run into problems, I'll ask the teacher or the librarian for help.")

Children who use this problem-solving method have a distinct advantage over less strategic-minded classmates. They think tactically, establish goals, and consider the pluses and minuses of all their decisions and actions. They learn from mistakes, bounce back from setbacks, and make pragmatic, expedient adjustments when appropriate. They link cause and effect, apply divide-and-conquer principles when faced with complex challenges, and persevere despite the occasional glitch. Because they can usually handle life's curve balls, they are successful in most of their endeavors. Success generates self-confidence, motivation, and conscientiousness. These qualities, in turn, generate more achievement.

For complex psychological reasons, some parents believe that they must insulate their child from life's problems. To protect their child from all frustration, disappointment, and anxiety, they may attempt to take ownership of every challenge or potential difficulty their child encounters and endeavor to run interference and deflect every potential upset. This behavior, which signals excessive fearfulness and a compelling need to be in control of a child's life, can have disastrous psychological implications. Parents who continually shield their children from problems unwittingly deny them vital opportunities to develop and refine their own problem-solving resources.

Certainly, the problems to which children are exposed should be calibrated with their chronological age. One cannot reasonably expect a six-year-old to handle issues he isn't yet developmentally or psychologically ready to handle. All children, however, should be encouraged to confront challenges and should be systematically taught how to solve problems. To insulate them from life's realities is a disservice. Overly protected youngsters pay a heavy price for their parents' loving, but misguided, behavior. Youngsters denied the opportunity to develop their own intellectual and emotional resources rarely evolve into independent, self-sufficient adults and rarely acquire healthy self-esteem (see Learned Helplessness; Self-Esteem and Self-Confidence).

Corrective Strategies

In School

1. If your child is not solving problems effectively, ask the teacher if the entire class might benefit from learning how to break down difficult problems and challenges into manageable pieces. Students could use the six problem-solving steps described above to deal with issues that affect the entire class. They might work together (see Studying with Friends) and practice applying the steps and developing problem-solving strategies. For example, the class might examine how a complex or difficult assignment could be successfully completed by the due date. The procedure could be reinforced by having students solve specific aspects of the problem individually and then share and compare their solutions with their classmates. Children who struggle in this area could be teamed with children who possess intuitive problem-solving abilities; so that they can observe and learn from watching the modus operandi of these "natural problem solvers."

2. Not knowing how to define problems accurately is a major barrier to effective problem solving. Children can often confuse the symptoms of a problem with the source of a problem. The DIBS Problem-Solving Method (see following) is a powerful, practical, and easy-to-use alternative to the six-step procedure presented earlier. This systematic, sequential method can be applied to a wide range of problems that children will encounter, both in school and outside of school. (DIBS is an acronym for the steps of the procedure.)

DIBS PROBLEM-SOLVING METHOD

Define the Problem:

TEACHER: "I have a problem. When I leave the classroom, work stops and many of you begin to misbehave."

Investigate the Causes:

TEACHER: "Let's look at what is causing this problem. Any ideas?"

STUDENTS: "We need to let off steam."
"Some kids like to misbehave."
"We never get to talk to each other in class."
"It's fun to get away with something."

Brainstorm Solutions:

TEACHER: "Let's brainstorm as many ideas as we can to help me solve my problem."

STUDENTS: "Three minutes each period of free talk time."
"An honor system in which everyone behaves and is quiet when the teacher leaves the room."
"A class monitor who will report children who misbehave."

Select a Solution to Try Out:

TEACHER: "Let's select an idea to try out and see if it solves the problem. How about three minutes of free talk time if the class completes the assigned work?"

The DIBS Method can be applied whenever the entire class or an individual student in class is experiencing a problem. Issues might include teasing, cheating, sharing responsibilities, or bullying. The key to making the system work is to define the problem accurately and to identify who actually "owns" the problem. Strategic problem solving can provide youngsters with a powerful tool for dealing with life's inevitable upsets. (For more about teaching children effective problem-solving skills, see *The Life-Smart Kid* and other relevant books in Resource List at back of the book.)

At Home

1.   The following guidelines will help your child acquire effective problem-solving skills:

• Link the problem-solving process with real-life situations. ("How can you get your older brother to stop teasing you?")

• Experiment with different strategies. ("Could you walk away when he teases you? Could you ask him to stop without getting angry?")

• Assess critically why some strategies are successful and others are unsuccessful. ("The approach you have been using in dealing with your brother is apparently not working. Do you have any ideas about why it isn't working? Do you think your brother understands that you truly want to end the teasing and that you are willing to make some changes in your own behavior?")

• Analyze strategies described in school materials ("Why did General Washington's plan for winning the Revolutionary War prove more effective than the British strategy?")

• Incorporate strategic thinking and problem-solving skills into all personal planning. ("How can you solve the problem of finding time to take guitar lessons and still get your school work done?")

2.   Urge your child to apply the DIBS Method to problems encountered in school and at home. For example, she could use DIBS to find a solution to the following problems: a sibling who borrows possessions without asking, a fight with a friend, a dilemma about how to play after-school sports with a friend and still find time to study for a test, or how to confront a friend who is lying, stealing, or revealing secrets. Remember

that it is often difficult for children (and adults!) to define a problem accurately and differentiate the actual problem from the symptoms and causes of the problem. A great deal of practice may be required before a child can say, "I'm upset because I think my friend Megan lied to me!" rather than "I'm mad because Megan is dumb or because no one likes me!" (For additional suggestions, see Critical Thinking; Smart Thinking.)

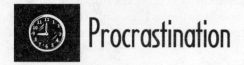

Procrastination

The child who chronically procrastinates generates stress and unpleasantness that affects everyone in the family. Exasperated parents may be convinced that the behavior is intentionally designed to torment them, but the real explanation is probably more complex.

Procrastination can be linked to one or more of the following underlying factors:

- Poor academic skills
- Poor time-management skills
- Inadequate goal orientation
- Disorganization
- Disinterest
- Poor study skills
- Laziness
- Desire for negative attention
- Low self-esteem
- Inadequate appreciation of cause-and-effect principles

Like their adult counterparts, children procrastinate when they want to avoid unpleasant, boring, difficult, or time-consuming jobs. For those with learning or study skills deficits, any academic assignment represents a distasteful challenge that they prefer to resist or avoid if possible. Repeated negative school experiences damage self-confidence, undermine motivation, and cause phobic reactions to homework and studying. Youngsters with learning problems can be especially adept at evading schoolwork. By

procrastinating, the struggling child temporarily deflects frustration, feelings of inadequacy, and pain. If he has reading problems, he will probably put off reading a book for a book report until the last minute. If he has language arts deficits, he will avoid writing his science term paper, and if he has concentration problems, he will avoid any academic task that requires focused, sustained effort (see Attention Deficit Disorder; Inadequate Study Time; Language Arts; Learning Disabilities; Negative Attitude toward School; Planning Ahead; Self-Esteem and Self-Confidence; Study Skills; Time Management; Working Independently).

Avoiding schoolwork is an appealing path of least resistance to a demoralized child. Excuses, rationalizations, and complaints that the work is boring or irrelevant are transparent defense mechanisms designed to protect the child from feeling incompetent. By putting off the work, he can pretend that the work does not exist and temporarily delude himself that he won't have to deal eventually with the repercussions. (In fairness, it should be noted that some schoolwork *is* indeed boring and irrelevant, and some teachers haven't taught a creative or stimulating lesson in twenty years. Children must nevertheless get the job done, despite the tediousness of the assignment or the teacher.)

Some children procrastinate because they do not know how to establish personal goals. These children, who typically learn and think passively, are usually described by exasperated parents and teachers as lazy, unmotivated underachievers. Lacking a sense of purpose and direction, they seem content to coast through school and life in cerebral neutral (see Goals; Passive Learning; Priorities; Underachievement).

Procrastination may also be linked to a poorly developed appreciation for basic principles of cause and effect. Children who habitually disregard potential consequences of their actions and decisions would probably disavow the obvious connection between poor school performance and their irresponsibility. Denying reality, rationalizing laziness, and deflecting responsibility for not doing the work are common, self-sabotaging traits that can become integral components of a child's personality (see Behavior and Attitude; Disregard of Consequences; Expectations and Performance Guidelines).

Low self-esteem and poor self-confidence also can cause children to procrastinate. An insecure child who is terrified by the prospect of failing and having to confront his deficiencies may be unconsciously compelled to avoid challenges and responsibilities. The child may rationalize his stalling behavior with excuses like: "The teacher didn't assign any homework." "I did it in school." "Don't worry. I'll get it done." "It's boring!" After convincing himself that the self-deceptions are true, he will then reject all evidence to the contrary. The illusion that everything is okay inevitably shatters when report cards are handed out (see Fear of Success/Failure/Competition; Grades).

Procrastination may also be linked to poor study and organizational skills. A child may have good basic academic skills, but may not know how to plan projects, organize materials, prioritize the steps required for completion, or budget time. Late, incomplete work testifies to a lack of order in the child's life (see Disorganization; Incomplete Assignments; Planning Ahead; Priorities; Study Skills; Time Management).

Children may also procrastinate because they know their parents will rescue them whenever they get into a bind. The attention and coddling they receive can actually become a more desir-

able reward than the pleasure they would derive from completing the work independently. The predictable payoff—the rescue—ironically encourages them to continue being irresponsible (see Learned Helplessness).

In some cases, chronic procrastination may be symptomatic of emotional or family problems. A depressed, angry, or resentful child may use nonadaptive behavior as a weapon against his concerned parents. This weapon can be especially potent when his parents place great value on diligence, effort, punctuality, and achievement. The child who chronically resorts to this form of passive aggression may feel that this is the only way he can safely vent his anger and unhappiness and get attention. Such a child clearly requires professional counseling (see Anger and Frustration; Passive Learning; Psychological Problems and Psychological Overlay).

Corrective Strategies

In School

1.   If you see your child procrastinating, explore strategies with the teacher that might motivate him to get his work done. Elementary school teachers are usually more than happy to work with parents on correcting students' self-defeating behavior. Junior or senior high school teachers may be less willing to participate in a behavior modification plan because they see far more children each day and have less time to devote to individual students. Moreover, many teachers in the upper grades feel that it is the student's responsibility to get the work done and that they are not obligated to "spoon feed" children who procrastinate. If you point out the underlying causes for your child's counterproductive behavior and suggest a collaborative effort to reorient him, his teacher may be more willing to cooperate, assuming the plan does not require a great deal of extra work on the teacher's part.

2.   To help you monitor your child, ask the teacher to complete a Daily Performance Checklist (see Monitoring Homework). The school

may already have such a checklist. Modify whichever one you use so it focuses on your child's particular deficits.

3.   If you believe your child is procrastinating because of academic or study skills deficits, ask for an evaluation by the Child Study Team or the school psychologist. If he doesn't qualify for testing or assistance, consider private tutoring, educational therapy, or enrollment at a private learning center (see Atypical Learning Problems; Learning Disabilities; Underachievement).

4.   (Junior High/High School, J/HS) If your child chronically procrastinates in school, a conference with the guidance counselor is critical. Counselors continually deal with this problem, and they should have a systematic method for monitoring and motivating students who procrastinate. Unfortunately, many high schools do not have effective programs and some are rather cavalier about providing support for underachieving, unmotivated students. If this is the case at your child's school, you may need to find a qualified private academic counselor or therapist. Ask your pediatrician, family physician, or the school principal for a referral.

At Home

1.   If it becomes apparent from teacher feedback, report cards, and your own observations that your child has acquired the habit of procrastinating, try to identify the reasons for the behavior. Your response to a child who procrastinates because of poor academic skills will be different from your response to a lazy or passively aggressive child. The Student Evaluation Checklist (see Learning Disabilities) will help you determine if your child has underlying academic deficits or a learning disability. If you are able to identify specific deficits, refer to relevant entries in this book for corrective strategies.

2.   If your child is procrastinating because he doesn't establish goals or doesn't know how to study, think smart, prioritize, manage time, or plan ahead, refer to these entries for corrective strategies.

3.   Helping your child learn how to manage time more effectively can be a vital antidote for chronic procrastination (see Goals; Inadequate Study Time; Planning Ahead; Study Breaks; Study Skills; Time Management). Actively involve your child in the process of creating his own personal study schedule. With the teacher's input, you may conclude that one hour and fifteen minutes is the average study time each night for most students in the class. Encourage your child to participate in designing a workable schedule and to commit to the study time; this is a critical part of the process of empowering your child. Active participation encourages responsibility, decreases resistance and resentment, and discourages passive learning. Establish the parameters, and be prepared to compromise when appropriate (see Monitoring Homework; Learned Helplessness; Passive Learning; Priorities).

Psychological Problems and Psychological Overlay

Children respond to the world around them on two interacting levels: the neurological and the psychological. On the neurological level, the brain receives, deciphers, assimilates, imprints, and reacts to external data from the five senses while concurrently reacting to internal data from the organs in the body. On the psychological level, the brain interprets external events and situations and creates internal impressions, thoughts, and emotions. The neurological and psychological levels of perception overlap; difficulty on one level often triggers difficulty on the other.

The dyslexic child who cannot read accurately or recall what she is reading is experiencing difficulty on the neurological (sensory) level of perception (see Atypical Learning Problems; Dyslexia; Learning Disabilities; Memorizing Information; Reading Comprehension; Underachievement; Visual Memory). If she becomes increasingly frustrated and demoralized and concludes the school battle is hopeless, her confidence, desire, and motivation will erode. At best, she may tolerate school. At worst, she will hate it (see Anger and Frustration; Negative Attitude toward School). As her frustration mounts and self-confidence deteriorates, she may compensate for her feelings of inadequacy by acting out, giving up, retreating into a defensive shell, or becoming resistant, hostile, irresponsible, or manipulative. A sensory processing dysfunction and its academic implications have now clearly spilled over into the psychological level of perception and have begun to distort her feelings about herself and the world around her.

Despite this spillover, the origins of the child's negative feelings and counterproductive behaviors, however, remain neurological.[1]

Nonadaptive and counterproductive behavior caused by emotional trauma or family dysfunction (for example, child abuse) are described as *psychological problems*. Nonadaptive behaviors caused by a learning disability (or other impediment) are described as *psychological overlay*. The more serious the child's learning problems are, the greater the risk of self-concept damaging psychological overlay.

Just as neurological (sensory) processing deficits can cause learning problems and trigger psychological overlay, so, too, can psychological problems cause sensory processing problems and trigger learning problems. An angry, depressed, insecure, or guilt-ridden child who has experienced emotional trauma will often have great difficulty concentrating, following her teacher's instructions, or reading accurately. Her inner turmoil may manifest itself as hyperactivity, distractibility, or careless mistakes. Because the symptoms of psychological problems and psychological overlay are similar, differentiating the

---

1. Use of the term *neurological problem* does not indicate brain damage. Most children with processing deficits do not have an organic impairment. Rather, they have a *perceptual processing dysfunction* that impedes the efficient decoding of sensory data. This dysfunction is not linked to intelligence. In fact, many children with perceptual deficits have superior intelligence (see IQ Test Scores).

underlying causal factors and making an accurate diagnosis can be challenging unless the struggling child is assessed by a well-trained diagnostician.

Profoundly unhappy children who lack self-esteem and feel undeserving of success rarely work at a level commensurate with their potential (see Behavior and Attitude; Self-Esteem and Self-Confidence). It is common for children who continually struggle in school to feel incompetent (psychological overlay). To confirm their unworthiness, these children may unconsciously sabotage themselves. Failure becomes a comfort zone for them where they can ensconce and protect themselves emotionally from adult expectations and demands they are convinced they cannot fulfill. By gravitating to other students who are also struggling academically, many of these youngsters are able to create an alternative identity and social order (see Peer Pressure).

Children with psychological problems may become so enveloped by sadness and preoccupied with emotional survival that they shut down in school. They may lose their emotional resilience and become incapable of learning efficiently (see Anger and Frustration; Bouncing Back from Setbacks and Learning from Mistakes; Fear of Success/Failure/Competition). Although their distractibility and escapist daydreaming may mimic the symptoms of ADD (see Attention Deficit Disorder), it would be inaccurate and misleading to attribute these symptoms to a neurologically based condition without first doing a comprehensive neuropsychological assessment.

Failure can be addictive. Children who struggle academically and experience a steady diet of embarrassment, frustration, reprimands, and demoralization because of neurological problems or psychological problems often become habituated to and accepting of negative payoffs. The coping mechanisms they use to protect their remaining vestiges of self-esteem—procrastination, denial, laziness, blaming, acting out, passivity, and daydreaming—offer no real protection. In fact, the behaviors guarantee continued poor performance. Of course, emotionally desperate children do not recognize this irony.

Children continually compare their accomplishments with those of their classmates. Even five-year-olds are keenly aware of how they rate on the performance scale. "Smart" kids do well and are praised by their teachers and parents. "Dumb" kids get into trouble, their teachers get angry at them, and their parents are disappointed in them. These conclusions may be simplistic, but they are essentially accurate. Tragically, the feelings of worthlessness experienced by struggling children in elementary school often persist throughout life and produce disastrous emotional, academic, and vocational consequences. Kids who see themselves as losers often live up to this negative self-perception.

Most parents lack the training and insight to differentiate the symptoms of underlying psychological problems from the symptoms of psychological overlay. Parents who are confused about what is causing their child's unhappiness and self-defeating, counterproductive behavior have three options:

- Make their own diagnosis.
- Hope the problem will correct itself.
- Consult a competent educational psychologist or mental health professional for an accurate diagnosis, and if appropriate, treatment.

Psychological problems and psychological overlay rarely disappear on their own. Children with psychological overlay require help from a resource specialist, educational therapy, and/or tutoring, and children with psychological problems require counseling or psychotherapy. In many cases, psychological overlay dissipates when children begin to succeed in school, assuming, of course, that learning assistance has been provided before significant emotional scarring has occurred.[2] If, however, the unhappiness and

---

2. Psychological overlay from learning problems can become a serious psychological problem if it is not treated. Older children who have been forced to struggle year after year in school can acquire profoundly warped perceptions of themselves and the world.

self-sabotaging behaviors persist despite learning assistance, providing a comprehensive psychological assessment is of critical importance.

Although the blatant symptoms of psychological problems and psychological overlay may assume different forms as children mature, the underlying issues will usually persist and continue to cause problems. If the underlying factors are not addressed, these self-defeating behaviors often become increasingly entrenched and debilitating. Not seeking professional help when the need is clearly indicated can have catastrophic consequences for the child and the entire family.

Corrective Strategies

In School

1.   Ask the teacher if he believes your child's unhappiness or counterproductive behavior is being caused primarily by school difficulties or by other psychological factors. Be prepared for the possibility that the teacher may not know the answer to this question. (This does not imply incompetence: Teachers are not trained psychologists!) Discuss your concerns with the school psychologist and request diagnostic testing to determine if your child has learning problems and/or underlying psychological problems.

2.   If it is the consensus of the school personnel that your child's frustration, negative attitude, and counterproductive behaviors are primarily attributable to learning problems (psychological overlay), request that she be provided with learning assistance (see Parents' Rights). If she is already in a resource program, and her skills and behavior are not improving, request a meeting with the school psychologist, resource specialist, and classroom teacher (see Communicating with the School; Conferencing with School Officials; Individual Educational Program [IEP]). Use this meeting to define specific academic and behavioral objectives and explore innovative strategies for achieving these objectives. For example, if your child is acting out on the playground because of academic frustration, develop a coordinated plan to reduce the frustration and modify the unacceptable behavior. You might design a simple checklist that the teacher could complete each day to inform you when your child has misbehaved.

If your child is clearly struggling academically, perhaps the quantity and difficulty level of the assigned academic work could be reduced (see Expectations and Performance Guidelines). If she misbehaves, she could go to a special time-out area. At the end of the time-out, the teacher might complete a simple checklist that asks if the child is ready to return to the playground and is willing to abide by agreed-upon behavior guidelines. She could have the child check off specific changes that she agrees to make (such as no teasing, fighting, or name-calling on the playground).

At Home

1.   The following inventory is designed to help you differentiate the more serious symptoms of psychological problems from symptoms of psychological overlay (behavior produced by a learning problem). If you identify red-flag symptoms, have your child assessed by a well-trained mental health professional who can evaluate the situation objectively.

PSYCHOLOGICAL PROBLEMS INVENTORY

Psychological Red Flags

- *Disorganized thinking*

- *Lack of orientation (being aware of time, place, and people)*

- *Delusions (persecution or grandeur: "My teacher hates me!")*

- *Sensory distortions (auditory and/or visual hallucinations)*

Nonadaptive Behaviors

- *Social withdrawal (seclusiveness, detachment, inability to form friendships, excessive sensitivity, unwillingness to communicate)*

- *Tantrums*

- *Superstitious activity (motor rituals that must be performed before doing a task)*

- *Extreme mood changes*

- *Excessive fantasizing*

- *Phobic reactions (fear of people or germs)*

- *Fixations (excessive and exclusive interest in something)*

- *Suicidal tendencies*

- *Chronic explosive anger or hostility*

- *Depression*

- *Excessive fearfulness*

- *Excessive anxiety*

- *Chronic manipulative behavior*

- *Chronic bullying*

- *Chronic lying*

- *Chronic stealing*

- *Chronic need to control others*

Physical Dysfunctions

- *Bed-wetting (in older children)*

- *Incontinence (in older children)*

- *Repeated stomachaches (also may be symptomatic of a physical problem)*

- *Sleep disturbances*

Children manifesting any of the behaviors described above are at risk, and treating their psychological needs should take priority over treating any learning problems they might have. (In many cases, emotional problems and learning problems can be treated concurrently.) The longer parents wait before providing help, the more extensive and debilitating the emotional damage may be.

2.   Psychological overlay caused by learning problems tends to produce less extreme symptoms than those appearing on the preceding list. The associated behaviors include: frustration, anger, acting out, resistance, resentment, irresponsibility, procrastination, laziness, denial, and blaming. Unfortunately, making an accurate diagnosis is complicated by the fact that some the symptoms of psychological overlay are also symptomatic of psychological or family problems. If you are unsure of the source of your child's symptoms, consult the school psychologist or a private mental health professional. Should your child's counterproductive behaviors and attitudes persist despite the best efforts of the teacher and resource specialist, seek outside professional help. This may involve educational therapy, family counseling, and/or psychotherapy (see Learning Disabilities).

3.   Talk to your child! Discuss events and upsets in her life nonjudgmentally. Share events and upsets in your own life. Share your own reactions and emotional responses, even the ones that are not "perfect." Discuss what makes you angry. Model introspection and self-awareness ("I remember how hurt I felt when I was not invited to the birthday party of one of the popular children in my third grade class. I felt embarrassed and left out. I was convinced no one liked me. Later, I realized that some of the kids I like the most were also not invited to the party. I realized that not everyone wants you to be their friend.") Communicate unequivocally to your child that you will always be there to help her sort out issues if she wants you to help. Be sensitive to her pain and stress, even if the source of these feelings might appear silly to you. Look for red flags that might indicate emotional problems. Be prepared to provide professional help if your intuition tells you that intervention is necessary.

4.   Children who manifest psychological overlay almost invariably suffer from low self-confidence (see Self-Esteem and Self-Confidence). Encourage your child to develop talents in nonacademic areas (dance, gymnastics, art, karate, and others). Accomplishments in these areas can be an important source of confidence and pride that offsets the painful trials and tribulations that your child may be experiencing in school.

Punctuation

The rules of punctuation have tormented students throughout the ages. Today, some teachers are less exacting and do not require their students to conform to all the traditional conventions for punctuating compound sentences, introductory prepositional phrases, series, and restrictive and nonrestrictive clauses. Despite the trend toward liberalization, students can expect to encounter at least some teachers who do insist on strict adherence to the rules.

In junior and senior high school, many teachers require students to apply basic punctuation rules properly in their expository writing. This is especially true in English classes. Students who learn the rules and use them consistently will usually get better grades on essays and reports than those who disregard them or use them inconsistently. A well-written term paper may merit an A on the basis of content and literary style, but if it is poorly punctuated, the teacher may give the student a B (see Essay Tests; Language Arts).

Learning punctuation rules and practicing them does not necessarily have to be an irrelevant, excruciatingly painful, mind-numbing experience for your child. The key to defusing your child's resistance to learning the rules and facilitating mastery is to make the self-editing process as interesting and challenging as possible. For example, you might suggest that punctuating an essay correctly be a contest in which your child pits his skills against the punctuation rules in much the same way he would pit his skills against a computer game. By suggesting that using punctuation in this way could actually be an enjoyable challenge, you can reframe a potentially negative experience and make it a positive one. Once your child becomes convinced he can win this contest handily, he will be more willing to expend the requisite time and effort to making sure he has punctuated his assignments correctly. Specific suggestions for teaching the rules and making the process more engaging are found in the following.

Corrective Strategies

In School

1.   If the teacher is concerned about your child's punctuation, ask her to specify particular rules that are problematic for your child. Request that she supply supplemental materials to use in school and/or at home to reinforce the rules and improve mastery. If your child is having a great deal of difficulty, ask the teacher if she could provide individualized help before or after class.

2.   Ask the teacher if she wants you to proofread your child's work to find punctuation mistakes. Some teachers do not want parents to proofread homework assignments and reports. If you do check over your child's work, you may first need to review the rules yourself.

At Home

1.   Make two copies of a page from a well-written, well-punctuated book or article. Count up

all the punctuation marks. Set one copy aside. Carefully white-out all the punctuation marks on the second copy and photocopy this page again. Go through the page without punctuation with your child and discuss where commas, periods, and quotation marks should be placed. You might say: "The word *and* in this sentence is followed by a second subject and second verb, making it a compound sentence (two independent clauses). You must put a comma before *and* because the rule says a compound sentence joined by the conjunctions *and, or,* or *but* requires a comma." Tell your child in advance how many punctuation marks you removed and see how many he can correctly replace. The more practice the better, but know when to stop for the day! Overkill can trigger resistance and resentment. If you are enjoying yourselves, repeat the activity several times.

2.   Play the same game with written work your child has already submitted. Count the original punctuation marks, white them out (along with any corrections by the teacher), photocopy the report, then go through it together. Compare the number of punctuation marks in the original with the second version. If you find that you lack the skills or patience to work with your child, consider hiring a qualified tutor.

3.   When helping your child proofread assignments, do not simply insert the missing commas, colons, and quotation marks for him. Explain succinctly why the punctuation is needed. Be patient. Write down another example of the same type of sentence (compound, series, introductory phrase) and leave out all the punctuation marks. Allow your child to use previously corrected sentences as models, and ask him to punctuate the new sentence properly.

4.   If you feel insecure about punctuation rules, go to a teacher supply store and request material specifically designed to reinforce punctuation rules. Materials you might want to review may be found in the Resource List at the back of the book.

5.   If your child is having difficulty remembering what a conjunction, adjective, adverb, or prepositional phrase is, encourage him to use his visual memory skills. For example, he might visualize a cherry tree with two cherries hanging from a stem that looks like the letter V. Suggest he associate the place where the two stems are joined (the fork) with the conjunction. Each cherry is a subject. Tell your child to picture *the fat* (adjective) *cherry* (noun) *fell* (the verb) *gently* (adverb) *to the ground* (prepositional phrase) *and* (conjunction) *the small* (adjective) *cherry* (noun and subject) *remained* (verb) *attached* (adverb) *to the stem* (prepositional phrase). (See Grammar; Memorizing Information; Visual Memory.)

Reading Aloud

Oral reading ability is one of the major criteria elementary school teachers use to evaluate academic achievement. Students who can read accurately, fluently, and with proper intonation are affirmed and rewarded. Those who lack these skills become acutely aware of their deficiencies each time they are asked to read aloud. If their associations with oral reading are traumatic, the embarrassment can produce feelings of inadequacy, reading phobias, and emotional scarring.

To read well, your child must acquire *phonics, word attack, blending,* and *visual tracking skills.* This means being able to recognize nonphonetic words (such as *rough*), anomalies (such as *psychology*), and common foreign words (such as *colonel, buoyant, faux pax, demitasse, crochet,* and *lieutenant*). (See Nonphonetic Words.)

There are two basic approaches to teaching children to read.[1] The most common is the *phonetic* or *sounding-out method* (see Phonics). This method teaches methods for "attacking" words that conform to consistent rules of spelling and pronunciation. Children use the rules to sound out individual phonemes (or syllables) then blend the sounds together to form words.

The second method encourages children to *learn words by sight.* Utilizing visual memory skills (see Visual Memory), students continually add to the storehouse of words they recognize by appearance. Practice is essential, of course, and most students require several exposures to difficult words before they can immediately recognize them.

Because of numerous phonetic anomalies in the English language, many teachers integrate both phonics and sight recognition in their instructional strategy: Children *sound out* words that conform to standard phonics rules and *memorize* those that do not.

Poor *visual tracking* (seeing letters, words, and syllables accurately) can make oral reading a nightmare for a child. To read efficiently, the child's eyes must be able to scan smoothly from left to right (called *ocular pursuit*). If his eye muscle control is deficient, he may transpose letters or omit letters, syllables, words, or even phrases when reading. *Static tracking* problems usually manifest themselves as letter and/or number reversals (*b* perceived as *d*, or *q* perceived as *g*). The child may also have up/down reversals (*6* perceived as *9*, or *n* perceived as *u*). *Kinetic tracking* problems usually manifest themselves as flipped words (*was* perceived as *saw* and *bad* perceived as

---

1. Other programs that have proven popular in some school districts include Whole Language and Read to Write. Many innovative reading methods, however, tend to be faddish. They enjoy popularity for a while and then disappear because the publishers' claims and the educators' and administrators' expectations are not validated by standardized achievement test scores. A good teacher can teach reading using a 1920s primer. Although publishers argue that the new programs are designed to compensate for inadequate teaching, an obvious motive for creating these new materials is to make existing programs obsolete and sell millions of new textbooks. That these programs actually improve reading skills is debatable.

dab). When tracking problems are chronic, the condition is usually referred to as *dyslexia* (see Dyslexia).

Children with oral reading deficits may also have difficulty hearing the difference between sounds (*e* may be perceived as *i*). Intensive phonetic discrimination training has proven very effective in improving the oral reading of children with auditory discrimination problems (see Auditory Discrimination).

Stress can also interfere with oral reading fluency. Shy or self-conscious children may become quite anxious when asked to read aloud. If these children have reading problems, their anxiety and fear of reading inaccurately may cause them to make errors which, in turn, will intensify their stress and insecurity. Developing a creative strategy to reduce their fears is vital (for example, before class begins, have them privately practice reading aloud to the teacher the same material they will be asked to read in class later). These tentative and insecure children must obviously be handled with extra sensitivity and must be given extra affirmation.

If your child is struggling with oral reading, any specific reading deficits must be identified before an effective assistance program can be developed (see Atypical Learning Problems; Auditory Discrimination; Auditory Memory; Learning Disabilities; Slow Reading; Visual Discrimination; Visual Memory). Once deficits are pinpointed, systematic instruction from a resource specialist, tutor, or private educational therapist, extra encouragement, and ample opportunities to practice are vital if your child is to become a competent, self-confident reader.

Corrective Strategies

In School

1.   If your child stumbles, falters, and/or reads inaccurately, and the teacher feels that the problem cannot be remedied in class, request an evaluation by the school psychologist, reading specialist, or resource specialist. It is a relatively easy task to identify specific reading deficits involving phonics, word attack, blending, and/or visual tracking. It is also a relatively simple procedure for a school psychologist, resource specialist, or educational therapist to determine if your child has visual memory, visual discrimination, auditory memory, or auditory discrimination deficits. If specific deficiencies are identified, request that your child be provided with remedial assistance (see Parents' Rights).

Once your child is tested and, ideally, assigned to a resource program, verify that the IEP (Individual Educational Program) pinpoints his specific deficits and indicates the remedial methods that will be used to correct these problems. The IEP should also target short-term and long-term remedial goals and provide a general time framework for completing the remedial process. If the administration will not evaluate your child or provide assistance, ask to see the school district's Parents' Rights Manual (see Parents' Rights). Your child's legitimate access to learning assistance is protected by federal law, and you may need to assert these rights aggressively if diplomacy fails (see Communicating with the School; Conferencing with School Officials).

2.   (Elementary School, ES) If your child is traumatized by reading aloud in class, request that he be excused from doing so until he and the resource (or reading) specialist have made headway in correcting his reading problems. Embarrassment can be psychologically damaging and could cause your child to become profoundly phobic about reading aloud. This would negate any potential advantage that might be derived from the extra practice time.

At Home

1.   If your child is to improve his oral reading skills, he must practice reading in a nonstressful, supportive context. If he has significant reading problems, he may be very sensitive and resistant. To overcome defense mechanisms, you must be especially patient and affirming. Orchestrating

successful and enjoyable reading experiences, communicating positive expectations, and calibrating the difficulty of the reading materials you use to your child's reading level are vital. Youngsters who realize that they're making progress are generally less resistant and defensive. The following guidelines will make reading sessions more productive and enjoyable for you and your child:

• Ask the teacher to indicate your child's current reading level. This can be obtained from standardized test scores (see Understanding Diagnostic Test Results), or from the observations of the teacher, resource specialist, tutor, or educational therapist.

• Select reading materials from the library or bookstore that are slightly below your child's current reading level. Ask the teacher or librarian to recommend appropriate books. Involve your child in the selection process. Choose books that your child finds interesting. If your child is reading at a basic primer level, you will find many high-interest books for children about sports legends, heroes and heroines, and historical figures intentionally written at low reading levels—with stimulating content. The librarian can help you find these books. Steer your child to easy-to-read materials at first. As he progresses, he can select more challenging books.

• If your child has significant problems, slowly read a sentence (or portion of a sentence) aloud. Have him follow along as you read by pointing to each word with his index finger.[2] Then ask him to read the same sentence, using his finger as a guide. This method of reading is especially im-

portant if he has visual tracking, word attack, or blending deficits (see Dyslexia). If he makes an error, use discretion: You do not need to correct every mistake. You want reading aloud to be a pleasant experience. Be patient, supportive, and affirming! Acknowledge progress and brainstorm strategies for learning difficult or nonphonetic words (see Nonphonetic Words). Your child could make his own personal flash cards of difficult words (see Memorizing Information; Spelling Problems).

• Keep the sessions short! Forcing your child to continue beyond his natural endurance levels will cause resistance and resentment. Also make the sessions fun. Quit for the day when either you or your child becomes tired, restless, or impatient. If reading aloud is difficult for your child, his self-confidence will probably be fragile. Resistance and defensiveness, common ego-protecting reactions to feelings of inadequacy, may assume the form of chronic yawning, distractibility, hypersensitivity, or irritability. Your goal is to help your child relinquish his negative associations with reading so that he doesn't become profoundly phobic about reading aloud. Praise and affirmation for progress are vital!

• The need to preread each sentence to your child before he reads will no longer be necessary as his skills improve. When appropriate, begin reading entire paragraphs aloud: you read a paragraph and he reads the next paragraph. At some point, your child will be ready to read the material aloud without you having to read first. If he prefers to continue the procedure of reading alternative paragraphs, let him do so. You want your child to have pleasant, successful associations with reading. These associations produce greater proficiency and build confidence.

• Carefully control the progression into more challenging reading materials. Do not push your child too quickly. To build his self-confidence, orchestrate repeated opportunities for success.

• Establish performance goals, with your child's active participation. You might say: "When you

---

2. Some teachers do not want children to use their fingers as a marker or guide, arguing that this procedure will undermine reading fluency and will become a "crutch." This position is ludicrous, particularly in the case of children who have tracking problems. To prevent them from using their finger is to deny them the chance to read more accurately. Later, when their ocular pursuit and word attack skills improve, they will be able to read without having to use their finger to control their eyes.

progress into third grade reading materials, we'll celebrate by going out for pizza."

2. If your child is not making sufficient progress despite your help (and that of the resource specialist), consider hiring a trained reading specialist, tutor, or educational therapist, or enrolling at a private learning assistance center.

3. (Junior High/High School, J/HS) Working with older students who have profound reading problems can pose a monumental challenge to concerned parents. If your child is resistant to your help or highly defensive, consider hiring a trained tutor or educational therapist who has had extensive experience working with teenagers with reading problems. Older students with a history of chronic reading difficulty may require counseling to help them examine and relinquish defensive, resistant, and counterproductive behaviors. The emotional wounds that can result from reading inadequacies can be deep, and patience and perseverance by parents are vital if these wounds are to heal without causing profound scarring. (See Behavior and Attitude; Bouncing Back from Setbacks and Learning from Mistakes; Negative Attitude toward School; Psychological Problems and Psychological Overlay; Self-Esteem and Self-Confidence.)

Reading Comprehension

The process of teaching children to read is akin to constructing a building. Basic decoding skills—phonics, word attack, blending, and sight word recognition—form the foundation of the structure (see Phonics). Simple comprehension skills (understanding and remembering facts and details) comprise the lower floors, and advanced comprehension skills (drawing inferences, thinking analytically and critically, and applying information) comprise the upper floors.

In grades K to 2, the primary focus of reading instruction is to teach children how to decipher or decode written symbols. Students who struggle to *make sense* of letters and words are often so exhausted by the effort that they have no intellectual energy left to think about what the words *mean* (see Dyslexia; Learning Disabilities; Reading Aloud; Visual Memory).

During the first three years of elementary school, the issues, concepts, and information children are expected to comprehend are relatively straightforward and uncomplicated. A child might read: "Human beings can survive several weeks without food and several days without water, but they can survive only several minutes without air." This information is easily understood, and the child can readily relate the data to her own observations and life experiences. As children progress into the upper grades and their vocabulary and reasoning skills expand, the complexity of the material they are expected to understand increases significantly.

In grade 3, the focus of reading instruction begins to shift. Decoding skills (phonics, word attack, and blending) are still being taught, of course, but children are now also expected to *retain* and *apply* the information they read. This shift from the basic reading of words to the utilization and application of information is reflected in textbooks and reading materials that increasingly emphasize comprehension and vocabulary development.

On the most basic level of reading comprehension, the *literal level*, students must be able to identify and remember facts and information. For example, they might read:

• Literal statement: The scientist carefully measured two chemicals, placed them in a flask, added purified water, and boiled the mixture for five minutes.

• Literal question: What did the scientist do?

A ninth grader taking a timed standardized reading test might be asked to read the following:

• Literal statement: Prior to the Second World War, Nazi Germany, which had formed an allegiance with fascist Italy called the Axis, began to invade the surrounding countries in Europe. In 1939, they invaded Poland. This was the first of many countries that Germany would ultimately annex. The invasion convinced the English government that war with the Axis powers was unavoidable. Later Germany invaded Hungary, Czechoslovakia, Latvia, Lithuania, and France.

• Literal question: The invasion of which country convinced England that war with Germany was unavoidable? (A) Hungary (B) France (C) Czechoslovakia (D) Poland

On the second level of reading comprehension, the *inferential level*, students must demonstrate that they can reason and apply logic. To draw inferences, they make conclusions based upon information that is implied but not expressly stated. For example, they might read:

• Inferential statement: The man and his son experimented with different lenses, angles, apertures, and speed settings as they tried to create the most pleasing visual effect.

• Inferential question: What do you think they were doing?

A fourth grader taking a timed standardized reading comprehension test might be asked to read the following statement and answer the following inferential question:

• Inferential statement and question: It hadn't rained for six months. The long drought was followed by a famine that caused great suffering for the farmers in the poor country. The famine was hardest on the young, the old, and the weak. Many: (A) survived (B) became wealthy (C) ate (D) died.

The preceding question probes the student's ability to infer from the context that famine is bad even though she may never have seen the word before and may not know its actual definition. The child who has difficulty with literal comprehension (remembering facts and information) also usually has difficulty drawing inferences.

On the highest level of reading comprehension, the *applicative level*, children must be able to use or apply information they read or hear. For example, they might read:

• Applicative statement: As they used their new computer, the woman and her daughter discovered the remarkable speed with which it could solve complex math problems and the ease with which they could use the computer for word processing.

• Applicative question: In what ways could the girl use the computer effectively to help her with schoolwork?

An eleventh grader taking a biology test might read the following statement and be asked to answer the following applicative essay question:

• Applicative essay statement: There are six major disadvantages to using pesticides. (1) They leave a residue; (2) they can kill the plants they were designed to protect; (3) they are difficult to apply evenly; (4) they can disturb the balance of nature; (5) they can cause pollution; (6) insects can develop resistance to the chemicals.

• Applicative essay question: Write an essay that examines alternative ways to protect crops that reduce dependency on pesticides. Refer to all the disadvantages of pesticides, and explain and justify the rationale for your alternatives. Incorporate information from your textbook, class lectures, and class discussions.

When students enter junior high, they are expected to be able to answer increasingly probing questions about the content and meaning of what they read and study. They must be able to relate what they are currently learning to what they have already learned and to demonstrate an understanding of assigned material on tests.

The pressure to demonstrate in-depth mastery of course content accelerates in high school. Although the ability to comprehend, reason, draw inferences, and apply information is linked to intelligence, virtually all students—even those who are mildly retarded—can improve their reading comprehension skills with systematic instruction. They can be taught how to ferret out key ideas and underlying issues, and how to assimilate the information they read more efficiently and effectively (see Critical Thinking; IQ Test Scores; Smart Thinking). Students who develop and refine their capacity to understand, remember, and use what they read are rewarded with good grades and typically find themselves on a track leading to college and ultimately to more challenging and rewarding careers.

In upper level courses, especially college preparatory classes, the ability to remember literal information does not guarantee good grades. Most teachers demand insight as well as factual knowledge. They want students to demonstrate that they can analyze, interpret, and critique what they read, and tests are designed to measure these skills (see Essay Tests; Identifying Important Information; Notetaking; Passive Learning; Study Skills; Underachievement).

Many students who can decode words with ease but struggle to understand and recall the content of their textbooks are usually not in the habit of *creating mental pictures* when they read. For example, they might read in their science textbook about the positive and negative ecological effects of building dams. The chapter may describe how tons of cement are poured to create the dam, how water is released, and how dams are used to control floods and improve farming. If these students cannot *visualize* the dam stretching across the river and cannot visualize how it is built, and how it works, then the words they are reading are little more than abstractions. Because they are not actively and intellectually engaged in digesting and assimilating the data, these students typically have difficulty understanding, recalling, and utilizing the information (see Passive Learning).

Teaching your child to form mental images when reading and to express these images in words can result in a significant improvement in reading comprehension skills. Your child will be able to use these imprinted images and words as reference points for understanding and recalling the content of the material being read. (Methods for teaching your child how to visualize and verbalize are described in Corrective Strategies).

You do not have to be a teacher or reading specialist to help your child improve reading comprehension. The requisites for providing effective help are basic: a willingness to become constructively involved, appropriate remedial materials, a well-thought-out assistance plan, positive expectations, and patience.

Corrective Strategies

In School

1. Ask the teacher to pinpoint your child's specific reading deficits. Be forewarned that many classroom teachers—especially junior and senior high school teachers—have had only limited training in diagnosing reading problems. They may recognize from classroom performance and scores on standardized and teacher-designed tests that your child is not comprehending well, but they may not know how to specify the deficiencies causing the problem. The following Reading Problems Inventory will help identify specific deficiencies.

READING PROBLEMS INVENTORY

This student:

	YES	NO
Has difficulty with phonics	___	___
Has difficulty blending sounds together	___	___
Has difficulty with sight word recognition	___	___
Has difficulty reading accurately	___	___
Reverses letters, numbers, or words	___	___
Omits letters or syllables	___	___
Skips over words or entire lines	___	___
Has difficulty understanding and/or recalling literal information (facts)	___	___
Has difficulty drawing inferences from material that is read (information implied but not stated)	___	___
Has difficulty using and applying information that is read	___	___
Has difficulty relating what is currently being learned to what has already been learned	___	___
Has difficulty identifying concepts and finding common threads that run through the content of what is read	___	___

If the teacher indicates that your child has problems in any of the areas on the inventory, request an evaluation by the school psychologist, resource specialist, or reading specialist (see Dyslexia). If your request for testing is denied or deflected, request to see the district's Parents' Rights Manual (see Parents' Rights).

2.   If your child has basic visual decoding deficits (symptoms: inaccurate reading, letter and word reversals, omitted syllables and words, letter transpositions, and losing her place when reading), it is vital that she be provided with assistance from a trained resource specialist, reading specialist, or private educational therapist. Commonly used teaching/remedial materials designed to correct visual tracking deficits are included at the back of the book (also see Dyslexia).

3.   If your child's comprehension is more than one year below grade level, ask the teacher to adjust academic expectations to your child's present skill level. Most teachers have the latitude to make reasonable accommodation to the needs of struggling students. You want your child to stretch, but you don't want her to become frustrated and demoralized by unreasonable demands. You must do everything in your power to prevent feelings of inadequacy because she is struggling to read or understand the material in her textbooks. The repercussions of continually struggling in (to the child) a hopeless situation can be psychologically devastating. If the student is to acquire the reading skills needed for academic success, he must be provided with a focused, well-conceived remedial strategy and a concerted, cooperative effort from everyone involved in the remedial process.

4.   Ask the teacher to assign materials in class and for homework specifically designed to improve reading comprehension skills. Remedial materials written at different grade levels are included in the Resource List at the back of the book.

5.   If you suspect that your child is having difficulty creating visual pictures to help her understand and recall the content of what she reads, do visualizing and verbalizing activities together. Ask her to describe something she has just read in a textbook. (You will also, of course, need to read the material!) If she has difficulty, ask her teacher if any staff at the school have been trained in the Visualizing/Verbalizing Method (developed by Nanci Bell at the Lindamood Center in San Luis Obispo, California). This program is specifically designed to develop your child's comprehension skills. (If no one is trained in this method, refer to suggestions below under At Home.)

6.   If you suspect your child has *inferential deficits*, ask the teacher for her opinion. If she concurs that your child does have inferential problems, ask if she can assign materials that can improve this skill. (See the Resource List at the back of the book for suggestions.)

7.   A comprehensive study skills program can help your child acquire practical methods for identifying, comprehending, retaining, and applying important information. Applicative comprehension skills can be developed with guided, systematic instruction, practice, and feedback. If your child's school does not offer such a program, strongly urge the administration to establish one.

At Home

1.   If the Reading Problems Inventory indicates that your child has basic visual decoding problems, remedial help in deficit areas will be required. Decoding errors, tracking problems, and blending, phonics, and word attack deficits can create serious roadblocks to reading comprehension. An effective and systematic remedial program can help children correct or effectively compensate for these problems. If you conclude that you lack the requisite skills, patience, or desire to work with your child, ask the teacher, school psychologist, or pediatrician for a referral to an effective tutor, educational therapist, or learning center. (See Dyslexia; Inaccurate Copying; Learning Disabilities; Nonphonetic Words; Phonics; Reading Aloud; Visual Memory.)

2.   When working with your child at home, keep sessions relatively short (ten to twenty min-

utes for younger children and twenty to twenty-five minutes for children grade 6 and above). When your child begins to become frustrated or resistant, quit for the day!

3.   If your child has difficulty drawing inferences or applying information when she reads, use real-life situations to help link implied but not directly stated consequences. For example you might say: "A seventh grader watched three hours of television and talked for more than an hour on the phone each evening. What kind of grades do you think she received on her report card? Why did you conclude this?" "He couldn't understand why the coach had benched him. He was the best player on the team. What could have possibly caused the coach to bench his best player? How many possible reasons can you come up with?" (See Disregarding Consequences).

4.   Read newspaper articles with your child and ask questions that encourage inferential and applicative thinking. (Example: "What might have caused this car accident to happen?" "Why do you think they lost the football game?" "Why are so many people upset about violence in movies?") With older children you might select articles that deal with such issues as gang violence, homelessness, pollution, drugs, and other relevant topics. Brainstorm how your child can use what she already knows about the issue to avoid or resolve the problem (Example: "How might he have avoided being victimized by the gang?") (See Critical Thinking. Also refer to *The Life-Smart Kid;* see Resource List at back of book.)

5.   Go to a teacher supply or educational software store and review parent-child interactive materials designed to develop comprehension skills. Some of these materials can be found in the Resource List.

6.   If the teacher's completed Reading Problems Inventory indicates that your child's decoding skills are satisfactory but that comprehension skills are deficient, you should help her develop the ability to make visual associations when she reads (see Memorizing Information; Spelling Problems; Visual Memory). As you read together, periodically stop your child and ask her to describe what she is reading in her own words. Use stimuli to encourage visualization: action ("Describe what is happening."); color ("Describe what colors you see when you think about this chemical process."); mood and feelings ("How do you think the Indians felt as they watched the settlers destroy the buffalo herds that provided them with food?"). If your child has difficulty visualizing, consider hiring a tutor trained in the Visualizing/Verbalizing Method. [You may want to contact the Lindamood Center in San Luis Obispo, California for referral to a trained tutor in your area. You may also want to purchase *Visualizing and Verbalizing for Language Comprehension and Thinking* (see Resource List).]

7.   An alternative for developing your child's capacity to form visual pictures and improve comprehension is to ask her to draw a *mind-map* or illustration as she reads. (This technique is also called *chunking*.) Let's assume your child is reading an article about lasers. Have her read the material once relatively quickly and begin to mind-map what she remembers of the content from this cursory reading. Then have her reread the material more slowly and carefully and encourage her to add any information she might have omitted. This method stimulates your child to think about what she is reading and to incorporate information she believes is important in a graphic representation.

Examine the two facsimile mind-maps that follow. Both visually encapsulate the information. One mind-map is clearly more artistic and creative than the other. This type of representation would probably appeal to students who are themselves artistic and creative, though your child does not have to be to use the method effectively and comprehend the content. The key is to represent and link information graphically, and by so doing enhance comprehension and retention. Because your child is more intellectually engaged, her comprehension and retention should signficantly improve. Encourage her to use colored pencils or pens and to be as colorful and creative as she wishes. You want the process to be

MIND-MAP SAMPLE #1

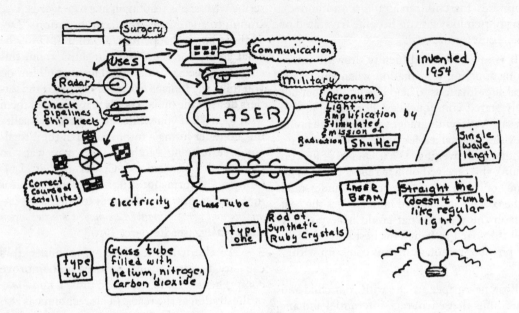

MIND-MAP SAMPLE #2

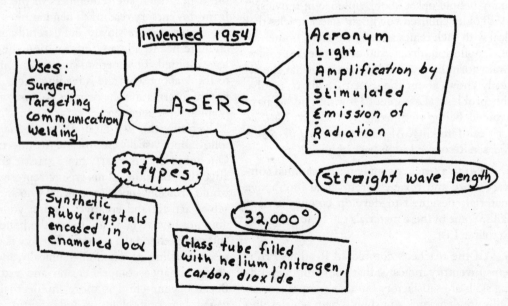

enjoyable, and you want to stimulate active participation. If your child omits facts that you think are important, discuss the facts. The mind-map does not have to contain every bit of information, nor does it have to be exactly as you would do it. Be patient! You are opening doors, and your child may be tentative and even resistant at first. You are asking her to think about what she is reading, and this may be difficult and threatening, especially if she is in the habit of passive thinking (see Passive Learning). If your child enjoys the method and practices mind-maps, comprehension and retention should improve.

8. If your child continues to struggle with reading comprehension and does not respond positively to strategies outlined here, consider hiring a tutor who knows how to teach applied study skills techniques (see Notetaking; Study Skills). Many reading and learning centers offer courses in study skills. Refer to *Study Smart, Think Smart* (elementary school) and *Getting Smarter* (high school) for strategies designed to improve study skills and applicative comprehension deficits (see Resource List). Also refer to corrective strategies in Critical Thinking.

If you enroll your child at a reading center, request that her specific reading comprehension deficits be identified. Using a procedure called *item analysis*, a reading specialist can analyze your child's incorrect responses and determine precise deficiencies. Insist that the instructional materials and remedial strategy address identified deficits. Many teachers believe that basic decoding and comprehension deficits must be remedied before attempting to correct higher level inferential deficits. This position is logical, but some teachers prefer to work on decoding and comprehension skills concurrently.)

9. Teaching your child how to take "standard" notes can also significantly improve his comprehension and retention of information. Refer to Notetaking for specific instructional strategies.

Recording Assignments

Students who do not properly and consistently record their homework assignments are settting themselves up for academic disaster. Deluding themselves that they can remember details, they play Russian Roulette with deadlines, page and exercise numbers, and formatting directions. If they bother to write down assignments, they do so haphazardly on whatever paper is available. The outcome is preordained: they miss deadlines, fail to complete assignments, forget to study for announced tests, and disregard important instructions. Their grades inevitably suffer the consequences of such nonadaptive behavior and poor tactical thinking (see Smart Thinking).

Children who are cavalier about recording assignments either do not recognize or choose to deny a basic academic cause-and-effect principle: poor grades are directly linked to irresponsibility. The same children also tend to be cavalier about other academic details, such as carefully proofreading essays, checking over math assignments, and submitting completed homework assignments on time (see Attention to Details; Behavior and Attitude; Disregarding Consequences; Incomplete Assignments; Monitoring Homework; Passive Learning; Study Skills; Underachievement; Working Independently).

A sixth grade teacher might announce orally or write the following assignment on the chalkboard:

SCIENCE ASSIGNMENT

Answer questions 1, 3, 5, 7 and 9, page 51. Complete sentences. Skip line between each answer. Name on the upper right hand line and date below it. Due tomorrow. Quiz Friday.

The child who writes in her binder: "Do questions page 51" has omitted vital information, and will probably not complete the assignment as instructed. She will also probably forget to study for the quiz.

Although some children figure out an effective system for recording assignments, other children require clear guidelines, practice, and supervision until the procedure becomes automatic. Those left to their own devices may never develop an efficient assignment recording system and are destined to spend a great deal of time trying to figure out what they are supposed to do.

If your child is not recording her assignments properly, you may be tempted to resort to nagging or punishment. This approach is usually ineffectual. The logical alternative is to teach your child how to record her assignments efficiently and to monitor her carefully until she demonstrates that she's mastered and internalized the procedures.

Corrective Strategies

In School

1.   Unless the teacher has a specific assignment recording sheet she wants all the students to use, you and your child should select or create your own version (see sample Assignment Sheet below). Ask the teacher to initial your child's Assignment Sheet each day to confirm that your child has properly recorded all necessary information.

2.   If you believe your child's entire class would benefit from systematic instruction in how to record data properly on an assignment sheet, you might diplomatically suggest to the teacher that assignment recording practice would be beneficial. Also suggest that children be carefully monitored until they can demonstrate that they have mastered the procedure. (Unfortunately, many high school teachers might not be amenable to this suggestion, as they may assume—often erroneously—that students have already mastered this skill in elementary school. Many high school teachers feel that students in the upper grades should not be "spoon-fed.")

3.   (ES) Ask your child's teacher(s) to initial an Assignment Monitoring Form each day. Make copies of the form and have your child tape it to the inside cover of her binder so it will not be lost. (See a variation of this form under Monitoring Homework.)

At Home

1.   Tell your child that you want her to record all her assignments on her Assignment Sheet and explain why you insist that she follow this procedure.

2.   Make certain that your child has a specific place in her binder for the Assignment Sheet. The sheet should probably be the first page in her notebook.

3.   Work out a system of abbreviations with your child to facilitate recording assignments

---

ASSIGNMENT SHEET

SUBJECTS	MON.	TUES.	WED.	THURS.	FRI.
_____	_____	_____	_____	_____	_____
_____	_____	_____	_____	_____	_____
_____	_____	_____	_____	_____	_____
_____	_____	_____	_____	_____	_____
_____	_____	_____	_____	_____	_____

Due Dates

Subject:

Tests

Reports

Teacher's initials　　　　_____　_____　_____　_____　_____

ASSIGNMENT MONITORING FORM

Week of: _____

	MON.	TUES.	WED.	THURS.	FRI.
Completed assignments due today.	_____	_____	_____	_____	_____
Submitted assignments on time.	_____	_____	_____	_____	_____
Work not completed.	_____	_____	_____	_____	_____
Teacher's initials	_____	_____	_____	_____	_____

(for example, *ex = exercise; p = page; thru = through; cmplt = complete; d = due; rpt. = report; sci = science; Fr = French; Sp = Spanish*, etc.). Abbreviations can be especially helpful when teachers dictate assignments. Emphasize to your child that she must be able to understand her own abbreviations!

4.   (ES) Have your child read the assignment sheet to you. This procedure will help you make certain she can decipher her own entries and that she understands what is due the next day. If she is having difficulty prioritizing tasks and managing time, see Planning Ahead, Priorities, and Time Management.

Repeating a Grade

Having a child repeat a grade is a major decision that should not to be taken lightly. In most cases, the recommendation for retention originates with a concerned teacher who is convinced that a struggling and/or developmentally immature child cannot handle the academic demands at the next grade level.

On the surface, the rationale for repeating a grade is logical: a second exposure to the course content, coupled with greater maturity, should improve the student's skills and allow him to have a more successful school experience. Those who favor this remedy contend that any possible negative psychological effects are more than offset by the benefits of a child being able to keep up with the class and, perhaps, excel.

Most children are retained in grades 1 to 4, although some may be held back in grades 5 through 8. In rare cases, students may be held back in junior or senior high school. The retention rate and policies in a school district often reflect not only the district's philosophy about how to handle struggling learners but also the resources available for dealing with academically deficient students (see Evaluating Special Education Programs; Mainstreaming and Special Day Classes).

Retention may be the only option when a child lacks the requisite skills to handle the work and does not qualify for learning assistance in the school resource program. Depending on state code and school district procedures, the local administration may be quite insistent that parents

acquiesce to their decision, or they may be content to present the pros and cons and leave the final decision about retention to the parents.

Private and parochial schools have their own guidelines and criteria for dealing with the issue of retention. Because many smaller private schools do not have on-site resource programs to help struggling learners, retention may be the only option for parents who want their struggling child to remain at the school. In some states, private school students may qualify for diagnostic assessment by the local school district psychologist and for resource help at the local public school. These students would either attend the public school for a period of time each week, or the district might send an itinerant resource specialist to the private school campus to provide on-site learning assistance services. Some private schools offer tutoring and educational therapy programs and either hire their own staff or contract with independent tutors and educational therapists. Parents of children participating in these learning assistance programs are usually charged an additional fee for these add-on services.

As states develop more stringent competency tests for high school graduation, arguments in favor of retention are heard with increasing frequency. Many districts are no longer willing to push students with poor skills through the system and contend that awarding high school diplomas to students with fifth grade skills makes the diploma meaningless and is a disservice to students who cannot possibly meet the demands of a competitive job market. Despite this supposed tightening of competency requirements, many states continue to graduate students from high school who are functionally illiterate.

High school students who cannot meet minimum academic skills requirements to graduate have several options: they can repeat classes, take intensive remedial courses, attend summer school, graduate late, drop out of high school at sixteen, or earn an equivalency diploma at a later date. Some states permit older teenagers to enter the community college system without having graduated from high school. Credit earned in courses can be used to fulfill high school degree requirements.

The decision to retain students does not always originate with the teacher. Convinced that their child lacks the developmental, emotional, and/or academic resources to handle the demands at the next grade level, parents may conclude that repeating the grade will allow their child to review and master important skills and avoid ego-damaging anxiety, stress, and pressure. Other parents have more pragmatic and strategic reasons for wanting their child to repeat a school year. They believe that greater maturity can provide a competitive academic advantage, produce a higher grade point average, and ultimately improve their child's chances of being admitted into a better or more prestigious university.

If you are considering having your child repeat a grade, you should carefully weigh the potential advantages against the following potential disadvantages:

• Negative psychological impact: Children may feel embarrassed, incompetent, and socially stigmatized. Some may erroneously conclude that they are mentally deficient. These reactions are less prevalent when children are retained in kindergarten or first grade.

• Disillusioning quick-fix solution: The immediate crisis may be temporarily relieved and children may do well for a while, but if underlying learning problems are not identified and corrected, these deficits could cause major academic problems down the road.

• Resistance to remaining in school: Retained children may be unwilling to attend high school when they are nineteen.

Retention can "buy time" for children with deficient academic skills and spare them from experiencing constant frustration and demoralization. The practice, however, is not a viable alternative to providing first-rate learning assistance that addresses and corrects the specific deficiencies causing the academic problems.

Although it is certainly true that some youngsters are developmentally immature and academically unready to handle the challenges of the next grade level, most students targeted for retention are not, in fact, developmentally immature. These youngsters have specific perceptual, concentration, attitudinal, intellectual, or study skills deficits that impede academic achievement. Labeling them immature may be convenient, but the description is usually inaccurate and misleading. To retain and recycle students who have specific, identifiable academic deficits without identifying and remedying their deficiencies only puts off "the day of reckoning." Retained children may do well for the next year or two and create the illusion that everything is okay, but the initial advantages of retention often diminish as learning disabled students progress through school.

Retention of children with learning problems could be the equivalent of burying a land mine shell that could explode with devastating impact in sixth, seventh, eighth, or ninth grade (see Atypical Learning Problems; Underachievement). Packing more soil on top of the shell (i.e., another year in second grade) may temporarily avoid detonation, but it does not eliminate the potential danger.

Corrective Strategies

In School

1. (Elementary School, ES) If you observe your child falling further and further behind in school, ask the teacher to alert you by midyear if she is considering retention. Emphasize that you do not want to be surprised in May. This forewarning

will give you time to procure help for your child, either within the school system or privately, and to determine if the assistance program is making inroads into resolving the specific deficits. Do not accept descriptions such as "immature" or "not ready to settle down" unless you are convinced the descriptions are accurate. Ask the teacher to identify in specific terms your child's learning and concentration deficits (see Attention Deficit Disorde; Keeping Up with the Class). The more precise the teacher's description, the more likely that your child's problems will be accurately diagnosed and treated (see Communicating with the School; Conferencing with School Officials; Parent-Teacher Conferences).

2. If the school argues that your child has significant academic deficits and uses this as a rationale for retention, ask what other options are available. Express your legitimate concerns about retention as a means for dealing with a child's learning deficits. If your child has not yet been assessed by the Child Study Team and/or evaluated by the school psychologist, request an evaluation (see Parents' Rights). Discuss with the teacher and, if appropriate, the principal, the long-range consequences of not properly identifying and remedying the underlying learning deficits that are causing your child's learning difficulties. Inquire about the success rate when other children struggling with similar deficits. Ask if you could speak with the parents of some of these children. Insist that remedial support from the resource specialist be provided if specific learning disabilities are identified. (Getting assistance for children with nonspecific learning disabilities is usually more problematic; see Atypical Learning Problems; Underachievement). Examine the social and psychological implications of repeating the grade and ask if your child might be provided with short-term counseling to make the experience less traumatic.

At Home

1. (ES) If your child's teacher is strongly in favor of retaining your child and you agree with this plan, begin to prepare your child well in advance. Tell your child that you want him to be successful in school and to feel good about his skills. Explain that some very bright children need more time to learn at first, but that later school becomes much easier for them. Your child will probably have concerns about losing friends, making new friends, and, perhaps, about being teased. Most children are keenly aware of their comparative abilities. Assure your child that repeating a year does not mean he is "dumb." Handling this issue incorrectly can have a profound effect on your child's self-concept, so allow him to express his feelings and never dismiss his feelings as "silly." Some children appear unconcerned about being retained, at least on the surface. Others may be quite troubled by the prospect. These youngsters will need repeated assurances that they are capable of doing well in school (see Bouncing Back from Setbacks and Learning from Mistakes; Self-Esteem and Self-Confidence).

2. If you are undecided about whether to retain your child, ask him how he feels about the idea. He may agree that it is a wise decision, or he may feel strongly that he does not want to be held back. Explore alternatives. Would he be willing to accept tutoring, educational therapy, or study skills help? Would he agree to put in more time studying? How could he organize himself and schedule his time more efficiently? You must make the final decision, but your child's input is important. If he is denying the reality of the situation or is unable to make a commitment to an assistance program, you will have to make a unilateral decision about retention.

Having your child repeat should be a last resort. If retention is necessary, you might want to transfer your child to another school in the district to assuage any social concerns he might have. If he doesn't want to start over and make new friends at another school, his wishes should be respected. He will need a great deal of affirmation and emotional support during the transition. You will need to monitor him closely to make sure the same problems do not recur. A second retention at a later date could be disastrous and should not even be considered. (Believe it or not, some schools actually recommend this!)

3.   Retention is not a magical cure for school problems. Repeating the year may, in some cases, be all that is needed to get a child on track, or it may be little more than a misguided stopgap measure. If you believe your child needs learning assistance, and the school is unwilling or unable to provide this help, you may need to seek private learning assistance from a qualified tutor, educational therapist, or independent learning center. Whether or not your child is retained, you will need to evaluate his progress and ask for periodic updates from his teacher. Most learning problems do not simply go away. You must be vigilant. If you observe your child is slipping further and further behind, you must find help, either within the system or from a qualified and talented private educational therapist.

Self-Esteem and Self-Confidence

A child's self-esteem is the composite of her feelings about herself and represents her unconscious assessment of her value as a human being. These unconscious feelings can be seen in the self-image (or self-concept) the child projects. Children with healthy self-esteem exhibit a positive self-image, and those with poor self-esteem exhibit a negative image. In some cases, this reflection of the child's unconscious feelings about herself is obvious. In other cases, the underlying feelings may be hard to discern, and the child may feel unconsciously compelled to camouflage her feelings.

The foundation for self-esteem is formed before birth and is comprised, on the most basic level, of inherited temperament, intelligence, and aptitude. During the first four years of life, the building blocks for the self-esteem superstructure are mounted on this foundation. The blocks consist of family values; child-rearing practices; life experiences; reasonable, clearly communicated parental expectations; fair and consistently applied rules; and social relationships (see Behavior and Performance Guidelines). The mortar that holds the blocks together is provided by the child's parents: a blend of love, appreciation, encouragement, affirmation, clearly defined limits and boundaries, and a sense of security. When the foundation is solid, the building blocks well-formed, and the mortar strong, a child develops self-esteem and a positive self-image and acquires faith and pride in her own power, connectedness, and uniqueness.

It is axiomatic that children cannot develop healthy self-esteem when they are physically or emotionally abused, denigrated, compared to more successful siblings, given confusing double messages, caused to feel guilt and shame, or permitted to work below their potential. These negative forces invariably cause a child to dislike and disrespect herself. The child enmeshed in self-hatred is fated to smash repeatedly against barriers throughout life. Her negative feelings inevitably distort her perceptions and judgment and undermine her attitude, behavior, motivation, effort, performance, commitment, perseverance, and emotional resiliency (see Behavior and Attitude; Fear of Failure/Success/Competition; Guilt; Negative Attitude toward School; Psychological Problems and Psychological Overlay).

The child with healthy self-esteem wants to succeed and because she appreciates and respects herself, she believes she *deserves* to succeed. She enjoys challenges, delights in developing her talents, and revels in her accomplishments. Radiating self-acceptance and self-appreciation, she voluntarily expends the effort and energy requisite to attaining her personal goals (see Smart Thinking).

In contrast, the child with poor self-esteem usually lacks faith in her ability to prevail. Because she does not accept or respect herself, she is convinced that others cannot possibly appreciate or love her. Feeling unworthy, she will avoid establishing personal performance goals and confronting challenges. She will lower her expectations and then perform congruently with these diminished expectations. Radiating negativity and self-deprecation, she may consciously or unconsciously sabotage herself with flawed choices and judgments and ineffectual effort (see Anger and Frustration; Effort and Motivation; Goals).

Achievement should not be confused with self-esteem. As psychologists and psychiatrists can certainly attest, achievers do not necessarily have good self-esteem. In fact, many people who consciously choose not to aspire to the traditional standards of success (money, power, or fame) may have far healthier self-esteem than their ostensibly more successful counterparts. These people may prioritize family, religion, art, charity, or harmony with nature over high-powered careers, exciting and frenetic lifestyles, pressure, anxiety, and the accolades of others.

Some people unconsciously use achievement as a surrogate for poor self-esteem. Defining themselves by their accomplishments, they may take pride in what they achieve quantitatively and/or qualitatively without giving any thought to who they are and how they achieve their successes. The deceptiveness of success is chronicled virtually every day in the media where countless stories describe famous actors, athletes, singers, musicians, lawyers, ministers, politicians, physicians, and business executives who self-destruct for seemingly irrational reasons. In virtually every case, their unhappiness and aberrant behavior can be directly traced to intrinsically flawed self-esteem.

Because academic or athletic achievement can create the impression that an achieving child possesses healthy self-esteem, parents must look beneath surface appearances as they attempt to assess their child's true feelings about herself. The self-confident athlete who excels on the basketball court may feel profoundly inadequate in other areas of her life. Despite her athletic successes, she may neither like nor respect herself, and poor self-esteem will directly influence her perceptions and actions. She may be shy and

withdrawn off the playing field and have difficulty establishing or maintaining friendships. She may have poor judgment, make little or no effort academically, take excessive physical risks, experiment with drugs, or gravitate toward friends who are on a collision course with the criminal justice system (see Disregarding Consequences; Passive Learning; Peer Pressure).

Being affirmed for achievements can certainly improve a child's self-confidence, but this acknowledgment does not guarantee that a child will acquire healthy self-esteem. Because self-esteem and self-confidence overlap, the two phenomena are often erroneously equated. A self-confident child may be convinced she can prevail over a range of challenges, obstacles, and problems. She may appear competent and poised, but she may actually be very insecure about her intrinsic value as a human being.

When a child's self-image is based exclusively upon her ability to achieve or upon the affirmation of others, her self-esteem is, at best, tentative. A series of even minor reversals could crush her self-confidence and crumble her tenuous self-esteem.

Setbacks and defeats can test the mettle and emotional resiliency of any child, even one with healthy self-esteem. Although the child with a good self-concept might temporarily falter and be saddened when confronted with a failure, her basic positive feelings about herself will nonetheless remain intact. Her emotional resilience will allow her to rebound from the setback, and her decision to persist in her efforts or strategically go around the obstacle will be based on an objective assessment of the situation and not an imprinted negative psychological script. (see Bouncing Back from Setbacks and Learning from Mistakes; Critical Thinking; Planning Ahead; Problem Solving; Smart Thinking).

Some parents believe they can "give" self-esteem to their child. Others believe that their child's self-esteem will grow in proportion to the attention, presents, or educational advantages they lavish on her. These parents will ultimately discover that self-esteem cannot be bestowed. Children must earn their own self-esteem and parents must create the context for them to do so.

Although you cannot *give* your child self-esteem, you can stimulate its development during the critical formative years by providing love, acceptance, affirmation, a sense of security, and by communicating faith in her ability to handle problems and challenges.[1] Your child will gain self-esteem and self-confidence by solving problems, prevailing over challenges, handling frustration, and dealing with setbacks. She will earn it by working hard, persevering, thinking strategically and acting honorably. As she develops her talents, and experiences her own power, she will acquire increasing self-sufficiency and self-appreciation. These are the benchmarks of healthy self-esteem.

Shielding children from trials, setbacks, uncertainties, frustration, and unhappiness does not enhance self-esteem. The opposite is true. The misguided attempts by overly protective parents to insulate their children from every unpleasantness undermines the development of self-esteem. Certainly, children require guidance and context-appropriate protection at critical junctures in their lives, but this does not mean that parents have the obligation or the right to take ownership of their child's problems. Children must develop their own survival skills. They must learn to rebound from defeats, handle glitches, overcome obstacles, and neutralize opponents. Allowing them to falter occasionally is an essential part of the process of preparing them to cope successfully with life and achieve greater maturity (see Learned Helplessness).

By allowing your child to grapple with a controlled amount of frustration, you cast a vote of confidence in her. The opportunity to prevail over age-appropriate trials and challenges is vital to developing initiative, resourcefulness, re-

siliency, perseverance, and self-respect. Encouraging independence does *not* preclude you from being concerned and involved, providing assistance in a crisis, or helping your child sort out a problem and analyze the issues (see the DIBS Problem-Solving Method in Problem Solving). As your child improves her analytical thinking and problem-solving skills and takes increasing responsibility for her own welfare, she will become self-reliant and self-assured. Reveling in her accomplishments, she will feel competent, powerful and focused, and her self-esteem and self-confidence will grow commensurately (see Problem Solving; Working Independently).

Corrective Strategies

In School

1.   (Elementary School, ES) If your child lacks self-esteem and/or self-confidence, and her negative experiences in school are contributing to tenuous self-concept, confer with her teacher. If your child is struggling academically, brainstorm ways to provide opportunities to achieve and improve her self-confidence. Request an evaluation by the school psychologist if you believe she would benefit from learning assistance (see Parents' Rights). If your child does not qualify for help in the resource program, be prepared to provide private tutoring or educational therapy. To build your child's self-confidence, the teacher might encourage her to do extra-credit projects that capitalize on her natural artistic, musical, or athletic talents. Perhaps the teacher could occasionally make your child a class monitor or ask her to keep track of certain class records. School achievement and affirmation do not guarantee that your child will develop healthy self-esteem, but they can certainly be a major factor in helping her acquire more self-confidence.

2.   (Junior High/High School, J/HS) Junior and senior high school teachers may not be as supportive of your attempts to orchestrate opportunities for your child to improve her

---

1. See Corrective Strategies for suggestions about how you can take a proactive role in helping your child acquire self-esteem and self-confidence.

self-confidence. Teachers in the upper grades see many more students each day than their elementary school counterparts. Most prioritize the content of their courses and their students' performance on tests. Some teachers may be willing to create opportunities for your child to win in school, but others may not be cooperative or even sympathetic. In such cases, it may be appropriate to discuss your concerns with the school counselor, school psychologist, and/or principal. They may be able to elicit the teacher's cooperation or, if appropriate, recommend an evaluation by a therapist or social worker. (Some enlightened districts have social workers and therapists on staff.) Unfortunately, issues involving self-esteem and self-confidence are often overlooked at the high school level. Parents unable to elicit support in the school will need to seek private counseling or educational therapy (see Negative Attitude toward School; Psychological Problems and Psychological Overlay).

At Home

1.   You cannot *give* your child self-esteem, but you *can* intentionally create a context at home that encourages the development of self-esteem. The guidelines are:

- Express your love, acceptance, and pride
- Create a secure and stable home environment
- Establish reasonable and consistent standards and expectations
- Insist that your child assume reasonable, age-appropriate responsibilities
- Express faith in your child's talents and ability to prevail and succeed
- Communicate honestly
- Be sensitive and empathetic to your child's feelings and fears
- Clearly define your family's values and expectations
- Be consistent
- Orchestrate opportunities for success

- Encourage independence and self-sufficiency
- Permit your child to experience a reasonable amount of frustration and encourage her to persevere (see Anger and Frustration)
- Provide emotional and/or academic support
- Acknowledge and affirm your child's accomplishments
- Urge self-expression
- Validate your child's feelings and ideas even if you are not in complete agreement
- Listen nonjudgmentally when you communicate

2.   You can also intentionally create a context at home that is conducive to your child developing self-confidence. The guidelines are:

- Encourage your child to establish personal short- and long-term goals
- Help your child develop a practical strategy for attaining goals and handling problems
- Encourage your child to take on new challenges that improve skills and abilities
- Emphasize that the payoffs for taking responsibility for solving problems and prevailing over challenges are pride and a sense of achievement
- Provide academic and/or psychological support if underlying learning or emotional issues are preventing your child from developing good self-esteem
- Express faith in your child's ability to handle problems and challenges
- Provide selective guidance and appropriate feedback

These strategies for improving self-esteem and self-confidence can significantly improve the likelihood that your child will feel secure, appreciate her talents, feel deserving of success, and perceive herself as worthy, powerful, and competent. If you feel overwhelmed by the challenge of implementing a systematic self-esteem and self-confidence-building strategy, consider enrolling in a parenting class, parenting skills workshop, or parent support group. These programs are frequently offered at local community centers, YMCAs, adult education departments in your school district, or community colleges.

3.   Chronic poor self-esteem is symptomatic of underlying emotional problems. Serious self-esteem deficits will not disappear of their own accord. Even if a child with poor self-esteem is academically or athletically successful, she will probably derive limited enjoyment and satisfaction from her accomplishments. The child who dislikes herself and feels unworthy or "bad" will most likely continue to feel this way throughout life unless she receives help from a qualified mental health professional. The function of counseling or psychotherapy is to help the child examine, process, and resolve the underlying feelings responsible for her negative attitudes and perceptions. Providing help before poor self-esteem becomes entrenched is the best investment you can make in her future. If the self-esteem deficits are already entrenched, then the need to become proactive and procure help is all the more compelling.

 # Slow Reading

Children read slowly for many reasons. Some have difficulty decoding letters and words (see Dyslexia) or deciphering phonetic and/or non-phonetic words (see Nonphonetic Words; Phonics). Others have been trained by classroom teachers, reading specialists, and resource specialists to read (*track*) each word carefully. To help struggling students overcome or compensate for reading problems, these teachers may stop them whenever they make a mistake and insist that they sound out (*attack*) each syllable slowly and then carefully combine the sounds (*blend*) to form each word (see Reading Aloud).

Teachers committed to the meticulous *track/attack/blend/correct* procedure usually justify their method with two common rationales: 1) children who read imprecisely will continue to do so unless their errors are corrected, and 2) children must read accurately to comprehend what they are reading and develop self-confidence (see Reading Comprehension).

The practice of insisting that children read precisely and meticulously begins in kindergarten or first grade and is repeatedly reinforced throughout elementary school. In many schools, requiring reading accuracy from elementary students is a firmly entrenched institution and an integral part of the instructional methodology. Because of this methodology, slow reading is not limited to children with reading problems. In many schools, even fluent readers are also encouraged to read word-by-word. The practice is reinforced by the tradition of teachers having

students read aloud in class and meticulously correcting each mistake. For poor readers, this process can be traumatic and humiliating. It can trigger profoundly negative associations and cause children to become reading phobic.

Unfortunately, the syllable-by-syllable, word-by-word method can have negative consequences. Children who are continually corrected can become highly self-conscious and sensitive. Because they are so intent on compensating for their inaccuracies, these youngsters often reduce reading speed, and they may continue to read slowly and laboriously long after they have overcome their phonics, word attack, blending, and word-tracking deficits. The burdensome habit of sounding out each word meticulously and subvocalizing (hearing the sound of the word in one's mind) places them at a significant disadvantage in upper level classes where they will be required to do a great deal of reading.

The justification for having children read aloud is obvious. The procedure allows teachers to monitor students' progress, evaluate skills, and provide appropriate assistance. The downside of this practice is that children can become so habituated to vocalizing or subvocalizing words that they do so even when reading silently. This inevitably slows down their reading speed. (Seeing a child move his lips while reading silently is the telling sign that he is subvocalizing each word.)

Hearing words in one's mind when reading can, of course, be one of life's more aesthetically pleasing experiences. The sounds produced by pronouncing beautiful poetry or prose carefully and rhythmically can be exalting. There are times, however, when students must be able to activate their "reading turbo charger" and complete assignments quickly. Being able to *speed-read* in these situations can be a vital academic resource.

When students speed-read, they are actually skimming or scanning sentences and chunks of information without being restrained by the need to subvocalize. They learn to assimilate and remember visual information without having to hear the words in their mind. At first, children may find skimming disconcerting because it contradicts what they have been taught in school and forces them out of their reading comfort zone. After years of indoctrination and practice, the systematic vocalization and subvocalization of words can become a hard-to-break habit.

Are children truly *reading* when they are skimming pages in textbooks? The answer to this question depends upon your definition of reading. Certainly, youngsters—even those is grades 3 and 4—can learn how to assimilate information by skimming, and their brains can be trained to recall visual data that is not subvocalized.

Speed-reading can be a valuable academic resource for students faced with many assignments and a finite amount of time to complete the work. One important advantage of the procedure is that it allows youngsters to preview a textbook chapter or an encyclopedia entry quickly and get an overview before actually studying the material. Students can use the method to identify important information that they may want to examine more carefully at a later time. The technique is also a highly effective resource when studying and reviewing for tests, doing library research, or getting an overview of what is being covered on an exam.

Speed-reading should be used selectively, as there are some disadvantages. Because the brain is trying to get an overview and assimilate the most obvious information, skimming does not lend itself to critical thinking nor to a careful evaluation of content. Despite these disadvan-

tages, the ability to read quickly is an important academic (and vocational) tool that allows students to sort through the plethora of information they must confront in an increasingly "data-loaded" world. Students who can activate on command their speed-reading ablities have a distinct competitive advantage over students who can only plod laboriously through the reams of material they are assigned in upper level courses.

Corrective Strategies

In School

1.   The first step in determining why your child is reading slowly is to ascertain if he has *decoding problems* (tracking, visual discrimination, blending, word attack, or phonics deficits; see Nonphonetic Words; Phonics; Visual Memory). If you suspect that your child has decoding problems, ask for an evaluation by the school psychologist or resource specialist to determine if he qualifies for help available in school (see Parents Rights). If your child is already in a reading assistance program to correct reading deficits, ask the resource specialist if one of her remedial goals is to help your child increase reading speed. Be forewarned that the specialist may want to resolve decoding problems before concentrating on increasing speed. It is likely that she is aware of the Catch-22: by attempting to improve accuracy, she risks reducing reading speed. When forced to prioritize, most specialists stress accuracy over speed, at least during initial stages of the remedial process.

2.   If your child reads slowly but does not have decoding deficits, ask if the school offers a speed-reading course or can integrate a speed-reading component into the regular curriculum. Some schools offer speed-reading as an elective, after-school, or summer program.

At Home

1.   If you suspect that your child has decoding problems or that a learning disability is reducing reading speed, refer to the Student Evaluation

Checklist (see Learning Disabilities), and the Reading Problems Inventory (see Reading Comprehension) to help identify underlying deficits that may be causing the problem. Once deficiencies are identified, refer to corrective strategies in relevant entries in this book.

2.   Do an experiment with your child. Have him place the first two fingers together to use as a pacing device. Then have him quickly scan a page from one of his textbooks, encouraging him not to subvocalize (hear himself pronounce the words in his mind). Tell him to pretend that his

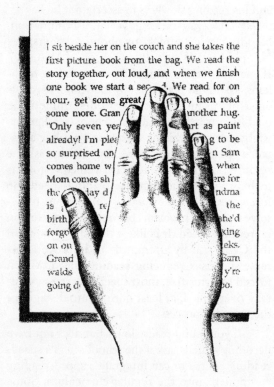

eyes are a camera and try to take a quick picture of the information his eyes are scanning. Play a game and see how many bits of information he can remember after one scan. Then have him speed-read the page again and give a verbal summary. Now turn the tables, and you scan the next page and give him a verbal summary. Emphasize that the objective is not to remember everything, but rather to get an overview of what is being said. Explain that when he studies, he would need to read more carefully, possibly in conjunction with notetaking. Speed-reading requires practice, and breaking the subvocalization habit initially requires effort.

Remember to affirm your child for progress. Your enthusiasm for mastering the procedure should be contagious. Explain that skimming or speed-reading is appropriate only under certain conditions. You might say: "Skimming a unit in your textbook will let you know what the material is about. This overview will give you a better idea about what you need to learn. Skimming can also be a great help when you review for tests. After skimming, however, reading the material again carefully and slowly and reading over your notes are extremely important. The student who studies smart combines both procedures."

3.   (Junior High/High School, J/HS) If you conclude that your child's slow reading is chronic and is impeding his academic progress, consider enrolling him in a private speed-reading class. These courses are offered at learning centers in many towns and cities.

Smart Thinking

A high IQ does not guarantee a cakewalk through school or through life. To succeed academically, your child must be able to use her intelligence. This pragmatic application of intelligence is the essence of smart thinking.

An important distinction must be made between smartness and intelligence. A highly intelligent child may be able to solve algebra problems in fourth grade, but may have had two bicycles stolen because she wasn't smart enough to lock them to the school bike rack (see IQ Test Scores).

The child who thinks smart has a distinctive modus operandi when faced with challenges, obstacles, problems, and opportunities. She characteristically:

- Concentrates on getting the job done efficiently and effectively and with a minimum amount of grief

- Establishes goals and priorities (see Goals; Priorities)

- Develops a practical strategy for getting from point A to B to C (see Planning Ahead)

- Calculates the odds

- Plans strategically

- Applies cause-and-effect principles (see Disregarding Consequences)

- Neutralizes obstacles

- Anticipates potential problems

- Develops a plan for handling possible glitches (see Planning Ahead; Problem Solving)

- Bounces back from defeats (see Bouncing Back from Setbacks and Learning from Mistakes)

- Learns from both positive and negative experiences

- Focuses intellectual and physical energy on attaining objectives

- Figures out how to survive and prevail in a challenging and competitive world

When confronted with a problem, smart children ask themselves, consciously or unconsciously, five key questions:

- What am I trying to achieve?

- What are the possible problems?

- How can I get the job done?

- How can I avoid mistakes?

- How can I increase my chances of success?

The smart child's analytical, critical, and strategic thinking are integral components in her response to all challenges and problems. The child may not always be consciously aware of her thinking process, but her astute judgment calls testify to the fact that her functional thinking mode is operating at full throttle (see Critical Thinking).

The smart child realizes that the shortest distance between two points is a straight line, but at the same time she also realizes that the path to her objective is not always going to be direct. In some situations, she may need to make detours. She will also need to make interim stops along the way. She intuitively understands that a short-term goal (for example, a B+ on the next French test) is a stepping stone to achieving her long-term goal (a good enough grade point average to be accepted at the Air Force Academy). If her objective is to become the starting pitcher on her softball team, she might spend hours pitching a ball through a tire suspended from a tree limb to improve her accuracy. She voluntarily commits the time and effort because she believes this strategy will help her attain the payoff she desires.

Another key trait distinguishes the smart child from her less successful classmates: she carefully considers—in advance—the possible and probable consequences of her decisions and actions. If she makes a mistake or suffers a setback, she assesses the situation and makes the necessary strategic adjustments. The not-so-smart child does not learn from negative experiences, and as a consequence is destined to repeat the same mistakes (see Bouncing Back from Setbacks and Learning from Mistakes).

The child who thinks smart is keenly aware of what is happening around her and uses these observations and insights to guide her actions. If her history teacher has emphasized the civil rights movement in lectures, the smart student devotes extra time to studying civil rights issues in detail as she prepares for the next test. She will review previous tests and quizzes and, based upon the previous test questions, the teacher's hints, and the issues emphasized during class discussions, she will try to anticipate what questions the teacher is likely to ask. She will establish her goal (e.g., the grade she desires), plan ahead, and allocate sufficient time to study (see Planning Ahead; Preparing for Tests; Priorities; Study Skills; Time Management).

The not-so-smart-thinking child responds very differently to responsibilities and challenges. She might forget to attach a bibliography to her history term paper, check over her math prob-

lems for errors, or review newly assigned vocabulary words before the French test (see Disorganization; Negative Attitude toward School).

A discrepancy between IQ (intelligence quotient) and *SQ* (smartness quotient) may be attributed to the fact that IQ tests are designed to measure a child's potential to succeed in school.[1] The tests do not assess the practical application of intelligence, nor do they assess whether or not a child will choose to develop and use her full intellectual abilities.

Students who float through life intellectually anesthetized usually become habituated to passive, ineffectual thinking. The long-term academic and vocational implications of this cerebral dulling can be disastrous. These students are destined to discover a painful fact of life: teachers (and employers) are not going to give the most coveted rewards to passive thinkers and passive workers. Good grades, career advancements, and raises are allocated to those who think smart, work assiduously, and produce.

Historically, it has been the traditional role of parents to impart wisdom to their children and to teach them how to "use their heads." Unfortunately, many parents today lack the time or inclination to meet this compelling obligation. Perhaps they are too consumed with earning a living, paying bills, and surviving emotionally in a pressure-cooker world. Perhaps they don't realize how vital their guidance is to their child's intellectual development. Because so many parents fail to serve as primary mentors, schools have tried to fill the void. They have done so with limited success. The intense pressure on teachers to teach academic skills and maintain discipline leaves little time for training students how to think strategically, or, at least, this is the rationale often offered for not providing this training. Ironically, teaching students thinking skills could easily be an integral and dynamic component of the course

---

1. *SQ* is a term coined by the author. Currently, there is no standardized (normed) test that measures strategic intelligence.

content. For example, a high school history teacher might ask students to list pros and cons and potential consequences that the Founding Fathers considered as they wrestled with the decision to break away from England. This would ideally lead to a discussion of cause and effect, tactical thinking, planning, priorities, goals, problem solving, and ethics (see Critical Thinking; Disregarding Consequences; Planning Ahead; Priorities; Problem Solving).

Our society is paying a high price for not teaching children how to think. More and more children are making tragically flawed decisions, and these defective choices are producing disastrous repercussions. The rampant mindlessness of young people has reached epidemic proportions. Despite blatant risks, teenagers are smoking, driving while intoxicated, failing to practice safe sex, becoming pregnant, acquiring sexually transmitted diseases, joining street gangs, taking and dealing drugs, and killing each other. They are also committing suicide in record numbers. The explanation for this frightening epidemic of madness is quite simple: we are failing to teach our children what they need to know in order to handle life's pressures, challenges, and problems (see *The Life-Smart Kid*).

Virtually every child can be taught to think smarter and improve her analytical thinking skills. For this to happen, parents must intentionally create an environment at home—and teachers must intentionally create an environment in school—that offers repeated opportunities for children to practice tactical, strategic, and analytical thinking. With encouragement, guidance, acknowledgment, feedback, and affirmation, children can raise their "Smartness Quotient." As their SQ increases, their potential for success in school and in life will improve dramatically.

Corrective Strategies
In School

1.   If you suspect your child is not thinking smart in school and that strategic thinking deficiencies are having a negative impact on her aca-demic performance, ask the teacher to complete the inventories found under Disregarding Consequences and Bouncing Back from Setbacks and Learning from Mistakes (see pages 28 and 43). (Additional parent inventories that assess smart thinking can be found in the following in the At Home section.) The teacher's evaluation process should take no more than five minutes. If your child is in junior or senior high school, the teacher may not be able to evaluate your child in all areas because of limited exposure. Be diplomatic. Some teachers may feel you're putting them on the spot. Others may resent being asked to spend extra time to complete the inventories. Explain that you sincerely want to help your child do better in school. If you are to provide meaningful direction and help at home and support the teacher's efforts, you must have specific feedback about your child's performance and about any deficits that are impeding her progress. (Please note: because of the overlap of underlying causal factors, some behaviors and attitudes appear on more than one checklist.)

2.   Brainstorm with the teacher ways in which you might work together to help your child overcome any deficits identified on the inventories. See specific entries in this book for additional suggestions about how to help children manage time and establish goals and priorities. School workbooks that address these issues include *Getting Smarter* and *Study Smart, Think Smart*. For parent-oriented, interactive books that teach children to think smart, refer to *Smarter Kids*. These and other resources are listed at the back of this book.

At Home

1.   To identify specific areas in which your child is not thinking smart, fill out the same checklists you ask the teacher to complete (see pages 28 and 43). Your observations and perceptions may be different because you observe and interact with your child in a different context. This inconsistency does not invalidate your impressions or those of the teacher. (Please note: Some statements on the inventories are clearly

not relevant to children in the lower grades of elementary school.)

2.   If you want further insight into the effectiveness and efficiency of your child's thinking, complete the following inventories.

ATTITUDE INVENTORY

My child:	YES	NO
Seeks new challenges	____	____
Enjoys finding solutions to problems	____	____
Likes to be put to the test	____	____
Enjoys developing new skills and talents	____	____
Has faith in ability to succeed at any task	____	____
Perseveres until mastery is achieved	____	____
Takes pride in doing a first-rate job	____	____
Believes s/he deserves to win	____	____
Believes s/he is a valuable person	____	____
Believes s/he is capable	____	____

Problem Management Inventory

My child:	YES	NO
Repeats the same mistakes	____	____
Resists assistance	____	____
Tends to avoid confronting problems or challenges	____	____
Insists on getting his/her own way	____	____
Gives up easily	____	____
Blames others for his/her problems	____	____
Is unwilling to accept suggestions and help	____	____

Gets upset when frustrated	____	____
Cannot think clearly when upset	____	____
Has difficulty developing strategies for solving problems	____	____
Is disorganized	____	____
Is passive	____	____
Becomes defensive when a problem is pointed out	____	____
Procrastinates	____	____
Denies s/he has problems that are blatant	____	____

Goals Inventory

My child:	YES	NO
Establishes realistic goals	____	____
Is motivated	____	____
Plans ahead	____	____
Establishes priorities	____	____
Can develop a strategy for attaining defined objectives	____	____
Budgets and manage time effectively	____	____
Establishes interim goals	____	____
Can suspend immediate gratification to attain future goals	____	____
Continues to pursue goals despite occasional setbacks	____	____
Can handle frustration	____	____
Likes challenges and likes to be tested	____	____
Believes s/he can prevail over most problems and challenges	____	____
Is proud of accomplishments	____	____
Establishes a new goal once an objective is attained	____	____

Time Management Inventory

My child: YES   NO

*Leaves projects and assignment
to the last minute*   _____   _____

*Doesn't care about getting
things done on time*   _____   _____

Does not use a schedule   _____   _____

Hands in incomplete assignments   _____   _____

*Does not hand in assignments
when due*   _____   _____

*Has difficulty estimating how
much time a project requires*   _____   _____

Lacks planning skill   _____   _____

*Is often under stress caused by
poor time management*   _____   _____

*Schedules too many things to
do at one time*   _____   _____

*Does not leave enough time for
reviewing and proofreading*   _____   _____

Is chronically late   _____   _____

---

3.   Select some of the behaviors described in these inventories and create a checklist for your child to complete. Don't list all the negative traits, as this is certain to demoralize your child and/or make her defensive and resistant. Choose statements that she can understand, that are relevant to problem areas, and that are applicable to her level of maturity. Use her responses as a catalyst for discussion. Define one or two key problem areas (selecting too many behaviors to correct will overwhelm her) and explore possible solutions (see DIBS Problem-Solving Method in Problem Solving). Listen to your child! She may have excellent ideas about how to correct the problems. For example, she might suggest that she design a simple checklist to indicate that she has completed all her homework. If she does not

offer solutions, suggest ideas to her. For additional strategies, refer to relevant entries in this book (such as Planning Ahead; Priorities; Time Management). For a comprehensive methodology to help you enhance your child's strategic thinking skills, consult *The Life-Smart Kid* (see Resource List at the back of the book).

4.   If your child is having difficulty with the principles of cause and effect, you might do an activity entitled "Possible and Probable Consequences." Below find examples of hypothetical scenarios you might explore together.

POSSIBLE AND PROBABLE CONSEQUENCES

What might happen if . . .

(Elementary School, ES) The oil level in the engine is too low.

CONSEQUENCE: _____
_____

Is this consequence possible or probable?

A child rides her bicycle at night without a light.

CONSEQUENCE: _____
_____

Is this consequence possible or probable?

(Junior High School, JHS) A kid jumps from a rock into a river without checking out the depth of the water and the speed of the current.

CONSEQUENCE: _____
_____

Is this consequence possible or probable?

(High School, HS) You go to a party where the parents are not home, and kids are drinking beer on the front lawn.

CONSEQUENCE: _____
_____

Is this consequence possible or probable?

---

5.   Using the preceding as models, make up other scenarios that would be relevant to your child. Keep the tone upbeat and enjoyable and avoid lecturing and sermonizing. Focus on discussing issues and examining your child's thinking and evaluative process. Offer insights when appropriate, but don't expect your child to "get it" the first time you do this activity. Changing behaviors and attitudes, especially those that are entrenched, requires time and patience. For additional suggestions about how to improve your child's awareness of cause and effect principles, see Disregarding Consequences.

6.   If you suspect that your child's strategic thinking skills are being undermined by possible emotional or family issues, refer to Anger and Frustration, Behavior and Attitude, Effort and Motivation, Psychological Problems and Psychological Overlay, and Self-Esteem and Self-Confidence.

Speech Disorders

Children with speech disorders have difficulty pronouncing letters and words properly. Subtle disorders manifest themselves as relatively common articulation problems. The symptoms include: omitting sounds (e.g., *at* instead of *cat*) or substituting one sound for another (e.g., *pag* for *bag*). Children may also distort words (e.g., *furog* for *frog*) or sounds such as *r* and *l*. Other symptoms include *lisping, stuttering, stammering,* and *cluttering*. These disturbances in speech rhythm may be caused or exacerbated by physiological, genetic, or emotional factors. In extreme cases, the child's communication may be incomprehensible.

There are many theories about the origins of speech disorders. Although most children with these problems are physically normal; approximately 15 percent have measurable physiological or neurological abnormalities. Research suggests that children who stutter have a higher incidence of central nervous system dysfunction. Those born prematurely or multiple births appear more predisposed to speech problems. Attempts to pinpoint the specific factors responsible for speech disorders, however, are controversial, and some authorities contend that there are no clearly defined causes. Advances in brain research may provide greater insight into the origins and neurological dynamics of these disorders.

In some cases, interference in basic sound production can be linked to deficiencies in specific muscles or organs that produce sound. Some youngsters with speech disorders also have motor coordination deficits, developmental delay, and behavior problems. The counterproductive behaviors sometimes associated with speech disorders may include resistance to help, rebelliousness, and acting out. These responses are common psychological defense mechanisms that struggling children use to protect themselves from feeling inadequate and defective. Ironically, self-conscious, emotionally vulnerable children with speech problems are frequently so enmeshed in defense mechanisms that they do not realize their behavior calls attention to the very deficiencies they are trying to hide (see Psychological Problems and Psychological Overlay; Self-Esteem and Self-Confidence).

Articulation skills are acquired sequentially. A three-year-old may say *wawa* instead of *water* because he has not yet acquired the ability to pronounce the *t* sound. This characteristic is not necessarily symptomatic of a speech disorder, and parents should not be alarmed. As the child matures, his articulation skills should improve. If problems persist, parents should consult their pediatrician who may refer the child to a speech pathologist for a comprehensive speech and language diagnostic evaluation.

Minor articulation problems often disappear by age eight or nine. Children should be monitored closely, however. The chart below indicates the approximate developmental stages at which children acquire specific articulation skills. Significant delays should alert parents to the need for professional speech evaluation. Children manifesting clear symptomatology of speech disorders qualify for an evaluation by a school district speech pathologist. If the school district refuses to provide this evaluation or acknowledge that a child has a speech problem, parents can begin protest procedures, or have their child privately assessed and treated (see Parents' Rights).

DEVELOPMENT OF ARTICULATION SKILLS

AGE	SOUNDS
3 years and 5 months	*b,p,m,w,h*
4 years and 5 months	*t,d,g,k,ng,y*
5 years and 5 months	*f,u,s,z*
6 years and 5 months	*sh,l,th*

A four-year-old's difficulty pronouncing the *l* sound should not cause concern. A six-year-old's inability to pronounce the sound *b* accurately, however, is a red flag that signals an articulation problem. Such a child should be professionally evaluated.

Speech disorders can be a serious source of embarrassment for children. The child who struggles to communicate intelligibly is often self-conscious, apprehensive, and insecure. The struggle can lead to teasing by other children, undermine self-confidence, and warp self-perceptions. Speech therapy is vital to protect such a child from emotionally debilitating self-consciousness, pain, and trauma (see Anger and Frustration).

Although the child with a serious speech problem is usually identified by his parents, teacher, or pediatrician and targeted for speech therapy in school, the child with less severe deficits may slip through the diagnostic/treatment net. He may only have difficulty articulating one or two sounds (for example, the *r* sound), and his parents and teacher may assume that the problem will correct itself naturally. Some parents may even find certain articulation problems "cute." They may overlook chronic "baby talk" and assume that their child will ultimately outgrow the problem. This attitude will delay vital treatment.

You must be vigilant even if your child is receiving speech therapy in school. Because of limited resources in many school districts, your child may be "bumped" out of the program before the problem is completely resolved. Be prepared to resist this cost-expedient action on the part of the school district.

Articulation problems become less "cute" as children mature and can undermine self-confidence, affect educational progress, and limit career choices and advancement. Common sense dictates that intervention is essential before serious emotional damage occurs. Rebuilding a defeated child's self-image is far more challenging, time-consuming, heart-wrenching, and costly than early diagnosis and treatment.

Corrective Strategies

In School

1.   If your child is having difficulty articulating sounds, insist that he be evaluated by the school speech pathologist (see Parents' Rights). If he doesn't qualify for help or the program is full, consider private speech therapy. The classroom teacher does not have the specialized training to help your child. If she continually corrects him in class, she may unwittingly cause him to feel embarrassed, self-conscious, and inadequate.

At Home

1.   Children with speech and language problems require highly specialized treatment. If your child is in a speech therapy program, ask the therapist if you should provide additional help at home. Do not continually correct your child's articulation errors. If he perceives your corrections as nagging, he will most likely become self-conscious, resistant, resentful, and defensive. To protect himself, he will begin to tune out your criticism. Because your child is highly sensitive to your attitude and the tone of your voice, you

must create an affirming and supportive context when you correct his articulation errors. If the speech pathologist feels you can help, ask for guidelines. Be patient! Articulation problems can be tenacious, and your child may not respond as quickly as you would like.

2.   Ask the school speech pathologist if there are tapes, workbooks, and/or computer programs that you can use to help your child at home. Ask for materials that are fun. Remember to make your interactive sessions enjoyable!

3.   If any child (or adult!) should tease or make fun of your child in your presence, clearly and unequivocally communicate that this is unacceptable. Such teasing will cause your child to feel embarrassed, self-conscious, and inadequate.

4.   If your child is denied help in school, or is not making as much progress as you want, seek a qualified private speech pathologist. One or two hours per week should be sufficient, and the investment could speed up the remedial process and avert psychological damage.

Spelling Problems

Millions of students are poor spellers. For some, weekly spelling tests are the nemesis. They conscientiously study assigned words, and on the morning of the test they carefully review the words one last time with their mother or father. Then they take the test, and disaster strikes. A pattern of red marks on their graded paper confirms that they did not master many of the words they so diligently studied.

Other students have little difficulty memorizing words for spelling tests, but cannot spell words correctly in reports and essays. And there are those unfortunate children who spell poorly in all contexts.

Spelling problems are usually attributable to two major sources: *auditory discrimination* deficits (hearing the difference between spoken sounds) and *visual memory* deficits (being able to remember what is seen). Children who cannot hear the difference between *band* and *bend* or who cannot see in their minds the spelling of nonphonetic words such as *receive* are prime candidates for being poor spellers. There are phonetic rules— *i* before *e* except after *c*—but few children remember these rules when taking a test or writing a report.

Another characteristic of English contributes to spelling problems. Our language abounds with spelling exceptions. *Alignment* is spelled with one *l*, whereas *alliance* is written with two, even though the two words have similar pronunciations. Unfortunately, there are no phonics rules to help children remember the proper spelling of these words (see Nonphonetic Words; Phonics).

The inherent difficulty in spelling English words correctly is compounded by the fact that many common words are frequently mispronounced. For example, most Americans pronounce *prerogative* as *perogative*. Because of this mispronunciation, the word is usually misspelled. There are many other examples of imprecise American pronunciation. Little or no verbal distinction is made between words ending in *-ant* (*reliant*) and *-ent* (*talent*) or between words ending in *-able* (*delectable*) and *-ible* (*fallible*). The spelling challenge is compounded by an additional imprecision in pronunciation: *delectable* is often pronounced *dillectable*.

Another distinctive characteristic of the English language contributes to spelling confusion: Whereas the pronunciation of English has evolved, the spelling has not. Hundreds of years ago, words such as *thought, through, fought, although*, and *rough* were pronounced precisely as they are spelled. (In Middle English, the words were spoken with a guttural sound similar to German.) Because there is no longer a clear relationship between spelling and pronunciation, these words are now classified as nonphonetic and children are expected to learn them by sight. Poor spellers quickly discover in first grade that there are innumerable examples of nonphonetic words assimilated (English words such as *could* and *through*, and foreign words such as *lieutenant* and *rouge*) that can make their lives miserable. Children, however, need not resign themselves to being incompetent spellers. The fundamentals of good spelling—the ability to discriminate the sounds of phonetic words and visualize the spelling of nonphonetic words—can be systematically taught. With good instruction and sufficient practice, your child can learn to compensate for any lack of natural spelling talent.

Corrective Strategies

In School

1. If your child has chronic spelling problems on spelling tests and/or written assignments, request that her hearing be evaluated by the school district audiologist or by her pediatrician. If the tests indicate that your child does not have a hearing loss, ask that she be tested by the school psychologist, resource specialist, or reading specialist to identify a possible auditory discrimination or visual memory problem. Assert your right to have her evaluated if your request is denied (see Parents' Rights), or have her tested privately.

2. If your child has auditory discrimination deficits and is struggling to differentiate basic sounds such as *i* and *e*, *o* and *u*, and *p* and *b*, she will require specialized assistance. Ask if there is a teacher at the school trained in the Lindemood Auditory Discrimination In-Depth Program, published by Developmental Learning Materials. (See Parents' Rights, if you are told your child does not qualify for help.) A wide range of other remedial materials, audio tapes, and computer software designed to develop auditory discrimination skills is available to schools. Check teacher supply stores and retail bookstores. Also refer to the Resource List at back of the book.

3. If your child has visual memory problems, ask the resource teacher use materials specifically designed to develop these skills. As is the case with auditory discrimination materials, a wide range of workbooks, flash cards, videos, and computer software designed to develop visual memory skills is available to schools. Review materials sold at teacher supply stores and retail

bookstores and refer to the Resource List at back of the book.

4. Ask your child's teacher or resource specialist if she thinks it would be beneficial for you to work with your child at home. If she agrees that this would be helpful, ask if the child's school can lend you materials specifically designed to improve spelling.

At Home

1. Children learn differently. The first step in improving your child's spelling skills is to help her discover her own most successful learning style. Is she a *visual, auditory, tactile,* or *kinesthetic* (learns by feel or by using her body as a dancer or natural athlete might) learner? To help make this determination:

• Ask your child's teacher for an opinion about your child's preferred learning style.

• Observe how your child learns school and nonschool related material (e.g. a new dance step or a cooking procedure). Does she learn by observing the procedure, by describing it in words, or by practicing it hands-on?

• Ask your child which learning modality is easier and which she prefers to use.

• If you and your child are unsure about how she learns best, experiment together. You might select four words that are unfamiliar to your child. (The level of difficulty of these words should be roughly equivalent.) Ask her to learn the definition of the first word by reading it silently several times (*this capitalizes on the visual modality*). Then you read the second word and its definition to her. Have her repeat the definition aloud several times (*this capitalizes on the auditory modality*). Now have her write the third word and its definition several times (*this capitalizes on the tactile modality*). Finally, have her act out the definition of the fourth word. She might, for example, pretend she's *despairing* (*this capitalizes on the kinesthetic modality*). Wait a few minutes and give her a fun, nonstressful quiz. Be careful not to appear judgmental or critical if she forgets words. Emphasize that the procedure is only an experiment. Through observation, "quiz" performance, and feedback from your child attempt to determine which learning modality is the most comfortable and productive for her.

• Request that the resource specialist or school psychologist administer the *Learning Styles Inventory* published by Creative Learning Press, Inc.

• Refer to *In Their Own Way* by Thomas Armstrong (Jeremy D. Tarcher Inc., 1987) for more information about learning styles.

Auditory learners typically prefer to repeat the spelling of words verbally. They should be encouraged to spell the words aloud. A tape recorder can be used for verbal drilling.

Tactile/Kinesthetic learners generally prefer to write the letters of words repetitively. They should be encouraged to trace words in the air using their entire arm and shoulder in the process. Creative kinesthetic learners enjoy hands-on learning in which they pretend and act as a means of learning information. For younger children, writing spelling words on a cookie sheet containing Plasticine clay or tracing the letters gently on sandpaper can be an effective tactile experience.

Visual learners learn best by reading words repetitively, subvocalizing, and perhaps writing down information. For the reasons discussed in the introduction to this section, visual learners have the ability to see information in their minds and this gives them a distinct advantage when they spell.

2.   Whenever possible, children should be encouraged to capitalize upon their preferred learning style. Some types of information, however, can be best learned by utilizing a particular modality, and this modality may not be the preferred one. Spelling is a perfect example. Although an auditory learner should be encouraged to use a tape recorder and repeat words aloud, she may discover that this preferred method does not produce the desired results. By encouraging her to develop visualization skills, you are providing her with an additional learning resource, which will be invaluable when she is required to memorize large quantities of information.

To help your child develop her visualization skills, have her write each of her spelling words on individual index cards using colored pencils or felt pens. Tell her to use any colors she wants. If

she prefers, she can write eachl letter of the word in different colors. Have her hold the word slightly above eye level. The word should be positioned either slightly to the right or the left of the child's line of vision so the child's eyes are pointing slightly to the right or left side. (See illustration, poage 238.)

Let your child experiment to determine which side produces the best results. (Looking up and to the right or left helps your child access and represent information visually, as the eyes naturally go upward and to the preferred side when information is being processed visually.) Have your child study the word until she thinks she knows it. Then have her close her eyes and see if she can still "see" the word in her mind or on the inside of her closed eyelids in the colors she has chosen. If she can't, have her open her eyes and study the word again.

Once she can see the word in her mind's eye, have her spell it aloud to you. Then have her write it. She can choose the same colors or different colors when she writes the word. Follow this procedure for five to ten words, and then give a review quiz. Encourage your child to close her eyes and visualize the words when taking an actual test in school or when writing a difficult word in a report. This technique can also be used for remembering number facts, definitions, historical dates, math equations, verb conjugations, and chemical formulas.

3.   You might want to purchase spelling development materials (tapes, computer software, workbooks, etc.) for use at home. These materials are generally available in teacher supply stores. Refer to the Resource List at the back of this book for suggestions.

Study Breaks

Sparks fly in many families when the issue of study breaks is discussed. Confrontations can become especially heated when parents are convinced their child is taking too many breaks, and the child is convinced that repeated trips to the kitchen, interludes on the phone, and diversions with TV and the stereo are not negatively affecting the quality of his study and schoolwork.

Most parents have traditional attitudes about study breaks. They believe that the quality of their child's studying must suffer if he cannot sustain his concentration and effort. They want him to sit down and work conscientiously until he completes his homework. Although they can accept an occasional break, they do not want him to get up from his desk every five minutes.

Before chronic disagreements about study breaks can be resolved, parents must ask themselves four key questions:

• How much time should our child realistically be expected to study before taking a break?

• What underlying learning or concentration deficits could be causing our child to take excessive breaks?

• Is the quality of our child's work suffering because of taking too many breaks?

• How can we help our child improve his study stamina?

Traditional parental attitudes about study breaks must be applied selectively when a child has a chronic concentration problem A youngster who lacks effective impulse control will have difficulty focusing for more than a few moments on any subject that does not interest him (see Attention Deficit Disorder). Any object or stimulus in the environment can attract his attention. He might begin to play with a pencil, become engrossed in tapping his fingers on the table, drift off into a daydream, or attempt to participate in a conversation in another room (see Distractions while Studying.) If he is hyperactive, he will fidget, repeatedly drop objects and retrieve them, and continually get up from or fall out of his chair. He will use any pretext to go into the kitchen for a snack, to make a gratuitous comment, to ask an irrelevant question, daydream, or to wander into the TV room (see Passive Learning).

Youngsters with underlying learning problems are especially likely to interrupt their studying. This behavior is either a conscious or unconscious escape mechanism. Frustrated by the continual battle to decipher, comprehend, and complete assignments, they grasp at any opportunity to stop working. Most of these children are not consciously aware they are using interruptions to avoid work, and those who are aware may not be able to control their behavior. To struggling, demoralized children who lack good academic skills and self-confidence, interrupting their studying can be a compelling temptation (see Atypical Learning Problems; Dyslexia; Effort and Motivation; Keeping Up with the Class; Learning Disabilities; Underachievement).

Children with poor study habits often take excessive study breaks. They rarely establish goals or priorities and have difficulty managing time (see Time Management), planning (see Planning Ahead; Priorities), and preparing for tests (see Preparing for Tests). Because they lack self-discipline and are uninvolved and disorganized, these children are delighted to interrupt their homework as often as possible (see Disorganization; Goals; Negative Attitude toward School; Priorities; Procrastination; Study Skills).

Deciding if you need to monitor your child's studying demands a judgment call (see Learned Helplessness, Monitoring Homework). Your child's academic performance should be your primary criterion for intervention. If, after reviewing his grades and homework assignments, you conclude that he's working below his potential and that his marginal performance is attributable to poor study habits and excessive study breaks, it is vital that you establish reasonable study break guidelines. If, however, your child is doing good work despite many study breaks, it is advisable not to intervene. Your child may learn best with short bursts of intense studying. The maxim, "don't fix it if it isn't broken" applies in this situation. To impose study break guidelines when there is no need could be counterproductive and precipitate an unnecessary showdown.

Corrective Strategies

At Home

1.   How long children are able to sustain concentration and study without a break will vary according to the age of the child and the nature of the child's academic or study skills deficits. As a general rule, children with no presenting underlying learning problems or attention deficit disorder should be able to study for the following sustained periods:

- 10 minutes (1st and 2nd grade students)
- 15 minutes (3rd and 4th grade students)
- 15 to 20 minutes (5th and 6th grade students)

- 20 to 25 minutes (6th through 8th grade students)
- 25 to 40 minutes (8th through 12th grade students)

These numbers are not chiseled in stone. Some second graders can study for twenty minutes, and some sixth graders can study for forty-five minutes without a break. If the work is taxing, they may take more frequent breaks. Ask the teacher what would be an appropriate study routine for your child based upon her observations and experience. Your child's age, skills, and concentration span must be factored into the study break equation. Increase study time in small increments, and involve your child in the process of establishing the guidelines and working toward meeting mutually agreed-upon standards. The guidelines should be realistic. Insisting that a seven-year-old study for thirty-five minutes without a break is as unreasonable and unfair as insisting that a twelve-year-old with attention deficit disorder or a learning disability study independently for thirty-five minutes without a break. Praise, acknowledgment, and incentives for sustained effort should be integral components in the behavior modification process.

2.   Explain to your child why you feel repeated study breaks can reduce efficiency and undermine his concentration. Tell him that you want to set up an experiment to see if increasing the amount of study time between breaks will improve his schoolwork. When you propose the experiment, do so positively and without expressing disappointment in your child's current study style. Establish a reasonable and realistic goal, perhaps a study period of 10 minutes between breaks and then increase the time in 2 to 5 minute increments per week, working up to 25-minute study periods (an appropriate goal for a child in eighth grade or above) without a break. Base your target study time on your child's chronological age and the general guidelines above.

Set an egg timer for 10 minutes the first day of the experiment, and encourage your child to work for this amount of time without a break. It would be strategic to establish an incentive program in which your child can earn points toward a prize or special treat after studying for the agreed-upon time without looking up. The next day have your child set the timer for 11 minutes. Over the next five weeks, slowly build to the defined goal of 25 minutes. To document improvement (ideally, there will be improvement!), keep track of changes in your child's school performance. The record is an integral part of this experiment.

Repeatedly acknowledge and affirm your child for progress and express positive expectations that he can achieve his performance and study goals. (For more suggestions, see Disorganization; Distractions while Studying; Inadequate Study Time; Monitoring Homework; Passive Learning; Planning Ahead; Procrastination; Smart Thinking; Time Management.)

3.   Hyperactive children and those with concentration problems will have difficulty meeting the standards described above. When working with your child on modifying poor study habits, remember that the way in which you communicate is pivotal. Your words can trigger cooperation and insight or resistance and resentment. Frontal attacks and disparaging comments ("Well, if you wouldn't get up every five minutes, maybe you could pass your next history test") are guaranteed to produce a negative reaction. The more strategic alternative is to examine the issues in a cooperative, nonemotionally charged, and nonaccusatory manner and to develop a well-conceived plan that can help your child improve his concentration and study for more sustained periods. (For suggestions about how to help children who have difficulty concentrating, see Attention Deficit Disorder.)

STUDY TIME/STUDY BREAKS EXPERIMENT

DATE	AMOUNT OF STUDY TIME between BREAKS	GRADES (HOMEWORK TESTS, REPORTS)
----------	------------------------------------	---------------------------------------
----------	------------------------------------	---------------------------------------
----------	------------------------------------	---------------------------------------
----------	------------------------------------	---------------------------------------
----------	------------------------------------	---------------------------------------
----------	------------------------------------	---------------------------------------
----------	------------------------------------	---------------------------------------

Studying with Friends

Studying with a friend or friends can be an effective strategy if the students are serious and diligent and have clearly defined goals. Although the procedure may not always be an appropriate substitute for individual studying, the collective synergy of a study group can be especially helpful in preparing for tests. Students can capitalize on each other's insights, learning strengths, and skills. They can help each other identify important information, understand complex concepts, and memorize key facts. They can ask each other facsimile test questions, compare notes, and share the burden of outlining a chapter or developing a diagram that ties the important information together (see Memorizing Information; Notetaking; Reading Comprehension).

When study groups are composed of conscientious students, a "let's get serious and learn this" dynamic is created. The group dynamic can be a powerful learning tool. Students with good test-taking skills who can anticipate what the teacher is likely to ask on an exam can teach their critical and strategic thinking process to their study partners (see Critical Thinking; Identifying Important Information; Preparing for Tests; Smart Thinking; Study Skills).

Study groups have been used by law and business graduate students for decades, and many elementary and secondary school teachers have only recently "discovered" the technique. Labeled *cooperative learning*, the practice of having students break up into small groups in the classroom is becoming increasingly popular, and many teachers now incorporate study groups as an integral part of their instructional methodology.

If your child wants to study with a friend or friends, you must make a judgment call as to whether or not she is sufficiently mature, conscientious, and motivated to profit from the procedure. Be alert to hidden agendas. Children who use study groups primarily to socialize defeat the intent of the process and will derive little or no good from it.

As an experiment, allow your child to study cooperatively. Look at the chemistry of the group. If it appears to consist of at least some serious students who are getting good grades, this should allay many of your concerns. If cooperative learning works for your child, encourage continued use of the method.

Corrective Strategies

In School

1.   If cooperative learning is not encouraged in your child's class, and you believe it might be an effective learning tool, discuss the advantages of the procedure with your child's teacher. Some teachers might consider this "interference" or an invasion of their territory. Others may be resistant to any innovative teaching procedure regardless of who broaches the subject. Be guided accordingly. If you sense resistance or resentment, back off. You might find it more strategic to discuss the matter with the principal.

At Home

1.   Show your child how to use cooperative studying as an effective method for preparing for tests. Pretend you are one of her classmates. Work together at identifying key information in her notes and textbook. Ask each other questions. Make up a practice test and discuss which information the teacher is likely to include on his test. Ask her if she would like to try the method with a classmate who is serious about doing well in school. Discuss the temptation to get sidetracked and talk about unrelated issues when friends study together. Brainstorm how to handle this temptation (for example, a twenty-five-minute session followed by a ten-minute break for talking or a snack). Observe portions of the session (without being too obvious).

Be especially diplomatic and discrete when observing older students. They may be particularly sensitive to and resentful of any type of adult interference. Discuss your observations, elicit feedback from your child, and brainstorm ideas for improving the procedure. If it is clear that your child is not yet sufficiently mature to study with a friend, discourage her from doing so for now. An alternative might be to help her figure out how to "fix" the problem so that she and her study partners can study productively (see DIBS Problem-Solving Method in Problem Solving).

2.   When your child studies with a friend or friends, urge them to ask each other questions and make up practice tests (multiple choice, short answer, true/false, and, perhaps, essay tests). The method will help them review and identify important information. Encourage them to think like teachers when they study, and try to anticipate what's likely to be on the test (see Test Anxiety). Urge your child to record and compare her test performance when she studies cooperatively and when she studies alone. The results should indicate whether or not group studying is effective for her.

 Study Skills

The commonly held belief that intelligence determines school success discounts the role of focused effort and efficient study skills in the academic achievement equation. It is certainly true that the ability to grasp concepts, understand abstractions, perceive relationships, and recall information can facilitate learning and enhance school performance, but it is also true that a superior IQ does not guarantee superior achievement. Brilliant children may perform marginally in school while their less-than-brilliant classmates may do exceptionally well (see Critical Thinking; IQ Test Scores; Reading Comprehension; Smart Thinking).

In addition to being highly motivated, diligent, and self-disciplined, achieving students share other key characteristics that set them apart from underachieving and nonachieving students. They consistently:

- Define personal goals
- Establish priorities
- Record assignments accurately
- Manage time efficiently
- Plan ahead
- Identify important information when they study
- Develop an effective system for remembering information
- Take good notes from textbooks and lectures
- Engage actively in what they are learning

- Organize their materials
- Meet deadlines
- Proofread carefully and check for errors
- Anticipate what is likely to be on the next test

These pragmatic, academic achievement-oriented traits comprise the nuts and bolts of good study skills (see Attention to Details; Disorganization; Distractions while Studying; Effort and Motivation; Goals; Grades; Identifying Important Information; Inadequate Study Time; Note-taking; Planning Ahead; Preparing for Tests; Priorities; Recording Assignments; Study Breaks; Studying with Friends; Time Management; Working Independently).

Underachieving students have a very different modus operandi. Because most of these children learn passively, studying for them means little more than mindlessly turning the pages of their textbooks and notes. The consequences of their marginal involvement in the learning process are predictable: deficient skills, marginal mastery of course content, and poor grades (see Disregarding Consequences; Negative Attitude toward School; Passive Learning).

They may not admit it, but many teachers consciously or unconsciously ascribe to the theory that the "cream rises to the top." Believing that bright, capable children will naturally discover how to study efficiently and effectively, they devote little time to the formal systematic teaching of study skills.

Those youngsters who do figure out on their own how to study effectively join an elite, primarily middle-class "academic fraternity/sorority" whose members are on a track that leads to first-rate colleges and rewarding careers. Unfortunately, many other capable children never make it into this exclusive club because no one took the time to teach them systematically how to study productively (see Keeping Up with the Class).

It is axiomatic that students' school experiences can have a profound impact on their evolving self-concepts. Youngsters who struggle through twelve years of school often bear deep emotional scars that attest to academic trials and tribulations. Chronic frustrations, painful associations, phobias, and lack of confidence underscore how a poor school track record can cause youngsters to devalue their talents and intellect and alter their educational and career aspirations (see Bouncing Back from Setbacks and Learning from Mistakes; Self-Esteem and Self-Confidence).

Exceptions exist. Some students do poorly in the academic arena but continue to feel good about themselves and are successful in life. In almost every instance, these youngsters have other abilities and interests that buffer them from the impact of chronic academic frustration and demoralization. They may be good athletes, talented artists, or natural mechanics. Those who think smart figure out how to capitalize on their natural talents.

Despite these exceptions, positive school experiences significantly increase the likelihood of children having self-confidence, elevated expectations, and motivating educational and career aspirations. Negative experiences have the opposite effect. They diminish confidence and reduce expectations and aspirations. That a student who does poorly in school might conclude she is inadequate and incompetent is understandable. Although this conclusion may be erroneous, the child has little or no concrete evidence to prove otherwise (see Anger and Frustration; Behavior and Attitude; Expectations and Performance Guidelines).

Youngsters who are struggling in school because they lack good study skills have several options. They can:

- Persevere until they somehow prevail
- Figure out how to compensate for deficiencies
- Develop other talents and pursue areas of interest in which they can excel
- Lower expectations and aspirations
- Develop ego-protecting defensive behaviors
- Give up and shut down academically

Most children choose the path of least resistance. If they are doing poorly in school, they will often do everything in their power to avoid studying. By deluding themselves that they are not really failing if they don't try, these youngsters attempt to protect themselves emotionally and deny or deflect the unpleasant realities of their situation.

That children with the greatest need to study are usually the most resistant to studying is, of course, ironic. These marginally performing youngsters are usually described by their exasperated, despairing parents and teachers as unmotivated, lazy, irresponsible, and disorganized. These descriptive adjectives are actually quite accurate. Children with poor study habits and deficient study skills characteristically procrastinate; submit sloppy, incomplete and late assignments; blame others; deny that they have problems; and either become helpless or resistant to help. Their counterproductive behavior accentuates the very deficiencies they are trying to hide or deny, but because they are so enmeshed in their self-protecting system, they rarely recognize the paradox (see Atypical Learning Problems; Inadequate Study Time; Incomplete Assignments; Learning Disabilities; Psychological Problems and Psychological Overlay; Underachievement).

Logic dictates that all students should receive systematic instruction in how to study properly as an integral part of their education and that study skills instruction should occur *before* self-defeating habits, attitudes, and behaviors become entrenched. A compelling argument can be made for requiring students in elementary school to practice and apply study skills in every subject area. Two reasonable corollaries would be to stipulate that study skills competence be a precondition for advancement to junior high school, and that high school students who have not mastered the techniques be obligated to take an intensive remedial course.

If your child is struggling in school because of suspected study skills deficits, it is naive and risky to assume that she will somehow naturally figure out on her own how to study and learn more efficiently. The safer course would be to make certain she is taught the nuts and bolts of effective studying. If she is already doing well in school, having her review and practice basic study skills and teaching her advanced test-preparation and test-taking skills will help her become an even better student.

Corrective Strategies

In School

1.   To determine if your child has a study skills problem, ask the teacher to take a few minutes to complete the following Study Skills Inventory.

STUDY SKILLS INVENTORY

Code: 0 = Never   1 = Rarely   2 = Sometimes
       3 = Often   4 = Always

This student:

Works independently	_____
Is well organized	_____
Establishes short-term goals (A on the next quiz)	_____
Establishes long-term goals (B+ in English for the semester, or going to college)	_____
Establishes priorities	_____

Records homework assignments	_____
Plans ahead	_____
Manages time well	_____
Uses a study schedule	_____
Identifies important information when studying	_____
Remembers important information when taking tests	_____
Comprehends the assigned material when studying	_____
Takes good notes from textbooks	_____
Takes good notes from lectures	_____
Anticipates what is likely to be asked on tests	_____
Can study 10 minutes without a break (grades 1 to 2)	_____
Can study 15 minutes without a break (grades 3 to 4)	_____
Can study 20 minutes without a break (grades 5 to 6)	_____
Can study 25 minutes without a break (grades 6 to 8)	_____
Can study 30 minutes without a break (grades 9 to 12)	_____
Reviews conscientiously for tests	_____
Checks over assignments to find errors	_____
Has confidence in academic skills	_____

A pattern of 0's and 1's are red flags that indicate your child has a significant study skills problem and requires systematic instruction. A pattern of 2's is common in underachieving children and should alert you to the need for closer monitoring of your child's study habits—in school and at home. Use the inventory selectively with children in the lower grades of elementary school. Your child is not yet expected to have mastered some of the skills on the list. These skills, however, should be introduced as your child progresses into the upper grades. If she demonstrates that she is not assimilating the skills, express your justifiable concerns to her teachers and brainstorm some practical solutions to the problem.

2.   If the teacher indicates that your child has poor study skills, ask for suggestions about how to help your child acquire these critically important skills. Most children can significantly improve their study skills and academic performance with focused, intensive instruction, perceptive feedback, and sufficient practice. Parents who unite and demand that their school provide systematic study skills instruction as part of the curriculum generally discover that squeaky wheels get the oil. The noise, however, may have to be loud enough to disturb a complacent and sometimes myopic educational bureaucracy!

At Home

1.   If the inventory completed by your child's teacher indicates study skills deficits, make up a priority list of skills your child needs to master. For example, the teacher may have identified problems with disorganization, incomplete assignments, notetaking, and preparing for tests. Refer to these entries in this book, and use appropriate corrective strategies.

2.   (Elementary School, ES) If your child is in grades 1 to 4, you can prevent potential academic problems by teaching her good study skills before she may actually need them. This is the educational equivalent of practicing preventative medicine. Begin working with your child on goal setting, recording assignments, and planning ahead. Make sessions short and fun. For example,

you might actively involve your child in planning the next family vacation or her own birthday party. Help her establish priorities, make up lists, budget time, and create schedules. (See Planning Ahead; Time Management).

3.   Encourage your child to get in the habit of making up a checklist before beginning a major project such as a term paper or studying for a midterm or final exam. She should list all the steps she needs to complete and when she needs to complete them. As she accomplishes each task, she would then check it off the list. This process is a key component in the development of effective study habits.

4.   Brainstorm with your child a personalized study procedure for the next history, science, or math test. Discuss how to identify important information, recall data, and forecast what the teacher is likely to ask on the test (see Critical Thinking; Identifying Important Information; Preparing for Tests; Reading Comprehension). Explore different learning and memorization techniques to master the material (see Auditory Memory; Memorizing Information; Visual Memory). Examine different notetaking techniques (see Notetaking). Plan a study schedule together (see Planning Ahead; Time Management). Make up practice tests and answer the questions together. Quiz each other on the subject matter (see Preparing for Tests). Modeling pragmatic study and test-preparation techniques will provide your child with a framework. Be careful not to get into the habit of studying for every test with your child. This might cause excessive dependence on you (see Learned Helplessness). Once she has demonstrated that she knows how to study, turn her loose!

Teacher–Child Conflict

Teachers and students do not always get along. The friction, usually attributable to a child's misbehavior, negative attitude, or lack of effort, may involve relatively minor issues such as talking in class or more serious issues such as cheating, fighting, or stealing. Behaviors certain to upset teachers include: disruptiveness, irresponsibility, aggressiveness, chronic distractibility, hyperactivity, disrespect, hostility, dishonesty, profanity, resistance, laziness, and chronic dependency (see Anger and Frustration; Attention Deficit Disorder; Disregarding Consequences; Effort and Motivation; Expectations and Performance Guidelines; Learned Helplessness; Negative Attitude toward School; Psychological Problems and Psychological Overlay).

Smart students who understand cause-and-effect principles realize that their teachers have the ultimate authority, and they rarely, if ever, challenge this power hierarchy. They recognize and accept the facts of life: students are usually held accountable when they are in conflict with teachers, and teachers have the prerogative to enforce their rules and standards (see Smart Thinking).

Not-so-smart children are often oblivious to the power structure and the predictable repercussions for testing the rules. They may talk in class, act silly, distract other students, talk back, get into fights on the playground, or pass notes when the teacher's back is turned. They may not submit their homework or hand in work that is late, incomplete, and shoddy. Other traits that increase the risk of student-teacher tension include

not recording assignments, failing to study adequately, and actively or passively resisting help and guidance (see Behavior and Attitude; Passive Learning).[1]

Teachers are not necessarily blameless in every conflict situation. The assumption that all teachers are skilled, creative, inspirational, caring, enthusiastic, insightful, and nurturing may be comforting, but it is naive. Certainly, many highly competent teachers possess these traits and do the best job possible under often less-than-perfect conditions, but many others are burned out and intolerant of students who require extra effort, guidance, empathy, support, or patience. Their teaching style and attitude, and the fact that they may not have taught a creative and dynamic lesson in years, often triggers negative energy in the classroom, leaches enthusiasm and joy from the learning experience, and precipitates misbehavior, boredom, negative attitudes, and teacher-student strife. A teacher's reaction to disagreements, deportment problems, and conflict directly mirrors her values, attitudes,

---

1. Students' self-defeating behaviors and attitudes may be symptomatic of psychological overlay, often associated with a learning disability. Academically demoralized children who lack self-esteem and self-confidence often unconsciously resort to counterproductive behavior so they can function congruently with their negative self-concept (see Psychological Problems and Psychological Overlay; Self-Esteem and Self-Confidence).

training, teaching philosophy, and feelings about children.

Some teachers prioritize obedience, decorum, and course content. Others prioritize the development of self-confidence, active learning, critical thinking, and creativity. They believe that when children enjoy learning and are affirmed for their accomplishments, they rarely misbehave. When problems arise, as they must inevitably, these teachers intentionally model how to use reasoning and communication skills to resolve the problems. Recognizing that positive reinforcement (praise and affirmation) is generally more effective in shaping behavior than negative reinforcement (threats and punishment), the enlightened teacher might say, "I know that you'll continue working and not talk when I leave the room. You've repeatedly showed me that you're responsible, hardworking, and trustworthy." If the teacher's assumption proves wrong, and the students misbehave, she will use the misconduct as an opportunity to explore the important issues of responsibility and trust (see the DIBS Problem-Solving Method, page 190).

Whenever possible, wise teachers make every effort to defuse conflict and reorient negative behavior and resistance. Their modus operandi is to identify causal factors and develop a strategy that addresses and resolves underlying issues. Rather than taking a child's acting out behavior personally and resorting to traditional teacher weapons—punishment, denial of privileges, detention, and so on—they seek more creative and constructive solutions. Although they have rules and enforce their standards, they avoid letting problems degenerate into conflicts that they must win because they have all the power and that children must lose because they have no power. By encouraging children to confront problems, examine issues, accept responsibility, and think analytically, they stimulate insight and awareness and model how to respond rationally to conflict.

Unfortunately, some teachers wittingly or unwittingly create showdowns with misbehaving children. The deportment problems of many of these children are attributable to insecurity and inadequate self-esteem, self-confidence, and academic skills. Other children act out in school because they have emotional or family problems. Wise teachers realize that student–teacher conflict is inevitable when they choose to perceive students' nonadaptive behavior and misconduct as an affront and a challenge to their authority.

Certainly, misbehavior can disrupt the class, interfere with teaching, and elicit teacher resentment. Children must be apprised of the rules, standards, and behavior guidelines. They require direction and occasional "attitude adjustments." At issue is whether reprimands, punishment, and showdowns are the most effective ways to rein in children and help them become better citizens in the classroom and, later, in society.

Most teachers willingly accept their primary responsibilities to develop their students' academic skills and reinforce society's position on such key issues as effort, diligence, and attention to details. There are, however, many misconceptions about other supposed teacher responsibilities and obligations. Parents must realize that:

• Classroom teachers are not surrogate parents. It is not their job to impart basic values and attitudes that should be taught at home.

• Classroom teachers are not police officers. It is not their job to discipline students who are chronically out of control, hostile, manipulative, disrespectful of authority, or antisocial.

• Classroom teachers are not psychotherapists. It is not their job to "cure" children who manifest chronic oppositional behavior and have significant personality or conduct disorders (see Psychological Problems and Psychological Overlay).

A society that expects teachers to fulfill these roles is destined to be sadly disillusioned.

Being reasonable and empathetic does not preclude teachers from defining behavior guidelines and rules, imposing reasonable and appropriate punishment, or implementing firm and consistent academic standards. Each situation must be judged on its merits. Cooperative problem solving may be indicated in one context, and the imposition of unilateral authority may be indicated in another.

Most teacher-child conflicts can be resolved when:

- The problem or conflict is accurately defined
- The underlying issues are identified
- Communication channels are intentionally opened
- Parents and teachers work together at finding reasonable solutions to teacher-child conflicts
- The student's feelings are acknowledged
- The student is actively engaged in the process of finding solutions to the problem or conflict

Just as children who are preoccupied with defending themselves may not realize (or may deny) that their attitudes and behaviors are causing conflict, so, too, teachers can become so preoccupied with defending their own position that they, too, lose perspective. Once they begin to perceive a child as an enemy, intervention is essential.

While it is more typically the student who alienates the teacher with misbehavior or a negative attitude, sometimes the situation is reversed. When an entire class loses respect for a teacher, the disrespect is usually earned. Children who are continually yelled at and who perceive their teacher as unfair, inconsistent, prejudiced, or incompetent often respond by misbehaving. If the teacher clearly prefers girls to boys, she can expect to antagonize the boys in her class. Misconduct may be the most accessible retaliatory weapon available, and misbehavior may express the class's collective sense of injustice.

Improved communication is an essential key to resolving conflict between a teacher and a child. Both parties must be willing to assess their positions, attitudes, and actions and make changes intended to improve relations. Teachers who are convinced that their way is the only correct way and those who are inflexible, unwilling to analyze disagreements objectively, and resist altering their preconceptions, attitudes, or approach erect major barriers to communication. These teachers signal their intransigence and refusal to engage in a rational problem-solving process when they proclaim, "I've been teaching for twenty years, and I'm not about to change my methods to accommodate your child. When he improves his behavior in my class, the conflict will be resolved."

Many children lack the insight and communication skills to resolve conflicts with teachers, so parents must be prepared to step in and help define the issues causing the conflict. They must help their child identify the teacher's values and priorities and the rationale for her position. They must help their child explore how to make reasonable and expedient accommodations to the teacher's wishes. At the same time, parents may need to help the teacher understand the factors contributing to the conflict without justifying their child's behavior. They must make every effort to see the situation from the teacher's perspective. If she has thirty other students in class, managing a child who requires an inordinate amount of time and effort could legitimately cause her to feel guilty about depriving other students of their fair share.

If your attempts to help your child resolve a conflict with the teacher prove unsuccessful, request a conference with the school psychologist, counselor, and/or principal (see Communicating with the School; Conferencing with School Officials). Transferring your child to another class should be a last resort. Although this may resolve the immediate problem, it may only be a temporary solution. If your child chronically misbehaves and the underlying issues are not identified and resolved, he will probably soon find himself in conflict with his new teacher.

When you model for your child how to resolve disagreements, communicate effectively, and think analytically and strategically, you avail yourself of an unparalleled opportunity to help your child become "life-smart." The child who learns how to deal successfully with people in authority and who learns how to resolve conflicts has acquired a invaluable resource that he will be able to use throughout his life.

Corrective Strategies

In School

1.   If your child is in conflict with his teacher, it is vital that you acquire as much specific information as possible. A well-focused parent-teacher conference will provide this data (see Parent-Teacher Conferences). At this juncture, you have two options: you can encourage your child to work out problems with the teacher on his own (see suggestions below), or you can take an active role in resolving the problem. The extent of your involvement should reflect the nature of the conflict; your child's level of confidence, maturity, communication skills, and insight; and his teacher's attitude. If you decide to serve as a mediator or facilitator, you and the teacher must define the problem or the conflict accurately and identify the underlying issues (see DIBS Problem-Solving Method on page 190).

Once the problem is defined and the causal factors identified, you and the teacher can brain-

storm solutions to the conflict. It may be appropriate for your child to attend this meeting with the teacher, or it may be more appropriate for the initial conference to be held without your child present so that you and the teacher can talk openly and frankly.

Your own attitude will undoubtedly play a major role in the outcome of the conference. If you are accusatory and hostile, the teacher is likely to be defensive, resistant, and resentful. If the teacher is uncooperative and unwilling to work with you despite your sincere efforts to be diplomatic and objective, involve the principal in subsequent discussions.

2.   (Elementary School, ES) If you believe your child's attitude or behavior are primarily responsible for the conflict, you and the teacher should develop a behavior modification program to use in school and at home. The following checklist will provide daily feedback about your child's behavior, and the information can be used to make discussions with the teacher more substantive and meaningful. Examine areas of concern with your child and brainstorm ideas for reducing friction and conflict (see Problem Solving). One op-

DAILY BEHAVIOR CHECKLIST

Code: 0 = Never   1 = Rarely   2 = Sometimes   3 = Often   4 = Always

	MON.	TUES.	WED.	THURS.	FRI.
Pays attention in class					
Raises hand in class					
Behaves on the playground					
Follows instructions					
Completes assignments					
Pays attention					
Is respectful					
Obeys class rules					
Works independently					

tion is to give your child a reward if he achieves a targeted performance score for the week. The initial targeted score should be realistic and raised incrementally. The checklist can be altered and categories substituted to pinpoint specific issues producing friction in the classroom. Experiment with involving your child in the process of determining what specific behaviors and attitudes should be included on the checklist.

3.   Consult the school counselor or principal if you need more suggestions about how to resolve the conflict between your child and his teacher. If you and the teacher are having difficulty communicating or working together and if it becomes apparent that the conflict is not resolvable despite the efforts of the principal to mediate, you may need to request that your child be placed in another class.

4.   Chronic, extreme misbehavior is usually symptomatic of emotional or family problems. In some instances, this behavior may be attributable to Attention Deficit Disorder. Consult with your pediatrician or family physician, who may refer you to a psychiatrist, psychologist, or neurologist for diagnostic evaluation.

At Home

1.   Discuss with your child the feedback you are getting from the teacher about the conflict. Be prepared for your child to deny responsibility and blame the teacher entirely for the problem. This reaction in many cases is a transparent psychological defense mechanism and is quite common. Like their adult counterparts, children are often reluctant to acknowledge counterproductive behavior. Your job is not to take sides, but to help your child identify the issues; understand the teacher's values, priorities, and concerns; and identify the attitudes and behaviors that the teacher feels are contributing to the conflict. Your child must accept that the teacher has the power

in her classroom. He may feel the teacher is unfair (and you may concur), but he must learn to accommodate to the realities of the existing power hierarchy. Helping him recognize and accept that life is not always fair is an important part of the process of preparing him to deal with the real world—where conditions are never perfect.

Your child's ability to make the best of a bad situation is a vital survival skill in a competitive and often harsh and unforgiving world. If, however, you honestly believe the teacher is unfair and the situation is unresolvable, you need to support your child in your dealings with the school. There are no absolute formulas about how to resolve teacher-child conflicts. Sometimes you will need to defend your child. In other instances, you may need to be a conflict mediator, or you may need to encourage your child to make strategic accommodations to the teacher's desires.

2.   Urge your child to discuss with the teacher the issues that are causing conflict (such as an unfair grade on a report or test, or a feeling that the teacher is embarrassing him in class). At the same time, realize that your child may feel apprehensive about broaching these subjects and confronting an authority figure. Questioning and perhaps challenging an adult can be an intimidating prospect for a child. Helping your child create a strategy that addresses the issues and his concerns can be an important learning experience. Rehearsals can be invaluable in refining your child's technique, reducing anticipatory anxiety, and developing his confidence. Model how your child could bring up the subject. ("Mrs. Lantham, I'd like to talk to you about how I feel when you criticize my handwriting in front of the class.") Have your child play the role of the teacher. Then switch roles. Be patient and affirming as your child struggles to express feelings and improve communication skills.

 # Test Anxiety

The prospect of having to take a test will generate some anxiety and apprehension for virtually all students. For most children, these qualms and misgivings are manageable. Once they begin to take the test, they calm down. For others, the foreboding and angst they experience during the test may be so debilitating that it undermines the validity of the test as an accurate measure of their knowledge and skills. The excessively test-anxious child is often convinced in advance he will do poorly. Such catastrophic expectations have an unfortunate tendency to be self-fulfilling. The foreboding may begin days before the test and intensify as D-day approaches. While waiting for the test to be handed out, a voice inside screams: "I know I won't be able to answer the questions!" Finally, he receives his copy, and he quickly scans it. Overwhelmed by panic, he can find no relationship between the test questions and the material he studied. His brain shuts down. He forgets how to spell words he knew how to spell that morning at the breakfast table. He cannot remember how to add mixed fractions, despite having done dozens of similar problems in class and for homework. He cannot recall important dates, math formulas, chemical symbols, vocabulary definitions, irregular verb conjugations, grammar rules, or biology phyla. His worst nightmare becomes a reality (see Self-Esteem and Self-Confidence).

Chronic, excessive test anxiety can usually be traced to one or more of the following factors:

- Poor preparation
- Deficient academic skills
- Poor stress management skills
- Inadequate study skills
- Negative experiences with tests
- Negative expectations about performance
- Negative associations with school and learning
- Low self-confidence

It is virtually impossible to assess accurately the skills of a child who is paralyzed by fear. Even less extreme test-associated stress can cause students to think and work inefficiently and produce poor scores on standardized tests (nationally normed) and poor grades on teacher-designed test (see Understanding Diagnostic Test Results).

If you believe your child's marginal test performance is at least in part attributable to test anxiety and test phobias, it is vital that you help your child develop pragmatic methods for handling stress. The first step in dealing with any phobic reaction is to identify the factors causing the fear. The starting point in this identification process is an objective assessment of the test-anxious child's academic skills and study skills. If a diagnostic evaluation by the school psychologist or an independent psychologist or educational therapist confirms significant academic deficits or a learning disability, remedial assistance must be provided (see Atypical Learning

Problems; Learning Disabilities; Parent's Rights; Underachievement.)

The child who is convinced he does not comprehend the course content is understandably going to be demoralized and apprehensive about taking tests. Each poor grade will confirm his feelings of incompetence and intensify his test-taking fears. Lacking the skills to do well, his stress will increase and his self-confidence will diminish until he becomes paralyzed by dread and feelings of futility. He may give up and refuse to study, or he may simply go through the motions of studying. To prevent this shutdown, intervention by an educational therapist, resource specialist, or private tutor is vital (see Effort and Motivation; Evaluating Special Education Programs; Self-Esteem and Self-Confidence).

Poor study skills can also be a primary source of test anxiety. Although marginally performing students may not always be willing to admit it, most realize that they don't know how to study and prepare for tests effectively. Their chronically poor grades provide concrete evidence of their inefficient study habits. Teaching these marginally performing students good study skills is essential to building their academic self-confidence and reducing test anxiety (see Distractions while Studying; Identifying Important Information; Notetaking; Planning Ahead; Preparing for Tests; Problem Solving; Smart Thinking; Study Breaks; Study Skills; Time Management).

Some children's test-taking fears cannot be attributed to specific underlying learning or study skills deficits. These students would benefit from learning basic relaxation techniques to reduce foreboding and from learning specific test-preparation and test-taking techniques to enhance performance (see Bouncing Back from Setbacks and Learning from Mistakes; Essay Tests; Identifying Important Information; Visual Memory). Also see relaxation techniques described below.

Once your child learns to study strategically and reduce stress before and during tests, his faith in himself and his abilities should improve.

A successful track record and self-confidence are two of the most powerful antidotes for test anxiety. If excessive fears persist despite your best efforts to help reduce foreboding, consult a mental health professional. Psychological counseling may be required to help your child identify underlying emotional issues that may be generating pressure, anticipatory dread, and performance-detracting anxiety (see Anger and Frustration; Fear of Failure/Success/Competition; Psychological Problems and Psychological Overlay).

Corrective Strategies

In School

1.   If your child is test phobic and you suspect that his poor performance is linked to specific academic deficits, learning problems, or study skills deficits, request an evaluation by the school psychologist or resource specialist. If your suspicions are confirmed, your child will require learning assistance and/or study skills instruction before you can expect his test anxiety to diminish. (See Learning Disabilities; Parents' Rights; Study Skills).

2.   (Elementary School, ES) If you believe other children in the class are also experiencing excessive test anxiety, ask the teacher if he would be willing to give occasional practice tests. Providing test-phobic children with opportunities to take practice tests can significantly lower their stress level. The objective of these dry runs is to demonstrate that test taking need not trigger fear. Encouraging children to make up their own practice tests when they study will also reduce anxiety and help them study more effectively. Practice tests intentionally designed not to be too difficult can provide a major boost to self-confidence. Good teachers want their students to win in school, and they do everything in their power to improve their chances of being successful. As students become more confident, skilled, and test-wise, teachers can make the academic demands more stringent and tests more challenging.

3. Request that the teacher show your child an effective test-taking system. Good test-taking strategies can play an instrumental role in reducing test phobias and improving children's performance. An effective and practical system would include the following steps:

• Take a few deep breaths with your eyes closed to calm your nerves. (Do not take more than two or three, as this could cause you to hyperventilate and become dizzy.)

• Visualize yourself doing well on the test.

• Quickly scan the entire test so that you know what is being covered.

• Calculate approximately how much time you can spend on each question or each section of the test.

• Answer the easiest questions first.

• If an essay is required, make a short and quick outline (a thumbnail outline) of what you want to include (see Essay Tests).

• Be alert for trick questions that seem too easy.

• If you feel butterflies while taking the test, close your eyes for a few seconds, breathe, feel yourself relax, and calmly remind yourself that you studied hard and know the material.

• If possible, allow time to check over your answers.

• Write clearly and neatly so your answers can be read.

At Home

1. Work with your child to design sample tests and quizzes that cover the material being studied. After reading the material, ask each other questions. Ask probing questions about the content of the work, write down test questions, and make up a facsimile test. Each of you should take the test. Initially, these practice tests should be intentionally designed to allow your child to succeed. As his self-confidence improves, make up harder tests that parallel the types of tests he takes in school.

2. Practice anxiety-reducing relaxation techniques with your child. Have him close his eyes and become conscious of his breathing. Urge him to feel his chest expand and contract. Have him take two or three deep breaths. The entire process should not take longer than a minute. Urge him to use the technique before a test is handed out. He should not be self-conscious about using this relaxation method. No one in the class need even know he is doing it.

3. Review the six test-taking steps described above. Have your child study the steps until he knows them. Then have him practice the procedure when he takes the practice tests you create together.

Time Management

The ability to manage time is vital to effective, efficient, and productive studying. Good time management skills become increasingly important as children progress into the upper grades and academic demands become more stringent. This is especially true in the case of high school students taking AP (advanced placement) and college preparatory courses. Most discover (to their dismay) that there are a seemingly infinite number of academic projects and obligations and a distressingly finite amount of time to fulfill these obligations.

Students who manage time poorly invariably have poor planning skills (see Planning Ahead). They typically fail to allow sufficient time to prepare for tests, check for errors on homework assignments, do required library research for term papers, read a required book for a book report, or proofread their essays (see Attention to Detail; Inadequate Study Time; Preparing for Tests; Procrastination; Smart Thinking). Students with poor time management skills share other counterproductive traits that undermine their school performance. Most do not establish goals and priorities, record assignments properly, create a study strategy, organize materials, or meet deadlines (see Goals; Recording Assignments; Priorities; Study Skills). Their nonstrategic academic style produces continual crises. Ironically, those students with the greatest need to improve their planning and time management skills are the ones who seem most cavalier about their defi-ciencies and the resulting predicaments. Some are simply oblivious to the consequences of inefficient time management (see Behavior and Attitude; Disregarding Consequences; Passive Learning). Others are in denial and do not want to confront the implications of their poor planning and disorganization.

Students who refuse to admit they have poor time management skills will be forced to face reality in junior and senior high school. Their time-budgeting deficiencies can make completing a history term paper on time or studying for an algebra final a nightmare. Some students become so overwhelmed, discouraged, and demoralized that they simply shut down (see Bouncing Back from Setbacks and Learning from Mistakes; Effort and Motivation; Fear of Failure/Success/Competition; Self-Esteem and Self-Confidence). Some spin their wheels and lurch ahead spasmodically. Others become increasingly dependent on their parents (see Learned Helplessness; Monitoring Homework).

With good instruction, constructive feedback, sufficient practice, and affirmation for progress, your child can acquire effective planning skills. The first step in helping her develop a more efficient time-management system is to provide a practical, easy-to-implement method for defining and prioritizing obligations and for budgeting time (see Priorities). The next step is to demonstrate how this system can make life easier and allow more free time. Once she sees the value of planning ahead and managing her time effi- ciently, she will be far more receptive to using the system voluntarily (see Planning Ahead).

Corrective Strategies

In School

1. (Elementary School, ES) If you feel your child's entire class might benefit from formal in- struction in time management, diplomatically suggest that the teacher consider including a seg- ment on planning skills in the curriculum. For example, students might plan a class project and design a schedule that incorporates basic time management principles. Students would priori- tize the steps and determine the estimated time requirements for each step. This data could then be plotted into a flow chart.

At Home

1. Study the sample schedule below with your child. Explain that the schedule indicates how one student has chosen to use her time and make sure she gets her work done.

2. Help your child complete her own Weekly Schedule. This hands-on practice will demon- strate how she can budget the time necessary to complete her homework assignments and still have free time. After you both agree on the ap- proximate amount of homework time required on a typical school night, your child should de- cide when she wants to study (see Inadequate Study Time). Empowerment is important and can usually defuse "I'm an oppressed child" resis- tance. Insist that your child maintain the sched- ule for a minimum of two weeks. Discourage deviations and manipulations, as these will defeat the intent of the scheduling process. If your child has agreed to study from 6:15 until 7:00, she should keep this commitment. Wanting to watch a TV show is an unacceptable excuse. After two weeks, allow your child to make adjustments in the schedule. Then she must keep to the revised schedule for at least two more weeks.

3. Monitor your child to make sure she is keeping to her schedule. Discuss any problems that arise. Do not nag or give sermons about re- sponsibility, as your child is likely to tune out ad- monitions and lectures. Have your child list the

SAMPLE WEEKLY SCHEDULE

TIME	MON.	TUES.	WED.	THURS.	FRI.
3:00 –3:30	Free	Free	Free	Free	Free
3:30 –4:00	Free	Free	Free	Free	Free
4:00 –4:30	Study	Study	Study	Study	Study
4:30 –5:00	Study	Study	Study	Study	Study
5:00 –5:30	Free	Free	Free	Free	Free
5:30–6:15	Dinner	Dinner	Dinner	Dinner	Dinner
6:15 –7:00	Study	Study	Study	Study	Study
7:00 –9:00	Free	Free	Free	Free	Free
9:00 –9:30	Sleep	Sleep	Sleep	Sleep	Sleep

MY WEEKLY SCHEDULE

TIME	MON.	TUES.	WED.	THURS.	FRI.
3:00–3:30	_____	_____	_____	_____	_____
3:30–4:00	_____	_____	_____	_____	_____
4:00–4:30	_____	_____	_____	_____	_____
4:30–5:00	_____	_____	_____	_____	_____
5:00–5:30	_____	_____	_____	_____	_____
5:30–6:00	_____	_____	_____	_____	_____
6:00–6:30	_____	_____	_____	_____	_____
6:30–7:00	_____	_____	_____	_____	_____
7:00–7:30	_____	_____	_____	_____	_____
7:30–8:00	_____	_____	_____	_____	_____
8:00–9:00	_____	_____	_____	_____	_____
9:00–9:30*	_____	_____	_____	_____	_____

Adjust bedtime for older children.

projects, chores, and assignments she needs to complete each week. Set up a way to reward her if she completes tasks on time. A Projects and Assignments Check-off Sheet could give points for completed work. These points could be applied to winning a prize. Household chores could also earn points. Rewarding your child is not a bribe. Your objective is to modify counterproductive behavior. Remember to express positive expectations and to give lots of praise!

4.   Do planning activities with your child. For example, have your child plan her own birthday party or a family project. Write down target dates for completing each step. Establish a list of priorities. Figure out the amount of time required to do each step. With older children, you might plan a relatively substantial project, such as weatherproofing the porch or building a dog run. List the steps involved and agree who is responsible for completing each step. Then make up a schedule that indicates when the work is to be started, how much time is to be spent each day, and projects a completion date. Discuss the rationale for your time estimates. This will help your child understand how to budget time realistically and effectively (see Planning Ahead).

Underachievement

At any given moment in classrooms throughout the United States, millions of students are working below their full potential. Approximately 1.8 million of these children have specific, identifiable learning deficits and are officially classified as *learning disabled* (or *learning different*).[1] Millions of others with less specific, more puzzling learning problems also work below their potential. These students are usually classified as *underachievers* (see Atypical Learning Problems; Dyslexia; Learning Disabilities.)

Economics has forced many school districts to reserve learning assistance programs for students with serious academic deficiencies and quantifiable learning disabilities. These children represent between 3 percent and 15 percent of the student population (depending upon who is making the estimate). Underachieving children with hard-to-identify problems may represent an additional 30 percent. In most school districts, marginally performing youngsters plod through twelve years of school without receiving substantive help. The consequences of this neglect are predictable: legions of poorly educated and, in some cases, emotionally scarred students arrive each year at the end of the educational production line unprepared to compete in a highly competitive and technologically advanced society.

The subtle, enigmatic, or intermittent deficits that cause underachievement may manifest in only one content area or in several academic subjects. One child may read aloud well but may have poor comprehension. Another may read inaccurately but may miraculously have good comprehension (see Reading Aloud; Reading Comprehension). A third child may get decent grades in history, English, and science but may spell atrociously and do terribly in math. Although these students are struggling academically and working below their potential, their deficits may not be considered serious enough to qualify them for learning assistance in school. These programs are generally reserved for children with more debilitating problems.

Some insightful educators argue persuasively that children struggle in school because teachers have not developed effective and creative teaching strategies. [See *In Their Own Way* by Thomas Armstrong (Tarcher, 1987) and *The Learning Mystique* by Gerald Coles (Pantheon, 1987).] They contend that there would be far fewer underachievers if schools would develop individualized teaching strategies that capitalize on how each child learns best and if schools would improve curricula, enhance teacher training, raise the standards for tenure, and increase teacher salaries.

It is difficult to fault this logic. Motivated, dynamic, well-paid, well-trained, creative teachers could certainly achieve better results in small classes of children with similar skills. The results would be even better if they individualized the curriculum and if parents actively supported the educational process and monitored and encour-

---

1. Gene L. Maeroff. *The School-Smart Parent* (Times Books, 1989).

aged their children at home. Unfortunately, these ideal conditions are the exception rather than the rule. Classrooms often contain thirty or more students representing a wide spectrum of abilities, cultures, and personalities.[2] Active parental support of the educational process is becoming less and less common. Parents are increasingly preoccupied with earning a living, paying the rent or the mortgage, making car payments, and keeping the family intact. Under these less-than-perfect conditions, teachers still must somehow do their jobs competently. They must creatively jury-rig their teaching methods, adjust their expectations to conform with the facts of life in their classrooms, and impart important skills and information to their students.

Because of the extensively reported qualitative crises in American education and the dismal academic skills of many students, teachers are being asked to rethink their methods, objectives, and assumptions. They are being asked to be more creative and to modify their curricula and instructional strategies so that they can more effectively reach children who learn differently. Some teachers are receptive to this pressure to improve the educational delivery system. Others are quite resistant. After years on the academic front line, many of the more resistant are set in their ways, reactionary to change, and wary of educational fads that periodically sweep the country and just as quickly disappear. They are also wary of outside consultants and experts in ivory towers and "think tanks" who critique them and make unsolicited suggestions about how they could teach better. Their reaction to the proposal that they develop new, creative curricula and individualize their teaching strategies is: "No way! I'm already overworked, underpaid, and unappreciated."

---

2. Cultural diversity is not in itself a negative condition in the classroom. In fact, the opposite is true. Diversity contributes to greater awareness, sensitivity, and appreciation of other values and styles. Diversity can, however, be a challenge to the teacher when the represented cultures do not place equal value on educational achievement. Creative, talented teachers can usually figure out how to overcome this challenge.

The net effect of our less-than-perfect educational system is that underachievers who do not meet the rigid standards for a specific learning disability often slip through holes in the safety net. As they proceed through school, subtle, unresolved learning deficits usually become increasingly problematic. By the time they reach high school, their unresolved "minor" deficiencies may have become major educational impediments and may be compounded by psychological damage and seriously undermined self-confidence (see Anger and Frustration; Psychological Problems and Psychological Overlay; Self-Esteem and Self-Confidence).

Even under imperfect conditions, your child must still get the job done and become educated. He must adjust to his teacher's standards, guidelines, and expectations, just as one day he will need to adjust to the demands of the competitive, imperfect world beyond the classroom (see Behavior and Attitude; Effort and Motivation; Expectations and Performance Guidelines). He must learn number facts, recognize verbs and adjectives, and know about Benjamin Franklin. He must learn to write legibly, spell correctly, comprehend what he is reading, express his ideas, solve algebraic equations, write grammatically correct sentences, and conjugate irregular Spanish verbs. If he cannot make these expedient, strategic accommodations to the system, he will suffer (see Disregarding Consequences; Grades; Handwriting; Keeping Up with the Class; Language Arts; Math; Passive Learning; Smart Thinking; Spelling Problems; Teacher–Child Conflict).

Children are programmed by nature to achieve. The impetus to solve problems, develop abilities, overcome obstacles, prevail over challenges, and apply talents creatively and strategically is requisite for human survival and testifies to the uniqueness and distinctive capabilities of the species. The spirit of achievement causes bridges to be built, vaccines to be discovered, symphonies to be written, new technology to be developed, and beautiful art to be created. When children are unmotivated and content not to achieve, something is profoundly amiss, and the causal factors must be identified. The alternative is to allow these children to tread water and waste their potential. This alternative is clearly unacceptable.

The thousands of hours your child will spend in the classroom must have a profound impact on his self-image, self-confidence, expectations, aspirations, and career choices. Although achievement, per se, does not guarantee happiness and psychological adjustment, chronic underachievement significantly increases the probability of unhappiness (see Negative Attitude toward School). By helping your underachiving child identify the specific deficits that are impeding his progress, by showing him how to solve problems and remove barriers, and by providing guidance, emotional support, and quality control, you can play a key role in helping him achieve at a level commensurate with his true ability.

Corrective Strategies

In School

1.   Before you can develop a strategy for helping your child work up to his ability, you must identify specific deficits that might be causing him to underachieve. To help you in this detective work, refer to the table of contents. Check off those areas in which your child might be deficient and read the descriptions of symptoms in each problem area. If you feel that your child has a deficiency, discuss the issue with your child's teacher. If she concurs, explore together if it would be feasible to implement some of the corrective strategies in class.

2.   If you suspect that your child may have a learning disability, ask his teacher(s) to complete the Student Evaluation Checklist (pages 128–130). If the teacher identifies a pattern of deficits that suggests a learning disability, refer to relevant entries in this book. To determine if your child qualifies for learning assistance, request an evaluation by the Child Study Team and the school psychologist (see Parents' Rights).

At Home

1.   Once you have identified specific problems that may be causing your child to underachieve, make a priority list of issues that can be addressed at home. Refer to appropriate entries in this book and examine specific corrective strategies. Begin with only one problem (such as spelling or time management). Don't attempt to remedy all of your child's deficits at once as this could undoubtedly trigger resistance and resentment.

2.   If you conclude that you lack the requisite skills or patience to provide the learning assistance your child needs to work up to full potential, consider hiring a qualified and dynamic tutor or educational therapist. If you believe that underlying psychological or family issues are impeding your child, it is imperative that you consult a mental health professional. To disregard or deny the problem could have disastrous implications. If you intuitively sense that your child is at risk, it is vital that you intervene before self-sabotaging behavior and underachievement become entrenched habits that last throughout life (see Psychological Problems and Psychological Overlay).

Understanding Diagnostic Test Results

The diagnostic tests given by school psychologists, resource specialists, speech therapists, and classroom teachers are designed to provide important information about a child's academic strengths and weaknesses. These data are a vital component in the process of developing an effective remedial strategy, targeting educational goals, and creating reasonable criteria for evaluating the efficacy of learning assistance programs (see Evaluating Special Education Programs; Individualized Educational Program [IEP]; Learning Disabilities; Mainstreaming and Special Day Classes).

Because there are so many different types of learning problems, educators and psychologists have developed a broad spectrum of diagnostic tests designed to identify specific academic and perceptual processing deficits. These tests range from quick screening assessments to comprehensive, multifaceted evaluations. Most schools use a standard "package" of commonly administered and highly accurate tests. In theory, the more precise the identification process, the more focused and effective the learning assistance program can be. Unfortunately, the testing protocols in most schools are often far more effective in diagnosing the deficits than the remedial procedures are in correcting identified problems.

A good diagnostic workup can assess perceptual decoding efficiency (how well children decode auditory, visual, and kinesthetic sensory data), IQ, word recognition, vocabulary, reading comprehension, inferential reasoning, spelling, math conceptual and computational skills, visual and auditory memory, expressive language, visual-motor skills, and motor coordination. Certain tests are usually administered by the school psychologist and others by classroom teachers, resource specialists, and speech pathologists.

A glossary of common testing terms and educational jargon can be found below. These terms often appear on diagnostic test reports and may also be used during an IEP (Individualized Educational Program) meeting. The codes indicate who typically administers a particular test.

CT = Classroom Teacher   *PSY = School Psychologist*

RS = Resource Specialist   *SP = Speech Pathologist*

• Achievement Test: A test designed to measure how much your child has learned after instruction in specific content areas. These tests are usually standardized and nationally normed. ("Standarized Test" and "Norms" are defined on pages 264 and 265.)

• Aptitude: An ability, capacity, or talent in a particular area such as music or mathematics. Aptitude is a specialized facility to master a particular skill.

• Criterion-Referenced Test: A test, usually designed by a teacher or publisher, that measures your child's mastery of specific subject matter that has been presented in school. The scores are not standardized (nationally normed) but can provide the teacher and you with useful information about what your child has and has not learned. CT

• Diagnostic Test: A test that pinpoints your child's academic or perceptual strengths and weaknesses. The results are generally used to plan a learning assistance strategy to correct identified weaknesses. PSY/RS/SP

• Grade Equivalent: A ranking of test performance based on a raw score that statistically compares your child's correct answers with those of other children in the same grade. The score is expressed in terms of years and months (with nine months making up each school year). For example: a grade equivalent score (G.E.) of 2.8 means that a child's test performance compares with that of other children in the eighth month of second grade.

• Intelligence Quotient (IQ): An index designed to predict academic success. The IQ test compares your child's verbal and nonverbal performance (or learning potential) with that of other children of the same age. This comparison yields a statistically derived score called IQ. The test does not measure abilities that many educators now consider to be components of intelligence: creativity, artistic talent, musical aptitude, leadership, strategic planning, social skills, self-knowledge, or motivation. An IQ score between 85 and 115 is considered average. A score between 70 and 85 is low average, while 115 to 130 is considered high average. A score below 70 indicates probable mental retardation, and a score above 130 indicates probable giftedness. Scores may vary depending on the IQ test administered, and scores can be influenced by rapport with the examiner and by emotional, cultural, and perceptual factors (see IQ Test Scores). PSY

• Mastery Test: See Criterion-Referenced Test. CT

• Mean Score: The mathematical average of all students' test scores on a particular test. One half

of the students taking the test score above the mean and one half score below.

• Mental Age: A score on a mental abilities test which statistically compares your child's performance level to that of other children. The score differentiates your child's chronological age from her mental age. For example: your child's chronological age may be 10.6 (10 years, 6 months), but the number of her correct answers on the test may statistically compare with that of children whose age is 11.8. Her total correct answers generate a statistical mental age score six months above her chronological age. Your child would, thus, be considered to have above average intelligence.

• Norms: A statistical frame of reference on a standardized test that enumerates performance on the test by pupils of specific ages and in specific grades in school. Through the use of norms, your child's score can be compared nationally to the scores of other students of the same age or in the same grade.

Some tests allow an even more precise comparison. They may offer norms for children living in specific geographic areas or even for all children attending private schools.

• Percentile: A score which indicates your child's relative position within a defined group by ranking all students who have taken the test. A score at the fiftieth percentile is generally considered to be at grade level. A score at the fortieth percentile would be approximately one year below grade level. A score at the sixtieth percentile would be approximately one year above grade level.

• Power Test: An untimed test with items usually arranged in order of ascending difficulty that determines your child's level of performance in a particular subject area. CT

• Raw Score: The total number of correct answers on a test.

• Readiness Test: A test that measures your child's mastery of requisite skills before she proceeds to the next academic level. This test is typically used by kindergarten teachers to determine if your child is academically and developmentally prepared to function effectively in first grade. CT/RS

• Reliability: A statistical representation of how well a test consistently produces the same results.

• Scaled Score: A ranking system chosen by the publisher of a test which is derived from the raw scores obtained by students taking the test. A different scale is established for each test. For example, one test might have a scale from 1 to 19 while another might have a scale from 1 to 70. To interpret a scaled score, you must know the mean score and the standard deviation for that test.

• Standard Deviation: A measure of how much your child's score varies from the mean score of all students taking the test.

• Standard Score: A statistical ranking of your child's performance on a standardized test based on the raw score she achieved relative to the performance of a large sample of students of the same age and/or grade level.

• Standardized Test: A test with specific and uniform instructions for administering, timing, and scoring that is given to large numbers of children at one time. The test may be an achievement test that evaluates your child's skills in specific areas, an IQ test, or a diagnostic test. The testing instrument statistically compares your child's performance with that of a large sample of students of the same age and/or grade level. On some tests, local norms are also provided for comparing your child's scores with those of other children of the same socioeconomic background. The norms, established by a standardization process, are used by teachers and school psychologists to determine a child's relative level of performance and achievement. CT/RS/PSY/SP

• Stanine: A statistical ranking of your child's performance on a standardized test on a scale of 1 through 9. The mean score is 5 and a score from 3 to 4 is generally considered low average.

A score from 6 to 7 is considered high average. Frequently, the results on a standardized test will be reported in both a stanine score and a percentile score. The higher the stanine score, the higher the percentile score will be.

• Survey Test: A test that measures general achievement in an academic area. It is not as comprehensive or specific as a criterion-referenced test. CT

• Validity: The accuracy with which a test measures that which it has been designed to measure.

Corrective Strategies

In School

1. If you are to play a constructive, contributory role in the remedial process, you must understand your child's academic strengths and weaknesses, identify any underlying deficits, and concur with the objectives of the learning assistance program and the choice of corrective methods. Test results can guide you in selecting the most appropriate program for your child, evaluating progress, communicating with the classroom teacher and resource specialist, and providing appropriate support and assistance at home.

It is crucial that the person evaluating your child take the time to explain carefully the test results and any technical data or jargon in comprehensible terms. If you are perplexed or have reservations, don't hesitate to ask questions and to express concerns. You may need several explanations before you agree to a remedial strategy. Do not feel "dumb" if you need clarification. You are your child's primary advocate, and you must have comprehensive information if you are to fulfill this vital function. Take the time to review the preceding information about terminology and tests, and even bring this book with you to the meeting. If you are going to participate effectively in the extremely important IEP meeting (when the results of the diagnostic tests administered to your child are discussed), you must comprehend the significance of the scores. Primed with an understanding of the issues and a knowledge of the jargon, you can more intelligently, rationally, and, if necessary, forcefully assert your rights and those of your child! (See Communicating with the School; Conferencing with School Officials; Evaluating Special Educational Programs; Individual Educational Program [IEP]; Parents' Rights).

At Home

1.   If you are dissatisfied with the testing procedures, test interpretation, the proposed learning assistance strategy, or the denial of learning assistance services, you may consult a professional outside of the school system. This person should be able to explain and interpret the test results, offer a "second opinion," and suggest alternative options for addressing your child's learning needs, such as private learning assistance (see Atypical Learning Problems; Underachievement).

2.   If you feel your child's educational needs are not being met, discuss your concerns with the school authorities. You may need to involve the superintendent if you do not get satisfaction at the local level. Consult the district's Parents' Rights Manual. In dispute situations that cannot be easily resolved, you may need to hire a parent advocate to represent you at the IEP and in subsequent dealings with the school district. Advocates are educational or clinical psychologists or educational therapists who are knowledgeable about learning problems and well-versed in educational law. Their function is to represent your child's interests during the planning stages of the remedial strategy. In a worst case scenario, you may be forced to hire an attorney who is an expert in educational law. Your advocate can most likely refer you to such a person.

Your child's interests will be best served if you work with the school district constructively and cooperatively. Make every effort to be reasonable and to negotiate calmly if there is a disagreement about the test interpretation, proposed remedial strategy, or educational services being offered or denied your child. Communicate your position rationally and calmly, and listen carefully and objectively to the responses of the educators and administrators. If their explanations, conclusions, interpretations, rationales, and recommendations don't make sense, you have a right to question and challenge their position. If possible, do so diplomatically.

If you cannot reach agreement, move to the next phase of the protest procedure (see Parents' Rights for a more complete explanation of your options and prerogatives). An adversarial situation with possible legal action should be a last resort. Ideally, as an informed and reasonable parent, you will be able to avoid this unpleasantness. Should you become convinced that the district is unwilling to address your child's legitimate needs and rights, do not hesitate to represent her forcefully and aggressively. This may trigger a showdown with the school administration, but sometimes you have no better alternative.

Verbal Expression

Children are continually responding to stimuli received through the five senses (*decoding*) and selecting words to express perceptions, feelings, and thoughts (*encoding*). Their choice of words and the quality of their expressive language skills are influenced by five interrelated factors: intelligence, natural language aptitude, home environment, social environment, and educational experiences (see Language Arts; Language Disorders; Speech Disorders; Vocabulary).

As with most problems, expressive language difficulties range from the subtle to the severe. Profound communication disorders are often symptomatic of a condition called *dysphasia* or, in extreme cases, *aphasia* (virtual total inability to use language). Because both of the these neurologically based conditions erect major barriers to communication, children afflicted with them require intensive language therapy. In some cases, a severe expressive language disability may be linked to *autism*, a perplexing disorder that causes children to become emotionally distant, noncommunicative, and either nonemotive or inappropriately emotive. (This condition is not related to dysphasia or aphasia.)

Most children have more subtle expressive language deficits. Although mildly inarticulate children may require language therapy, most can improve their verbal skills dramatically if they are provided with systematic instruction, patient guidance, and sensitive, empathetic feedback. Children who struggle to express themselves must practice using language in school and at home. They must be constructively (and selectively) critiqued and repeatedly affirmed and acknowledged for progress. Even children with relatively minor communication problems can be extremely sensitive about language deficiencies. Their struggle to express themselves can cause insecurity and trigger feelings of inadequacy, anxiety, and vulnerability (see Psychological Problems and Psychological Overlay; Self-Esteem and Self-Confidence).

The more significant a child's communication deficits, the more defensive, verbally tentative, and language phobic she is likely to become. To protect herself, she may resist discussing her feelings, thoughts, and observations. She may respond grudgingly to direct questions, answer in monosyllables, and avoid speaking in public. This reticence ironically calls attention to the very inadequacies the child is unconsciously trying to hide. Unless her specific language deficits (vocabulary deficits, grammar and syntax errors, or disorganized thinking) are identified and treated, the chronically noncommunicative youngster is at risk for becoming increasingly isolated from other children and, perhaps, from her family. It is critical that she be evaluated by a speech pathologist to determine if language therapy and/or psychological counseling are required to help her overcome her communication deficits and anxiety.

Some children may actually be quite articulate in private conversation but traumatized by the prospect of speaking in front of others. To overcome their fears and anxiety, these tentative, insecure, or chronically shy children must be gently coaxed to communicate and repeatedly affirmed and praised. Their parents and teachers must also make a special effort to convince them that they are not being critically judged. Allaying their fears and building their self-confidence will require time, patience, emotional support, planning, affirmation, and carefully orchestrated and deliberately acknowledged successes.

Parents and teachers should intentionally create opportunities for all children, especially those with poor communication skills, to express their ideas and feelings. When responding to children who make unclear statements, good judgment and discretion are vital. Sometimes it is appropriate *not* to correct the errors. In other instances, providing sensitive, supportive, selective, and constructive feedback can help children significantly improve their communication skills.

It is imperative that verbally tentative, insecure children be drawn into family discussions. As they become more self-confident and competent, they should be gently urged to participate in class debates, give short speeches and oral presentations, discuss current events, and summarize verbally what they have read in their textbooks. Although initially these experiences will undoubtedly trigger anxiety in children who are phobic about speaking in public, this anxiety can usually be overcome with encouragement, affirmation, and praise for progress.

Excessively fearful children require special treatment, extra coaching, rehearsals, encouragement, acknowledgment, praise, and instruction in basic relaxation and visualization techniques (see Test Anxiety). A series of engineered successes can be a powerful elixir for building self-confidence and a powerful antidote for stage fright.

Children who have learned to communicate effectively possess an invaluable resource that they will be able to use throughout their lives. Although teaching effective verbal skills should clearly be one of our highest educational priorities for all students, these skills are not being emphasized in American schools. Unless this situation changes, our high schools will continue to crank out graduates with a working vocabulary of perhaps two thousand words. Struggling to express their most basic feelings and thoughts comprehensibly, these youngsters will characteristically preface each incoherent statement they utter with the words "you know." Unfortunately, these inarticulate teenagers are destined to discover that their inadequate expressive language skills will exclude them from many of the most coveted careers and vocations.

Corrective Strategies

In School

1.   Ask your child if she participates in class discussions, verbal question and answer periods, and class debates and is required to give oral reports and speeches. If you conclude that she is not being provided with sufficient opportunities to develop communication skills, discuss your concerns with the teacher or, if appropriate, the principal. Urge the school administration to set up programs designed to help students improve their expressive language. If you are dissatisfied with the response, enlist other parents in your crusade and attend school board meetings to express your concerns publicly.

2.   If you believe your child has an expressive language problem, request an evaluation by the school speech pathologist. (Consult with your pediatrician for a second opinion or a referral to a private diagnostician.) Suggest to the teacher that he coax your child gently to express her ideas and feelings in a nonstressful, noncompetitive context. If she is very shy, reticent, or language deficient, her teacher will need to be especially patient, nurturing, affirming, and supportive. Opportunities to speak in front of other children should be orchestrated, and the process of building your child's skills and self-confidence should proceed in small, controlled increments. For example, initially your child might be asked to talk for only fifteen to thirty seconds about her vacation or a project she is working on. The teacher may need to help her, but he should not correct

her in front of other children, as this might cause embarrassment; feedback should be given privately after class. Competent, sensitive teachers realize that they have a responsibility to create a supportive classroom context in which students are required to be sensitive to the feelings of any child expressing his or her ideas.

3. If your child's school does not have a debating club, suggest to the principal that one be established at each grade level. Opportunities to debate should also be created in the classroom. Acting out historical events described in textbooks can also provide a wonderful opportunity for public speaking and for acquiring confidence. The students might assume the roles of King George and his advisers and generals. Other students could play the roles of George Washington and the Founding Fathers. A script could be written by the students. Each side would present its position. The same process could be used to debate such issues as the use of insecticides, nuclear power plants, offshore drilling, and disarmament.

At Home

1. By deliberately creating opportunities at home for communication and the expression of feelings and ideas, and by providing constructive feedback, support, and criticism, you can play a vital role in developing your child's verbal skills. Practice can usually compensate for a lack of natural talent in almost any endeavor. The dinner table is an excellent context for family discussions about the day's events. Youngsters who participate in discussions and who hear their parents express themselves almost invariably become more articulate than those who do not have these experiences. If your child responds to the question "What happened in school today?" by saying "Nothing," be more specific without sounding like you are a detective grilling a suspect. You might say: "Tell me what the teacher said about the field trip," or "How did you solve those fraction problems that were giving you trouble?" "What are you going to cover in your science re-

port?" There are two guiding principles for engaging shy, reticent, defensive children: avoid making the discussions stressful and know when to stop.

2. Debate issues with your child—strip mining, logging, women reporters in men's locker rooms, whatever strikes you). Be careful not to overwhelm her with your superior communication skills, vocabulary, and knowledge. Newspaper articles can be a great catalyst for discussion. If your child is interested in sports, read aloud something from the sports page. Your objective is to develop verbal skills, not reading skills. Ask thought-provoking questions: "What do you think about this decision to fire the manager?" Encourage her to organize her thoughts. If her ideas do not appear logical or sequential, you might respond: "I'm not sure I understand. Could you explain it again?" Use this approach sparingly, or you risk making your child defensive and impeding communication. Know when to listen and when to back off. Do not interrupt your child. Make the session fun and do not make the discussions too drawn out. Your child's attention span is shorter than yours. Let her know that you appreciate her ideas. Support, affirm, and acknowledge her not only for progress, but also for effort! Praise her when she makes a good point and effectively communicates her position. Children can sense when you want them to succeed. Your goal is not to win the debate! Your goal is to build your child's skills and confidence.

3. (Elementary School, ES) To develop your child's telephone communication skills (a vital asset!), call home and engage her in conversations. Ask her to describe everything that happened that day in school. For some children, talking on the telephone and not seeing the face of the person they are speaking to poses a significant challenge. These children tend to "freeze" as soon as they pick up the phone.

4. Encourage your child to expand her vocabulary by intentionally using new words in her daily communication. Demonstrate how carefully

chosen words can express ideas with precision (see Vocabulary).

5.   Periodically set aside time after a TV show for a family discussion. The discussion could be about issues in a *Bill Cosby* or *Simpsons* episode, or any movie, network special, TV news story, or sit-com. Encourage your child to express ideas and feelings. If you disagree, do not become critical. Use discretion in presenting an opposing viewpoint. Your goal is to stimulate, not stifle, communication and the exchange of ideas.

6.   If your child has chronic expressive language difficulties and is unresponsive to the strategies described above, consult with your pediatrician. A neurological examination and comprehensive assessment by a private speech and language specialist may be advisable (see Language Disorders). Psychological counseling may also help if your child's reticence and apprehension about expressing herself are deeply entrenched and appear to have reached phobic proportions.

Visual Memory

Most teachers expect their students to assimilate prodigious amounts of written information. The range of material children are required to recall includes facts, formulas, rules, definitions, dates, and conjugations. Youngsters with good visual retention clearly have a distinct advantage in classes where the retention of facts and details from textbooks and lecture notes are emphasized.

Good visual memory skills are a particularly valuable resource when children spell. The child who can "see" words in her mind is invariably a better speller than the student who tries to sound out words or tries to apply the rules of spelling and phonics (see Memorizing Information; Nonphonetic Words; Spelling Problems; Visual Memory). The capacity to imprint a mental picture of a word can significantly reduce errors and is especially useful when spelling words that are commonly mispronounced (*prerogative*), nonphonetic (*allegiance*, *through*, and *bought*), or foreign (*sergeant* and *lieutenant*).

It is revealing that people with exceptional visual recall are often referred to as having a "photographic memory." This analogy is quite accurate. Those who possess a photographic memory are able to imprint a visual image of words, symbols, and dates in their brain in much the same way that a camera imprints visual images on a roll of film. Their eyes are the equivalent of the camera lens and the brain is the equivalent of the film inside.

Having good visual memory skills can be an invaluable asset in virtually every subject area in school. The child who can see in her mind the date when the Declaration of Independence was signed, the formula for sulfuric acid, the conjugation of the French word *savoir*, or the formula for determining the circumference of a circle will have little difficulty recalling this information.

There are, of course, other ways to learn and recall information. Auditory learners prefer to imprint spoken or subvocalized information in their minds by repeating the information verbally until they have memorized it (see Auditory Memory). As a general rule, however, visual imprinting is a more effective tool for memorizing large quantities of factual data written in textbooks, in notes, and on the chalkboard.

Good visual memory skills do not guarantee good reading comprehension. A student may be able to remember and regurgitate facts and may do well on multiple choice and true/false tests that stress details, but she may not understand the facts or be able to apply them (see Identifying Important Information; Reading Comprehension).

Although rote memorization has a place in the educational process, a primary emphasis by teachers on the memorization of information discourages critical thinking. The cerebral RPMs (revolutions per minute) required to answer the question, "When was the cotton jenny invented and who invented it?" are considerably fewer than those required to answer the question, "Discuss the long-term effects of the Industrial Revolution on our present culture and cite specific inventions that have affected the American lifestyle and economy." (See Critical Thinking; Study Skills; Preparing for Tests).

Students tend to forget quickly information that is poorly understood, not reinforced by discussion and application, and/or perceived as irrelevant. Most children who are required to memorize the names of the bones in the hand will forget this information soon after taking a test. Their long-term retention usually increases significantly if they assemble a model of the hand (kinesthetic/tactile learning), draw diagrams (visual learning), discuss and describe the information verbally (auditory learning), and interact with other students in a cooperative learning context. When active and enthusiastic multisensory learning is reinforced by having students intentionally create visual pictures in their minds, recall will be even better.

Smart students capitalize on their natural and preferred learning styles and learning strengths. If they are required to memorize a great many facts, dates, names, or formulas, they strategically use those learning modalities (visual, auditory, tactile/kinesthetic) that will help them recall the information (see Smart Thinking). This tactical pragmatism distinguishes achieving students from nonachieving and underachieving students (see Behavior and Attitude; Negative Attitude toward School; Passive Learning; Underachievement).

With adequate instruction and sufficient practice your child can significantly improve critically important visual memory skills, even if she is not a natural visual learner. In appropriate learning situations, she can learn to use her eyes and brain like a camera. This ability to imprint visual pictures is an invaluable resource that will serve her throughout her life.

Corrective Strategies

In School

1.   If you suspect that your child has visual memory deficits, request that she be evaluated by the Child Study Team, school psychologist, or resource specialist. Highly accurate tests can be used to identify deficiencies. If weaknesses are confirmed by testing, request that the resource specialist provide remedial assistance. If help is denied, consult the school district's Parents' Rights Manual, which spells out the official guidelines and criteria for admission to the resource program (see Parents' Rights).

2.   Discuss with the classroom teacher and/or the resource specialist specific teaching materials that can improve your child's visual memory skills. Also refer to the Resource List at back of this book.

At Home

1.   Urge your child to create visual pictures whenever she needs to memorize information. Encourage her to close her eyes and "see" in her mind the definition of a word she needs to memorize or the conjugations of an irregular Spanish verb. Suggest that she visualize words, dates, and formulas in her favorite colors as she memorizes. When studying, have her hold the paper containing the material she is learning above eye level and look up as she imprints the information. This technique facilitates visual recall. For other techniques that develop visualization skills, refer to corrective strategies under Spelling Problems.

2.   Encourage your child, when appropriate, to capitalize on her natural abilities and use her preferred learning modality. For example, if she learns best using the kinesthetic/tactile modality (through movement and manipulating objects), have her act out the definition of a word she is learning to spell or trace the letter of the word in the air using her whole arm. Have her use Scrabble squares to form words. Suggest that she cut her own cardboard squares from index cards and use these to record scientific symbols or historical facts. Active, participatory learning is clearly preferable to passive learning. Urge your child to be creative, but impress upon her that there will be times when she would be strategic to use the visualization techniques described above to rein-

force her preferred learning modality, and to help her memorize specific material that may not lend itself to her natural learning style.

3. Go to your local teacher supply store and ask to see materials specifically designed to develop visual memory skills (see Resource List at the back of the book). Also ask your child's teacher(s) or resource specialist to recommend workbooks and/or educational computer software that address your child's visual memory deficiencies.

Vocabulary

To communicate effectively, children must be able to access the words that can express their feelings, ideas, and insights. The more expansive their vocabulary, the more precise and effective their communication skills will be.

The hundreds of thousands of bright, potentially capable teenagers who graduate each year from high school with inadequate vocabularies are the legacy of a society and an educational system that does not prioritize good communication skills (see Verbal Expression). Many youngsters complete their educations virtually incapable of communicating cogently and coherently.

The traditional method for developing students' vocabulary skills is, at best, uninspiring and, at worst, mind-numbing. Teachers typically assign a list of new words each week and require students to look up and memorize the definitions. Children are instructed to use the words in sentences or paragraphs and given weekly vocabulary tests to measure their mastery. Once they have supposedly learned the new assigned vocabulary, the words are seldom reviewed, and students are rarely required to use them again. The outcome of this inadequate instructional system and lack of practice is predictable: the meaning of the words is soon forgotten.

The *memorize, use in a sentence, take a test* ritual extracts the joy children derive by participating actively, creatively, and dynamically in the process of enriching their vocabularies. Children who learn words mechanically cannot possibly be seduced by the beauty, precision, and potential of the English language.

There are, of course, exceptional teachers who do a first-rate job of developing vocabulary skills. Their enthusiasm for language is contagious and inspires students to improve their vocabulary and communication skills. Unfortunately, too many teachers approach vocabulary development as a painful chore, and their students respond accordingly.

In many school districts, the primary concern of administrators, teachers, parents, and school boards is to improve students' scores on reading and vocabulary tests. In an annual ritual, the standardized test performance of the local school is compared to that of schools in other districts and states. These test results have become the major criteria for measuring the efficacy of local educational programs, and because of the political implications, many teachers are overtly or covertly pressured to "teach to the tests." In the frenzy to raise scores and supposedly demonstrate teaching excellence, the issue of retention and application of vocabulary skills is often overlooked (see Understanding Diagnostic Test Results).

Listening to children communicate confirms that most youngsters use few words to express their thoughts and feelings. The typical high school graduate has a working vocabulary of perhaps two thousand words. In daily communication, most children use fewer than one thousand words. (Two of the most common of these words are "you know.") Our beleaguered educational system cannot be held exclusively responsible for this sad state of affairs. Insufficient encouragement and few opportunities to use communication skills at home and negative social pressures deter children from developing verbal skills. In our society, and especially in certain teenage subcultures, having and using a good vocabulary is equated with pretentiousness, and youngsters are often reluctant to use "big" words for fear of social rejection. Even educated adults may hesitate to use precise vocabulary because they do not want to be considered pedantic or superior (see Verbal Expression).

Vocabulary skills must be continually practiced and applied in school and at home. Children who hear their parents use language effectively around the dinner table, who are encouraged to express their feelings, perceptions, and ideas, and who are acknowledged and affirmed for developing communication skills and for expanding their vocabulary invariably become more articulate than children who are permitted to coast through life with a working vocabulary of one thousand words.

If parents and teachers truly want children to acquire a precise, rich vocabulary, they must encourage them to use effective language in their daily communication. It may not be realistic to expect a teenager to use the words *convoluted, protracted,* or *irrepressible* when chatting with friends, but it is realistic and desirable to encourage children to use such words when discussing issues in class or around the dinner table. By providing guidance, modeling, systematic instruction, encouragement, and feedback, creative parents and teachers can play a significant, proactive role in improving the expressive language and vocabulary skills of virtually every child.

Corrective Strategies

In School

1.   If you suspect that your child is not acquiring good vocabulary skills, express your concerns to the teacher. Ask if there are any creative materials or methods to help your child (and other students) develop better verbal skills. Materials specifically designed to achieve this objective are included in the Resource List at the back of this book.

2.   (Junior High/High School, J/HS) If you have concerns about the vocabulary development methods used in your child's class, ask the teacher to describe the program and its objectives. Diplomatically express any concerns you have, being careful not to make the teacher feel attacked or denigrated.

At Home

1.   Establish a family tradition of looking up in the dictionary and introducing one interesting new word each day. By using the dictionary and demonstrating your appreciation for language, you cannot help "infecting" your child with your enthusiasm. Be supportive of his use of new words, and effusively affirm and acknowledge progress. Everyone should try using the word at least twice during dinner. Make the process fun. You might say: "In the movie we rented yesterday, one of the lawyers said 'I'm not your adversary.' What do you think *adversary* means? Let's look it up. I'll use the word in a sentence. Now you make up a sentence using the word." (Help your child if necessary.)

Keep a dictionary handy. Purchase one written specifically for children. Review previously used words as a game or contest. ("For one point, can you remember the definition of *adversary*, and for an extra point use it in a sentence?") Learning the definitions of new words is only a small part of the mastery process. The litmus test is being able to use the words in conversation. Remember, your child will probably require many exposures and a great deal of practice before he'll be able to recall and use new words easily.

2.   Purchase from your local bookstore or teacher supply house vocabulary development workbooks, games, flash cards, and/or computer software appropriate to your child's grade level (see Resource List).

3.   Play word games with your child. Make two copies of a list of twenty-five words and their definitions. Pick the words yourself or use a vocabulary development book. Have your child look at the words and definitions on his list while you say: "I'm thinking of a word that means *hardworking.*

It begins with the letters *in* and ends with the letter *s*. Your child would get 1 point for figuring out the word *industrious* and a bonus point for using the word in a sentence. (The points could be used for winning a prize.) Now have your child take a turn. He gives the clues, and you figure out the word and use it in a sentence. Don't make the words too difficult. Intentionally use the new words in conversation during the week and urge your child to use them. Vocabulary materials you might want to examine are included in the Resource List at the back of this book.

4.   Encourage your child to use a thesaurus when writing reports, essays, and term papers. Explain that eliminating reduncancies and intentionally inserting precise vocabulary in a report can significantly improve the quality of the writing. If he uses a word processing program on his computer, make sure the software includes a thesaurus option.

5.   See Verbal Expression for additional strategies to develop your child's language and vocabulary skills.

Working Independently

In fourth grade a major shift occurs in the classroom: teachers expect students to work with increasing independence. Those children who require constant supervision are destined to have significant academic difficulties in junior and senior high school.

Parents alarmed by their child's lack of independence may attempt to compensate by becoming excessively involved in monitoring his work and in helping him with his assignments (see Monitoring Homework). Although their intentions may be noble, these parents are unwittingly discouraging the development of self-sufficiency. Overly protected, continually rescued children may misconstrue their parents' motives and conclude that their parents want them to remain dependent. In some cases, this perception may be accurate, for some parents actually do have an unconscious need to create and perpetuate a symbiotic relationship with their child (see Learned Helplessness).

The emotional and vocational consequences of excessive dependency can be catastrophic. Children addicted to having their parents serve as on-call academic paramedics will be tempted to call for help whenever they encounter any challenge or problem. Being continually assisted, protected, nagged, cajoled, and consoled may become their primary payoff. The dependency guarantees attention and sympathy. Once a child becomes firmly ensconced in this comfort zone, he will often vigorously resist all attempts to help him become self-sufficient.

Children with learning difficulties are at the greatest risk for becoming dependent on their parents and teachers. Those not receiving learning assistance or not responding positively to assistance are especially at risk, academically and emotionally. If they cannot do the work and are falling further and further behind, they will become increasing discouraged, frustrated, and demoralized. Because of the continual struggle to survive academically, they will be very tempted either to give up or to demand constant help and support from their parents (see Anger and Frustration; Behavior and Attitude; Self-Esteem and Self-Confidence).

The parents of a learning disabled child are faced with an obvious dilemma. They realize their child needs help, but they also realize that if they provide too much help he could become overly needy. Extricating themselves from the "dependency loop" requires careful planning and the willpower to resist rescuing their child every time he encounters a glitch. (See Bouncing Back for Setbacks and Learning from Mistakes; Fear of Failure/Success/Competition).

A powerful natural instinct impels parents to protect a weak and vulnerable child. If you suspect that your protective instinct is excessive and not in your child's best interests, or if you suspect that you might be unwittingly encouraging your child's dependency, examine objectively your own psychological needs and "hidden agenda." A red flag should go up if you are continually using the pronouns *we* and *our*. ("We have a spelling test tomorrow," or "We have to do our math problems now.")

A child's "security blanket" must be withdrawn in carefully planned stages. Removing the support system too abruptly could trigger anxiety, resentment, insecurity, resistance, and shutdown.

Corrective Strategies

In School

1.   If you observe your child having difficulty working independently, the following step-by-step procedure will help you develop a strategy for correcting the situation.

• Ask the teacher, school psychologist, and resource specialist to help you realistically assess your child's current academic skills and needs.

• Make certain that necessary remedial assistance is provided in school or in a private after-school program (see Parents' Rights).

• Adjust your expectations and performance guidelines to your child's skill level (see Expectations and Performance Guidelines).

• Request that the teacher adjust the difficulty of the assignments to your child's current skill level.

• Request that the teacher and/or resource specialist provide guidance about the type and extent of assistance you should furnish at home (for example, should you proofread his book reports?)

• Objectively examine your child's behavior and your family's dynamics. If appropriate modify your responses to discourage excessive dependency.

2.   If your child is receiving extra assistance and has become overly dependent, discuss this issue with the teacher and/or resource specialist. Define specific, realistic academic and behavioral objectives that take into consideration his current academic skill levels. For example, after your child does several sample math problems and clearly understands the concepts, expect him to complete the remaining problems without any help. This "weaning" process may initially cause

some anxiety, but you must prepare your child to deal with the real world where he cannot expect someone always to be there to hold his hand. If he makes "silly" mistakes because his teacher is not continually monitoring his work, he will simply have to redo the work.

3. If your child can do the assigned work but insists on being helped by his teacher, suggest that she deflect his request. She might say: "I believe you can do this on your own. I will evaluate the work after you hand it in and if you do not understand something, we can go over it together." If your child continually asks "Is this right?" she might respond, "What do you think?" The teacher's refusal to be manipulated may make your child unhappy, but modifying his self-defeating behavior is far more critical than his grade on an assignment.

At Home

1.   For academically needy children, some at-home help will undoubtedly be necessary. You must strike a balance between appropriate and excessive help. Consult your child's teacher, resource specialist, and/or school psychologist for suggestions about how to accelerate improvement in specific academic deficit areas and about how best to provide assistance. Progress reports and periodic conferences are vital. You may also want to consult an independent educational therapist or psychologist for ideas about how to help your child catch up and modify nonadaptive behaviors.

2.   (Junior High/High School, J/HS) Helping academically deficient junior and senior high school students can be difficult for parents, especially when the material requires you to use skills you have not practiced in twenty-five years. You may conclude it is advisable to hire a tutor to help your child with homework and studying. Discuss any concerns you have about excessive dependency with the tutor. Even a highly skillful tutor can be manipulated into providing too much help.

3.   Be realistic and patient. Dependency "scripts" cannot be changed overnight. If your child continually requests help, and you are con-

vinced he can do the work, you might respond: "I believe you know how to do this on your own. I am willing to check it over after you've completed it." If he makes spelling mistakes, check the lines where errors are found and have him find the errors himself. If he can't, so be it. Being rescued is habit-forming! Helping him become more self-sufficient is, in the long run, more important than correcting every one of his spelling mistakes.

4. Discuss with your child your concerns about the need to be able to work independently and brainstorm together how he could begin to do more work on his own. You might say: "Now that you understand how to do these problems, how much of this math assignment can you do without any help?" If he is reluctant to work on his own, propose an experiment and create a system for rewarding him for independence. ("If you can do all these yourself, we'll go out for an ice-cream cone.")

5. If your child is struggling to do his work because he lacks important skills, you will have to make a judgment call about how much help to provide. If his skills are very poor, consider hiring a qualified tutor. The tutor should be able to assess his skills and determine the true extent of his needs.

 # Resource List

ALTERNATIVE TEACHING STRATEGIES

(see Atypical Learning Problems, Communicating with the School, Keeping Up with the Class, Negative Attitude toward School, Passive Learning, Teacher–Child Conflict)

Armstrong, Thomas, *In Their Own Way* (Los Angeles: Jeremy D. Tarcher, 1987).

Coles, Gerald, *The Learning Mystique* (New York: Pantheon, 1987).

Gardener, Howard, and Jensen, Eric, *Frames of Mind* (New York: Basic Books, 1983); *Student Success Secrets* (Hauppauge, NY: Barron, 1989).

Jensen, Eric, *You Can Succeed* (Hauppauge, NY: Barron, 1989).

Macroff, Gene L., *The School Smart Parent* (New York: Times Books, 1989).

ATTENTION DEFICIT DISORDER

(see Atypical Learning Problems, Dyslexia, Mainstreaming, Parents' Rights, Understanding Diagnostic Test Results)

Goldstein, Sam, and Goldstein, Michael, *Hyperactivity: Why Won't My Child Pay Attention?* (New York: John Wiley & Sons, 1992).

McCarney, Stephen B., *The Attention Deficit Disorders Intervention Manual* (Columbia, MO: Hawthorne Educational Services, 1989 and 1994); *The Parent's Guide to Attention Deficit Disorders*, 2nd Edition (Columbia, MO: Hawthorne Educational Services, 1995).

Rief, Sandra F., *How to Reach and Teach ADD/ADHD Children* (Englewood Cliffs, NJ: The Center for Applied Research in Education, Prentice-Hall, 1993).

Taylor, John, *Helping Your Hyperactive/Attention Deficit Child* (Rocklin, CA: Prima Publishing, 1990).

Quinn, Patricia O., and Stern, Judith M., *The "Putting on the Brakes" Activity Book for Young People with ADHD* (New York: Magination Press, 1993).

GRAMMAR

(see Phonics, Punctuation)

Auld, Janice L., *Cut & Paste Phonics* [gr. 1–3] (Belmont, CA: Fearon Teacher Aids, 1985).

Burch, Marilyn, *Phonics Seatwork* [gr. 1–2] (Belmont, CA: Fearon Teacher Aids, 1985).

Criscuolo, Nicholas, *Boost Skills with Practice* [gr. 3–6] (Belmont, CA: Fearon Teacher Aids, 1987); *Brush Up on the Basics* [gr. 2–5] (Belmont, CA: Fearon Teacher Aids, 1987).

Freeman, Sara, *Nouns, Verbs & Adjectives* [gr. 1–2] (Palo Verdes Estates, CA: Frank Schaffer Publications, 1990).

Hoeber, Margaret, *Nouns, Verbs & Adjectives* [gr. 2–3] (Palo Verdes Estates, CA: Frank Schaffer Publications, 1990).

Knoblock, Kathleen, *Compounds & Contractions* [gr. 2] (Palo Verdes Estates, CA: Frank Schaffer Publications, 1987).

Laird, Stanley, *Hands-on Grammar* [gr. 4–12] (Belmont, CA: Fearon Teacher Aids, 1978).

Manhard, Stephen, *The Goof-Proofer* [all grades] (New York: Collier Books, 1985).

Rodgers, Molly, and Zimmer, Linda M., *Grammar* [gr. 5–7 up] (Columbus, OH: Essential Learning Products, 1990).

Shiotsu, Vicky, *Compounds & Contractions* [gr. 1] (Palo Verdes Estates, CA: Frank Schaffer Publications, 1987).

Terban, Marvin, *Checking Your Grammar* [all grades] (New York: Scholastic, 1993).

Games and Activities

"Capitalization & Punctuation Activity Cards" [gr. 1–2] (Palo Verdes Estates, CA: Frank Schaffer Publications).

"Punctuation Bingo" [gr. 1–6] (St. Paul: Trend Enterprises).

"Punctuation Patterns" [gr. 1–3] (Baltimore: Media Materials).

LANGUAGE ARTS

(see Essay Tests, Verbal Expression, Vocabulary)

Akers, Deborah, and Von McInnis, *Writing Power Plus* [gr. 1–6] (Belmont, CA: Fearon Teacher Aids, 1986).

Chin, Beverly, *On Your Own: Writing Progress* [gr. 11–adult] (Englewood Cliffs, NJ: Prentice-Hall, Cambridge Adult Education, 1990).

Corbett, Paula, *Fantasy Fling* [gr. 5–8] (Santa Barbara, CA: Learning Works, 1984).

Dean, John D., *Writing Wells* [gr. 5 up] (Belmont, CA: Fearon Teacher Aids, 1985).

Evans, Marliyn, *Guided Report Writing* [gr. 3–6] (Monterey, CA: Evan-Moor Corp, 1987).

Hamilton, Sally, *Spin Your Wheels* [gr. 4–6] (Santa Barbara, CA: Learning Works, 1982).

Johnson, Eric, *You Are the Editor* [gr. 5 up] (Belmont, CA: Fearon Teacher Aids, 1981).

May, Robert R., and Cerny, Sarah P., *Power Writing* [gr. 1–8] (Mount Laurel, NJ: Learn Inc., 1979).

Phelps Terasaki, Diana, and Phelps, Trisha, *Teaching Written Expression* (Novato, CA: Academic Therapy Publications, 1980).

Price, Bren T., *Basic Composition Activities Kit* (Englewood Cliffs, NJ: Center for Applied Research in Education, Prentice-Hall, 1982).

Robertson, Debbie, *Blast Off with Book Reports* [gr. 3–8] (Carthage, IL: Good Apple, 1985).

Wenrtcek, Ginger, *Leaping Lizards Language Arts* [gr. 2–4] (Belmont, CA: Fearon Teacher Aids, 1986).

LEARNING THE ALPHABET

(see Auditory Discrimination, Memorizing Information, Phonics, Spelling Problems, Visual Memory)

Coudron, Jill, *Alphabet Fun and Games* [gr. pre-K–3] (Belmont, CA: Fearon Teacher Aids, 1984); *Alphabet Puppets* [gr. K–3] (Belmont, CA: Fearon Teacher Aids, 1979); *Alphabet Activities* [gr. pre-K–3] (Belmont, CA: Fearon Teacher Aids, 1952); *Alphabet Stories* [gr. pre-K–3] (Belmont, CA: Fearon Teacher Aids, 1982).

Foust, Sylvia, *Beginning Book of Letters and Consonant Sounds* [gr. K–2] (Belmont, CA: Fearon Teacher Aids, 1986); *Beginning Book of Vowel Sounds* [gr. K–2] (Belmont, CA: Fearon Teacher Aids, 1986).

Gruber, Barbara, *Alphabetizing Activities* [gr. 1–2] (Palo Verdes Estates, CA: Frank Schaffer Publications, 1988).

Tauber, Annette, *Alphabet* [gr. pre-K–K] (Palo Verdes Estates, CA: Frank Schaffer Publications, 1987); *Alphabet Dot-to-Dot* [gr. pre-K–K] (Palo Verdes Estates, CA: Frank Schaffer Publications, 1987).

Games and Learning Materials

"Basic Word Skills Activity Cards" [age 4–7] (Palo Verdes Estates, CA: Frank Schaffer Publications).

"Bearamores Go to the Big City" [gr. pre-K–1] (Baltimore: Media Materials).

"Bearamores Learn Letter Sounds" [gr. pre-K] (Baltimore: Media Materials).

"Beginning Sounds" [gr. K–2] (Baltimore: Media Materials).

"Easy Blends and Digraphs" [Age 4–7] (Palo Verdes Estates, CA: Frank Schaffer Publications).

"Easy Consonants" [Age 4–7] (Palo Verdes Estates, CA: Frank Schaffer Publications).

"Easy Picture Word Opposites" [Age 4–7] (Palo Verdes Estates, CA: Frank Schaffer Publications).

"Easy Picture Words—Sets" [Age 4–7] (Palo Verdes Estates, CA: Frank Schaffer Publications).

"Easy Sight Words" [Age 4–7] (Palo Verdes Estates, CA: Frank Schaffer Publications).

"Easy Special Vowels" [Age 4–7] (Palo Verdes Estates, CA: Frank Schaffer Publications).

"Easy Vowels" [Age 4–7] (Palo Verdes Estates, CA: Frank Schaffer Publications).

"Phonetic Quizmo" [gr. 1–3] (Baltimore: Media Materials).

"Picture Word Bingo" [Age 4–7] (Palo Verdes Estates, CA: Frank Schaffer Publications).

"Short and Long Vowel—Do-Mi-No-Es" [Age 4–7] (Palo Verdes Estates, CA: Frank Schaffer Publications).

"Sight Word Bingo" [Age 4–7] (Palo Verdes Estates, CA: Frank Schaffer Publications).

"You Can Read Phonetic Drillcards" [gr. K–3] (Baltimore: Media Materials).

LEARNING DISABILITIES

(see Attention Deficit Disorder, Atypical Learning Problems, Dyslexia, Mainstreaming, Parents' Rights, Understanding Diagnostic Test Results)

Cronin, Eileen M., *Helping Your Dyslexic Child* (Rocklin, CA: Prima Publishing, 1994).

Dias, Peggy, *Diamonds in the Rough* (E. Aurora, NY: Slosson Educational Publishers, 1989).

Greene, Lawrence J., *Kids Who Underachieve* (New York: Simon and Schuster, 1986); *Learning Disabilities and Your Child* (New York: Fawcett, 1987).

Harwell, Joan M., *Complete Learning Disabilities Handbook* (Englewood Cliffs, NJ: Center for Applied Research in Education, Prentice-Hall, 1989).

Hays, Marnell L., *Oh Dear, Somebody Said "Learning Disabilities"!* (Novato, CA: Academic Therapy Publications, 1978).

Henzl, Elizabeth M., *Visual Aural Discrimination* [gr. 1–12] (Novato, CA: Ann Arbor Publications, 1973).

Justus, Fred, *Visual Discrimination* [gr. 1–2] (Jonesboro, AR: ESP, 1979).

Levinson, Harold M.D., *A Solution to the Riddle of Dyslexia* (New York: Springer-Verlag, 1983); *Smart but Feeling Dumb* (New York: Warner, 1988).

Love, Maria, *20 Decoding Games* [gr. 1–3] (Belmont, CA: Fearon Teacher Aids, 1982).

McCarney, Stephen B., and Bauer, Angela Marie, *The Learning Disability Intervention Manual*, Revised Edition (Columbia, MO: Hawthorne Educational Services, 1989).

Osman, Betty B., *Learning Disabilities—A Family Affair* (New York: Warner, 1985).

Valett, Robert E., *The Remediation of Learning Disabilities* (Belmont, CA: David S. Lake, 1978).

MATH

Fisk, Sally, *Primary Fractions* [gr. 1–3] (St. Louis: Millikin Publications, 1984).

Herlihy, Ruth, *Math Workbook: Drill & Practice* [gr. 1–6] (St. Louis: Millikin Publications, 1980); *Decimals Workbook: Drill & Practice* [gr. 5–7] (St. Louis: Millikin Publications, 1980).

Howell, Will C., *Grid and Bear It* [gr. 1–3] (Belmont, CA: Fearon Teacher Aids, 1989); *Grid and Graph It* [gr. 4–6] (Belmont, CA: Fearon Teacher Aids, 1987).

Kay, Peggy, *Games for Math* [gr. K–3] (New York: Pantheon Books, 1987).

Kirkpatrick, Vicky, *Addition/Subtraction with Regrouping* [nongraded] (St. Louis: Millikin Publications, 1984).

Nance, Beverly, *Beginning Algebra* [gr. 6–8] (St. Louis: Millikin Publications, 1989).

Panchyshyn, Robert, and Moore, Eula Ewing, *Developing Key Concepts for Solving Word Problems* [gr. 3–4] (Chicago: Barnell Loft [SRA Technology], 1989).

Parson, Judith N., *Math-A-Dot* [gr. 1–5] (Belmont, CA: Fearon Teacher Aids, 1974); *Math-A-Draw* [gr. 1–5] (Belmont, CA: Fearon Teacher Aids, 1983).

Ryan, John J., *Developing Key Concepts in Math* (Chicago: Barnell Loft [SRA Technology], 1986).

Taylor, Loretta, and Taylor, Harold, *Understanding Fractions* (Palo Alto, CA: Dayle Seymore Publications, 1981).

Vervoort, Gerardus, and Mason, Dale J., *Beginning Calculator Math* [gr. 5–7] (Belmont, CA: Fearon Teacher Aids, 1980); *Intermediate Calculator Math* [gr. 6–8] (Belmont, CA: Fearon Teacher Aids, 1980); *Advanced Calculator Math* [gr. 7–10] (Belmont, CA: Fearon Teacher Aids, 1980).

Games and Learning Activities

"Addition, Multiplication, Division, Subtraction Flash Cards" [gr. 1–5] (St. Paul: Trend Enterprises).

"Arithmetic Quizmo" [gr. 1–7] (Baltimore: Media Materials).

"Castles and Keys" [gr. 1–3 or 4–6] (Baltimore: Media Materials).

"Count Your Change" [gr. 1–4] (Baltimore: Media Materials).

"Divisor Countdown" [gr. 5–7, reading level 4.0] (Baltimore: Media Materials).

"Flannel Board Cut-Outs" [gr. K–1] (Baltimore: Media Materials).

"Fractions are Easy as Pie" [gr. 2–6] (Baltimore: Media Materials).

"Fraction Discs" [gr. 4–6] (Baltimore: Media Materials).

"Geometric Shapes" [gr. pre-K–3] (Baltimore: Media Materials).

"Learning Multiplication Facts" [gr. 1–3] (Baltimore: Media Materials).

"Make Your Own Flash Cards" [gr. pre-K] (St. Paul: Trend Enterprises).

"Math Lotto" [gr. K–3] (Baltimore: Media Materials).

"Mark on Wipe off Math Cards" [gr. K–4] (Baltimore: Media Materials).

"Menu Madness" [gr. 4–8, reading level 3.0] (Baltimore: Media Materials).

"Numbers 0–25 Flash Cards" [gr. K–1] (St. Paul: Trend Enterprises).

"Numbers 0–100 Flash Cards" [gr. K–1] (St. Paul: Trend Enterprises).

"Prime Factor Scramble" [gr. 5–7, reading level 4.0] (Baltimore: Media Materials).

"Prime Number Checkers" [gr. 5–7, reading level 4.0] (Baltimore: Media Materials).

"Tangram & Pattern Cards" [gr. 3–adult] (Baltimore: Media Materials).

"Tell Time Quizmo" [gr. 1–4] (Baltimore: Media Materials) .

"Telling Time" [gr. 1–3] (St. Paul: Trend Enterprises).

"Tigo Game" [gr. 4 up] (Baltimore: Media Materials).

"Toy Money" [gr. K–4] (Baltimore: Media Materials).

PHONICS

(see Auditory Discrimination, Auditory Memory, Dyslexia, Learning Disabilities, Nonphonetic Words, Phonics, Reading Aloud, Spelling, Slow Reading, Visual Memory)

Bernstein, Rosella, *Sound Out* [gr. K–1] (Englewood Cliffs, NJ: Center for Applied Research in Education, Prentice-Hall, 1993).

Caroll, Jeri A., and Kear, Dennis J., *Writing Fun with Phonics* [gr. pre-K–2] (Carthage, IL: Good Apple, 1992).

Dolche, Edward W., and Dolche, Marguerite P., *Dolche Proper Word Lists*, Set I & II [gr. 1–6] (Allen, TX: Developmental Learning Materials, 1987).

Greene, Lawrence J., *Key Word Inventory* [gr. 1–6] (San Jose, CA: Developmental Learning Products, 1981).

Games and Learning Activities

Auditory Discrimination

"Sounds Lotto" [gr. pre-K–1] (Baltimore: Media Materials).

Visual Discrimination

"Creature Factory" [ages 4–9] (Dominguez Hill, CA: Educational Insights).

"Mix & Match Bears" [gr. pre-K–2] (Baltimore: Media Materials).

"Play Scenes Lotto" [gr. pre-K–3] (Baltimore: Media Materials).

"Teddy Bear Search" [gr. pre-K–1] (Baltimore: Media Materials).

READING COMPREHENSION

(see Auditory Memory, Critical Thinking, Identifying Important Information, Learning Disabilities, Logic, Notetaking, Preparing for Tests, Reading Aloud, Study Skills, Visual Memory)

Bell, Nanci, *Visualizing & Verbalizing for Language Comprehension and Thinking* [all ages] (Baldwin, NY: Lowell and Lynwood, 1978).

Boning, Richard A., *Multiple Skills Series* [gr. 1–6] (Baldwin, NY: Lowell and Lynwood, 1978); *Specific Skill Series: Detecting the Sequence* [gr. 2–12] (Chicago: Barnell Loft [SRA Technology], 1977); *Specific Skill Series: Drawing Conclusions* [gr. 2–12] (Chicago: Barnell Loft [SRA Technology], 1977); *Specific Skill Series: Getting the Facts* [gr. 2–12] (Chicago: Barnell Loft [SRA Technology], 1977); *Specific Skill Series: Getting the Main Idea* [gr. 2–12] (Chicago: Barnell Loft [SRA Technology], 1977); *Specific Skill Series: Locating the Answer* [gr. 2–12] (Chicago: Barnell Loft [SRA Technology], 1977); *Specific Skill Series: Using the Context* [gr. 2–12] (Chicago: Barnell Loft [SRA Technology], 1977).

Boning, Richard A., Boning, Charles R., and Higgins, John F., *Interactive Reading Program–Clues to Cloze* [gr. 1–6] (Chicago: Barnell Loft [SRA Technology], 1989).

Ceaser, L.D., *The Big Book of Comprehension Capers* [gr. 1–3] (Belmont, CA: Fearon Teacher Aids, 1986); *Comprehension Capers Series: Intent on Inferences* [gr. 4–6] (Belmont, CA: Fearon Teacher Aids, 1986); *Comprehension Capers Series: Main Ideas Maneuvers* [gr. 1–3] (Belmont, CA: Fearon Teacher Aids, 1986); *Comprehension Capers Series: Making Inferences* [gr. 1–3] (Belmont, CA: Fearon Teacher Aids, 1986).

Liddle, William, *Reading for Concepts* (New York: McGraw Hill, 1977).

Love, Maria, *20 Reading Comprehension Games* [gr. 4–6] (Belmont, CA: Fearon Teacher Aids, 1977).

McAllister, Elizabeth, *Primary Reading Skills Activities Kit* [gr. K–1] (Englewood Cliffs, NJ: Center for Applied Research in Education, Prentice-Hall, 1987).

Miller, Wilma, *Complete Reading Disabilities Handbook* (Englewood Cliffs, NJ: Center for Applied Research in Education, Prentice-Hall, 1993).

Stelluto, Donna, *On Your Own: Reading* [gr. 11–adult] (Englewood Cliffs, NJ: Cambridge Adult Education, Prentice-Hall, 1990).

Tierney, Robert J., Readence, John E., and Dishner, Ernest K., *Reading Strategies and Practices: A Compendium* [all grades] (Needham Heights, MA: Allyn and Bacon, 1990 and 1995).

Wittenberg, William H., *Identifying Inferences* [gr. K–12] (Chicago: Barnell Loft [SRA Technology], 1986).

SPELLING

(see Auditory Discrimination, Auditory Memory, Memorizing Information, Spelling Problems, Visual Memory)

Abbatino, Vincent, *Spellbound* [gr. 1–6] (New York: Vantage, 1990).

Barr, Linda, *Spelling & Writing* [gr. 1–4] (Columbus American Education, 1991).

Feinstein, George W., *Programmed Spelling Demons* [gr. 1–6] (Englewood Cliffs, NJ: Prentice-Hall, 1984).

Kottmeyer, William, and Claus, Audrey, *Basic Goals in Spelling* [gr. 5–8] (New York: McGraw Hill, 1984).

Wittenberg, William H., *Diagnostic and Prescriptive Spelling Program* [gr. 2–8] (Chicago: Barnell Loft [SRA Technology], 1980).

Games and Learning Activities

"Match and Spell—Match the Animals & Spell Their Names" [gr. K–3] (Otto Maier Verlag).

"Castles and Keys" [gr. 1–3 and 4–6] (Baltimore: Media Materials).

STUDY SKILLS

(see Attention to Details, Behavior and Attitude, Critical Thinking, Disregarding Consequences, Distractions while Studying, Effort and Motivation, Essay Tests, Expectations and Performance Guidelines, Goals, Grades, Identifying Important Information, Inadequate Study Time, Incomplete Assignments, Learned Helplessness, Memorizing Information, Monitoring Homework, Negative Attitude toward School, Notetaking, Preparing for Tests, Priorities, Procrastination, Recording Assignments, Smart Thinking, Test Preparation, Time Management)

Flippo, Rona, *Test Wise* [gr. 11 up] (Belmont, CA: Fearon Teacher Aids, 1988).

Greene, Lawrence J., and Jones-Bamman, Leigh, *Getting Smarter* [gr. 6–12] (Belmont, CA: Fearon Teacher Aids, 1985).

Greene, Lawrence J., *Smarter Kids* [gr. 1–12] (New York: Fawcett Crest, 1987); *Study Smart, Think Smart* [gr. 4–8] (Englewood Cliffs, NJ: Center for Applied Research in Education, Prentice-Hall, 1992).

Ohme, Herman, *Learn How to Learn* [gr. 9–college] (Palo Alto, CA: California Educational Plan, 1986).

THINKING

(see Critical Thinking, Disregarding Consequences, Identifying Important Information, Logic, Problem Solving, Smart Thinking)

Anderson, Valerie, and Bereiter, Carl, *Thinking Games 1 & 2* [gr. 4–7] (Belmont, CA: Fearon Teacher Aids, 1980).

Black, Howard and Sandra, *Building Thinking Skills II* [gr. 4–7] (Pacific Grove, CA: Midwest Publications, 1987).

Gregorich, Barbara, *Logical Logic* [gr. 7–12] (Santa Barbara, CA: The Learning Works, 1985).

Greene, Lawrence J., *Smarter Kids* [gr. 1–12] (New York: Fawcett Crest, 1987); *Study Smart, Think Smart* [gr. 4–8] (Englewood Cliffs, NJ: Center for Applied Research in Education, Prentice-Hall, 1992); *The Life-Smart Kid* [gr. 1–12] (Rocklin, CA: Prima Publishing, 1995).

Harnader, Anita, *Critical Thinking* [gr. 4–7] (Pacific Grove, CA: Midwest Publications, 1976).

Hopkins, Lee Bennett, and Shapiro, Annette, *Creative Activities for the Gifted Child* [gr. 1–6] (Belmont, CA: Fearon Teacher Aids, 1969).

Karnes, Merle B., *Primary Thinking Skills* [gr. K–2] (Pacific Grove, CA: Midwest Publicaitons, 1976).

Meredith, Paul, and Landin, Leslie, *100 Activiites for Gifted Children* [gr. 1–6] (Belmont, CA: Fearon Teacher Aids, 1957).

Pavlich, V., and Rosenast, E., *Do Something Different* [gr. 4–7] (Belmont, CA: Fearon Teacher Aids, 1987).

Post, Beverly, and Eads, Sandra, *Digging into Logic* [gr. 5–8] (Belmont, CA: Fearon Teacher Aids, 1987); *Logic Anyone?* [gr. 5–8] (Belmont, CA: Fearon Teacher Aids, 1982); *Logic Anyone? Workbook* [gr. 5–8] (Belmont, CA: Fearon Teacher Aids, 1982).

Prizzi, Elaine, and Hoffman, Jeanne, *Re: Thinking* [gr. 5 up] (Belmont, CA: Fearon Teacher Aids, 1989).

Schoenfield, Mark, and Rosenblatt, Jeannette *Adventure with Logic* [gr. 5–7] (Belmont, CA: Fearon Teacher Aids, 1985); *Discovering Logic* [gr. 4–6] (Belmont, CA: Fearon Teacher Aids, 1985); *Playing with Logic* [gr. 3–5] (Belmont, CA: Fearon Teacher Aids, 1985).

Symonds, Martha, *Think Big* [gr. 4–6] (Santa Barbara, CA: The Learning Works, 1977).

Williams, Wayne, *Quizzles* [gr. 5 up] (Palo Alto, CA: Dale Seymour Publications, 1982); *More Quizzles* [gr. 5 up] (Palo Alto, CA: Dale Seymour Publications, 1984).

Thinking Games and Activities

"Critical Thinking Activity Cards" [gr. 2–3] (Palo Verdes Estates, CA: Frank Schaffer Publications).

"Four-Scene Sequence Cards [gr. pre-K–3] (Baltimore: Media Materials).

"Pick Pairs Game" [gr. pre-K–3] (Baltimore: Media Materials).

"Sequencing Activity Cards" [gr. 1–2] (Palo Verdes Estates, CA: Frank Schaffer Publications).

"Smart Choices" [gr. 6 up] (St. Paul: Trend Enterprises).

"Space Race" [age 3–6] (Palo Verdes Estates, CA: Frank Schaffer Publications).

"Three-Scene Sequence Posters [gr. pre-K–3] (Baltimore: Media Materials).

VOCABULARY

(see Auditory Memory, Essay Tests, Language Arts, Language Disorders, Memorizing Information, Verbal Expression, Visual Memory)

Allman, Barbara, *Vocabulary Building* [gr. 1] (Palo Verdes Estates, CA: Frank Schaffer Publications, 1987).

Bell, Nanci, *Vanilla Vocabulary* [level 1, gr. 1–3; level 2, gr. 4–6; level 3, gr. 7–9; level 4, gr. 10–adult] (Paso Robles, CA: Academy of Reading Publication, 1993).

Criscuolo, Nicholas, and Herman, Barry E., *Fun with Words* [gr. 2–5] (Belmont, CA: Fearon Teacher Aids, 1988).

Gill, Nancy, *Vocabulary Boosters* [gr. 4 up] (Belmont, CA: Fearon Teacher Aids, 1985).

Glicksberg, Joy Brumby, *Crosswords for Language Arts* [gr. 1–5] (Belmont, CA: Fearon Teacher Aids, 1985).

Heymsfeld, Carla, *Digging into Language* [gr. 4 up] (Belmont, CA: Fearon Teacher Aids, 1983).

Knoblock, Kathleen, *Basic Word Vocabulary* [gr. 1–2] (Palos Verdes Estates, CA: Frank Schaffer Publications, 1989).

Love, Maria, *20 Word Structure Games* [gr. 2–5] (Belmont, CA: Fearon Teacher Aids, 1983).

Marshall, Kim, *The Kim Marshall Series: Vocabulary* [gr. 5–6] (Cambridge, MA: Educators Publishing Service, 1981).

Mueser, Anne Marie, and Mueser, John Alan, *Practicing Vocabulary in Context* [gr. 2–8] (New York: Random House, 1989).

Muncy, Patricia Tyler, *Word Puzzles* [gr. 4 up] (Belmont, CA: Fearon Teacher Aids, 1974).

Robinson, Joan, *The Roots of Language Series: Word Building* [gr. 4–9] (Belmont, CA: Fearon Teacher Aids, 1980); *The Roots of Language Series: Word Wise* [gr. 4–9] (Belmont, CA: Fearon Teacher Aids, 1989).

Runjamin, Rosmary E., *New Dimensions in Dictionary Practice: Creative Lessons for Reinforcement and Enrichment* [gr. 4–6] (Belmont, CA: Fearon Teacher Aids, 1987).

Wentrcek, Ginger, *Dandy Dictionary Skills: Motivating Work Sheets and Dictionary Practice* [gr. 2–4] (Belmont, CA: Fearon Teacher Aids, 1986).

Games and Learning Activities

"Economo Word Builder" [gr. K–3] (Baltimore: Media Materials).

"Sentence Builder" [gr. 1–3] (Baltimore: Media Materials).

"Vocabulary Quizmo" [gr. 5–8] (Baltimore: Media Materials).